THE FOURTEENTH AMENDMENT AND THE PRIVILEGES AND IMMUNITIES OF AMERICAN CITIZENSHIP

This book presents the history behind a revolution in American liberty: the 1868 addition of the Privileges or Immunities Clause of the Fourteenth Amendment. This exhaustively researched book follows the evolution in public understanding of "the privileges and immunities of citizens of the United States" from the early years of the Constitution to the critical national election of 1866. For the first ninety-two years of our nation's history, nothing in the American Constitution prevented states from abridging freedom of speech, prohibiting the free exercise of religion, or denying the right of peaceful assembly. The suppression of freedom in the southern states convinced the Reconstruction Congress and the supporters of the Union to add an amendment forcing the states to respect the rights announced in the first eight amendments. But rather than eradicate state autonomy altogether, the people embraced the Fourteenth Amendment that expanded the protections of the Bill of Rights and preserved the Constitution's original commitment to federalism and the principle of limited national power.

Kurt T. Lash holds the Guy Raymond Jones Chair in Law at the University of Illinois College of Law where he directs the Program on Constitutional Theory, History, and Law. A graduate of Yale Law School, Lash has served as the Chair of the Association of American Law Schools' Section on Constitutional Law, and his work has been cited by state and federal courts of all levels, including the United States Supreme Court. He has authored numerous articles and books on constitutional history and law, and his work has been published by the *Stanford Law Review*, *Georgetown Law Journal*, *Texas Law Review*, *Virginia Law Review*, *Northwestern University Law Review*, and *The Chicago Law Review Online*. He is the author of *The Lost History of the Ninth Amendment* (2009) and the forthcoming edited collection of historical materials, *The Reconstruction Amendments: Essential Documents*.

The Fourteenth Amendment and the Privileges and Immunities of American Citizenship

KURT T. LASH

University of Illinois College of Law

CAMBRIDGE
UNIVERSITY PRESS

CAMBRIDGE
UNIVERSITY PRESS

32 Avenue of the Americas, New York NY 10013-2473, USA

Cambridge University Press is part of the University of Cambridge.

It furthers the University's mission by disseminating knowledge in the pursuit of education, learning and research at the highest international levels of excellence.

www.cambridge.org
Information on this title: www.cambridge.org/9781316507520

© Kurt T. Lash 2014

First published 2014
First paperback edition 2015

A catalogue record for this publication is available from the British Library

Library of Congress Cataloguing in Publication data
Lash, Kurt T., author.
The Fourteenth Amendment and the Privileges and Immunities of American Citizenship /
Kurt Lash, University of Illinois College of Law.
    pages   cm
Includes bibliographical references and index.
ISBN 978-1-107-02326-0 (hardback)
1. United States. Constitution. 14th Amendment – History.   2. Privileges and immunities –
United States.   3. Federal government – United States.   4. Civil rights – United States.
5. United States. Constitution 14th Amendment – History.   I. Title.
KF4558 14th.L37   2014
342.7308′5–dc23   2013042146

ISBN 978-1-107-02326-0 Hardback
ISBN 978-1-316-50752-0 Paperback

Contents

Preface

What are our constitutional rights as American citizens, and where do they come from? If asked, most US citizens would probably point to some or all of the first ten amendments to the United States Constitution, the Bill of Rights: the rights of free speech, free press, and the free exercise of religion; protections against unreasonable searches and seizures, the taking of property without just compensation, the deprivation of life or liberty without due process of law. Although many Americans might think these rights protect them against the wrongful actions of any official with a badge, those most familiar with the Constitution know that the Bill of Rights binds only the national government. Under the original Constitution, states and state officials remained free to abridge speech, impose religious orthodoxy, imprison without due process, and take private property without paying a dime.

Today, of course, courts in the United States *do* apply the Bill of Rights against both state and federal officials. They do so because of the addition of the Fourteenth Amendment. Adopted in the aftermath of the Civil War, the Fourteenth Amendment declares (among other things): "No state shall make or enforce any law abridging the privileges or immunities of citizens of the United States, or denying any person life, liberty or property without due process of law." Unlike the Bill of Rights, this amendment expressly requires state officials to respect the rights of national citizenship. According to the Supreme Court, this includes most of the provisions in the Bill of Rights. So, for example, both state and federal officials must respect your freedom of speech and your right to free exercise of religion.

What is not clear, however, is *why* the Fourteenth Amendment forces the states to follow the federal Bill of Rights. The justices of the Supreme Court and the finest minds in the American legal academy have disputed the matter for more than a century.[1] Not even the members of the current US Supreme Court agree with one another regarding which provision in the Fourteenth Amendment prevents the state police from knocking down your door when you speak against your governor, seek solace from your God, or take refuge in your home.[2]

Initially, the Supreme Court rejected the idea that the Fourteenth Amendment applies the Bill of Rights against the states.[3] In the early twentieth century, however, the Supreme Court reversed course and began to "incorporate" certain federal rights against the states into the Court's reading of the Fourteenth Amendment's declaration that "nor shall any state deprive any person of life, liberty or property without due process of law."[4] One by one,

---

[1]   For a small sample of the debate over the Bill of Rights and the Fourteenth Amendment, see United States v. Cruikshank, 92 U.S. 542 (1876) (Waite, C.J.) (the Fourteenth Amendment does not apply the Bill of Rights against the states); Gitlow v. New York, 268 U.S. 652 (1925) (Sanford, J.) (the Fourteenth Amendment's Due Process Clause applies some of the Bill of Rights against the states); Adamson v. California, 332 U.S. 46, 59 (1947) (Frankfurter, J., concurring) (the Fourteenth Amendment does not apply any of the Bill of Rights against the states); *id.* at 68 (Black, J., dissenting) (the Fourteenth Amendment applies all of the first eight amendments against the states); Charles Fairman, *Does the Fourteenth Amendment Incorporate the Bill of Rights?*, 2 STAN. L. REV. 5 (1949) (the Fourteenth Amendment's Due Process Clause applies only those provisions from the Bill of Rights that are "implicit in the concept of ordered liberty" against the states); William W. Crosskey, *Charles Fairman, "Legislative History," and the Constitutional Limitations on State Authority*, 22 U. CHI. L. REV. 1 (1954) (the Fourteenth Amendment's Due Process Clause applies all of the first eight amendments against the states); MICHAEL KENT CURTIS, NO STATE SHALL ABRIDGE: THE FOURTEENTH AMENDMENT AND THE BILL OF RIGHTS (1986) (the Fourteenth Amendment's Privileges or Immunities Clause applies "fundamental" rights listed in the Bill of Rights against the states); RAOUL BERGER, THE FOURTEENTH AMENDMENT AND THE BILL OF RIGHTS (1989) (the Fourteenth Amendment does not apply any of the Bill of Rights against the states); Richard L. Aynes, *On Misreading John Bingham and the Fourteenth Amendment*, 103 YALE L. J. 57 (1993) (the Fourteenth Amendment's Privileges or Immunities Clause applies all of the first eight amendments against the states); AKHIL REED AMAR, THE BILL OF RIGHTS: CREATION AND RECONSTRUCTION (1998) (the Fourteenth Amendment's Privileges or Immunities Clause applies most of the first eight amendments against the states); McDonald v. Chicago, 130 S. Ct. 3020 (2010) (Alito, J.) (the Fourteenth Amendment's Due Process Clause applies the Second Amendment against the states); Philip Hamburger, *Privileges or Immunities*, 105 NW. U. L. REV. 61 (2011) (the Fourteenth Amendment does not apply any of the Bill of Rights against the states).

[2]   *Compare* McDonald v. Chicago, 130 S. Ct. 3020, 3031 (2010) (Alito, J.) (relying on the Due Process Clause of the Fourteenth Amendment as the textual vehicle for applying provisions of the Bill of Rights against the states) *with id.* at 3060 (Thomas, J., concurring) (arguing that the Privileges or Immunities Clause is the proper textual vehicle for applying provisions of the Bill of Rights against the states).

[3]   United States v. Cruikshank, 92 U.S. 542 (1875).

[4]   U.S. CONST. amend. XIV.

provisions like the Takings Clause,[5] the Freedom of Speech Clause,[6] and the Free Exercise Clause[7] were announced by the Court to be "fundamental liberties" protected against state action under the doctrine of "substantive" due process.

This reading of the Due Process Clause is in serious tension with the text. Rather than guaranteeing certain substantive rights, the text suggests that life, liberty, and property *may* be deprived so long as a state provides "due process."[8] Worse, this reading seems clearly contradicted by the Bill of Rights itself, which includes a Due Process Clause (in the Fifth Amendment) separate from the other rights listed in the first eight amendments,[9] indicating that the protections of the Due Process Clause do not include these other substantive rights. There is no evidence whatsoever that any framer of the Fourteenth Amendment believed the Fourteenth Amendment's Due Process Clause applied the Bill of Rights against the states, and the vast majority of Fourteenth Amendment scholars believe that the Court has chosen the wrong Clause (and the wrong doctrine) for incorporating the Bill of Rights.[10] When recently offered the opportunity to abandon the doctrine, the Court stood by substantive due process, not as a matter of a persuasive reading of the text, but simply due to the force of precedent and the doctrine of *stare decisis*.[11] In other words, the Court's current practice of enforcing the Bill of Rights against the states is due more to the inertia of past precedent than a result of a persuasive reading of the Constitution.

---

[5] Chicago, B. & Q. R. Co. v. Chicago, 166 U.S. 226 (1897).

[6] Gitlow v. New York, 268 U.S. 652 (1925).

[7] Cantwell v. Connecticut, 310 U.S. 296 (1940).

[8] In the famous formulation by John Ely, the phrase "substantive due process" is an oxymoron, a contradiction in terms with no more meaning than the phrase "green pastel redness." JOHN HART ELY, DEMOCRACY AND DISTRUST: A THEORY OF JUDICIAL REVIEW 18 (1980).

[9] U.S. CONST. amend. V ("[N]or shall any person . . . be deprived of life, liberty, or property, without due process of law.").

[10] Pro-incorporation scholars almost universally agree that the Privileges or Immunities Clause, not the Due Process Clause, is the text that binds the states to enforce the Bill of Rights. *See, e.g.*, AMAR, *supra* note 1, at 183; JACK BALKIN, LIVING ORIGINALISM 199–201 (2011); RANDY BARNETT, RESTORING THE LOST CONSTITUTION: THE PRESUMPTION OF LIBERTY 60, 194 (2004); CURTIS, *supra* note 1, at 2; Erwin Chemerinsky, *The Supreme Court and the Fourteenth Amendment: The Unfulfilled Promise*, 25 LOY. L. REV. 1143, 1151–52 (1992); Michael W. McConnell, *The Right to Die and the Jurisprudence of Tradition*, 1997 UTAH L. REV. 665, 692.

[11] McDonald v. Chicago, 130 S. Ct. 3020, 3030–31 (2010) (Alito, J.) ("We see no need to reconsider that interpretation here. For many decades, the question of the rights protected by the Fourteenth Amendment against state infringement has been analyzed under the Due Process Clause of that Amendment and not under the Privileges or Immunities Clause. We therefore decline to disturb the *Slaughter-House* holding.").

One suspects the reason the Supreme Court has avoided the Privileges or Immunities Clause is due to the failure of lawyers and legal scholars to articulate a historically plausible and judicially manageable interpretation of the "privileges or immunities of citizens of the United States." For example, in the 2010 case *McDonald v. Chicago*, the Supreme Court was presented with the rare opportunity to shift its Fourteenth Amendment individual rights jurisprudence from the embarrassment of "substantive due process" to the far more textually plausible Privileges or Immunities Clause. While making his argument before the Supreme Court, plaintiff's counsel was asked to define the limits of the Privileges or Immunities Clause. Although his client sought nothing more than incorporation of the Second Amendment, counsel nevertheless responded that "it's impossible to give a full list of unenumerated rights that might be protected by the Privileges or Immunities Clause."[12] The reply almost guaranteed that the Court's decision would *not* invoke Privileges or Immunities Clause, if only to avoid opening a Pandora's box of "impossible to fully list" unenumerated rights.[13]

But legal scholars have done no better in defining the scope of the "privileges or immunities of citizens of the United States." Despite widely divergent interpretations of the Privileges or Immunities Clause, almost all current Fourteenth Amendment scholars believe that the Clause was modeled on Article IV, Section 2 of the federal Constitution, which declares "[t]he Citizens of each State shall be entitled to all Privileges and Immunities of Citizens in the several States."[14] The most famous antebellum decision involving the so-called Comity Clause was a circuit court opinion written by George Washington's nephew, Bushrod Washington, in *Corfield v. Coryell*.[15] In *Corfield*, Judge Washington wrote that the provision protected "those privileges and immunities which are, in their nature, fundamental; which belong, of right, to the citizens of all free governments."[16] Because the same members of the Thirty-Ninth Congress who framed and adopted the Privileges or Immunities

---

[12] Transcript of Oral Argument at 5, United States v. McDonald, 561 U.S. 3025 (2010), *available at* http://www.supremecourt.gov/oral_arguments/argument_transcripts/08-1521.pdf.

[13] *See McDonald*, 130 S. Ct. 3020, 3030 (2010) (Thomas, J., concurring) ("[P]etitioners are unable to identify the Clause's full scope." [citing Tr. of Oral Arg. 5–6, 8–11]).

[14] U.S. CONST. art. IV, § 2. Just a small sample of current Fourteenth Amendment scholars who link the Privileges or Immunities Clause to the Comity Clause of Article IV includes AMAR, *supra* note 1, at 177–79; BALKIN, *supra* note 10, at 208–09; BARNETT, *supra* note 10, at 62–63; CURTIS, *supra* note 1, at 114–15; Hamburger, *supra* note 1, at 132–34.

[15] 6 F. Cas. 546 (C.C.Pa. 1823).

[16] *Id.* at 551.

Clause also frequently discussed *Corfield*, scholars have concluded that the Clause somehow embraces the case.[17] These scholars disagree about the particular manner in which *Corfield*ian "fundamental rights" bind the states, but all agree that the Comity Clause of Article IV and cases like *Corfield* are the lens through which we (and courts) should view the Privileges or Immunities Clause of the Fourteenth Amendment.

This book explains why this is wrong, both as a matter of text and as a matter of history. The Privileges or Immunities Clause of the Fourteenth Amendment is not based on the language of Article IV; it is based on the language of antebellum national treaties like the Louisiana Cession Act of 1803 and the 1848 Treaty of Guadalupe Hidalgo, and echoed in the Alaskan Cession Act of 1867. These acts declared the rights, privileges, and immunities "of citizens of the United States," a category of "privileges or immunities" altogether different from the rights of state citizenship protected under Section 2 of Article IV. As the framer of the Fourteenth Amendment, John Bingham, explained,

> Mr. Speaker, that the scope and meaning of the limitations imposed by the first section, fourteenth amendment of the Constitution may be more fully understood, permit me to say that the privileges and immunities of citizens of the United States, as contradistinguished from citizens of a State, are chiefly defined in the first eight amendments to the Constitution of the United States.[18]

These personal rights are "chiefly defined" in the Bill of Rights, but they include *all* constitutionally enumerated personal rights. More controversially, perhaps, the original meaning of the Privileges or Immunities Clause included only those rights enumerated in the Constitution. Neither Congress nor the country in 1866 wished to erase constitutionally established limits on federal power, including the limited powers of the federal courts. What was lacking was a constitutional provision expressly requiring the states to respect those rights placed in the Constitution by the people themselves and which had come to be viewed as representing the privileges and immunities of citizens of the United States.

---

[17] *See* AMAR, *supra* note 1, at 177–79; BALKIN, *supra* note 10, at 208–09; BARNETT, *supra* note 10, at 62–63; Curtis, *supra* note 1, at 114–15; McConnell, *supra* note 10, at 694. *But see* Hamburger, *supra* note 1, at 146 (agreeing that the Privileges or Immunities Clause should be read as modeled on the Comity Clause, but criticizing *Corfield* as a proper interpretation of Article IV).

[18] CONG. GLOBE, 42d Cong., 1st Sess. app. at 84 (1871).

METHODOLOGY

This book presents the history of a legal concept: the constitutional privileges and immunities of citizens of the United States. Although it includes analysis of key historical figures and events, the focus throughout is on the evolution of an idea and its entrenchment as fundamental law. This is, in other words, a book of *legal* history. The analysis in the chapters that follow presumes that law, as such, reflects particular social movements of the time but also plays a role in affecting and shaping those movements.[19] Law is itself a player in the drama of American history; it transcends the moment of its enactment and sets into motion future consequences that may or may not have been anticipated or intended by those who brought the law into being. This is true of all law, and it is particularly true of constitutional law.

To constitutionalize a subject or right means to place the matter beyond the reach of ordinary political decision making. The goal of one who frames and adopts a constitutional text is to constrain the options of future political actors and protect the future people from the self-interested or short-sighted decisions of future politicians. Put another way, a constitution is meant to "secure the blessings of liberty to ourselves *and our posterity*."[20] But those who frame constitutional text control neither its interpretation nor its actual operation. Political partisans inevitably seek to bend a legal text to their will, regardless of original or even *current* consensus understanding of the text. Times change and post-adoption events may illuminate issues and concerns unknown or underappreciated at the time of enactment, developments that affect how people read and understand constitutional text. At the very least, one may expect that politicians have an incentive to claim that the pressures of the moment illuminate needs unconsidered by the people of the past. There is no guarantee, in other words, that one's posterity will actually enjoy the blessings of liberty one seeks to secure by way of constitutional entrenchment.

Those who shaped the fundamental legal texts of American law understood the realities of time, passion, and politics. But they also shared an almost religious faith in the possibility of text-based constraints on the powers and actions of government officials. The American Constitution, a written and

---

[19] I agree with Ted White that law is, at the very least, partially autonomous from its cultural context and is therefore a proper object of historical investigation. *See* G. EDWARD WHITE, LAW IN AMERICAN HISTORY, VOL. 1, at 10 (2012) (arguing that law and American history have a reciprocal relationship and rejecting past schools of historical scholarship that treated law as nothing more than a nonautonomous "mirror of society").

[20] U.S. CONST. pmbl.

judicially enforceable charter of government power, is itself an expression of the newly formed faith of American revolutionaries in popular sovereignty.[21] Unlike their contemporaries in England, who had cast off the prerogative of Kings in favor of the sovereignty of the English Parliament, legal and political theorists in the Atlantic colonies embraced the idea that the people stand over and apart from their institutions of government.[22] Governments and political representatives are not the people themselves. They are no more than the people's agents, whose powers go no further than that authorized by the people in a written and enforceable constitution. A written constitution serves as a lasting expression of the people's will and declares the degree to which the people consent to the exercise of government power. The document both defines and limits the legitimate powers of the people's agents and continues to act as a constraint until such time as the people themselves alter or abolish their fundamental law through constitutional amendment or political revolution.

It is this lasting effect of entrenched principles of law, law immunized from the choices of transient political majorities, that makes constitutional law an especially appropriate choice for independent historical investigation. "Constitution" law not only plays the same partially autonomous role of all law, it is peculiarly designed to play such a role. Rather than merely mirroring the political choices of an age, it sets the terms for and, to a certain degree, the boundaries of future political choices. The same is true of all statutes and foundational documents which, even if not legally entrenched, nevertheless serve as constitutive elements of majoritarian political culture. Examples would include the Declaration of Independence, the Northwest Ordinance,[23] and, perhaps, major judicial opinions such as *Marbury v. Madison*[24] and *McCulloch v. Maryland*.[25] Political movements that plausibly frame their efforts in conjunction with these culturally embraced legal landmarks increase their odds of public acceptance and success. Likewise, political movements that appear out of step with constitutive laws and documents will pay a political price, and, to that degree, are less likely to succeed. Nor are these cultural legal landmarks limited to celebrated past events. Notorious past events, such as the Supreme Court's decision in *Dred Scott v. Sandford*,[26] may become a framing device for understanding proposed legal reforms. In all cases, the

---

[21] *See* GORDON WOOD, THE CREATION OF THE AMERICAN REPUBLIC, 1776–1787 (1998).

[22] *Id.* at 372–83.

[23] 1 U.S.C. lv (1787).

[24] 5 U.S. 137 (1803).

[25] 17 U.S. 316 (1819).

[26] 60 U.S. 393 (1857).

participants in legal movements have an incentive to frame their efforts in legal language that draws on popular understanding of constitutive or foundational documents, laws, and judicial opinions.

Consensus understanding of past law not only affects the likely success of later legal movements, but also shapes the legal rhetoric and the proposed legal language of later successful movements. If one seeks to discover the original public understanding of a legal text in general, and of a constitutional text in particular, one must understand the relationship between the officially adopted text and the historical antecedents that informed the framers' choice of that text and the likely public understanding of that text. For example, seen from afar, the language in the Fourteenth Amendment seems to have nothing to do with the second Bank of the United States, oyster raking in New Jersey, or the purchase of the Louisiana Territory. Zoom into the actual legal debates surrounding the adoption of the Amendment, however, and the reader discovers that the framers of the Amendment self-consciously framed their efforts in accordance with their understanding of the bank case *McCulloch v. Maryland*, the oyster case *Corfield v. Coryell*, and the rights conferred by the Louisiana Cession Act.

The goal of this book is to illuminate the original public meaning of the Privileges or Immunities Clause of the Fourteenth Amendment. I define "original meaning" as the likely original understanding of the text at the time of its adoption by competent speakers of the English language who were aware of the context in which the text was communicated for ratification.[27] Determining original meaning requires investigating historical events and texts antecedent to the proposed amendment in order to understand the full historical context in which a proposed text is debated and ratified. This is not an effort to recover the "true" or even "best" meaning of antecedent events and texts. Instead, the goal is to recover how these legal antecedents were broadly understood, correctly or not, at the time of the adoption of the Fourteenth Amendment.

As an investigation of the original public meaning of Section One of the Fourteenth Amendment, this book differs from earlier works on the historical Fourteenth Amendment. Beginning with the Fairman-Crossky debates

---

[27] *See* Lawrence B. Solum, *Originalism and Constitutional Construction*, FORDHAM L. REV. (2013) (manuscript at 6), *available at* http://papers.ssrn.com/sol3/papers.cfm?abstract_id=2307178 ("'Public Meaning Originalism' names the version of originalist theory holding that the communicative content of the constitutional text is fixed at the time of origin by the conventional semantic meaning of the words and phrases in the context that was shared by the drafters, ratifiers, and citizens.").

of the mid-twentieth century until very recently,[28] most work on the Four-teenth Amendment has sought to uncover the original intentions of the men who framed the text. This "framers' intent" scholarship fell into two broad cate-gories: those who found meaning in the views of particular men like Thaddeus Stevens and John Bingham, and those who rejected even the possibility of find-ing meaning due to the multiplicity of views espoused by different framers.[29] In recent decades, however, originalist scholarship has generally abandoned the search for framers' intent and instead seeks to uncover evidence of the original meaning of a text.[30] This is an empirical inquiry that looks for com-mon patterns of linguistic usage among competent speakers of the English language. Original meaning investigations have no guaranteed success: It may be possible to find evidence of historical consensus and original understanding in regard to some legal texts, less possible in regard to others, and perhaps not possible at all in regard to a few. And, in all cases, our understanding will be at best only partial. But the reality of incomplete knowledge does not prevent the legal historian from determining whether some meanings are more or less likely than others to have been the *original* meaning. Just as importantly, sometimes it will be possible to determine that certain textual understandings, even if theoretically possible, are not at all likely.

---

[28] *See* Richard L. Aynes, *Charles Fairman, Felix Frankfurter, and the Fourteenth Amendment*, 70 CHI.-KENT L. REV. 1197, 1243–56 (1995).

[29] *See, e.g.,* WILLIAM E. NELSON, THE FOURTEENTH AMENDMENT: FROM POLITICAL PRINCIPLE TO JUDICIAL DOCTRINE (1998).

[30] *See* Lawrence Solum, *Faith and Fidelity: Originalism and the Possibility of Constitutional Redemption*, 91 TEX. L. REV. 147, 148–53 (2012) (describing the history of originalist scholarship and the emergence of original meaning originalism).

Acknowledgments

By way of thanks, I am indebted to many individuals who have inspired me and helped me grapple with the original meaning of the Fourteenth Amendment. The path-breaking work of Gordon Wood has been foundational in my understanding of the American project of popular sovereignty and the role of written constitutions. While at Yale Law School, I had the great good fortune to learn from theorists like Akhil Amar and Bruce Ackerman, both of whom embraced the normative importance of discovering and keeping faith with the People's past constitutional commitments. Lawrence Solum has been a faithful and invaluable friend and colleague whose thoughtful work on contemporary originalism has helped shape my own views about the uses of history in the understanding and application of constitutional text. All historical work on the Privileges or Immunities Clause of the Fourteenth Amendment owes an enormous debt of gratitude to the work of Michael Kent Curtis and his influential efforts to provide historical support for the doctrine of incorporation. Others who have toiled diligently in the fields of Reconstruction and the Fourteenth Amendment and whose work and advice have greatly helped this project include Richard Aynes, Randy Barnett, Anthony Bellia, Michael Les Benedict, Garrett Epps, Philip Hamburger, John Harrison, Heidi Kitrosser, Gerard Magliocca, Earl Maltz, Jennifer Mason McAward, Michael McConnell, John McGinnis, William Nelson, William Van Alstyne, G. Edward White, Bryan Wildenthal, and Rebecca Zietlow. I also thank the *Georgetown Law Journal*, which previously published portions of Chapters 2, 3, and 4.

Finally, I gratefully and happily thank my wife, Kelly, whose constant love, friendship, and wisdom have made this and all other endeavors in my life a joy.

1

The Fourteenth Amendment

An Introduction

Here, in full, is the text of the Fourteenth Amendment:

Section One: All persons born or naturalized in the United States and
subject to the jurisdiction thereof, are citizens of the United States and
of the state wherein they reside. No state shall make or enforce any law
abridging the privileges or immunities of citizens of the United States;
nor shall any state deprive any person of life, liberty or property, without
due process of law; nor deny to any person within its jurisdiction the
equal protection of the laws.

Section Two. Representatives shall be apportioned among the several States
according to their respective numbers, counting the whole number of persons in each State, excluding Indians not taxed. But when the right to
vote at any election for the choice of electors for President and Vice President of the United States, Representatives in Congress, the Executive
and Judicial officers of a State, or the members of the Legislature thereof,
is denied to any of the male inhabitants of such State, being twenty-one
years of age, and citizens of the United States, or in any way abridged,
except for participation in rebellion, or other crime, the basis of representation therein shall be reduced in the proportion which the number
of such male citizens shall bear to the whole number of male citizens
twenty-one years of age in such State.

Section Three. No person shall be a Senator or Representative in Congress,
or elector of President and Vice President, or hold any office, civil or
military, under the United States, or under any State, who, having previously taken an oath, as a member of Congress, or as an officer of the
United States, or as a member of any State legislature, or as an executive
or judicial officer of any State, to support the Constitution of the United
States, shall have engaged in insurrection or rebellion against the same,

or given aid or comfort to the enemies thereof. But Congress may, by a
vote of two-thirds of each House, remove such disability.

Section Four. The validity of the public debt of the United States, authorized
by law, including debts incurred for payment of pensions and bounties for
services in suppressing insurrection or rebellion, shall not be questioned.
But neither the United States nor any State shall assume or pay any debt or
obligation incurred in aid of insurrection or rebellion against the United
States, or any claim for the loss or emancipation of any slave; but all such
debts, obligations and claims shall be held illegal and void.

Section Five. The Congress shall have power to enforce, by appropriate
legislation, the provisions of this article.

In five succinct paragraphs, the framers of the Fourteenth Amendment
set the conditions for the reconstruction of the United States. Section One
announces that, henceforth, states shall not abridge certain national rights,
privileges, and immunities. Sections Two, Three, and Four set the readmission
conditions for the recently defeated slave-holding states. Section Five confers
power on the federal government to enforce the Amendment.

Although Sections One and Five have played the most significant roles in
American constitutional law, the middle three sections shed important light
on the context and ultimate meaning of the Amendment as a whole. Their
texts are evidence of a recent national catastrophe: Clause after clause speaks
of "rebellion," "insurrection," and the betrayal of one's oath to the United
States. The bitter issue that divided the country goes unmentioned until the
final sentence in Section Four: *slavery*. This same sentence also suggests the
overall goal of the Amendment – repairing and reconstructing the United
States in the aftermath of a civil war in which the slaveholding states betrayed
their oaths and rebelled against the Union in order to preserve their "peculiar
institution."

Lincoln had been right. The government of the United States would not
"endure permanently half slave and half free . . . It will become all one thing
or all the other."[1] Not only had the national house been divided, its southern
members attempted to bring the house down altogether through secession
and the creation of an independent confederacy. When the Thirty-Ninth
Congress met in December of 1865,[2] the rebellion had been put down and

---

[1] Abraham Lincoln, House Divided Speech (June 16, 1858).
[2] The Thirty-Ninth Congress met in Special Session in March 1865 and witnessed the second
    inauguration of Abraham Lincoln. Lincoln was assassinated the next month, on April 15, 1865.
    The first official session of the Thirty-Ninth Congress was gaveled into order on December 4,
    1865.

the nation made wholly free but at a terrible cost. An estimated 620,000 soldiers, 2 percent of the national population, lost their lives in the conflict.[3] An equivalent percentage today would amount to 6 million men.[4] The South lay in ruins, and the nation mourned the recent assassination of a president who gave his last full measure of devotion to the cause of preserving the Union. Congress itself assembled in a room only half-full, the empty seats of the southern delegations serving as visible daily reminders of the unfinished business of rebuilding the nation.

Reconstruction was the watchword of the day.[5] The Thirty-Ninth Congress did not meet to accomplish a revolution; the revolutionaries had been put down. It was the seceding southern states that had tried to tear down the original structure and erect an entirely new nation, the Confederate States of America. The northern states, on the other hand, fought a war of preservation and (re)Union. The Union soldiers who died had been sent into harm's way so that the *existing* government "shall not perish from the earth." This bloody revolution died at Appomattox Court House, and the Thirteenth Amendment ended the evil that had torn the nation apart. The Fourteenth Amendment was about putting the nation back together again.

Today, the Fourteenth Amendment appears revolutionary. Adopted at a midpoint between the Founding and the modern age, the Amendment appears to signal a decisive break from the localism of the Founding and an embrace of the nationalism that now dominates American constitutional law. As we shall see, this is neither how most of the framers of the Amendment envisioned their task nor how they understood the text. Meeting amongst the rubble of the worst catastrophe in American history, the members of the Thirty-Ninth Congress sought to reassemble the pieces of a shattered country. The effort did not involve abandoning the original Constitution – abandonment was the sin of the seceding States. Rather, the task was to rebuild and restore the Constitution and do so in manner that ensured the States could never again claim the right to rend the fabric of the Union or deny its people their *existing* rights as American citizens.[6] Nothing about this project required abandoning the original idea of constitutional federalism. Indeed, it had been the slave

---

[3] Drew Gilpin Faust, This Republic of Suffering: Death and the American Civil War *xi* (2008).

[4] *Id.*

[5] One of the first actions of the Thirty-Ninth Congress was to establish the Joint Committee on Reconstruction. *See* Cong. Globe, 39th Cong., 1st Sess. 47 (1865).

[6] Consider again the language of Section One: "No state shall make or enforce any law abridging the privileges or immunities of citizens of the United States." U.S. Const. amend. XIV, § 1, cl. 2. The text presumes an existing set of national privileges and immunities.

power that had abandoned federalism by insisting that all states, north and south, accept slavery, and they had demanded federal legislation to protect it from both legal and social interference.[7] Northern Republicans justifiably believed that the slave power had simultaneously violated the principles of national freedom and shredded constitutional federalism. Reconstructing the Union meant restoring both to their proper balance.[8]

The North, of course, had its own revolutionaries. Radical abolitionists like William Lloyd Garrison famously burned the Constitution, calling it a "covenant with death and an agreement with hell." John Brown led a raid on the federal armory in Harpers Ferry in a failed effort to distribute arms to slaves and trigger a general uprising. Less violently, countless individuals in the North actively flouted national law by participating in the so-called Underground Railroad, which helped escaped slaves find their way to freedom in the North. Prior to the Civil War, however, such ideas and efforts remained the exception, not the rule. Northerners generally viewed radical abolitionists like Garrison with disdain.[9] The railroad to freedom remained "underground," even in the North, for a reason – it was in violation of federal law. John Brown, of course, was hanged, without the slightest effort by northern officials to plead his case, much less intervene on his behalf.[10] It was not until after the assault on Fort Sumter that the North as a whole resorted to violence. Even then, the first northern efforts to end the Civil War not only promised the continuation of slavery in the states, but the Union expressly promised its constitutional protection.[11]

It took a war to change opinion in the North. By 1865, abolition was no longer a radical idea. Lincoln's Emancipation Proclamation ended slavery

---

[7] The slave states insisted on the right to carry their slaves throughout the Union, and they demanded northern states suppress the inflammatory publications of abolitionists. *See* MICHAEL KENT CURTIS, FREE SPEECH, "THE PEOPLE'S DARLING PRIVILEGE": STRUGGLES FOR FREEDOM OF EXPRESSION IN AMERICAN HISTORY 150–51 (2000).

[8] As John Bingham declared during the debates of the Thirty-Ninth Congress, "I would say once for all that this dual system of national and State government under the American organization is the secret of our strength and power. I do not propose to abandon it." CONG. GLOBE, 39th Cong., 2d Sess. 450 (1867).

[9] CURTIS, *supra* note 7, at 129.

[10] According to William Seward's biographer, Walter Stahr, "Republicans did not support John Brown; on the contrary, Seward denounced Brown's invasion of Virginia as treason and pronounced his execution to be 'necessary and just.'" WALTER STAHR, SEWARD: LINCOLN'S INDISPENSIBLE MAN 183 (2012).

[11] Introduced by the lame-duck Congress in 1861 as part of a final effort to prevent secession, the infamous "Corwin Amendment" would have entrenched slavery as a matter of constitutional law. *See* H.R.J. Res. 13, 36th Cong., 2d Sess. (1861) ("No amendment shall be made to the Constitution which will authorize or give to Congress the power to abolish or interfere, within any State, with the domestic institutions thereof, including that of persons held to labor or service by the laws of said State.").

in the South and grafted the noble cause of freedom to the efforts of the Union Army.[12] Once victory was assured, Congress presented the country with the Thirteenth Amendment without even bothering to wait for Lee's signature at Appomattox.[13] Although Lincoln himself would not live to see its enactment, his vice president, Andrew Johnson, eagerly took up the cause of the Thirteenth Amendment and secured its ratification at the earliest possible moment.[14] Johnson's embrace of the Thirteenth Amendment did not represent the ascendancy of radical Republicanism. If anything, his administration's announcement in December of 1865 that the Thirteenth Amendment had been ratified was a profoundly conservative act.[15] To the consternation of radical Republicans, in determining whether the requisite number of states had ratified the Amendment, Johnson's secretary of state William Seward had counted the votes of the *still excluded* southern states. Thus, in a remarkable historical irony, the death of slavery coincided with the announcement that the southern slaveholding states had survived.[16]

Not every member of the Thirty-Ninth Congress approved. Charles Sumner famously insisted that, by seceding from the Union, the southern states had committed suicide.[17] Some Republicans argued that the southern states had cast off their status as members of the Union and should be combined into a smaller number of federally controlled districts.[18] These, however,

---

[12] *See* AKHIL REED AMAR, AMERICA'S CONSTITUTION: A BIOGRAPHY 356–57 (2005).

[13] The Amendment, having been previously approved by the Senate in 1864, was approved by the House and sent to the states for ratification on January 31, 1865. *See* CONG. GLOBE, 38th Cong., 2nd Sess. 531 (1865). Lee's surrender at Appomattox Courthouse occurred on April 9, 1865. *See* HARRY HANSEN, THE CIVIL WAR: A HISTORY 633–34 (Signet Classic 2002) (1961).

[14] Proclamation of Sect'y of State William Seward, No. 52, 13 Stat. 774 (Dec. 18, 1865); *see also* Andrew Johnson, First Annual Message, Dec 4, 1865, in 6 A COMPILATION OF THE MESSAGES AND PAPERS OF THE PRESIDENTS 1789–1897, at 358 (GPO 1897) (James D. Richardson, ed.).

[15] *See* BRUCE ACKERMAN, WE THE PEOPLE: TRANSFORMATIONS 150–59 (1998).

[16] *Id.*

[17] In February 1862, Charles Sumner introduced a Resolution adopting what came to be known as the "state suicide theory":

> Resolved, That any vote of secession or other act by which any State may undertake to put an end to the supremacy of the Constitution within its territory is inoperative and void against the Constitution, and when sustained by force it becomes a practical abdication by the State of all rights under the Constitution, while the treason which it involves still further works an instant forfeiture of all those functions and powers essential to the continued existence of the State as a body-politic, so that from that time forward the territory falls under the exclusive jurisdiction of Congress as other territory, and the State being, according to the language of the law, felo-de-se, ceases to exist.

CONG. GLOBE, 37th Cong., 2d Sess. 737 (Feb 11, 1862); *see also* ERIC L. MCKITRICK, ANDREW JOHNSON AND RECONSTRUCTION 110–13 (1960); David Currie, *The Civil War Congress*, 73 U. CHI. L. REV. 1131, 1211 (2006).

[18] *See* MCKITRICK, *supra* note 17, at 99 (discussing Thaddeus Stevens' "conquered province" theory).

were the positions of a minority. Most congressional Republicans rejected the theory of "state suicide" and continued to look forward to the day when the original Union would be restored. Unlike President Johnson, however, these more moderate Republicans believed that the southern states should remain excluded until Congress could ensure southern protection of individual freedom and the establishment of republican (small "r") governments.[19] For these members, the issue became how to best balance the newly ascendant idea of national liberty with an older principle of constitutional federalism.

As had been true at the time of the adoption of the original Constitution, some influential members of the political class viewed the United States in wholly nationalist terms. In the 1790s, for example, men like Pennsylvania's James Wilson denied the idea of state sovereignty and advocated broad national authority to regulate any matter affecting the national interest.[20] At the time of the Founding, however, wholly nationalist theories like Wilson's were held by a minority. Instead, the framers adopted a federalist Constitution of limited enumerated powers with the remainder reserved to the people in the several states. In the aftermath of the Civil War, the country faced a similar choice between unmediated nationalism and a balanced system of federalism. Another James Wilson, this one hailing from Iowa, once again called for the abolition of state sovereignty and the adoption of federal power over any matter affecting civil liberties in the states.[21] But just as the Founding generation rejected Wilsonian nationalist visions of government, so moderates in the Thirty-Ninth Congress turned away every effort to erase or even significantly undermine the dualist conception of American government. This was not a revolution. This was Reconstruction.

The idea that the original Constitution established a dual or federalist system of government can be contested, of course, and has been contested from the time of the Founding. Following the adoption of the Constitution (although not before), ardent nationalists not only denied that states retained any remnant of sovereign autonomy, but they also claimed that the states had never possessed sovereign autonomy in the first place.[22] On the other side of the spectrum, some antebellum state rights advocates insisted that states

---

[19] *Id.* at 113–14.
[20] See Kurt T. Lash, "Resolution VI": The Virginia Plan and Authority to Resolve Collective Actions Problems Under Article I, Section 8, 87 NOTRE DAME L. REV. 2123, 2154 (2012).
[21] *See infra* Chapter Three.
[22] *See* Chisholm v. Georgia, 2 U.S. (2 Dall.) 419, 470–71 (1793) (Jay, J.); *see also* JOSEPH STORY, COMMENTARIES ON THE CONSTITUTION (1833).

retained the sovereign right to nullify federal law,[23] and others insisted that the states retained the right to leave the Union altogether.[24]

The historical plausibility of either claim, Nationalist or Nullifier, is not the subject of this book. Instead, I seek to identify the views of the Constitution by members of Congress and the public at the time of the adoption of the Fourteenth Amendment. As one might expect, these views fall along a continuum, from ardent nationalist to almost as ardent state rightist (the fully secessionist views of men like Calhoun died with the slave power). I will claim, however, that a consensus emerged around a moderate position that sought to restore the original Constitution *as the moderates understood the original Constitution*, albeit on a firmer foundation.

To date, historical accounts of the Fourteenth Amendment have tended to emphasize the voices of those members of the Thirty-Ninth Congress whose views seem most like the view of the post-New Deal Supreme Court. From that perspective, the speeches of radical Republicans like Thaddeus Stevens, Charles Sumner, Lyman Trumbull, and Samuel Shellabarger seem almost prophetic in their broad vision of national power and individual liberty. In fact, men like these were revolutionaries.[25] By saying so, I do not mean to suggest that their views were so unacceptably out of the mainstream that they were not taken seriously. Indeed, had events transpired in only a slightly different manner, for example by forestalling consideration of the Fourteenth Amendment until after the Republican gains in the fall elections of 1866, there is reason to think that the Radical Republican agenda might have succeeded.

As events actually transpired in the spring of 1866, however, radical Republicans were forced into a tactical retreat. The final versions of the Fourteenth Amendment and the Civil Rights Act of 1866 were shaped by Republican moderates. Accordingly, the content and original understanding of these texts are altogether different from that which would have been the case had the radical Republicans prevailed. The text of the Fourteenth Amendment, in particular, reflects a view of the American constitutional republic as remaining neither wholly national nor wholly federal.[26] Whether their ideas

---

[23] *See* South Carolina, Ordinance of Nullification (Nov. 24, 1832), *available at* http://avalon.law. yale.edu/19th_century/ordnull.asp.

[24] *See* Secession Speech of Judah P. Benjamin, CONG. GLOBE, 36th Cong., 2d Sess. 212 (1860) (statement of Sen. Benjamin).

[25] McKITRICK, *supra* note 17, at 118 ("[T]here were men who, in their less guarded moments, blurted out that as far as they were concerned the country *was* in a state of revolution and that the constitution had nothing to do with the case.").

[26] *See* EARL M. MALTZ, CIVIL RIGHTS, THE CONSTITUTION, AND CONGRESS, 1863–1869, at 30 (1990) ("[The task of Reconstruction] was further complicated by the Republicans firm attachment to the basic structure of federalism."); WILLIAM E. NELSON, THE FOURTEENTH

about liberty and national power reflected an accurate understanding of the original Constitution, the moderates successfully translated their vision of constitutional government properly conceived into enduring constitutional text.

By claiming that Republican moderates committed to preserving a federalist Constitution controlled the legislative and constitutional outcomes of the Thirty-Ninth Congress, I am saying nothing particularly new. Historians have made this same observation for decades.[27] What has not been recognized, however, is the degree to which federalism played a role in shaping the language and original meaning of the Fourteenth Amendment. The moderate Republicans of the Thirty-Ninth Congress chose certain words and phrases that, if applied according to their original meaning, both protect individual liberty and preserve a constitutional balance of power.

One such phrase declares "the privileges or immunities of citizens of the United States." From a distance, this phrase looks very much like its lexicographical cousin, the so-called Comity Clause of Article IV, which protects the "privileges and immunities of citizens in the several states." As we shall see, however, these two provisions are not the same; they reflect different legal concepts and protect different kinds of rights.

AMENDMENT: FROM POLITICAL PRINCIPLE TO JUDICIAL DOCTRINE 27–39 (1988) (discussing the continued commitment to principles of federalism in the Reconstruction Congress).

[27] According to Eric Foner, moderates "accepted the enhancement of national power resulting from the Civil War, but they did not believe the legitimate rights of the states had been destroyed, or the traditional principles of federalism eradicated." ERIC FONER, RECONSTRUCTION: AMERICA'S UNFINISHED REVOLUTION 1863–1877, at 242 (1988); *see also* MALTZ, *supra* note 26, at 60 ("The disposition of the Freedmen's Bureau Bill and the apportionment amendment demonstrated that only those civil rights measures that received virtually unanimous support from mainstream Republicans could be adopted."); NELSON, supra note 26, at 114 ("Most Republican supporters of the [Fourteenth] amendment, like the Democrat opponents, feared centralized power and did not want to see state and local power substantially curtailed."); Michael Les Benedict, *Preserving the Constitution: The Conservative Basis of Radical Reconstruction*, 61 J. AM. HIST. 65, 67 (1974) ("[M]ost Republicans [during Reconstruction] never desired a broad, permanent extension of national legislative power.").

2

On Antebellum Privileges and Immunities

I. ON THE NATURE OF RIGHTS AT THE TIME OF THE FOUNDING

Having inherited a conception of rights rooted in medieval English common law,[1] American legal theorists at the time of the Founding faced the task of translating common law terms and ideas into the political and legal context of post-Revolutionary America.[2] In the middle to late eighteenth century, most Englishmen embraced the general Whig understanding of rights as running against the crown.[3] From the Magna Carta, to the Petition of Right, to the English Bill of Rights, the perceived danger was one of arbitrary and unconstrained executive (royal) power.[4] Although some of the more radical Whig writing warned about the dangers of the legislative branch as much as the executive,[5] most Englishmen in the mid-eighteenth century were not as concerned about the powers of Parliament as they were about the prerogatives of the King. Parliament, after all, stood as the body representing the people of England – why should the people constrain themselves?[6] Accordingly, English rights in the mid-eighteenth century were thought best protected

---

[1] Gordon S. Wood, *The History of Rights in Early America*, in THE NATURE OF RIGHTS AT THE AMERICAN FOUNDING AND BEYOND 233, 233 (Barry Alan Shain ed., 2007).

[2] For example, the first major American edition of *Blackstone's Commentaries* was a self-conscious effort by the author to translate English common law into the context of American constitutionalism. *See* ST. GEORGE TUCKER, BLACKSTONE'S COMMENTARIES: WITH NOTES OF REFERENCE TO THE CONSTITUTION AND THE LAWS, OF THE FEDERAL GOVERNMENT OF THE UNITED STATES, AND THE COMMONWEALTH OF VIRGINIA (Phila., Birch & Small 1803).

[3] *See* John Phillip Reid, *The Authority of Rights at the American Founding*, *in* The Nature of Rights of the American Founding and Beyond 67, 68 (Barry Alan Shain ed., 2007); *see also* Edmund S. Morgan, Inventing the People: The Rise of Popular Sovereignty in England and America 101–21 (1988).

[4] Wood, *supra* note 1, at 235.

[5] Gordon S. Wood, The Creation of the American Republic 1776–1787, at 14–15 (1969).

[6] Wood, *supra* note 1, at 235–36.

through mechanisms that ensured that life, liberty, and property would not be arbitrarily denied but regulated only by way of laws enacted by the people's representatives in Parliament.[7] As time went on, this deference to the English legislative assembly evolved into the general idea of Parliamentary supremacy.[8]

Americans, on the other hand, were drawn to the more radical Whig tradition that saw all branches of government as potential sources of tyranny and abuse. The self-serving and sometimes corrupt actions of the post-Revolutionary state governments fueled the emergence of a particular strain of popular sovereignty that viewed the people as both sovereign and distinct from their institutions of government, including the legislative branch.[9] As Gordon Wood has chronicled, the idea of popular sovereignty maintained that governments lawfully exercised only those powers delegated to them by the people themselves through a written constitution.[10] These constitutions not only described the general structure of state government, they also usually included a written declaration of rights to ensure that certain actions and activities fell beyond the unenumerated police powers of state governments.[11]

The proposed Federal Constitution, on the other hand, was presented by its advocates as granting the federal government only certain enumerated powers.[12] This is why, the Federalists explained, the document's drafters in

---

[7] JOHN LOCKE, TWO TREATISES OF GOVERNMENT AND A LETTER CONCERNING TOLERATION §§ 138–40, at 161–63 (Ian Shapiro ed., Yale Univ. Press 2003) (1689) (discussing the rights to freedom from arbitrary government and deprivation of property only by consent of the people's representatives); 1 WILLIAM BLACKSTONE, COMMENTARIES *137–38 (discussing the necessity of courts to protect against arbitrary executive deprivations of life, liberty, and property, and to ensure the enforcement of the law of the land).

[8] Wood, *supra* note 1, at 235–36.

[9] Wood, *supra* note 5, at 372–89.

[10] *Id.*

[11] *Id.*

[12] *See, e.g.,* THE FEDERALIST NO. 39 (James Madison) ("In this relation then the proposed Government cannot be deemed a *national* one; since its jurisdiction extends to certain enumerated objects only, and leaves to the several States a residuary and inviolable sovereignty over all other objects"); THE FEDERALIST NO. 45 (James Madison) ("The powers delegated by the proposed Constitution to the federal government, are few and defined. Those which are to remain in the State governments are numerous and indefinite"); James Madison, Virginia Ratifying Convention (June 15, 1788), *in* 3 DEBATES IN THE SEVERAL STATE CONVENTIONS ON THE ADOPTION OF THE FEDERAL CONSTITUTION 455 (Jonathan Elliot ed., 2d ed. 1836) ("With respect to the supposed operation of what was denominated the sweeping clause, the gentleman, he said, was mistaken; for it only extended to the enumerated powers. Should Congress attempt to extend it to any power not enumerated, it would not be warranted by the clause."); Alexander Hamilton, New York Ratifying Convention (June 28, 1788), *in* 2 ELLIOT'S DEBATES, *supra* this note, at 362 ("[W]hatever is not expressly given to the federal head, is reserved to the members. The truth of this principle must strike every intelligent mind."); *see also* Calder v. Bull, 3 U.S. (3 Dall.) 386, 387 (1798) (Chase, J.) ("[T]he several State Legislatures retain all

Philadelphia saw no need to include a written declaration of rights.[13] No power over subjects like speech, religion, and press had been delegated to the federal government, and thus, according to the fundamental principles of popular sovereignty, all nondelegated powers and rights would be retained by the people in the states.[14] Although Federalists ultimately acquiesced to the calls for a national Bill of Rights,[15] the addition of the Ninth and Tenth Amendments ensured that the basic idea of retained nondelegated powers and rights remained an express aspect of the Federal Constitution.[16] As the Maryland General Court explained in 1797, under the Federal Constitution "[a]ll power, jurisdiction, and rights of sovereignty, not granted by the people by that instrument, or relinquished, are still retained by them in their several states, and in their respective state legislatures."[17] The scope of conferred federal power was a matter of continual debate in the early years of the Constitution as Congress debated matters such as the establishment of a national bank[18] and the authority to criminalize seditious speech.[19] Nevertheless, even the most aggressive proponents of federal power accepted the basic concept of enumerated federal authority.[20] Although the states faced certain restrictions under Article I, Section 10, according to Chief Justice John Marshall in

---

the powers of legislation, delegated to them by the State Constitutions; which are not expressly taken away by the Constitution of the United States."); Gibbons v. Ogden, 22 U.S. 1, 195 (1824) (Marshall, C. J.) ("The enumeration presupposes something not enumerated.").

[13] *See* James Wilson, State House Yard Speech (Oct. 6, 1787), *in* 1 COLLECTED WORKS OF JAMES WILSON 171, 172 (Kermit L. Hall & Mark David Hall eds., 2007).

[14] *Id.*

[15] *See* James Madison, Speech in Congress Proposing Constitutional Amendments (June 8. 1789), *in* JAMES MADISON: WRITINGS 437, 442–43 (Jack Rakove ed., 1999).

[16] *See* U.S. CONST. amend. IX ("The enumeration in the Constitution, of certain rights, shall not be construed to deny or disparage others retained by the people."); *Id.* amend. X ("The powers not delegated to the United States by the Constitution, nor prohibited by it to the States, are reserved to the States respectively, or to the people."). For a discussion of how the Ninth and Tenth Amendments originally worked in tandem to preserve the people's retained right to local self-government, see KURT T. LASH, THE LOST HISTORY OF THE NINTH AMENDMENT (Oxford U. Press 2009).

[17] Campbell v. Morris, 3 H. & McH. 535, 554 (Md. 1797).

[18] *See, e.g.,* Madison, *supra* note 15, at 480 (speech opposing the National Bank).

[19] See James Madison, Report on the Alien and Sedition Acts (Jan. 7, 1800), in WRITINGS, supra note 15, at 608, 631–55; John Marshall, The Address of the Minority in the Virginia Legislature to the People of that State, Containing a Vindication of the Constitutionality of the Alien and Sedition Laws (Dec. 1798), in JOHN MARSHALL: MAJOR OPINIONS AND OTHER WRITINGS 34, 34–47 (John P. Roche ed., 1967).

[20] *See, e.g.,* Gibbons v. Ogden, 22 U.S. 1, 195 (1824) (Marshall, C.J.) ("The enumeration presupposes something not enumerated."); Alexander Hamilton, Opinion on the Constitutionality of the Bank (Feb. 23, 1791), *reprinted in* 3 THE FOUNDERS' CONSTITUTION 247, 248–49 (Philip B. Kurland & Ralph Lerner eds., 1987).

Barron v. Baltimore, the provisions of the Bill of Rights bound only the federal government.[21] This left the subject matter of the Bill of Rights, and personal rights in general, under the care and protection of state majorities.

Whether secured by federal or state law, the actual substance of rights at the time of the Founding included a rich mix of liberties, advantages, exemptions, privileges, and immunities.[22] Today, rights are most often conceived as individual in nature. At the time of the Founding, however, rights could be individual,[23] majoritarian,[24] collective,[25] or governmental.[26] Sources of law included natural law,[27] the law of nations,[28] common law,[29] positive law, or,

---

[21] 32 U.S. (7 Pet.) 243, 247–28 (1833).

[22] For a general discussion of the variety of rights in play at the time of the Founding, see LASH, *supra* note 16, at 82–83; RICHARD A. PRIMUS, THE AMERICAN LANGUAGE OF RIGHTS 78–91 (1999).

[23] *See, e.g.,* 1 ANNALS OF CONG. 732 (Joseph Gales ed., 1834) (statement of Rep. Theodore Sedgwick) (discussing the unenumerated individual right of a man "to wear his hat if he pleased" or "go to bed when he thought proper").

[24] LOCKE, *supra* note 7, §§ 95–99, at 141–43 ("When any number of men have so consented to make one community or government, they are thereby presently incorporated, and make one body politic, wherein the majority have a right to act and conclude the rest.").

[25] *See* THE DECLARATION OF INDEPENDENCE para. 2 (1776) (declaring the people's collective right of revolution).

[26] *See* EMMERICH DE VATTEL, THE LAW OF NATIONS bk. 1, ch. 3, § 31, at 94 (Thomas Nugent trans., Bela Kaposey & Richard Whatmore eds., Liberty Fund, Inc. 2008) (1758) (discussing "[t]he rights of a nation with respect to its constitution and government"); Lord Mansfield, Speech in the House of Lords (1770), *in* William Scott, LESSONS IN ELOCUTION 262 (1788) (Early Am. Imprints, Series 1, no. 21451) (claiming that a proposed bill "is no less than to take away from two thirds of the legislative body of this great kingdom, certain privileges and immunities of which they have been long possessed").

[27] *See, e.g.,* James Madison, *Notes for Speech in Congress* (June 8, 1789) ("Contents of Bill of Rhts... 3. *natural rights*, retained – as Speech, Con...."), *in* 12 PAPERS OF JAMES MADISON 193, 194 (Charles F. Hobson & Robert A. Rutland eds., 1979).

[28] *See generally* DE VATTEL, *supra* note 26. Vattel was one of the most frequently cited legal authorities of the Founding generation and long afterward. David Gray Adler, *Court, Constitution and Foreign Affairs, in* THE CONSTITUTION AND THE CONDUCT OF AMERICAN FOREIGN POLICY 19, 137–38 (David Gray Adler & Larry George eds., 1996) ("During the Founding period and well beyond, Vattel was, in the United States, the unsurpassed publicist on international law.... From the day Vattel's treatise arrived in America in 1775, it was invariably invoked as authoritative on matters of international law by the likes of Alexander Hamilton, James Madison, James Wilson, Edmund Randolph, Thomas Jefferson, John Marshall, Joseph Story and James Kent, among others.").

[29] *See, e.g.,* TUCKER, *supra* note 2. Like Vattel's work on the Law of Nations, Tucker's edition of *Blackstone's Commentaries* was a standard and frequently cited legal authority in the period between the Founding and the Civil War. *See* David T. Hardy, *The Lecture Notes of St. George Tucker: A Framing Era View of the Bill of Rights*, 103 Nw. U. L. REV. 1527, 1527 (2009) (Tucker's edition of Blackstone's Commentaries became "the standard work on American law for a generation" and he "remained the most frequently cited American legal scholar for over two decades").

quite commonly, a combination of all the above.[30] "Bearers of rights," to use Richard Primus's phrase, potentially included everything from individuals and groups to local, state, and national governments.[31]

Making the picture even more complicated, after the Founding, an individual rights bearer could be both a citizen of the United States and a citizen of a particular state.[32] This created a situation in which the same right could have a different nature and scope depending on who asserted the right and against whom the right was asserted. For example, the federal Bill of Rights originally bound only the federal government. Thus, in 1791, one might have an *individual* constitutional right against a *federal* law forbidding criticism of the government but only a local *majoritarian* right against a *state* law forbidding the same act.[33] In such a case, one might have a judicially enforceable right against the federal government but not against a law passed by a majority of the state legislature. One might argue, and many did, that the natural right to freedom of expression is the same regardless of the government institution. Historically, however, one's legal protection differed depending on whether the asserted right ran against the state (as a matter of state citizenship) or against the federal government (as a matter of federal citizenship).[34]

This brief survey only scratches the surface of the broad subject of rights at the time of the Founding.[35] It is important, however, that we have a general understanding of this taxonomy of rights. Antebellum religious, political,

---

[30] *See generally* Reid, *supra* note 3. John Reid reminds us that, despite the common use of the language of natural rights during the revolutionary period, natural law was generally used as an additional authority for the rights being claimed by the colonists – rights that mainly involved being treated equally with those royal subjects in England. *Id.* at 86. According to Reid, "[t]he chief utility of nature as a source of rights was to give civil rights an authority independent of human creation." *Id.* at 93. As far as the substance of natural rights goes, it was rarely argued that specific rights existed on the authority of nature alone; most often natural rights were "equated with British constitutional and positive law and with English common law." *Id.* at 96. The rhetoric of natural law provided an additional source of authority for those rights demanded by the colonists equal to the rights of the British.

[31] Primus, *supra* note 22, at 85.

[32] Article I, Section 8 conferred upon Congress the power to establish national citizenship by way of its power to establish uniform rules of naturalization, while Article IV (both implied and as a matter of later interpretation) referred to preexisting and ongoing rights associated with state citizenship. U.S. Const. art. I, § 8; *id.* art. V.

[33] *See* Madison, *supra* note 15, at 631–55.

[34] *See, e.g.,* Calder v. Bull, 3 U.S. (3 Dall.) 386, 387 (1798). For an analysis of the state-autonomy aspects of *Calder,* see Lash, *supra* note 16, at 177–81.

[35] For more detailed discussion of rights at the time of the Founding, see generally Primus, *supra* note 22, at 78–91; The Nature of Rights at the American Founding and Beyond 233, 233 (Barry Alan Shain ed., 2007): Wood, *supra* note 5.

social, and legal literature is soaked in the rhetoric of rights. Terms like "rights," "advantages," "privileges," and "immunities" appear in a variety of contexts and in reference to a variety of liberties. The manner in which the terms were used in one context may tell us much, little, or nothing at all about how the terms were used or understood in a different context.[36] This does not make the search for historical understanding impossible, but it does suggest that one must be sensitive to the legal context in which the terms were deployed.

A. *"Privileges" and "Immunities" in Antebellum America*

Political and legal usage of the terms "privileges" and "immunities" evolved alongside the terms "rights" and "liberties" and were put to the same varied use. Throughout the late eighteenth and early nineteenth centuries, one finds countless examples of the terms "rights," "advantages," "liberties," "privileges," and "immunities" used interchangeably and often at the same time.[37] As early as 1606, for example, Virginia's colonial charter spoke of the protected "Liberties, Franchises, and Immunities" of English citizens in Virginia.[38] According to the 1765 Resolves of the Virginia House of Burgesses, colonists were entitled to "all the Liberties, Privileges, Franchises, and Immunities, that have at any Time been held, enjoyed, and possessed, by the people of *Great Britain*," and "all Liberties, Privileges, and Immunities . . . as if they had been abiding and born within the Realm of *England*."[39] The Declaration of Rights

---

[36] Scholars like Michael Kent Curtis have done important work showing how the individual terms "privileges" and "immunities" were sometimes used in reference to the rights listed in the first eight amendments to the Constitution. *See, e.g.*, MICHAEL KENT CURTIS, NO STATE SHALL ABRIDGE: THE FOURTEENTH AMENDMENT AND THE BILL OF RIGHTS 161–63 (1986). My effort here is to show how these words, when used in combination, took on a particular meaning distinguishable from their uses as individual terms.

[37] *See* Michael Kent Curtis, *Historical Linguistics, Inkblots, and Life After Death: The Privileges or Immunities of Citizens of the United States*, 78 N.C. L. REV. 1071, 1095 (2000) (noting that "[t]he words 'rights' and 'privileges' were used interchangeably" in colonial America).

[38] *See* THE FIRST CHARTER OF VIRGINIA (1606) ("[King James I grants to] all and every the Persons being our Subjects. . . . all Liberties, Franchises, and Immunities, within any of our other Dominions, to all Intents and Purposes, as if they had been abiding and born, within this our Realm of *England*, or any other of our said Dominions."), *reprinted in* 7 THE FEDERAL AND STATE CONSTITUTIONS, COLONIAL CHARTERS, AND OTHER ORGANIC LAWS 3783, 3788 (Francis Newton Thorpe ed., Wash. Gov't Printing Office 1909); *see also* 16 THE PARLIAMENTARY DEBATES FROM THE YEAR 1803 TO THE PRESENT TIME 144 (London, Hansard 1812) ("That the Liberties, Franchises, Privileges, and Jurisdictions of Parliament, are the ancient and undoubted birthright and inheritance of the subjects of England.").

[39] JOURNALS OF THE HOUSE OF BURGESSES OF VIRGINIA, 1761–1765, at 360 (John Pendleton Kennedy ed., 1907).

of the Continental Congress likewise insisted that the colonists were "entitled to all the rights, liberties, and immunities of free and natural-born subjects, within the realm of England" and "to all the immunities and privileges granted [and] confirmed to them by royal charters."[40]

According to legal sources written in the early years of the Republic, the words "privileges" and "immunities" often meant the same thing.[41] Dictionaries of the time also equated the terms.[42] Also, just as rights at the time of the Founding referred to an extremely broad range of activities, sources, and bearers, so, too, one can find privileges and immunities associated with everything from individual rights to corporate powers, sometimes in the same source. For example, in one section of his *Commentaries*, Blackstone uses the individual terms "privileges" and "immunities" in reference to individual natural rights,[43] whereas in a different section of the same book he uses the combined phrase "privileges and immunities" to refer to the government-conferred collective rights of corporations.[44] This last example is instructive in that it is a harbinger of how the combined terms "privileges and immunities" came to be used in legal, political, and social literature of antebellum America as a phrase denoting specially conferred rights and advantages.

B. *The Pairing of "Privileges and Immunities"*

Although one can find the single word "privilege" used in a variety of contexts, at the time of the Founding, dictionaries generally defined the term as denoting

---

[40] 1 JOURNALS OF THE CONTINENTAL CONGRESS 1774–1789, at 68 (Worthington Chancey Ford ed., Wash. Gov't Printing Office 1904).

[41] According to the Maryland General Court in 1797, the terms "[p]rivilege and immunity are synonymous, or nearly so." Campbell v. Morris, 3 H. & McH. 535, 553 (Md. 1797); *see also* Douglass' Adm'r v. Stevens, 2 Del. Cas. 489, 501 (1819) ("By the second section of the fourth article of the Constitution of the United States the citizens of each state shall be entitled to all the privileges and immunities of the citizens in the several states. The words 'privileges' and 'immunities' are nearly synonymous. Privilege signifies a peculiar advantage, exemption, immunity. Immunity signifies exemption, privilege."); Robert G. Natelson, *The Original Meaning of the Privileges and Immunities Clause*, 43 GA. L. REV. 1117, 1133 (2009) ("[I]t appears that 'immunity' and 'privilege' were reciprocal words for the same legal concept.").

[42] *See, e.g.*, William Perry, THE ROYAL STANDARD ENGLISH DICTIONARY 411, 442 (1st Am. ed., Worcester, Mass., Thomas 1788) (Early Am. Imprints, Series 1, no. 21385) (defining "Right" as a "just claim; justice; interest; prerogative, privilege," and "Privilege" as a "publick right; peculiar advantage"); PHILADELPHIA SCHOOL DICTIONARY, OR EXPOSITOR OF THE ENGLISH LANGUAGE 105, 152 (3rd ed., Phila., Johnson 1812) (defining "Privilege" as a "[p]eculiar advantage" and "Immunity" as a "privilege, exemption").

[43] 1 BLACKSTONE, *supra* note 7, at *129 (describing personal rights as "private immunities" and "civil privileges").

[44] *See id.* at *468 (discussing the "privileges and immunities" of corporations).

a "publick right" or a kind of unique or special advantage.[45] This same definition applied to the combined terms "privileges and immunities." For example,
when Blackstone used the phrase "privileges and immunities" in reference to
the conferred rights of corporations, he meant those institutions on whom
legislatures or parliaments conferred special rights not generally available to
all others.[46] Early American legal sources echoed this "specially conferred
rights" understanding of the paired terms. Early court decisions explained that
"[p]rivilege signifies a peculiar advantage, exemption, immunity; immunity
signifies exemption, privilege," whereas the paired terms referred to a set of
"peculiar advantages and exemptions."[47]

From the time of the Founding right up to and beyond the Civil War,
one finds countless references to the specially conferred "privileges and

---

[45] *See supra* note 42; *see also* Natelson, *supra* note 41, at 1130 (discussing early dictionary definitions
of "privileges" as having four components "(1) a benefit or advantage; (2) conferred by positive
law; (3) on a person or place; (4) contrary to what the rule would be in absence of the privilege"
[citation omitted]).

[46] According to Blackstone:

> We have hitherto considered persons in their natural capacities, and have treated of their
> rights and duties. But, as all personal rights die with the person; and, as the necessary
> forms of investing a series of individuals, one after another, with the same identical rights,
> would be very inconvenient, if not impracticable, it has been found necessary, when it is
> for the advantage of the public to have any particular rights kept on foot and continued,
> to constitute artificial persons, who may maintain a perpetual succession, and enjoy a
> kind of legal immortality.

> These artificial persons are called bodies politic, bodies corporate, (*corpora corporata*)
> or corporations: of which there is a great variety subsisting, for the advancement of
> religion, of learning, and of commerce; in order to preserve entire and for ever those
> rights and immunities, which, if they were granted only to those individuals of which
> the body corporate is composed, would upon their death be utterly lost and extinct. . . . If
> [a college] were a mere voluntary assembly, the individuals which compose it . . . could
> neither frame, nor receive any laws or rules of their conduct; none at least, which would
> have any binding force, for want of a coercive power to create a sufficient obligation.
> Neither could they be capable of retaining any privileges or immunities: for, if such
> privileges be attacked, which of all this unconnected assembly has the right, or ability, to
> defend them? And when they are dispersed by death or otherwise, how shall they transfer
> these advantages to another set of students, equally unconnected as themselves? . . . But
> when they are consolidated and united into a corporation, they and their successors are
> then considered as one person in law. . . . [T]he privileges and immunities, the estates
> and possessions, of the corporation, when once vested in them, will be forever vested,
> without any new conveyance to new successions. . . .

1 BLACKSTONE, *supra* note 7, at *467–68.

[47] Campbell v. Morris, 3 H. & McH. 535, 533 (Md. 1797).

immunities" of kings,[48] diplomatic emissaries,[49] private societies,[50] churches,[51] artillery companies,[52] ecclesiastics,[53] Christian apostles,[54] and corporations,[55]

[48] *See, e.g.,* Marshall V. Lovelass, REPORTS OF CASES RULED AND DETERMINED BY THE COURT OF CONFERENCE OF NORTH-CAROLINA 217, 234 (Duncan Cameron & William Norwood eds., Raleigh, Gales 1805) (Early Am. Imprints, Series 2, no. 9035) ("[A]lthough the King cannot be sued, yet his aliene may be, for he does not partake of his privileges or immunities.").

[49] *See* DE VATTEL, *supra* note 26, at bk. 4, ch. 7, at 696–729. In 1801, a New York court declared that the law of nations did not grant "to consuls who enter into trade, any particular privileges or immunities above those enjoyed by the native subjects of the country." United Ins. Co. v. Arnold, Court for the Trial of Impeachments and the Correction of Errors 7 (Albany, N.Y., Webster 1801) (Early Am. Imprints, Series 2, no. 1033).

[50] In 1783, the Society of Cincinnati published a defense of the society, reminding readers that it lacked the "privileges or immunities" granted to corporations. *See* A REPLY TO A PAMPHLET, ENTITLED, CONSIDERATIONS ON THE SOCIETY OR ORDER OF CINCINNATI 18 (Annapolis, Green 1783) (Early Am. Imprints, Series 1, no. 18149).

[51] *See An Act to Alter the Name of the Second Presbyterian Church of Newark* (Jan. 31, 1811), *in* ACTS OF THE THIRTY-FIFTH GENERAL ASSEMBLY, OF THE STATE OF NEW-JERSEY 402, 402 (Trenton, Wilson 1811) (Early Am. Imprints, Series 2, no. 23525) ("[N]othing in this act contained shall in any manner or degree invalidate or impair any rights, powers, privileges or immunities to which the said body politic and corporate are entitled by the said act of incorporation and the said supplement thereto.").

[52] *See, e.g., An Act, Regulating the Militia in this Colony, in* ACTS AND LAWS OF THE ENGLISH COLONY OF RHODE-ISLAND AND PROVIDENCE PLANTATIONS, IN NEW-ENGLAND, IN AMERICA 179, 189 (Newport, Hall 1868) (Early Am. Imprints, Series 1, no. 10749) ("*PROVIDED always*, That nothing in this Act contained shall extend, or be construed to extend to take away or diminish any of the Liberties, Privileges, or Immunities of any independent or Artillery-Company or Companies established by Law in this Colony; but that the same, according to their Establishment, be preserved to them entire, any Thing herein contained to the contrary.").

[53] *See* 1 JOHN GIFFORD, THE HISTORY OF FRANCE, FROM THE EARLIEST OF TIMES, TILL THE DEATH OF LOUIS SIXTEENTH 500 (Phila., Bioren & Madan 1796) (Early Am. Imprints, Series 1, no. 30489) (discussing the "particular privileges or immunities, granted by the pope to ecclesiastics").

[54] *See* DAVID OSGOOD, A DISCOURSE ON THE VALIDITY OF THE PRESBYTERIAN ORDINATION 12 (Cambridge, Hilliard 1802) (Early Am. Imprints, Series 2, no. 2830) ("At the height of their exaltation however, [the Apostles] acknowledged themselves in all other respects, to be but *earthen vessels*, on a par with one another and with their Christian brethren in general, subject alike with them, both to the same infirmities and to the same laws, having no exclusive privileges or immunities.").

[55] *See, e.g.,* ACT OF INCORPORATION, CONSTITUTION, BY-LAWS, &C OF THE ASSOCIATED MECHAN-ICS AND MANUFACTURERS OF THE STATE OF NEW-HAMPSHIRE 4–5 (Portsmouth, N.H., Tread-well 1810) (Early Am. Imprints, Series 2, no. 19389) ("*And be it further enacted*, That the said corporation, shall have a common seal, such as shall be determined on by a major vote at any meeting, and which seal shall be affixed to grants of real estates that may be made by the corporation, and to grants of privileges or immunities to any member, and to certificates."). The references to the privileges and immunities of corporations are far too many to list, a fact not surprising in light of the references in *Blackstone's Commentaries. See supra* note 44 and accompanying text.

including incorporated towns and municipalities.[56] This last group was so thoroughly associated with conferred privileges and immunities that dictionaries of the day defined "disfranchise" as meaning "to deprive cities, & c. of chartered privileges or immunities."[57]

Antebellum legal documents, court cases, newspaper articles, and treatises repeatedly placed adjectives like "special,"[58] "peculiar,"[59] "exclusive,"[60] and

---

[56] The 1772 laws of New York protected the "Powers, Pre-eminences, Privileges or Immunities over, or in Respect to the said Township of Harlem." LAWS OF NEW-YORK, FROM THE YEAR 1691, TO 1773 INCLUSIVE, at 714 (N.Y., Gaine 1772).

[57] JOSEPH HAMILTON, JOHNSON'S DICTIONARY OF THE ENGLISH LANGUAGE 71 (2d ed., Newburyport, Thomas & Whipple 1806) (Early Am. Imprints, Series 2, no. 10643); *see also* SUSANNA ROWSON, A SPELLING DICTIONARY 42 (2d ed., Portland, Me., A & J Shirley 1807) (Early Am. Imprints, Series 2, no. 35815) (children's version of *Johnson's Dictionary* with the same definition of "disfranchise").

[58] *See, e.g.,* J. V. Smith, *Ohio Constitutional Convention.* OHIO DAILY STATESMAN, Feb. 14, 1851, at 2 [hereinafter Smith, *Ohio Constitutional Convention* (Feb.)] (reporting on a proposed clause in the Ohio Bill of Rights providing that the legislature may have a right "to alter, revoke, repeal or abolish . . . any grant or law conferring special privileges or immunities, upon any portion of the people, which cannot reasonably be enjoyed by all"); J. V. Smith, *Ohio Constitutional Convention.* OHIO DAILY STATESMAN, Mar. 1, 1851, at 2 [hereinafter Smith, *Ohio Constitutional Convention* (Mar.)] (reporting on a proposal to remove a portion of a proposed amendment to the Ohio Bill of Rights stating "and no special privileges or immunities shall ever be granted injurious to the public, and which cannot reasonably be enjoyed by all"); *The Constitutional Convention,* FREEDOM'S CHAMPION (Atchison City, Kan.), July 23, 1859, at 1 (discussing an article from Kansas's Bill of Rights that was adopted at Kansas's Constitutional Convention stating that "(n)o special privileges or immunities shall ever be granted by the Legislature which may not be altered, revoked or repealed by the same body"); *Virginia Legislature – House of Delegates Convention,* RICHMOND ENQUIRER (Va.), Jan. 15, 1829, at 1 (citing statement of Representative Mason of Frederick: "But, sir, under what sanction can individuals of the same community, holding a peculiar species of property, or any particular district of country, stipulate in like manner for *especial privileges or immunities* to that property, as a pre-requisite to the formation of a common government?" [emphasis added]).

[59] *See* Douglass' Adm'r v. Stevens, 2 Del. Cas. 489, 501 (1819) ("By the second section of the fourth article of the Constitution of the United States the citizens of each state shall be entitled to all the privileges and immunities of the citizens in the several states. The words 'privileges' and 'immunities' are nearly synonymous. Privilege signifies a peculiar advantage, exemption, immunity. Immunity signifies exemption, privilege."); Campbell v. Morris, 3 H. & McH. 535, 553 (Md. 1797) (discussing "[t]he peculiar advantages and exemptions contemplated under [Article IV]"); PHILADELPHIA SCHOOL DICTIONARY, *supra* note 42, at 152 (defining "Privilege" as a "[p]eculiar advantage" and "Immunity" as a "privilege, exemption"); *see also* Magill v. Brown, 16 F. Cas. 408, 428 (C.C.E.D. Pa. 1833) (No. 8,952) ("The words 'privileges and immunities' relate to the rights of persons, place or property; a privilege is a peculiar right, a private law, conceded to particular persons or places. . . . ").

[60] In 1841, *The Emancipator* called for "[e]qual rights, equal and exact justice to all men, and no exclusive privileges or immunities." *The Necessity of a Liberty Party,* THE EMANCIPATOR (N.Y.), Nov. 11, 1841, at 112.

"particular"[61] in front of the paired terms "privileges and immunities" in order to highlight the unique nature of such conferred rights. These "peculiar" rights might include natural rights or any other variety and combination of conferred liberties. The paired terms did not refer to a defined set of rights but rather indicated the existence of a unique set of liberties or advantages, the particular content of which differed depending on the context and the group at issue.

Having "privileges and immunities" was not always something to be celebrated.[62] Newspaper editorials during the Jacksonian era commonly decried "the possession of privileges or immunities, in which ninety-nine hundredths of the community, by the very nature of their situation, are denied all participation,"[63] and they vilified the "'privileged order'. . . on whom the law confers certain privileges or immunities not enjoyed by the great mass of the people."[64] In 1841, *The Emancipator* called for "[e]qual rights, equal and exact justice to all men, and no exclusive privileges or immunities."[65] Legislatures during this period drafted constitutional amendments that expressly opposed the granting of special privileges and immunities to corporations. For example, the members of the 1851 Ohio Constitutional Convention drafted a proposed addition to the state Bill of Rights that declared that "[n]o special

---

[61] *See* Corfield v. Coryell, 6 F. Cas. 546, 552 (C.C.E.D. Pa. 1823) (No. 3,230) (discussing the "particular privileges and immunities" protected under Article IV); Campbell, 3 H. & McH. at 554 (stating that a "particular and limited operation is to be given to [the privileges and immunities clause of Article IV]"); United Ins. Co. v. Arnold, *supra* note 49, at 7 (denying a diplomat any "particular privileges or immunities above those enjoyed by the native subjects of the country"); 1 GIFFORD, *supra* note 53, at 500 (discussing the "particular privileges or immunities, granted by the pope to ecclesiastics, with the permission of their sovereigns").

[62] An 1803 editorial in the *Aurora General Advertiser* declared that neither state legislatures nor the federal Senators they elected possessed special or "exclusive rights, powers and immunities" other than those "granted to them by the people." Editorial, *A Vindication of the Democratic Constitutions of America*, AURORA GEN. ADVERTISER (Phila.), Aug. 20, 1803, at 2. In 1820, a Mr. Grundy offered the following resolution in the Tennessee legislature:

> Whereas, the Congress of the United States will probably at their present session, take into consideration the propriety of establishing a uniform system of Bankruptcy throughout the United States, and whereas this General Assembly consider every measure, which bestows on one class of our citizens, rights, privileges or immunities, which are withheld from others, as unjust and impolitic. . . .

> *Resolved*, That our Senators in Congress be instructed, and our Representatives requested, to use their best exertions to prevent the passage of any act or acts calculated to violate the principles laid down in the preamble to this resolution.

Legislature of Tennessee, AGRIC. INTELLIGENCER, & MECHANIC REG. (Boston), Jan. 21, 1820, at 23.

[63] *The Cry of the Poor Against the Rich*, OHIO STATESMAN (Columbus), July 10, 1839, at 4.

[64] *Banks, a Privileged Order*, WIS. ENQUIRER, Oct. 17, 1840, at 1.

[65] The Necessity of a Liberty Party, *supra* note 60.

privileges or immunities shall ever be granted, injurious to the public" and provided that the legislature could "alter, revoke, or repeal or abolish . . . any grant or law conferring special privileges or immunities, upon any portion of the people, which cannot reasonably be enjoyed by all."[66]

In sum, although antebellum use of the single terms "privileges" and "immunities" occurred in an almost bewildering array of contexts, use of the *paired* terms "privileges and immunities" seems to have been generally reserved to a description of specially conferred rights. Put another way, "privileges and immunities" did not refer to the natural rights belonging to all people or all institutions but referred instead to particular rights conferred on a certain group or a particular institution.

II. THE PRIVILEGES AND IMMUNITIES "OF CITIZENS IN THE SEVERAL STATES"

Antebellum discussion of the rights of citizenship offers a particularly focused example of how the phrase "privileges and immunities" was understood in American law during the period between the Founding and the Civil War. The very concept of citizenship involves issues of group membership and the identification of rights associated with that membership. Just as different groups and institutions could have different "privileges and immunities," the citizens of various governments also had uniquely defined rights and advantages.

A. *State Citizenship: The Comity Clause of Article IV*

One of the greatest sources of friction between Britain and the American colonies was the colonists' belief that they had been denied the equal privileges and immunities of English citizens – rights they had "purchased" through the grueling and perilous act of emigrating from England and colonizing America.[67] The colonists, like all English citizens, expected the equal enjoyment of the privileges and immunities of English common law as long as they lived under the British flag.[68] English citizens traveling in foreign countries

---

[66] Smith, *Ohio Constitutional Convention* (Feb.), *supra* note 58, at 2; *see also* Smith, *Ohio Constitutional Convention* (Mar.), *supra* note 58, at 2 (reporting on a proposal to remove the following portion of a proposed amendment to the Ohio Bill of Rights: "and no special privileges or immunities shall ever be granted injurious to the public, and which cannot reasonably be enjoyed by all").

[67] *See* Reid, *supra* note 3, at 77.

[68] *See, e.g.*, 1 JOURNALS OF THE CONTINENTAL CONGRESS 1774–1789, *supra* note 40, at 68 ("That our ancestors, who first settled these colonies, were at the time of their emigration from the mother country, entitled to all the rights, liberties, and immunities of free and natural-born subjects, within the realm of England."); THE FIRST CHARTER OF VIRGINIA, *supra* note 38, at

enjoyed only those privileges and immunities secured to them by international treaty.[69]

Following the Revolution, the conferred rights of citizenship transferred to the newly independent states. State laws determined conditions of citizenship and naturalization, and state citizens expected the equal enjoyment of those privileges and immunities secured to them by their state's constitution.[70] Prior to the adoption of the Federal Constitution, however, it was not at all clear what privileges or immunities they could expect when traveling to, or through, other states. It seemed inappropriate to establish "visitation" rights by treaty – such an approach would create friction with nonparticipating states, and it would have the effect of treating the sojourning citizen as if he were an alien from a foreign country, a status that would deprive the traveler of a number of rights commonly enjoyed by citizens, including the right of entrance and the right to own and dispose of real property.

Article IV of the Articles of Confederation attempted to remedy the situation by declaring:

> The better to secure and perpetuate mutual friendship and intercourse among the people of the different States in this Union, the free inhabitants of each of these States, paupers, vagabonds, and fugitives from justice excepted, shall be entitled to all privileges and immunities of free citizens in the several States; and the people of each State shall have free ingress and regress to and from any other State, and shall enjoy therein all the privileges of trade and commerce, subject to the same duties, impositions, and restrictions, as the inhabitants thereof respectively; provided that such restrictions shall not extend so far as to prevent the removal of property imported into any State, to any other State, of which the owner is an inhabitant; provided also, that no imposition, duties, or restriction, shall be laid by any State on the property of the United States, or either of them.[71]

3788 ("[King James I grants to] all and every the Persons being our Subjects . . . all Liberties, Franchises, and Immunities, within any of our other Dominions, to all Intents and Purposes, as if they had been abiding and born, within this our Realm of *England*, or any other of our said Dominions."); Reid, *supra* note 3, at 67 (quoting Rhode Island Governor Stephen Hopkins as stating "[t]he British subjects in America have equal rights with those in Britain. . . . They do not hold those rights as a privilege granted them, nor enjoy them as a grace and favor bestowed, but possess them as an inherent, indefeasible right, as they and their ancestors were freeborn subjects, justly and naturally entitled to all the rights and advantages of the British constitution").

[69] *See, e.g.*, Pa. Gazette, June 19, 1766, at 2 (reporting news of a treaty between Great Britain and Sweden stating that "(t]he two Powers shall reciprocally enjoy, in the Towns, Ports, Harbours and Rivers of their respective States, all the Rights, Advantages, and Immunities, which have been, or may be henceforth enjoyed there by the most favoured Nations").

[70] *See* Wood, *supra* note 5, at 127–43.

[71] *See* Articles of Confederation, art. IV, § 1 (1788).

A streamlined version of this provision became Article IV of the Federal Constitution: "The Citizens of each State shall be entitled to all Privileges and Immunities of Citizens in the several States."[72]

At the time of its enactment, there was little in the way of substantive discussion regarding the meaning and potential application of Article IV, Section 2. James Madison indicated that it clarified the language of the older Article IV.[73] Alexander Hamilton rather unhelpfully explained that it formed "the basis of the Union" and that federal courts should be available to ensure an "equality of privileges and immunities to which citizens of the Union [would] be entitled."[74] As we shall see, at the time of the Civil War, the particular meaning of this Clause became a matter of serious discussion and debate. Its addition to the federal Constitution attracted little controversy, however, probably due to its roots in the Articles of Confederation.[75]

Early court decisions reflected five possible approaches to Article IV, with one quickly emerging as the dominant interpretation. First, the Clause could be read as binding the federal government, not the states, with a requirement that federal legislation not discriminate on the basis of state citizenship. Second, the Clause could be read as referring to a set of national rights that all states were bound to respect. Third, the Clause could be read to require states to grant all citizens visiting from other states the same rights that the visitors had received in and brought with them from their home state. Fourth, the Clause could be read as requiring states to grant visiting citizens *all* of the same privileges and immunities that the state conferred on its own citizens.

---

[72] U.S. CONST. art. IV, § 2, cl. 1.

[73] *See* THE FEDERALIST No. 42, at 269 (James Madison) (Clinton Rossiter ed., 1961) ("In the fourth article of the Confederation, it is declared 'that the *free inhabitants* of each of these States, paupers, vagabonds, and fugitives from justice excepted, shall be entitled to all privileges and immunities of *free citizens* in the several States; and *the people* of each State shall, in every other, enjoy all the privileges of trade and commerce,' etc. There is a confusion of language here which is remarkable.").

[74] THE FEDERALIST No. 80, at 478 (Alexander Hamilton) (Clinton Rossiter ed., 1961). Hamilton misquotes the provision as "the citizens of each State shall be entitled to all the privileges and immunities of citizens of the several States." *Id.* The error, however, does not affect his general point about the value of having a neutral (federal) tribunal available for trying cases involving disputes between citizens from one state and citizens from another state.

[75] James Madison described the Article as simply clearing up some of the ambiguous language of the Articles of Confederation. *See* THE FEDERALIST No. 42, *supra* note 73, at 269–71 (describing how Article IV of the proposed Constitution avoided the confused and legally problematic language of the related provision in the Articles of Confederation). In the first constitutional treatise, St. George Tucker had little to say about the clause beyond the fact that it was based on the earlier provision in the Articles of Confederation and would not apply to individuals made citizens by state law but not made citizens in conformance with a law establishing a uniform federal law of naturalization. *See* 1 TUCKER, *supra* note 2, app. at 365.

Fifth, the Clause could be read as requiring states to grant visiting citizens *some* of the same privileges and immunities that the state conferred on its own citizens. Although these are not the only possible interpretations of the Clause,[76] they appear to be the only options that were seriously considered. It was the fifth possible interpretation that came to dominate case law and scholarly commentary from the Founding until Reconstruction.

In 1797, the Maryland General Court provided what became the most influential interpretation of the privileges and immunities clause of Article IV for the next sixty years. The case, *Campbell v. Morris*, involved a claim that Maryland's attachment process for out-of-state citizens violated the privileges protected under Article IV.[77] Judge Chase[78] rejected the claim in an opinion that construed the Clause as requiring no more than equal access to a limited set of state-protected rights:

> The peculiar advantages and exemptions contemplated under this part of the constitution, may be ascertained, if not with precision and accuracy, yet satisfactorily[.]
>
> It seems agreed, from the manner of expounding, or defining the words immunities and privileges, by the counsel on both sides, that a particular and limited operation is to be given to these words, and not a full and comprehensive one. It is agreed it does not mean the right of election, the right of holding offices, the right of being elected. The court are of opinion it means that the citizens of all the states shall have the peculiar advantage of acquiring and holding real as well as personal property, and that such property shall be protected and secured by the laws of the state, in the same manner as the property of the citizens of the state is protected. It means, such property shall not be liable to any taxes or burdens which the property of the

[76] One could, for example, read the Clause as requiring all states to protect a certain set of rights, and to protect them in an equal manner, regardless of state citizenship, a kind of "full and equal" protection of substantive national liberties. Some arguments were made along these lines during the Reconstruction Congress, but no case or commentary adopted such a reading in the period between the Founding and the Civil War.

[77] 3 H. & McH. 535 (Md. 1797).

[78] There is some question whether United States Supreme Court Justice Samuel Chase authored this opinion. If he did, then Chase was doing double duty serving on both the US Supreme Court and the Maryland court. There was, however, another "Chase" on the Maryland court at the time the opinion was issued, Jeremiah T. Chase. Regardless of the true author, a number of later antebellum courts appear to have believed Samuel Chase authored the opinion. *See* Anderson v. Baker, 23 Md. 531, 624 (1865) (attributing the decision to "C. J." Chase, an appellation only Samuel and not J. T. would have had at the time that *Campbell* was decided); Opinion of Judge Appleton, 44 Me. 521, 548 (1857) (same). The later attribution to Samuel Chase may account for the prominent place of the decision in antebellum Comity Clause jurisprudence.

citizens is not subject to. It may also mean, that as creditors, they shall be on the same footing with the state creditor, in the payment of the debts of a deceased debtor. It secures and protects personal rights.[79]

Two aspects of Judge Chase's opinion are especially important, given their impact on later court decisions. First, Chase read Article IV as protecting only those rights recognized by state law. Property rights under Article IV, for example, are protected "in the same manner as the property of the citizens of the state is protected."[80] Second, the set of rights that must be equally extended to sojourning citizens of other states is a subset of the rights conferred on the citizens of the state. In other words, not all state-conferred rights counted as Article IV "privileges and immunities," with one particular exception being the political rights of suffrage.[81] Finally, as would later courts, Chase limited the rights of Article IV to "personal rights" – a category that excluded corporations from the protections of Article IV.[82]

Other courts and commentators during the early decades of the nation echoed Judge Chase's "equal but limited" reading of Article IV's privileges and immunities. In 1811, the author of the first official treatise on the United States Constitution, St. George Tucker, described Article IV as bestowing on out-of-state citizens a limited degree of equal access to state-granted privileges.[83] In 1812, the highest court in New York upheld the existence of a state monopoly against a claim by an out-of-state citizen that the monopoly violated the Privileges and Immunities Clause of Article IV. The panel of judges deciding the case included future Supreme Court Justice Smith Thompson, New York

---

[79] *Campbell*, 3 H. & McH. at 553–54.

[80] *Id.*

[81] Some scholars have suggested Judge Chase in *Campbell* read Article IV to protect a set of substantive fundamental personal rights, such as property rights, regardless of whether the rights had been protected under state law. *See, e.g.*, Douglas G. Smith, *The Privileges and Immunities Clause of Article IV, Section 2; Precursor of Section 1 of the Fourteenth Amendment*, 34 San Diego L. Rev. 809, 845 (1997); David R. Upham, Note, *Corfield v. Coryell and the Privileges and Immunities of American Citizenship*, 83 Tex. L. Rev. 1483, 1501–02 (2005). At least one abolitionist pressed this reading of Chase's opinion at the time of the Civil War. *See* 2 John Codman Hurd, The Law of Freedom and Bondage in the United States 343 (Boston, Little, Brown & Co. 1862). However, despite frequent citation to the decision, no court read Chase's opinion as presenting a theory of fundamental personal rights. Instead, it was regularly paired with other judicial opinions that read Article IV as protecting a limited set of state-conferred rights.

[82] *See, e.g.*, Tatem v. Wright, 23 N.J.L. 429, 445–46 (N.J. 1852); Commonwealth v. Milton, 51 Ky. (12 B. Mon.) 212, 216–17 (1851).

[83] *See* Hadfield v. Jameson, 16 Va. (2 Munf.) 53, 56 (1811) (in an opinion written by Tucker, explaining that Article IV entitled citizens from other states to the same judicial remedies available to citizens of Virginia).

Chief Justice James Kent, and future New York Governor Joseph Yates, all of whom voted to uphold the monopoly. Yates's opinion stressed the equal state-conferred rights reading of Article IV:

> To all municipal regulations, therefore, in relation to the navigable waters of the State, according to the true construction of the Constitution, to which the citizens of this State are subject, the citizens of other states, when within the state territory, are equally subjected; and until a discrimination is made, no constitutional barrier does exist. The Constitution of the United States intends that the same immunities and privileges shall be extended to all the citizens equally, for the wise purpose of preventing local jealousies, which discriminations (always deemed odious) might otherwise produce. As this Constitution, then, according to my view, does not prevent the operation of those laws granting this exclusive privilege to the appellants, they are entitled to the full benefit of them.[84]

Chief Justice Kent took the same position on Article IV:

> The provision that the citizens of each state shall be entitled to all privileges and immunities of citizens in the several states, has nothing to do with this case. It means only that citizens of other states shall have equal rights with our own citizens, and not that they shall have different or greater rights. Their persons and property must, in all respects, be equally subject to our law. This is a very clear proposition, and the provision itself was taken from the articles of the confederation.[85]

With the exception of a small minority of courts who read Article IV as restricting the powers of the federal government,[86] prior to 1823, almost every court

---

[84] Livingston v. Van Ingen, 9 Johns. 507, 561 (N.Y. 1812) (Yates, J.).

[85] *Id.* at 577 (Kent, C. J., opinion). Kent made the same point in his *Commentaries on American Law*:

> The article in the constitution of the United States, declaring that the citizens of each state were entitled to all the privileges and immunities of citizens in the several states, applies only to natural-born or duly nationalized citizens; and if they remove from one state to another, they are entitled to the privileges that persons of the same description are entitled to in the state to which the removal is made, and to none other.

2 JAMES KENT, COMMENTARIES ON AMERICAN LAW pt. 4, at 35 (7th ed., N.Y., Kent 1851).

[86] Although the vast majority of cases decided in this early period of the Republic follow Judge Chase's equal state-conferred rights reading of Article IV, two cases appear to read Article IV as a constraint on the powers of Congress, forbidding any federal grant of special privileges or immunities to citizens of a particular state. *See* Douglass's Adm'r v. Stevens, 2 Del. Cas. 489, 502 (1819) ("The privileges and immunities to be secured to all citizens of the United States are such only as belong to the citizens of the several states, which includes the whole United States; and must be understood to mean such privileges as should be common, or the same in every state, which seems to limit the operation in the clause in the Constitution to

to consider the issue adopted the same reading of Article IV: The Privileges and Immunities Clause secured to sojourning state citizens equal access to a limited set of state-conferred rights.[87] These rights did not include political rights such as suffrage, and they excluded any liberty not granted by the state to its own citizens.

B. Corfield v. Coryell

In many ways, Justice Bushrod Washington's 1823 opinion in *Corfield v. Coryell*[88] is more important for how it was later construed than for what it actually held. The case was a prosaic dispute over the right of a boat crew from Philadelphia to gather New Jersey oysters.[89] The key issue in the case involved whether New Jersey's law prohibiting all but New Jersey residents from "raking" oysters violated the Article IV privileges and immunities of the boatmen from Philadelphia.[90] Justice Washington ruled that the oysters were held in common ownership by the people of New Jersey and that the privileges and immunities of Article IV did not include the right of out-of-state citizens to abscond with the property of New Jersey residents.[91]

Justice Washington's decision in favor of New Jersey law was not controversial at the time or for many years. For decades, *Corfield* was cited as simply one of many antebellum cases limiting the scope of Article IV privileges and immunities. In arriving at his conclusion, however, Washington described the privileges and immunities of citizens in the states with such expansive

---

federal rules, and to be designed to restrict the powers of Congress as to legislation, so that no privilege or immunity should be granted to one citizen of the United States but such as should be common to all. It is not that the citizens in any state shall be entitled to all the privileges of citizens in each state."); Kincaid v. Francis, 3 Tenn. (Cooke) 49, 53–54 (1812) ("It seems to us most probable that this clause in the Constitution was intended to compel the general government to extend the same privileges and immunities to the citizens of every State, and not to permit that government to grant privileges or immunities to citizens of some of the States and withhold them from those of others; and that it was never designed to interfere with the local policy of the State governments as to their own citizens.").

[87] By state-conferred, I mean that it was up to the people of each state to determine whether the right ought to be recognized and protected. Natural rights scholars might object that privileges and immunities often included so-called natural rights that are recognized, not conferred. But states often differed with one another as to whether a given government action violated a claimed natural right (the establishment of religion, for example). The key to being a protected privileges or immunity thus did not turn on whether the right was, as a matter of a theory, a natural right, but whether the people of a given state affirmatively protected the claimed right.

[88] 6 F. Cas. 546 (C.C.E.D. Pa. 1823) (No. 3,230).

[89] *Id.* at 547–48.

[90] *Id.* at 550.

[91] *Id.* at 552.

language that Reconstruction-era proponents of civil rights frequently quoted the case in support of federal efforts to protect fundamental liberties in the former Confederate states.[92] It is because *Corfield* plays such an important role in the debates over the Privileges or Immunities Clause of the Fourteenth Amendment that it is important to take a close look at the key section of Justice Washington's opinion.

Here is the passage that would attract so much attention decades later, in 1866:

> The next question is, whether this act infringes that section of the constitution which declares that "the citizens of each state shall be entitled to all the privileges and immunities of citizens in the several states?" The inquiry is, what are the privileges and immunities of citizens in the several states? We feel no hesitation in confining these expressions to those privileges and immunities which are, in their nature, fundamental; which belong, of right, to the citizens of all free governments; and which have, at all times, been enjoyed by the citizens of the several states which compose this Union, from the time of their becoming free, independent, and sovereign. What these fundamental principles are, it would perhaps be more tedious than difficult to enumerate. They may, however, be all comprehended under the following general heads: Protection by the government; the enjoyment of life and liberty, with the right to acquire and possess property of every kind, and to pursue and obtain happiness and safety; subject nevertheless to such restraints as the government may justly prescribe for the general good of the whole. The right of a citizen of one state to pass through, or to reside in any other state, for purposes of trade, agriculture, professional pursuits, or otherwise; to claim the benefit of the writ of habeas corpus; to institute and maintain actions of any kind in the courts of the state; to take, hold and dispose of property, either real or personal; and an exemption from higher taxes or impositions than are paid by the other citizens of the state; may be mentioned as some of the particular privileges and immunities of citizens, which are clearly embraced by the general description of privileges deemed to be fundamental: to which may be added, the elective franchise, as regulated and established by the laws or constitution of the state in which it is to be exercised. These, and many others which might be mentioned, are, strictly speaking, privileges and immunities, and the enjoyment of them by the citizens of each state, in every other state, was manifestly calculated (to use the expressions of the preamble of the corresponding provision in the old articles of confederation) "the better to secure and perpetuate mutual

---

[92] *See, e.g.,* CONG. GLOBE, 39th Cong., 1st Sess. 1117–18 (1866) (remarks of Rep. Wilson).

friendship and intercourse among the people of the different states of the Union."

But we cannot accede to the proposition which was insisted on by the counsel, that, under this provision of the constitution, the citizens of the several states are permitted to participate in all the rights which belong exclusively to the citizens of any other particular state, merely upon the ground that they are enjoyed by those citizens; much less, that in regulating the use of the common property of the citizens of such state, the legislature is bound to extend to the citizens of all the other states the same advantages as are secured to their own citizens. A several fishery, either as the right to it respects running fish, or such as are stationary, such as oysters, clams, and the like, is as much the property of the individual to whom it belongs, as dry land, or land covered by water; and is equally protected by the laws of the state against the aggressions of others, whether citizens or strangers. Where those private rights do not exist to the exclusion of the common right, that of fishing belongs to all the citizens or subjects of the state. It is the property of all; to be enjoyed by them in subordination to the laws which regulate its use. They may be considered as tenants in common of this property; and they are so exclusively entitled to the use of it, that it cannot be enjoyed by others without the tacit consent, or the express permission of the sovereign who has the power to regulate its use.[93]

During the Reconstruction Congress, Justice Washington's reference to "fundamental" rights belonging to "the citizens of all free governments" became embroiled in debates over Congress's power to define and protect federal civil rights in the states.[94] No such issue was before the Court in *Corfield*. Instead, Washington's opinion focused on an issue that all sides conceded involved a right conferred as a matter of state law. The out-of-state oyster gatherers argued that, because New Jersey allowed its own citizens to rake oysters, this same right must be granted to sojourning visitors as a privilege or immunity protected under Article IV. As Washington phrased it, the claim was that out-of-state citizens should enjoy state-conferred oyster gathering rights "merely upon the ground that they are enjoyed by [in-state] citizens," and that "the [New Jersey] legislature is bound to extend to the citizens of all the other states the same advantages as are secured to their own citizens."[95] Justice Washington rejected such a broad reading of Article IV: Not all, but only *some* state-conferred rights fell within the scope of Article IV.

Washington then expounded on what he believed ought to be considered privileges and immunities of citizens in the States. His list differs in some

---

[93] *Corfield*, 6 F. Cas. at 551–52.
[94] *See infra* Chapter 4.
[95] *Id.* at 552.

respects from that of Judge Chase (particularly in regard to the rights of suffrage), but the precise content of the list is not as important to our analysis as is the source of such rights. Washington describes Article IV privileges and immunities as those that have "at all times, been enjoyed by the citizens of the several states which compose this Union, from the time of their becoming free, independent, and sovereign."[96] By grounding Article IV privileges and immunities in liberties that were granted by pre-Constitutional American states, Washington limited his list to rights recognized and secured by the states. As was true of liberties granted under the original state constitutions, Washington's list contains a mix of natural, common law, civil, and political rights, covering everything from travel and trade to equal taxes, suffrage, and the pursuit of happiness.[97] However, the list includes only those privileges and immunities that states "at all times" had provided their own citizens.

It is possible that Justice Washington intended to refer to those state-conferred substantive rights that not only *had* been granted but that, constitutionally, *had to be* granted by states. If so, he did not say. Nor did any court or commentator prior to the Civil War read *Corfield* as referring to any kind of nationally mandated set of substantive rights.[98] It was only after 1865 that radical Republicans[99] attempted to use *Corfield*'s language in support of federal protection of fundamental rights.[100]

On its face, then, Washington's theory of the rights protected under Article IV's Privileges and Immunities Clause mirrors that of Judge Chase in *Campbell* and Chancellor Kent in *Livingston*.[101] All three decisions described Article IV's privileges and immunities as a set of state-secured rights, and all three rejected

---

[96] *Id.* at 551.

[97] *See id.* at 551–52. For a critical accounts of Washington's opinion, see Natelson, *supra* note 41, at 1122–24; Philip Hamburger, *Privileges or Immunities*, 105 Nw. U. L. Rev. 61, 79 (2011). I take no position in this paper regarding whether Washington's account reflects the original understanding of Article IV. My goal is to determine how these words and phrases were understood at the time of the adoption of the Fourteenth Amendment, regardless of the original understanding of the Comity Clause.

[98] *See* Natelson, *supra* note 41, at 1124–25 (noting the lack of antebellum cases unambiguously embracing a substantive "natural rights" reading of *Corfield*).

[99] See *infra* Chapter 4. Advocates of a woman's right to vote also would later call on Washington's language in *Corfield*. *See* 2 Elizabeth Cady Stanton et al., History of Woman Suffrage 453 (Rochester, N.Y., Mann 1887) (citing Bushrod Washington's *Corfield* opinion in support of women's suffrage); *see also* Reva B. Siegel, *She the People: The Nineteenth Amendment, Sex Equality, Federalism and the Family*, 115 Harv. L. Rev. 947, 972 n.68 (2002).

[100] *See, e.g.*, Smith v. Moody, 26 Ind. 299 (1866). In *Moody*, a newly elected panel of Republican judges upheld the Civil Rights Act and arguably interpreted *Corfield* as referring to fundamental national rights. *Id.* at 302, 307.

[101] Some scholars treat *Corfield* as an outlier among a more dominant trend of judicial interpretation of Article IV. *See, e.g.*, Earl M. Maltz, *Fourteenth Amendment Concepts in the Antebellum*

the idea that sojourning state citizens must be granted *all* the rights of state citizenship. Where these cases diverge is in their description of which rights fell within that limited set. For example, Justice Washington believed that the rights of state-regulated suffrage fell within the circle of privileges and immunities, whereas Judge Chase did not. The basic theory of Article IV, however, is the same.

Later antebellum judicial opinions that cited *Corfield* treated the case as following the same reasoning as *Campbell* and *Livingston*, with the cases often cited in tandem.[102] In fact, with only a couple of

Era, 32 AM. J. LEGAL HIST. 305, 337–38 (1988) (describing *Corfield* as a widely cited but "somewhat equivocal exception" to the dominant trend in antebellum case law regarding Article IV privileges and immunities). This was probably true in regard to Washington's brief reference to state-regulated suffrage as an Article IV privilege and immunity. *See* DAVID P. CURRIE, THE CONSTITUTION IN CONGRESS: THE JEFFERSONIANS, 1801–1829, at 405 n.133 (2001); John Harrison, *Reconstructing the Privileges or Immunities Clause*, 101 YALE L. J. 1385, 1417 (1992). Judge Chase certainly disagreed with Washington on this point. *See* Campbell v. Morris, 3 H. & McH. 535, 554 (Md. 1797). Despite this disagreement on particular substance, however, Washington's basic theory of Article IV was widely viewed as being no different from that presented in *Campbell*, *Livingston*, and other "equal access to state-conferred rights" cases, as illustrated by the common practice of citing some or all three cases in tandem. *See, e.g.*, Wiley v. Parmer, 14 Ala. 627, 632 (1848). For a discussion of Washington's opinion in *Corfield* as an attempt to exclude blacks from privileges and immunities, see Hamburger, *supra* note 97.

[102] In 1848, Alabama Chief Justice Henry Collier collected the cases and explained:

By the second section of the fourth article of the federal constitution, it is enacted, that "the citizens of each State, shall be entitled to all privileges and immunities of citizens in the several States." It has been held that the intention of this clause was to confer on the citizens of each State a genera] citizenship; and to communicate all the privileges and immunities, which the citizens of the same State would be entitled to under the like circumstances. Corfield v. Cargill [Corfield v. Coryell], 4 Wash. C. C. Rep. 371; Livingston v. Van Ingen, 9 Johns. Rep. 507. In Campbell v. Morris, 3 Har. & McH. Rep. 535, it was said that the terms *privilege and immunity* are synonymous, or nearly so; *privilege*, signifies a peculiar advantage, exemption, immunity; *immunity*, signifies exemption, privilege. A particular and limited operation is to be given to the words "immunities and privileges" in this section of the constitution, and not a full and comprehensive one.... The object of the entire provision was to secure to the citizens of all the States the peculiar advantage of acquiring and holding real as well as personal property, and to provide that such property shall be protected and secured by the laws of the State in the same manner as the property of the citizens of the State is protected.

Wiley, 14 Ala., at 631–32. *See also* Baker v. Wise, 57 Va. (16 Gratt.) 139, 215–17 (1861) (although noting the lack of any full and authoritative interpretation of the clause, citing both *Corfield* and *Campbell* as representative cases and applying *Campbell*'s equal access to state-conferred privileges and immunities analysis in upholding as reasonable the discriminatory treatment

exceptions,[103] all of the cases identified in this article discussing Article IV privileges and immunities between the Founding and the Civil War read Article IV as referring to a limited set of state-law secured rights.[104] The decisions come from both north and south of the Mason-Dixon Line. In the 1827 case *Abbott v. Bayley*, for example, the Chief Justice of the Massachusetts Supreme Court provided an extended discussion of Article IV privileges and immunities that distinguished state-secured rights from federal rights and explained how Article IV left the regulation of life, liberty, and property to the state legislatures:

> The jurisdiction of the several States as such, are distinct, and in most respects foreign. The constitution of the United States makes the people of the United States subjects of one government *quoad* every thing within the national power and jurisdiction, but leaves them subjects of separate and distinct governments. The privileges and immunities secured to the people of each State in every other State, can be applied only in case of removal from one State into another. By such removal they become citizens of the adopted State without naturalization, and have a right to sue and be sued as citizens; and yet this privilege is qualified and not absolute, for they cannot enjoy

---

of process for nonresidents). For additional cases citing *Corfield* alongside of *Campbell, Livingston*, or both, see United States v. New Bedford Bridge, 27 F. Cas. 91 (C.C.D. Mass. 1847) (No. 15,867); Atkinson v. Phil. & T.R. Co., 2 F. Cas. 105 (C.C.E.D. Pa. 1834) (No. 615); Oliver v. Wash. Mills, 93 Mass. (11 Allen) 268 (1865). Although there are a number of cases involving disputes over waterways, tidelines, and fisheries that cite *Corfield* alone, I have managed to find only four cases prior to the Civil War (three of them again involving fisheries or clams) that discussed the Privileges and Immunities Clause and cited to *Corfield* but not to *Campbell* or *Livingston*. See Bennett v. Boggs, 3 F. Cas. 221, 226 (C.C.D.N.J. 1830) (No. 1,319) (citing *Corfield* in favor of state right to regulate fisheries); Dunham v. Lamphere, 69 Mass. (3 Gray) 268 (1855) (citing *Corfield* and *Boggs*); State v. Medbury, 3 R.I. 138 (1855); Commonwealth v. Milton, 51 Ky. (12 B. Mon.) 212 (1851). All four adopt the same equal access to a limited set of state-conferred rights approach of *Campbell* and *Livingston*. In *Tatem v. Wright*, the New Jersey court cited to *Corfield* alone but only to illustrate that the privileges and immunities of Article IV extend to persons, not corporations. See 23 N.J.L. 429, 445–46 (N.J. 1852); *see also* Slaughter v. Commonwealth, 57 Va. (13 Gratt.) 767, 779 (1856) (containing a single sentence referencing *Corfield* for the proposition that corporations are not protected under Article IV). This, too, echoes the language of *Campbell*: "It secures and protects personal rights." *Campbell*, 3 H. & McH. at 554.

[103] A small number of cases read Article IV to forbid federal statutes that discriminated among the several states. *See supra* note 102 and accompanying text.

[104] For example, in an 1833 circuit opinion, United States Supreme Court Justice Henry Baldwin recapitulated much of this Article's discussion of the historical roots of both the terms "privileges" and "immunities," as well as the common usage of the paired terms as referred to a set of state-conferred rights. See Magill v. Brown, 16 F. Cas. 408, 428 (C.C.E.D. Pa. 1833) (No. 8,952).

the right of suffrage or of eligibility to office, without such term of residence as shall be prescribed by the constitution and laws of the State into which they shall remove. They shall have the privileges and immunities of citizens, that is, they shall not be deemed aliens, but may take and hold real estate, and may, according to the laws of such State, eventually enjoy the full rights of citizenship without the necessity of being naturalized. The constitutional provision referred to is necessarily limited and qualified, for it cannot be pretended that a citizen of Rhode Island coming into this State to live, is *ipso facto* entitled to the full privileges of a citizen, if any term of residence is prescribed as preliminary to the exercise of political or municipal rights. The several States then, remain sovereign to some purposes, and foreign to each other, as before the adoption of the constitution of the United States, and especially in regard to the administration of justice, and in the regulation of property and estates, the laws of marriage and divorce, and the protection of the persons of those who live under their jurisdiction.[105]

Similarly, an 1851 Kentucky court examined Justice Washington's expansive language in *Corfield* and explained that Washington referred only to a certain set of rights protected as a matter of state law:

The Constitution certainly intended to secure to every citizen of every State the right of traversing at will the territory of any and every other State, subject only to the laws applicable to its own citizens, of exercising there, freely but innocently, all of his faculties, of acquiring, holding, and alienating property as citizens might do, and of enjoying all other privileges and immunities common to the citizens of any State in which he might be present, or in which without being present he might transact business. But in securing these rights it does not exempt him from any condition which the law of the State imposes upon its own citizens, nor confer upon him any privilege which the law gives to particular persons for special purposes or upon prescribed conditions, nor secure to him the same privileges to which by the laws of his own State he may have been entitled.

In *Corfield v. Coryell*, Judge Washington characterizes the privileges and immunities secured by this clause as being such as are, "in their nature, fundamental, which belong of right to the citizens of all free governments and which have at all times been enjoyed by the several States

---

[105] 23 Mass. (6 Pick.) 89, 92–93 (1827). During the Reconstruction debates, radical Republicans like Representative Samuel Shellabarger of Ohio cited *Abbott* as representing the consensus understanding of the Privileges and Immunities Clause of Article IV. *See* CONG. GLOBE, 39th Cong., 1st Sess. app. 293 (1866) (remarks of Rep. Shellabarger).

which compose this Union, from the time of their becoming free, independent and sovereign." We suppose the same idea is conveyed when we say that they are such privileges and immunities, as are common to the citizens of any State under its Constitution and constitutional laws.[106]

In the brief and unanimous 1855 Supreme Court opinion *Connor v. Elliot,* Justice Curtis ruled that, because a Louisiana law controlling property rights arising out of marriage applied to all marriage contracts entered into within the state regardless of citizenship, there could be no violation of the Privileges and Immunities Clause of Article IV.[107] According to Curtis, there was no "need . . . to attempt to define the meaning of the word *privileges* in this clause of the constitution. . . . The law does not discriminate between citizens of the State and other persons; it discriminates between contracts only. Such discrimination has no connection with the clause in the constitution now in question."[108]

The Supreme Court's reluctance to define the particular privileges protected under Article IV left state courts to their own devices on that particular issue.[109] The lack of substantive specificity rarely mattered, however, because most cases were resolvable on a simple application of the equal-access-to-state-secured-rights approach of Judge Chase in *Campbell*. Cases that required a more substantive analysis of privileges and immunities also followed the approach of *Campbell* and *Corfield* and narrowed the reach of Article IV to

---

[106] Commonwealth v. Milton, 51 Ky. (12 B. Mon.) 212, 219 (1851) (citation omitted).

[107] 59 U.S. (18 How.) 591, 593–94 (1855) (holding that marriage contracts are governed by the law of the state in which they were enacted and that Article IV does not require the State of Louisiana to confer the same rights on parties to out-of-state marriage contracts that are conferred on parties to in-state marriage contracts).

[108] *Id.*

[109] Article IV received an occasional reference in antebellum Supreme Court cases. *See, e.g.,* Gibbons v. Ogden, 22 U.S. (9 Wheat.) 1, 69 (1824) ("The constitution does not profess to give, in terms, the right of ingress and regress for commercial or any other purposes, or the right of transporting articles for trade from one State to another. It only protects the personal rights of the citizens of one State, when within the jurisdiction of another, by securing to them 'all the privileges and immunities of a citizen' of that other, which they hold subject to the laws of the State as its own citizens; and it protects their property against any duty to be imposed on its introduction."). The references, however, continued to follow Judge Chase's equality of state-secured rights reading of Article IV and provided no guidance as to the specific rights covered by the Clause. *See* Baker v. Wise, 57 Va. (16 Gratt.) 139, 215 (1861) ("We have no authoritative expositions of this clause of the constitution giving us a full and complete definition of its terms; though, it has been, I think, clearly shown that they must be received in a qualified and restricted sense.").

a limited subset of locally recognized rights.[110] As the 1861 Virginia Supreme Court explained in *Baker v. Wise*:

> We have no authoritative expositions of this clause of the constitution giving us a full and complete definition of its terms; though, it has been, I think, clearly shown that they must be received in a qualified and restricted sense. Thus in the case of *Campbell* v. *Morris*, judge Chase says – " . . . It seems agreed from the manner of expounding or defining the words immunities and privileges by the counsel on both sides, that a particular and limited operation is to be given to these words, and not a full and comprehensive one. . . . " He added that "a restriction of the power of the State legislatures to establish modes of proceeding for the recovery of debts is not to be inferred from the clause under consideration. . . . "
>
> [Just as] differences between the modes of proceeding against the citizens or residents of other States and the modes of proceeding against their own citizens or inhabitants will be found in the laws of most of the States; and I know of no decision in which it has been held that, by such discriminations, the citizens of such other States are deprived of any of their rightful privileges and immunities. . . .
>
> In neither of these instances can it be said that the non-resident is deprived of any of the immunities of citizenship, in the sense contemplated in the

---

[110] For example, in 1855 the Chief Justice of the Rhode Island Supreme Court relied on *Corfield* in an opinion that rejected an attempt to read Article IV as requiring a state to grant visiting citizens *all* the rights and privileges granted by that state to its own citizens:

> Article 4, sec. 2, of the Constitution of the United States, provides "that the citizens of each State shall be entitled to all privileges and immunities of citizens in the several States." This section has been referred to in the argument, as though it conferred on the citizens of each State, all the privileges and immunities which the citizens of the several States enjoy. Such is neither its language nor its import. No Court or Legislature in the Union has ever given such a construction to it; but on the contrary, a marked distinction has ever been made by them between the rights and powers of the citizens of a State, and the rights and powers of all other persons resident within the limits of the State, whether they are citizens of other States or foreigners. To deny the right to every State to make such distinction would be to annihilate the sovereignty of the States, and to establish a consolidated government in their stead. But this section in its terms, confers on the citizens of each State, "all privileges and immunities of citizens in the several States," that is, the rights and powers of citizenship. They are not to be deemed aliens. They are not to be accounted as foreigners; or as persons who may become enemies. They are to have the right to carry on business, to inherit and transmit property, to enter upon, reside in and remove from the territory of each State, at their pleasure, yielding obedience to and receiving protection from the laws. Such are some of the privileges and immunities conferred by this section, and all that are granted by it are of the same character. That the right claimed by the defendant is not one of these, has been expressly decided in the cases of *Corfield* v. *Coryell* (4 Wash. p. 376.)[.]

State v. Medbury, 3 R.I. 138, 142–43 (1855).

constitution; he is held ultimately responsible for nothing that he would not have to meet were he a resident citizen of the State. . . . [111]

Justice Washington may have unduly restricted the scope of Article IV privileges and immunities by requiring them to be "fundamental." In fact, later courts and treatise writers sometimes described the Clause as requiring equal access to all civil rights, even if not all political rights.[112] On the other hand, in those few cases where courts struck down laws as violating the equality principle, one can find language that echoes Washington's dicta that protected rights involve especially important matters. For example, in the 1864 Delaware case *Gray v. Cook*, the Delaware Supreme Court struck down a discriminatory arrest statute as violating Article IV.[113] After quoting Judge Chase in *Campbell*, the court rhetorically asked:

> [I]f by law you exempt your own citizens from arrest on certain conditions, as for debt without fraud, which is a privilege or immunity, of no insignificant value and importance to every honest, but unfortunate debtor, not only in our own State, but in every State in the Union, how can you deny it to every citizen in every other State of the Union, against that express provision of the constitution to the contrary?[114]

By protecting rights "of no insignificant value and importance," the court sought "to put a citizen of another State on a par and an entire equality with every citizen in the State."[115]

In sum, as the country entered a period of civil war, the jurisprudence of the Privileges and Immunities Clause of Article IV, although not fully fleshed out, was theoretically clear and surprisingly stable.[116] Courts throughout this period

---

[111] Baker, 57 Va. (16 Gratt.) at 215–17 (citations omitted).

[112] *See, e.g.*, Lavery v. Woodland, 2 Del. Cas. 299, 307 (1817) (stating that, under Article IV, "[t]he Constitution certainly meant to place, in every state, the citizens of all the states upon an equality as to their private rights, but not as to political rights").

[113] 8 Del. (3 Houst.) 49, 60–62 (1864).

[114] *Id.* at 61.

[115] *Id.*

[116] Judicial opinions continued to follow this consensus approach during the Civil War. According to an 1865 decision of the Massachusetts Supreme Court:

> [Article 4, Section 2] was doubtless taken and condensed from art. 4, § 1, of the articles of confederation and perpetual union, adopted by congress July 9th 1778, and which formed the basis of a national government for the United States prior to the adoption of the constitution. It was thereby provided that the "people of each state should enjoy in any other state all the privileges of trade and commerce, subject to the same duties, impositions and restrictions as the inhabitants thereof respectively." The object of substituting the constitution for the articles of confederation was to make a more perfect Union. One of the most efficient methods of effecting this purpose was to vest in the

consistently read the cases of *Campbell, Livingston, Corfield, Abbott,* and *Baker* to embrace the same principle: the privileges and immunities of Article IV referred to a limited (if especially important) set of state-secured rights. Both courts and legal commentators rejected attempts to expand the circle of privileges and immunities to include *all* state level rights, and no court read Article IV as a reference to substantive national rights.[117] As Thomas Cooley

> general government the power to regulate not only foreign trade and commerce, but also that between the different states of the Union, and to secure an equality of rights, privileges and immunities in each state for the citizens of all the states. It is obvious that the power of a state to impose different and greater burdens or impositions on the property of citizens of other states than on the same property belonging to its own subjects would directly conflict with this constitutional provision. By exempting its own citizens from a tax or excise to which citizens of other states were subject, the former would enjoy an immunity of which the latter would be deprived. Such has been the judicial interpretation of this clause of the constitution by courts of justice in which the question has arisen.

Oliver v. Wash. Mills, 93 Mass. (11 Allen) 268, 280–81 (1865) (citing *Corfield* and *Coryell,* among others).

[117] *See* 1 JOHN BOUVIER, INSTITUTES OF AMERICAN LAW 66 (2d ed., Phila., Peterson & Co. 1854) ("[The Privileges and Immunities Clause of Article IV] evidently refers to the privilege or capacity of taking, holding, and conveying lands lying within any state of the Union, and also of enjoying all civil rights which citizens of any State were entitled to; but it cannot be extended to give a citizen of another state a right to vote or hold office immediately on his entering the state."). A number of cases other than the ones cited in this section also embraced this principle. *See* Costin v. Washington, 6 F. Cas. 612, 613–14 (C.C.D.C. 1821) (No. 3,266) ("[I]f there be a class of people more likely than others to disturb the public peace, or corrupt the public morals, and if that class can be clearly designated, [the government] has a right to impose upon that class, such reasonable terms and conditions of residence, as will guard the state from the evils which it has reason to apprehend. A citizen of one state, coming into another state, can claim only those privileges and immunities which belong to citizens of the latter state, in like circumstances."); Davis v. Pierse, 7 Minn. 13, 21 (1862) ("The main object of the section was to prevent each State from discriminating in favor of its own people, or against those of any other. . . . " [citing *Corfield* in support]); Sheepshanks & Co. v. Jones, 9 N.C. (2 Hawks) 211, 213 (1822) ("If our own laws do not permit our own citizens who are not freeholders in this State to serve on a Jury, it cannot be considered as the denial of a right or privilege to the citizens of another State, who are not freeholders here, to consider them disqualified. For, upon the supposition that the right to serve on a jury here was claimed by the citizen of another State, as a privilege or immunity, he must shew that it is enjoyed by our own citizens not otherwise qualified than himself; otherwise it would be a claim, not of privileges *equal* to, but *greater* than those of our own citizens."); Amy v. Smith, 11 Ky. (1 Litt.) 326, 335 (1822) ("[Article IV's Privileges and Immunities Clause] can not, upon any principle, be construed to secure to the citizens of other states, greater privileges, within this state; than are allowed by her institutions to her own citizens."); Barrell v. Benjamin, 15 Mass. (14 Tyng) 354, 358 (1819) (noting that, if a citizen of Massachusetts "has the privilege to sue any foreigner who may come within this state," then an out-of-state citizen "has the same privilege secured to him by the constitution"); Lavery v. Woodland, 2 Del. Cas. 299, 307 (1817) ("[Under Article IV, a]

wrote in his popular 1868 *Treatise on Constitutional Limitations*, Article IV was meant to "prevent discrimination by the several States against the citizens" of other states.[118] In his treatise, Cooley twice described Article IV as preventing discrimination against sojourning citizens and twice cited both *Corfield* and *Campbell* for this proposition.[119]

C. *Slavery and the Privileges and Immunities Clause*

The stability of Article IV jurisprudence in antebellum case law may be due at least in part to the fact that the *Campbell* doctrine did not clearly line up with either side in the debate over chattel slavery. Limiting the scope of privileges or immunities had the effect of maximizing the scope of state regulatory autonomy, a states' rights result that protected the policy-making powers of both free and slave states alike. Nevertheless, it was inevitable that Article IV would be caught up in the same subject that became a national obsession and ultimately triggered a bloody national clash of arms.

Slavery and Article IV privileges and immunities came together as slave owners attempted to carry their "property" across a free state on their way to a destination that permitted slavery. Slave owners argued that the principle of comity and the provisions of Article IV required free states to respect the home-state-granted "privileges and immunities" of holding slaves. Free states, of course, pressed for a far more limited reading of Article IV. When the Supreme Court issued its explosive opinion in *Dred Scott*, the reasoning of the Court appeared to buttress the claims of slave owners to the point of suggesting that owners had a constitutional right to carry slaves anywhere within the jurisdiction of the United States. Extending *Dred Scott*'s holding to states as well as territories would have the effect of nationalizing slavery. Such an extension appeared quite likely as Article IV-based suits by slaveholders

---

redress of the private or civil rights belonging to individuals is certainly one of the privileges secured to the citizens of other states. This redress, or the exercise of this privilege, must be commensurate with the wrong and must be adapted to it, and must be obtained or exercised in the same manner and form of suit as if he were a citizen of the state. The Constitution certainly meant to place, in every state, the citizens of all the states upon an equality as to their private rights, but not as to political rights. A citizen of another state may pursue the same legal remedy by suit or action at law, whenever his right is invaded, as a citizen of the state is entitled to, but he is not entitled to the same political rights.").

[118] Thomas M. Cooley, A Treatise on the Constitutional Limitations Which Rest Upon the Legislative Power of the State of the American Union 15 (Boston, Little, Brown & Co. 1868).

[119] *See id.* at 15 n.3, 397 n.2.

wound their way through state courts, any one of which would serve as perfect vehicle for a "second *Dred Scott*."

1. Slavery, *Dred Scott*, and Article IV

In his concurring opinion in the 1841 case *Groves v. Slaughter*, Supreme Court Justice Henry Baldwin briefly discussed Article IV privileges and immunities and their relationship to the regulation of slavery in the States.[120] As he had in his circuit court opinion in *Magill v. Brown*,[121] Justice Baldwin followed the standard interpretation of Article IV privileges and immunities as referring to a limited set of state-secured rights. Because chattel slavery was a creature of state law, each state remained free to adopt its own internal policy, subject only to the Article IV-imposed constraint that, if state residents could own slaves, then so could visiting citizens from other states.[122] However, Baldwin insisted that slaves being moved from one state to another must be considered articles of commerce among the several states until they arrived at their destination and therefore subject to what Baldwin believed was the federal government's exclusive power to regulate interstate commerce.[123] This meant that states had no power to free any slave brought within their borders if that slave was "commerce in transit" to another state that permitted slavery.[124] Baldwin's concurrence went well beyond what was necessary to decide the case,[125] but the argument suggested trouble might lie ahead for those states that wished to enforce local policy when it came to slaves brought within their jurisdiction.

---

[120] 40 U.S. (15 Pet.) 449 (1841).

[121] *See supra* note 104 (discussing *Magill's* focus on state-conferred rights).

[122] *Groves*, 40 U.S. (15 Pet.) at 515. ("Hence, it is apparent, that no state can control this traffic, so long as it may be carried on by its own citizens, within its own limits; as part of its purely internal commerce, any state may regulate it according to its own policy; but when such regulation purports to extend to other states or their citizens, it is limited by the Constitution, putting the citizens of all on the same footing as their own.").

[123] *Id.* at 516.

[124] *Id.* ("If, however, the owner of slaves in Maryland, in transporting them to Kentucky, or Missouri, should pass through Pennsylvania, or Ohio, no law of either state could take away or affect his right of property; nor, if passing from one slave state to another, accident or distress should compel him to touch at any place within a state, where slavery did not exist. Such transit of property, whether of slaves or bales of goods, is lawful commerce among the several states, which none can prohibit or regulate. . . . "); *see also* Mary Sarah Bilder, *The Struggle Over Immigration: Indentured Servants, Slaves, and Articles of Commerce*, 61 Mo. L. Rev. 743, 807–12 (1996) (discussing *Groves* and the antebellum legal debates about the status of persons as articles of commerce).

[125] *See* Gerard M. Magliocca, *Preemptive Opinions: The Secret History of Worcester v. Georgia and Dred Scott*, 63 U. Pitt. L. Rev. 487, 569–70 (2002) (discussing the breadth of Baldwin's opinion).

In *Dred Scott v. Sandford*,[126] the Supreme Court took a critical step toward making slavery a national right. Although *Dred Scott* specifically involved jurisdictional issues and whether slavery could be banned from the territories, Chief Justice Taney discussed Article IV as part of his analysis of whether the generation that adopted the Constitution considered blacks as current or potential citizens of the United States. In the following passage, Taney presents what he believes would be the unacceptable parade of horribles that would result from the recognition of blacks as potential citizens protected under Article IV:

> The legislation of the States therefore shows, in a manner not to be mistaken, the inferior and subject condition of that race at the time the Constitution was adopted, and long afterwards, throughout the thirteen States by which that instrument was framed; and it is hardly consistent with the respect due to these States, to suppose that they regarded at that time, as fellow-citizens and members of the sovereignty, a class of beings whom they had thus stigmatized; whom, as we are bound, out of respect to the State sovereignties, to assume they had deemed it just and necessary thus to stigmatize, and upon whom they had impressed such deep and enduring marks of inferiority and degradation; or, that when they met in convention to form the Constitution, they looked upon them as a portion of their constituents, or designed to include them in the provisions so carefully inserted for the security and protection of the liberties and rights of their citizens. It cannot be supposed that they intended to secure to them rights, and privileges, and rank, in the new political body throughout the Union, which every one of them denied within the limits of its own dominion. More especially, it cannot be believed that the large slaveholding States regarded them as included in the word citizens, or would have consented to a Constitution which might compel them to receive them in that character from another State. For if they were so received, and entitled to the privileges and immunities of citizens, it would exempt them from the operation of the special laws and from the police regulations which they considered to be necessary for their own safety. It would give to persons of the negro race, who were recognised as citizens in any one State of the Union, the right to enter every other State whenever they pleased, singly or in companies, without pass or passport, and without obstruction, to sojourn there as long as they pleased, to go where they pleased at every hour of the day or night without molestation, unless they committed some violation of law for which a white man would be punished; and it would give them the full liberty of speech in public and in private upon all subjects upon which

---

[126] 60 U.S. (19 How.) 393 (1856). Although all nine Justices wrote an opinion in *Dred Scott*, the seven Justices in the majority allowed Taney's opinion to be designated as the opinion of the Court.

its own citizens might speak; to hold public meetings upon political affairs, and to keep and carry arms wherever they went. And all of this would be done in the face of the subject race of the same color, both free and slaves, and inevitably producing discontent and insubordination among them, and endangering the peace and safety of the State.[127]

Chief Justice Taney is relying on the standard antebellum reading of the Privileges and Immunities Clause of Article IV. If states considered blacks to be within the meaning of "citizen" when they ratified the Constitution, then they would have understood that they were conferring on blacks the same rights extended to traveling citizens from other states, including the right to travel "without papers." This right to travel was a traditional aspect of the rights of comity, with roots extending back to the "Comity Clause" of the Articles of Confederation.[128] In addition to guaranteeing the right to travel to any state in the Union, the Comity Clause of the federal Constitution would further guarantee visiting black citizens the same rights under state law as those afforded to "white men." Here, Taney repeats this equality reading of privileges and immunities in terms of the rights of speech: if blacks were to be considered citizens under Article IV, this would give them "the full liberty of speech in public and in private upon all subjects *upon which its own citizens might speak.*"[129] Note that Taney follows the approach of John Marshall in *Barron v. Baltimore* and treats freedom of speech as a subject left to the control of state law, subject only to the equality constraint of the federal Comity Clause.

The final two rights mentioned by Taney involve the rights "to hold public meetings upon political affairs, and to keep and carry arms." Here, Taney does not use the language of equality, an omission that has led a number of scholars to read this particular passage as referring to fundamental rights.[130] If so, then this means that Taney read the privileges and immunities clause as protecting no more than equal state-secured rights when it comes to freedom of speech (long considered an individual natural right) but as protecting a *substantive*

---

[127] *Dred Scott*, 60 U.S. (19 How.) at 416–17.

[128] *See* ARTICLES OF CONFEDERATION, art. IV (1781) ("[A]nd the people of each State shall have free ingress and regress to and from any other State, and shall enjoy therein all the privileges of trade and commerce, subject to the same duties, impositions, and restrictions, as the inhabitants thereof respectively.").

[129] *Dred Scott*, 60 U.S. (19 How.) at 417 (emphasis added).

[130] *See, e.g.*, AKHIL REED AMAR, AMERICA'S CONSTITUTION: A BIOGRAPHY 387 (2005); DON E. FEHRENBACHER, SLAVERY, LAW AND POLITICS 188–90 (1981); Robert J. Kaczorowski, *Revolutionary Constitutionalism in the Era of the Civil War and Reconstruction*, 61 N.Y.U. L. REV. 863, 886 (1986); Rebecca E. Zietlow, *Congressional Enforcement of the Rights of Citizenship*, 56 DRAKE L. REV. 1015, 1023 (2008).

national right when it came to holding public meetings and the right to "keep and bear arms." This would be an idiosyncratic, two-tiered reading of Article IV and the Bill of Rights, one found nowhere prior to *Dred Scott* and never repeated by anyone afterward.

More likely, Chief Justice Taney viewed all of the rights he listed in that single paragraph as state-controlled rights subject to the equality principles of Article IV. In fact, all of the rights mentioned by Taney were rights commonly protected under state law at the time,[131] thus making them all subject to the "equal access to state-secured rights" protections of the *Campbell* equality reading of Article IV. Taney seems to have highlighted the last two rights in order to emphasize the dangerously destabilizing effect such public meetings (with armed blacks!) would have on enslaved blacks who might witness such an event, "inevitably producing discontent and insubordination among them, and endangering the peace and safety of the State." To be sure, Taney did believe in certain fundamental due process rights that American citizens carried with them into the territories, a belief that led Taney to strike down the Missouri Compromise. Taney's insistence that one such right was the right of property in the guise of chattel slavery was reversed several times over with the adoption of the Thirteenth and Fourteenth Amendments. His general theory of Article IV privileges and immunities, on the other hand, was quite conventional and remains the law to this day.

One particular aspect of Chief Justice Taney's claim about Article IV, however, was controversial. Although it was well-established that states could not discriminate against sojourning citizens *as* sojourning citizens, it was not clear whether states could discriminate against sojourning citizens on the basis of race.[132] Taney's parade of horribles in *Dred Scott* was premised on a reading of Article IV that would disallow discriminatory treatment of sojourning citizens even when the discrimination was based on race and not citizen status.[133] This issue would later trigger fierce debate among Republicans and Democrats prior to the Civil War and inspire a young John Bingham to

---

[131] *See* WILLIAM E. NELSON, THE FOURTEENTH AMENDMENT: FROM POLITICAL PRINCIPLE TO JUDICIAL DOCTRINE 118 (1988) ("American states in the mid-nineteenth century did, in fact, provide their citizens with most of the protections contained in the Bill of Rights").

[132] Justice Curtis, in dissent, argued that Taney was wrong about Article IV's application to race-based constraints. *See Dred Scott*, 60 U.S. (19 How.) at 583–84 (Curtis J., dissenting).

[133] *See also id.* at 480 (Daniel, J., concurring) ("He may emancipate his negro slave, by which process he first transforms that slave into a citizen of his own State; he may next, under color of article fourth, section second, of the Constitution of the United States, obtrude him, and on terms of civil and political equality, upon any and every State in this Union, in defiance of all regulations of necessity or policy, ordained by those States for their internal happiness or safety.").

make his first public statements on the meaning of Article IV.[134] This issue, however, goes only to the scope of the equality reading of Article IV. For now, it is important simply to point out that Taney's general approach to Article IV fits within the standard reading of the Clause as presented in cases like *Campbell*, *Livingston*, and *Corfield*.[135]

The main body of Taney's opinion in *Dred Scott* posed an immediate problem for free states. In holding that slave owners had a constitutional right to carry their "property" into any territory of the United States, Chief Justice Taney appeared to be laying the groundwork for the full nationalization of slavery.[136] All that was needed was a proper case to come before the Court involving a slave owner's claimed home-state-granted privilege and immunity to carry slaves into free states and territories.[137] That case appeared to be on the horizon when the New York courts decided *Lemmon v. The People*.

---

[134] *See infra* Chapter 4.

[135] The subject also came up, if only obliquely, in Justice Curtis's dissent, in which he argued that the language of Article IV, which dropped the reference to "free inhabitants" from the Articles of Confederation, suggested that the Framers believed that blacks "were entitled to the privileges and immunities of general citizenship of the United States." *Dred Scott*, 60 U.S. (19 How.) at 575–76. For a discussion of the opinion, including Justice Curtis's discussion of privileges and immunities, see Mark A. Graber, *Desperately Ducking Slavery: Dred Scott and Contemporary Constitutional Theory*, 14 CONST. COMMENT. 271, 311 (1997).

[136] *See Dred Scott*, 60 U.S. (19 How.) at 468 (Nelson, J., concurring) ("A question has been alluded to, on the argument, namely: the right of the master with his slave of transit into or through a free State, on business or commercial pursuits, or in the exercise of a Federal right, or the discharge of a Federal duty, being a citizen of the United States, which is not before us. This question depends upon different considerations and principles from the one in hand, and turns upon the rights and privileges secured to a common citizen of the republic under the Constitution of the United States. When that question arises, we shall be prepared to decide it."); *see also* Alfred Brophy, Note, *Let Us Go Back and Stand on the Constitution: Federal-State Relations in Scott v. Sandford*, 90 COLUM. L. REV. 192, 221 (1990) (arguing that the *Dred Scott* decision "catalyzed Northern fears of the nationalization of slavery").

[137] Abraham Lincoln was convinced that the *Dred Scott* decision was part of a broader conspiracy to nationalize slavery and warned of a "nice little niche, which we may, ere long, see filled with another Supreme Court decision, declaring that the Constitution of the United States does not permit a *state* to exclude slavery from its limits. . . . Such a decision is all that slavery now lacks of being alike lawful in all the States. Welcome or unwelcome, such decision *is* probably coming, and will soon be upon us, unless the power of the present political dynasty shall be met and overthrown. We shall *lie down* pleasantly dreaming that the people of *Missouri* are on the verge of making their State *free*; and we shall *awake* to the *reality*, instead, that the *Supreme* Court has made *Illinois* a *slave* State." Abraham Lincoln, "House Divided" Speech at Springfield, Ill. (June 16, 1858), *in* ABRAHAM LINCOLN: SPEECHES AND WRITINGS 1832–1858, at 426, 432 (Don E. Fehrenbacher ed., 1989). For a discussion of Lincoln's repeated warnings of a "second *Dred Scott*," see Michael Stokes Paulsen, *Lincoln and Judicial Authority*, 83 NOTRE DAME L. REV. 1227, 1247–66 (2008).

2. The *Lemmon* Slave Case[138]

The *Lemmon* case involved a family of Virginia slave owners who were in the process of moving to Texas with their eight slaves. While in New York awaiting a boat to New Orleans, Louis Napoleon, the black vice president of the American and Foreign Anti-Slavery Society,[139] managed to procure a writ of habeas corpus from a local magistrate, who subsequently ruled in late 1852 that the slaves must be freed according to a New York law that banned the importation of slaves and declared the freedom of any slave illegally brought into the state.[140] While the case was still making its way through New York's courts of appeal, the US Supreme Court issued its ruling in *Dred Scott*. The Supreme Court's decision in *Scott* prompted the New York legislature to adopt a set of resolutions that declared "[t]hat this State will not allow Slavery within her borders, in any form, or under any pretense, or for any time" and that "the Supreme Court of the United States, by reason of a majority of the Judges thereof, having identified it with a sectional and aggressive party, has impaired the confidence and respect of the people of the States."[141] The stage was now set for the final resolution of the case before the newly established New York Court of Appeals.

In their appeal, no doubt emboldened by the Supreme Court's decision in *Dred Scott*, the Lemmons argued that the Privileges and Immunities Clause of Article IV protected the right of slave owners to bring slaves into the State of New York, regardless of any state laws to the contrary.[142] According to the Court in *Dred Scott*, the Constitution itself recognized slavery as a property right, and the fundamental nature of that right stood as one of the privileges and immunities of citizens in the states that could not be abrogated by any state law. This "fundamental property rights" reading of Article IV would be repeated by other proponents of slavery in their attempts to force free states to allow the transit of slaves across their borders.[143]

---

[138] Lemmon v. People, 20 N.Y. 562 (1860).

[139] John D. Gordan, III, *The Lemmon Slave Case*, Hist. Soc'y Cts. St. N.Y., 2006, at 1, 8, *available at* http://www.courts.state.ny.us/history/programs-events/images/Judicial-Notice-Newsletter-04.pdf.

[140] *Id.* at 9–10.

[141] Editorial, Ga. Telegraph (Macon). Apr. 28, 1857, at 2 (ruefully reporting on the New York resolutions).

[142] *Lemmon*, 20 N.Y. at 580–83.

[143] According to a November 17, 1857 editorial in the *Washington Union*:

> The Constitution declares that "the citizens of each state shall be entitled to all the privileges and immunities of citizens in the several States." Every citizen of one State coming into another State has, therefore, a right to the protection of his person, and that property which is recognized as such by the Constitution of the United States, any law

The New York Court of Appeals rejected the pro-slavery fundamental rights reading of Article IV, opting instead to follow the traditional reading of the Comity Clause as requiring equal access to state-secured rights. In his concurrence, New York Judge (and future Chief Judge of the New York Court of Appeals) William B. Wright declared that Article IV "was always understood as having but one design and meaning, viz., to secure to the citizens of every State, within every other, the privileges and immunities (whatever they might be) accorded in each to its own citizens. It was intended to guard against a State discriminating in favor of its own citizens. A citizen of Virginia coming into New York was to be entitled to all the privileges and immunities accorded to the citizens of New York."[144] Because New York law prohibited the importation of slaves by anyone, including its own citizens, the trial court's order releasing the slaves was affirmed.[145]

Lemmon is an example of how states' rights principles occasionally worked against the spread of slavery. As counterintuitive from a modern perspective as it might seem, adopting a fundamental national rights view in *Lemmon* would have had the effect of laying the foundation for the nationalization of slavery.[146] In fact, this was precisely what many feared would occur if the Taney Supreme Court heard *Lemmon* on appeal from the state court.[147]

> of a State to the contrary notwithstanding. So far from any State having a right to deprive him of this property, it is its bounden duty to protect him in its possession.
>
> If these views are correct – and we believe it would be difficult to invalidate them – it follows that all State laws, whether organic or otherwise, which prohibit a citizen of one State from settling in another, and bringing his slave property with him, and most especially declaring it forfeited, are direct violations of the original intention of a Government which, as before stated, is the protection of person and property, and of the Constitution of the United States, which recognizes property in slaves, and declares that "the citizens of each State shall be entitled to all the privileges and immunities of citizens in the several States," among the most essential of which is the protection of person and property. . . . The protection of property being, next to that of person, the most important object of all good government. . . .

Cong. Globe, 35th Cong., 1st Sess. app. 199 (1858) (internal quotation marks omitted) (editorial read aloud in the assembly).

[144] *Lemmon*, 20 N.Y. at 626–27 (Wright, J., concurring).

[145] *Id.* at 632. For discussion of *Lemmon v. The People* and the Privileges and Immunities Clause aspects of the holding, see Paul Finkelman, An Imperfect Union: Slavery, Federalism, and Comity 302 (1981).

[146] Cases such as *Prigg v. Pennsylvania* presented the same alignment of freedom and state rights, with the Supreme Court choosing pro-slavery nationalism over anti-slavery localism. *See* Prigg v. Pennsylvania, 41 U.S. 539 (1842) (striking down state law protecting free blacks and runaway slaves as conflicting with Article IV and the Federal Fugitive Slave Law).

[147] There was considerable fear at the time that the New York court's decision in *Lemmon* would be appealed to the US Supreme Court, where its reversal would constitute the "second

Despite concerns that *Lemmon* would become the "second *Dred Scott*," war broke out and the Supreme Court never heard the case. It was not until after the Civil War and the abolition of slavery that the US Supreme Court next heard a case involving the Privileges and Immunities Clause of Article IV. In *Paul v. Virginia*, decided the year after the country ratified the Fourteenth Amendment, the Supreme Court maintained the traditional reading of Article IV and read the privileges and immunities of citizens in the states to include a limited set of state-secured rights.[148] Although Lincoln-appointed Justice Stephen Field could have cited any number of antebellum decisions in support of this reading of Article IV, Field chose a single citation to the pro-freedom decision of the state court in *Lemmon v. People*.[149]

D. *Summary*

By the time of Reconstruction, the consensus understanding of Article IV was that it referred to a limited set of state-secured rights. The record is not completely unanimous on this point; a very small number of cases read Article IV as limiting federal, not state, power, and pro-slavery advocates pressed for a reading of privileges and immunities that would force free states to allow the transitory presence of slaves. These, however, were in the distinct minority. Cases like *Campbell*, *Livingston*, and, to a lesser extent, *Corfield* were the most cited decisions, and their reasoning dominated judicial and scholarly discussion of Article IV.

The gist of the consensus view was that the privileges and immunities of citizens in the states differed from state to state; what was expected was that a

---

Dred Scott" decision that Lincoln and others had warned about, one that would nationalize slavery. *See, e.g., The* Dred Scott *Case*, 1 HARPER'S WKLY., 193, 193 (1857) (commenting on the possible future of the *Lemmon* case and complaining that "all these slave cases are sour enough"); *The Issue Forced upon Us*, EVENING J. (Albany), Mar. 9, 1857, at 2 ("The Lemmon case is on its way to this corrupt fountain of law. Arrived there, a new shackle for the North will be handed to the servile Supreme Court, to rivet upon us. . . . [It] shall complete the disgraceful labors of the Federal Judiciary in behalf of Slavery. . . . The Slave breeders will celebrate it as the crowning success of a complete conquest"); *see also* THEODORE SEDGWICK, A TREATISE ON THE RULES WHICH GOVERN THE INTERPRETATION AND APPLICATION OF STATUTORY AND CONSTITUTIONAL LAW 604 n.† (N.Y., Voorhies 1857) ("The Lemmon Case, as it is commonly called presents the transit question in one aspect distinctly, and is now before the Supreme Court of the State of New York on appeal. The case known as the Dred Scott Case, recently decided by the Supreme Court of the United States, is understood to have incidentally discussed this subject; but we have as yet no authoritative report of the judgment of the court. If the People v. Lemmon shall go up on appeal to the Federal tribunal, the case will, in all probability, call for a settlement of the law on this important question.") (citation omitted).

[148] 75 U.S. (8 Wall.) 168, 180 (1868).
[149] *See id.* at 180 n.16.

certain subset of these privileges would be extended as a matter of comity and constitutional requirement to visiting citizens of other states. As Representative Cushing explained during the debates over the admission of Arkansas to the Union:

> There are no two states in the Union in which municipal "rights, advantages and immunities" are precisely the same. It is, therefore, an impossibility to admit a new state to an equality, in this respect, with each and all of the original states. The citizens of each state are entitled, by the Constitution, to all the privileges and immunities of citizens in the several states. But it is the enjoyment of those privileges which is equalized, the privileges remaining locally diverse. A citizen of New York, who removes to Pennsylvania, does not carry the laws of New York with him, but is admitted to the benefit of those of Pennsylvania, just as if he had originally resided in the latter state.[150]

Writing in 1833, Joseph Story explained that Article IV was intended "to confer on [citizens of each state], if one may so say, a general citizenship; and to communicate all the privileges and immunities, which the citizens of the same state would be entitled to under the like circumstances,"[151] citing, among

---

[150] Caleb Cushing, Speech on the Bill for Admitting the State of Arkansas into the Union (June 9, 1836), *reported in* SALEM GAZETTE (Mass.), July 15, 1836, at 1. Arkansas had submitted a draft Constitution that included a clause providing: "The General Assembly shall have no power to pass laws for the emancipation of slaves, without the consent of the owners. They shall have no power to prevent emigrants to this State from bringing with them such persons as are deemed slaves by the laws of any one of the United States." *Id.* In his speech, Cushing addressed a proposed amendment to the Act of Admission by John Quincy Adams, which would have provided "that nothing in this act shall be construed as an assent by Congress to the article in the Constitution of the said State [of Arkansas] relating to slavery and to the emancipation of slaves." *Id.* (emphasis omitted). Arkansas was admitted as a slave state in June of 1836.

[151] 3 JOSEPH STORY, COMMENTARIES ON THE CONSTITUTION OF THE UNITED STATES § 1800, at 674–75 (Boston, Hilliard, Gray, & Co. 1833). In his own work, COMMENTARIES ON AMERICAN LAW, James Kent adopted the use of Washington's language in *Corfield*, including Washington's argument that privileges and immunities did not include all state-conferred rights, but only those deemed fundamental. *See* 2 KENT, *supra* note 85, pt. 4, at 35–36. William Rawle, in his 1829 treatise *A View of the Constitution of the United States of America*, says little about the Privileges and Immunities Clause beyond noting that it clarified the more ambiguous version in the Articles of Confederation and was not intended to allow any one state to control the rights granted to citizens when they traveled to a different state. WILLIAM RAWLE, A VIEW OF THE CONSTITUTION OF THE UNITED STATES OF AMERICA 84–85 (2d ed., Phila., Nicklin 1829). Beyond that, Rawle simply notes that "[i]t cannot escape notice, that no definition of the nature and rights of citizens appears in the Constitution." *Id.* at 85. Finally, in his treatise *Constitutional Law*, Thomas Sergeant describes the facts and holding of *Campbell*, as well as the debates over the admission of Missouri, before adding that "[i]t has been also held, that the above clause of the constitution means only, that citizens of other States shall have *equal* rights with the citizens of a particular state, and not that they shall have different, or greater rights. Their persons and property must be in all respects, subject to the laws of such state."

other sources, *Corfield v. Coryell* and *Livingston v. Van Ingen*.[152] During the Reconstruction Debates, radical Republicans elevated *Corfield* above all other Article IV precedents and attempted to use Justice Washington's expansive language in support of a national fundamental rights reading of Article IV. This was not, however, how either *Corfield* or the Privileges and Immunities Clause of Article IV was generally understood outside the halls of the Reconstruction Congress prior to the Civil War or during the years immediately following.

In a later chapter, I will explore in detail the use of *Corfield* and Article IV during the debates of the Thirty-Ninth Congress. For now, it is sufficient to note that both the provision and the case enjoyed a consensus understanding by the time of the Civil War. The next section considers a second strain of antebellum thought that also involved "privileges" and "immunities." This strain referred to an entirely separate set of rights than those understood to be protected under Article IV: the privileges and immunities of *citizens of the United States*.

III. THE PRIVILEGES AND IMMUNITIES "OF CITIZENS OF THE UNITED STATES"

The Comity Clause of Article IV deals with one particular set of "privileges and immunities": those belonging to the "citizens in the several states." As this section will show, a separate line of antebellum legal precedent focused on the privileges and immunities *of citizens of the United States*. This second set of "privileges and immunities" were altogether different from those protected under Article IV.

As "free and independent" governments,[153] post-Revolutionary American states enjoyed the sovereign right to recognize a unique set of rights for their own citizens. The adoption of the Federal Constitution added an additional layer of conferred rights so that citizens of the United States could enjoy two separate sets of government-enforced rights. This condition of dual citizenship allowed one to enjoy one set of rights as a federal citizen and an altogether different set of rights as a citizen of a particular state. As the Virginia Supreme Court of Appeals explained in 1811, "[the Constitution] clearly recognises the distinction between the character of a citizen of the United States, and of a

---

THOMAS SERGEANT, CONSTITUTIONAL LAW 393–94 (2d ed., Phila., Nicklin & Johnson 1830). Here, Sergeant adds a footnote citing, among other cases, *Livingston v. Van Ingen. See id.* at 394 n.(*i*).

[152] 3 STORY, *supra* note 151, § 1800, at 675 n.1.

[153] *See* The Declaration of Independence para. 5 (U.S. 1776).

citizen of any individual state; and also of citizens of different states."[154] One's privileges and immunities *qua* US citizen were simply not the same as one's privileges and immunities *qua* state citizen.[155]

A. *The Louisiana Cession Act of 1803*

The rights of national citizenship were most often discussed in the context of US treaties of cession. These agreements promised the inhabitants of newly acquired territory that, once they were fully admitted into the Union, they would enjoy all of the privileges and immunities of US citizens. The Treaty of Purchase between the United States and the French Republic of 1803 (the Louisiana Cession Act) presents one of the earliest and most consistently referred to examples of national rights in antebellum America. According to Article III of that Act:

> The inhabitants of the ceded territory shall be incorporated in the Union of the United States, and admitted as soon as possible, according to the principles of the Federal constitution, to the enjoyment of all the rights, advantages and immunities of citizens of the United States; and in the mean time they shall be maintained and protected in the free enjoyment of their liberty, property, and the religion which they profess.[156]

---

[154] Murray v. M'Carty, 16 Va. (2 Munf.) 393, 398 (1811). The Virginia court went on to hold that the privileges and immunities secured under Article IV did not include the political rights conferred upon state citizens. For an additional example of officials distinguishing national from state-conferred privileges and immunities, see CODE OF LAWS FOR THE DISTRICT OF COLUMBIA: PREPARED UNDER THE AUTHORITY OF THE ACT OF CONGRESS OF THE 29TH OF APRIL 1816, at 26 (Wash., D.C., Davis & Force 1819) (providing laws for the District of Columbia that granted each inhabitant "all the benefits, rights, privileges and immunities, secured to the citizens of Virginia and Maryland respectively by the respective constitutions and declarations of rights of those states respectively, and to all the benefits, rights, privileges and immunities of citizens of the United States so far as such benefits, rights, privileges, and immunities are consistent with the political and local situation of the inhabitants of the said District, and with the constitution of the United States.").

[155] Perhaps the clearest example of the dual aspect of citizenship rights can be found in the original understanding of the First Amendment. The Establishment Clause conferred on all US citizens an immunity from federal religious establishments. U.S. CONST. amend. I ("*Congress* shall make no law respecting an establishment of religion."). Whether one enjoyed a similar immunity from one's own state government, however, was a matter of state law. For a discussion of the law of state religious establishment at the time of the Founding, see generally PHILIP HAMBURGER, SEPARATION OF CHURCH AND STATE (2002); Kurt T. Lash, *The Second Adoption of the Establishment Clause: The Rise of the Nonestablishment Principle*, 27 ARIZ. ST. L. J. 1085 (1995).

[156] Treaty of Purchase between the United States of America and the French Republic, art. III, U.S.-Fr., Apr. 30, 1803, 8 stat. 200; *see also, The Same Old Case*, N.H. PATRIOT, Oct. 24, 1860, at 2 (citing an editorial written by the editor of the *Keene Sentinel* as stating that the terms of

As described at the time by a northern newspaper, Article III was an attempt to provide the inhabitants of the territory "all the *immunities & privileges of citizens of the United States.*"[157] According to members of Congress, Article III provided for "the privileges of citizens of the United States,"[158] and later political tracts explained that the Cession Act's phrase "rights, advantages and immunities" "undoubtedly means those privileges that are common to all the citizens of this republic."[159]

As noted previously, in the period between the Founding and the Civil War, phrases like "privileges and immunities," "rights, advantages and immunities," and "rights, privileges and immunities" were interchangeable. What transformed these phrases into particular terms of art was not the inclusion of one or more of the interchangeable terms like "rights," "immunities," "advantages," or "privileges" but the use of these terms in reference to a particular *group* – for example, the "rights, privileges, and immunities *of citizens in the states*" as opposed to the "rights, privileges, and immunities *of citizens of the United States.*"

Article III of the Cession Act adopted the common language of contemporary international treaties,[160] and it clearly influenced later American treaties involving territorial cession. For example, under the 1819 treaty with Spain by which the United States acquired the territory of Florida, inhabitants of the territory were guaranteed "the enjoyment of all the privileges, rights, and immunities, of the citizens of the United States."[161] Similarly, when Texas joined the Union, it did so with congressional understanding that the

---

the Louisiana Cession Act provided inhabitants of its territory with "[t]he privileges of citizens of the United States").

[157] *Louisiana Memorial*, E. ARGUS (Portland, Me.), Nov. 8, 1804, at 2 (emphasis added).

[158] *See* DEBATES IN THE HOUSE OF REPRESENTATIVES, ON THE BILLS FOR CARRYING INTO EFFECT THE LOUISIANA TREATY 60 (Phila., Palmer Bros. 1804) (Early Am. Imprints, Series 2, no. 7492) (remarks of Representative Gaylord Griswold).

[159] Marcus, An Examination of the Expediency and Constitutionality of Prohibiting Slavery in the State of Missouri 17 (N.Y., Wilet & Co. 1819); *see also* N.H. Sentinel, Oct. 20, 1804, *reported in* New Hampshire Patriot, Oct. 24, 1960, Vol. XIV, issue 701, page 2 (Concord New Hampshire) (noting that "by the terms of the cession [act, inhabitants] will be entitled to the privileges of citizens of the United States").

[160] *See, e.g.*, PA. GAZETTE, *supra* note 69 (reporting of a treaty between Great Britain and Sweden that stated that "[t]he two Powers shall reciprocally enjoy, in the Towns, Ports, Harbours, and Rivers of the respective States, all the Rights, Advantages, and Immunities, which have been, or may be henceforth enjoyed there by the most favoured Nations").

[161] *See* Treaty of Amity, Settlement, and Limits, Between the United States of America and his Catholic Majesty, U.S.-Spain, art. 7, Oct. 24, 1820– Feb. 19, 1821, 8 Stat. 252, 258. Additionally, the treaty included language noting that "[t]he treaty with Spain, by which Florida was ceded to the United States, is the law of the land, and admits the inhabitants of Florida to the enjoyment of the privileges, rights, and immunities of the citizens of the United States." *Id.* at 252 n.(a).

territory and the new state complied with the Cession Act's guarantee of all "rights, advantages, and immunities of United States citizens."[162] Additionally, in 1848, then-Secretary of State James Buchanan advised his diplomatic agent to include a provision like Article III of the Cession Act in any peace treaty with Mexico:

> [The treaty should include] an article similar to the third article of the Louisiana treaty. It might read as follows: "The inhabitants of the territory over which the jurisdiction of the United States has been extended by the fourth article of this treaty shall be incorporated in the Union of the United States, and admitted as soon as possible, according to the principles of the Federal constitution, to the enjoyment of all the rights, advantages, and immunities of citizens of the United States; and, in the mean time, they shall be maintained and protected in the free enjoyment of their liberty, property, and the religion which they profess."[163]

Buchanan's advice resulted in Article IX of the treaty between the United States and Mexico, commonly known as the Treaty of Guadalupe Hidalgo, which declared that inhabitants of the territory were entitled

> to the enjoyment of all the rights of citizens of the United States, according to the principles of the constitution; and in the mean time shall be maintained and protected in the free enjoyment of their liberty and property, and secured in the free exercise of their religion without restriction.[164]

---

[162] According to a proposed bill regarding the annexation of Texas:

> And whereas the then territory of Texas was a part of the said territory of Louisiana, ceded by France to the United States by the treaty aforesaid: And whereas the said territory of Texas was ceded by the United States to Spain by the treaty of Florida of the 22d February, 1819: And whereas the citizens of said territory have declared, vindicated, and established their independence as a nation, and erected for themselves an independent republic: and, as it is represented, are desirous of having said territory reannexed to these United States, and the citizens of said republic restored to the rights, privileges, and immunities guarantied by the said third article of the said treaty of Louisiana: And whereas a faithful adherence to the stipulations of treaties is the glory of a nation, and should be preserved inviolate; and good faith to France, and justice to the citizens of Texas, require that it shall be done.

Cong. Globe, 28th Cong., 2d Sess. 76 (1845); *see also* Legislative Acts and Proceedings, *in* Augusta Chronicle, Jan. 4, 1845, page 2 (reporting on the submission of "A Bill to authorize the people of Texas to form a territorial Government and a Bill to protect the people of Texas in all the rights and privileges of citizens of the United States").

[163] S. Exec. Doc. No. 30–52, at 83 (1848).

[164] *See* Treaty of Peace, Friendship, Limits, and Settlement with the Republic of Mexico, art. IX, U.S.–Mex., May 30, 1848, 9 Stat. 922, 930.

According to the 1843 Treaty with "Stockbridge Tribe of Indians," every member of that tribe "from that time forth are hereby declared to be citizens of the United States to all intents and purposes, and shall be entitled to all rights, privileges and immunities of such citizens."[165] In fact, American treaties conferring the rights of national citizenship continued to use the language of the Louisiana Cession Act up to the time of Reconstruction. The same Senate that adopted the Privileges or Immunities Clause of the Fourteenth Amendment also ratified the following 1867 Treaty ceding Alaska to the United States:

> The inhabitants of the ceded territory, according to their choice, reserving their natural allegiance, may return to Russia within three years; but if they should prefer to remain in the ceded territory, they, with the exception of uncivilized native tribes, shall be admitted to the enjoyment of all the rights, advantages, and immunities of citizens of the United States, and shall be maintained and protected in the free enjoyment of their liberty, property, and religion.[166]

In sum, declarations of the "rights and immunities" of national citizenship were a common feature of antebellum American law, particularly as it regarded the rights of US citizens in areas incorporated into the Union.[167] The words of Article III of the Louisiana Cession Act, which protected the "rights, advantages and immunities of United States citizens," were understood at the time as protecting the "immunities and privileges of United States citizens" or simply "the privileges of citizens of the United States."[168] Thus, when John Bingham

---

[165] 1 William Henry Wheaton & William Beach Lawrence, Elements of International Law appx. 900 (2d. annotated ed. 1863).

[166] Treaty Concerning the Cession of the Russian Possessions in North America by His Majesty the Emperor of All the Russias to the United States of America, U.S.–Russ., art. III, Mar. 30-June 20, 1867, 15 Stat. 539, 542.

[167] *See also* Treaty between the United States of America and the Ottawa Indians of Blanchard's Fork and Roche De Boeuf, June 24, 1862, 12 Stat. 1237 ("The Ottawa Indians of the United Bands of Blanchard's Fork and of Roche de Boeuf, having become sufficiently advanced in civilization, and being desirous of becoming citizens of the United States . . . [after five years from the ratification of this treaty] shall be deemed and declared to be citizens of the United States, to all intents and purposes, and shall be entitled to all the rights, privileges, and immunities of such citizens."); Treaty between the United States of America and Different Tribes of Sioux Indians, Art. VI, April 29, 1868, 15 Stat. 637 ("[A]ny Indian or Indians receiving a patent for land under the foregoing provisions, shall thereby and from thenceforth become and be a citizen of the United States, and be entitled to all the *privileges and immunities of such citizens*."). For these and additional examples of the terms "privileges" and "immunities" in antebellum treaties and their relevance to Section One of the Fourteenth Amendment, see McDonald v. City of Chicago, 130 S.Ct. 3020, 3068–70 (2010) (Thomas, J., concurring); AKHIL REED AMAR, THE BILL OF RIGHTS: CREATION AND RECONSTRUCTION 167–68 & nn. *.-2 (1998).

[168] As pointed out earlier, the terms "privileges" and "immunities" were words used interchangeably with terms like "rights" and "advantages." Thus, it is not surprising to find Article III of

added the phrase "privileges or immunities of United States citizens" to Section One of the Fourteenth Amendment, he used phrasing with roots extending as far back as the Louisiana Cession Act of 1803 and a common phrase in antebellum American law.

B. *Debating the Rights of National Citizenship: The Missouri Question*

One of the most extensive antebellum discussions involving the privileges and immunities of US citizens occurred during the debates over the admission of Missouri and congressional efforts to ban slavery in the state as a condition of admission.[169] The effort failed and Congress instead adopted a compromise that admitted Missouri as a slave state but banned slavery in any future state added north of the 36°30′ parallel.[170] During the debates over the Missouri question, the opponents and proponents of slavery traced out the positions that would ultimately dominate the increasingly bitter sectional debate over the next four decades.[171] As would later abolitionists, free-state advocates called on all manner of sources to defend the proposed ban on slavery in Missouri, including natural law, the Declaration of Independence, and the precedential ban of slavery in the Northwest Territories.[172] They also addressed the meaning of Article III of the Louisiana Cession Act and its protection of the rights, advantages, and immunities of United States citizens.

On February 13, 1819, New York Representative James Tallmadge proposed an amendment to the bill admitting Missouri that would ban future importation of slaves into the state and free all children of current Missouri slaves when

---

the Louisiana Cession Act's language of "rights, advantages and immunities" paraphrased as "immunities and privileges" or simply "privileges." For example, one can find Article IV of the Bill of Rights' reference to "privileges and immunities" described as a reference to the "rights, advantages, and immunities" conferred by a state on its own citizens. *See* Cushing, *supra* note 150. All of these phrases were interchangeable; the key difference was on which group the privileges and immunities (or rights, advantages, and immunities) were conferred.

[169] Tallmadge's amendment, see *infra* text accompanying note 195, was approved by the House but rejected by the Senate. When the House voted to reapprove the Amendment, the result was to put the matter over until the next Congress. *See* SEAN WILENTZ, THE RISE OF AMERICAN DEMOCRACY: JEFFERSON TO LINCOLN 224 (2005).

[170] For a discussion of the legal side of the congressional debate, see CURRIE, *supra* note 101, at 232–39. For the political side, see Graber, *supra* note 135, at 120; DANIEL WALKER HOWE, WHAT HATH GOD WROUGHT: THE TRANSFORMATION OF AMERICA, 1815–1848, at 147 (2007); WILENTZ, *supra* note 169, at 218–40.

[171] *See, e.g.*, Graber, *supra* note 135, at 122 ("Slaveholders in Congress during the Missouri debates anticipated the central themes of *Dred Scott*.").

[172] *See, e.g.*, *Debate on the Missouri Bill in the House of Representatives*, HILLSBORO' TELEGRAPH (Amherst, N.H.), Mar. 18, 1820, at 1 (providing comments of Representative Clifton Clagett of New Hampshire).

they reached the age of twenty-five.[173] Battle lines were quickly drawn both inside and outside Congress, with opponents of Tallmadge's amendment arguing that Congress had no power to make either slavery or abolition a condition for admitting a new state.[174] In particular, opponents argued that imposing such a restriction on the inhabitants of the states would deny them the "rights, advantages and immunities" promised to them under the Louisiana Cession Act, Missouri having been carved out of the original Louisiana Purchase.

Pro-slavery advocates like Missouri Delegate John Scott asked, "Can any gentleman contend . . . that, laboring under the proposed restriction, the citizens of Missouri would have the rights, advantages, and immunities of other citizens of the Union? Have not other new states, in their admission, and have not all the states in the Union, now, privileges and rights beyond what was contemplated to be allowed to the citizens of Missouri?"[175] "[I]f you compel Missouri to relinquish any of the rights of self-government enjoyed by the other States," argued Kentucky Representative Hardin, "her citizens will not enjoy the same privileges and immunities of citizens of the several states, through their respective State governments."[176] As Massachusetts Representative Henry Shaw explained:

> I voted against [Tallmadge's amendment] because I believed it a violation of the treaty of cession. By the third article of the treaty by which we acquired Louisiana, it is expressly stipulated, "that the inhabitants of the ceded territory shall be incorporated in the Union of the United States, and admitted, as soon as possible, according to the principles of the federal constitution, to the enjoyment of all the rights, advantages, and immunities of citizens of the United States citizens &c.["] . . . [A]nd yet Congress, by this amendment, says to Missouri, you shall not be admitted as a sovereign state, and your citizens shall *not* have the same *rights* and *advantages* that citizens of every state may have, and that the citizens of eleven states absolutely enjoy. A clearer and more palpable violation of a treaty, in my opinion, was never made.[177]

According to an editorial published in both the *St. Louis Enquirer* and *Kentucky Reporter*, Article III of the Louisiana Cession Act required Congress "to admit the people of the Missouri into the union, with all the rights, advantages,

---

[173] HOWE, *supra* note 170, at 147.

[174] *See Remonstrance of the Grand Jury of Howard County*, ST. LOUIS ENQUIRER, Aug. 4, 1819, at 2 (arguing that, per the terms of the Louisiana Cession Act, Congress could not condition the admission of Missouri on the banning of slavery).

[175] WILENTZ, *supra* note 169, at 228 (citing 33 Annals of Cong. 1200 (1819)).

[176] *See* 35 ANNALS OF CONG. 1083 (1820).

[177] Henry Shaw, Letter to the Editor, *The Missouri Slave Question*, DAILY NAT'L INTELLIGENCER (Wash., D.C.), May 8, 1819, at 2.

and immunities of the citizens of the United States."[178] As the controversy rever-
berated around the country, slaveholding states saw the danger of conceding
any measure of congressional power to regulate slavery. In Virginia, the House
of Delegates passed a Resolution that expressed the assembly's "common cause
with the people of the Missouri Territory" and supported Missouri's demand
to be admitted to the Union "upon equal terms with the existing States. How
else can they enjoy the rights, advantages, and immunities of other citizens of
the United States?"[179]

For their part, free-state advocates argued that the rights protected under
Article III of the Louisiana Cession Act were federal rights and not state-level
rights like slavery. Article III, wrote Daniel Webster, "cannot be referred to
rights, advantages and immunities derived exclusively from the State governments, for these do not depend on the federal Constitution."[180] Writing to the
people of Illinois, the pamphleteer Aristides asked,

> [I]f it were possible to consider slavery as a *right,* an *advantage,* or an *immunity,*
> with what propriety could it be classed among the rights, advantages, and

[178] Kentucky Reporter, *The Question of Slavery to the West of the Mississippi,* ST. LOUIS ENQUIRER,
June 9, 1819, at 2. The editorial continued:

> [B]y what authority can Congress impose upon them a restriction which has not been
> imposed by the constitution on the citizens of the other states? . . . [T]he *right* of "the
> citizens of the United States " to hold slaves, if not prohibited by their local constitutions
> and laws, is recognized in numerous articles of [the Constitution]. It being then clearly a
> *right and advantage* of the citizens of the United States, according to the principles of the
> federal constitution that they may hold slaves, unless they choose to deny themselves that
> right and advantage by their local institutions, how can Congress require a prohibition
> of slavery in the state of Missouri, without a manifest violation of the compact by which
> we are bound to grant such state all the rights and advantages which accord with the
> principles of the federal constitution?

Id.

[179] *Virginia Legislature: Missouri Question,* CAROLINA CENTINEL (Newbern, N.C.), Jan. 22, 1820,
at 2. A separate question involved whether the Treaty's promise that the inhabitants would also
"be maintained and protected in the free enjoyment of their liberty, *property,* and religion"
included the right to property in slavery. This particular question would reverberate for decades.
See, e.g., CONG. GLOBE, 34th Congress, 1st sess. app. 1265 (Mr. Kidwell) (arguing that property
rights protected in the Cession Act include the rights of property in slaves).

[180] Daniel Webster et al., A Memorial to the Congress of the United States, On the Subject of
Restraining the Increase of Slavery in New States to be Admitted Into the Union 15 (Boston,
Phelps 1819) (Early Am. Imprints, Series 2, no. 47390). Although Webster was one of four
signatories, he chaired the Committee that produced the report. According to his biographer,
"[t]he resulting memorial clearly bore the marks of Webster's hand" and can be considered
his "handiwork." Robert V. Remini, Daniel Webster: The Man and His Time 169 (1997). I
will follow Remini's lead and treat Webster as the prime, if not clearly the sole, author of the
Memorial.

immunities *of citizens of the United States,* when more than one half of those citizens do not enjoy this pretended right, advantage, or immunity?[181]

As Pennsylvania Representative Joseph Hemphill pointed out:

> If the right to hold slaves is a federal right and attached merely to citizenship of the United States, [then slavery] could maintain itself against state authority, and on this principle the owner might take his slaves into any state he pleased, in defiance of the state laws, but this would be contrary to the constitution.[182]

According to a report of the abolitionist Delaware Society, "[i]n the *character* of citizens of the United States, as members of the federal compact, slaves cannot be held. They can be held only by citizens of some particular States, deriving their power solely from the State government. On this point of distinction between citizens of the United States, and citizens of particular States, your committee can perceive no ground for contrariety of opinion."[183]

1. Federal Rights "Common to All"

The basic approach of the free-state advocates was to distinguish state-secured rights from the federal rights of the Louisiana Cession Act. "Any citizen who enjoys a right which another citizen in the United States does not enjoy," argued New Hampshire Senator David Morill, "acquires that right from some other source than the constitution of the United States."[184] The rights protected under Article III were federal rights derived from the Constitution and were common to all citizens throughout the United States. "If it were the right of a citizen of the United States, *as such*, to hold [slaves]," wrote "Philadelphian" Robert Walsh, "then they might be legally held in New York or Pennsylvania, as Georgia; since a *federal right* could not be impaired by the laws of any member of the confederacy."[185]

---

[181] Aristides, *To the People of Illinois,* EDWARDSVILLE SPECTATOR (Ill.), June 5, 1819, at 6.

[182] Joseph Hemphill, Speech on the Missouri Question in the House of Representatives (Feb. 5, 1820), *in* JOSEPH HEMPHILL, SPEECH OF MR. HEMPHILL ON THE MISSOURI QUESTION: IN THE HOUSE OF REPRESENTATIVES OF THE U. STATES 16 (Wash., D.C., Shaw & Shoemaker 1820) (Early Am. Imprints, Series 2, no. 48206).

[183] Report of a Committee of the Delaware Society (Sept. 29, 1819), *in* Minutes of the Sixteenth American Convention for Promoting the Abolition of Slavery, and Improving the Condition of the African Race 18, 25 (Phila., Fry 1819) (Early Am. Imprints, Series 2. no. 46985).

[184] David Morill, Remarks of Mr. Morill in the Senate of the United States on the Missouri Question (Jan. 17, 1820), *in* HILLSBORO' TELEGRAPH (Amherst, N.H.), Mar. 4, 1820, at 1.

[185] A Philadelphian, Free Remarks on the Spirit of the Federal Constitution, the Practice of the Federal Government, and the Obligations of the Union Respecting the Exclusion of Slavery From the Territories and New States 49 (Phila., Finley 1819); *see also* Shaw, *supra* note 177.

Over and over again, free-state advocates stressed that the immunities of US citizens were uniform throughout the country and "common to all." According to Joseph Blunt, writing under the pseudonym Marcus, Article III referred only to "those privileges that are common to all the citizens of this republic, not those depending upon state laws."[186] John Sergeant, in his speech on the Missouri Question, explained that "'the rights, advantages and immunities' of citizens of the United States . . . are the same throughout the United States."

> They are, therefore, independent of local rights, or those which depend on residence in a particular place. An inhabitant of a State has certain privileges arising from his inhabitancy of the State. An inhabitant of a territory, too, has certain privileges, which arise from his living in a territory. A citizen of the United States, who resides neither in a State or territory, but is out of the limits of the Union, enjoys neither of the privileges of a State or a territory, but he possesses the rights, privileges and immunities of a citizen of the United States, which are common to all the three descriptions of persons.[187]

In his *Memorial to Congress*, Daniel Webster declared,

> The rights, advantages and immunities here spoken of [in Article III] must, from the very force of the terms of the clause, be such as are recognized or communicated by the Constitution of the United States; such as are common to all citizens, and are uniform throughout the United States. The clause cannot be referred to rights advantages and immunities derived exclusively from the State Government, for these do not depend upon the federal Constitution.[188]

Although it is possible to understand "rights common to all" as referring to "rights commonly found in state law throughout the United States," this is not how the term was used by those seeking to ban slavery in the state of

---

[186] Marcus, *supra* note 159, at 17–18. Marcus continued:

> It is the privilege, and a great a glorious one, of a citizen of Massachusetts, that his security and comfort cannot be destroyed by a slave population. This privilege is denied to the citizens of Georgia. On this very subject the laws of the different states grant different rights. Therefore they are not federal but state rights, and the inhabitants of Missouri may be admitted to the enjoyment of the rights, advantages, and immunities of citizens of the U.S. with or without the power of slave holding.

Id. at 18.

[187] *See* John Sergeant, Speech on the Missouri Question, *reprinted in* 2 American Eloquence: A Collection of Speeches and Addresses by the Most Eminent Orators of America: With Biographical Sketches and Illustrative Notes 525 (Frank Moore, ed. 1857).

[188] Webster et al., *supra* note 180, at 15.

Missouri. According to Daniel Webster, these national privileges and immunities were those "recognized or communicated by the Constitution of the United States."[189] According to New Hampshire Senator David Morill, these were rights "derived from the constitution; and these are federal rights, enjoyed by every citizen, in every state in the Union."[190] These were rights, in other words, of US citizens *as* US citizens. As Rufus King explained, once Missouri became part of the Union, Article III of the Cession Act would guarantee its inhabitants "'all the rights, advantages and immunities' which citizens of the United States derive from the constitution thereof: – these rights may be denominated federal rights, are uniform throughout the Union, and are common to all its citizens."[191]

Although not necessary for their argument, free-state advocates occasionally addressed the nature of federal privileges and immunities protected under Article III of the Louisiana Cession Act. According to Senator Morill:

> The following are federal rights, namely, each state is entitled to two Senators – the legislatures shall choose them – they shall be privileged from arrest – each state shall appoint electors – the electors in each state shall meet on the same day and vote for two persons – the cognizance of controversies between two or more states – between a state and citizens of another state – between citizens of different states – between citizens of the same state, claiming lands under grants of different states, and between a state, or the citizens thereof, and foreign states. . . . These are all secured to Missouri, and all other rights derived from the constitution of the United States.[192]

The national rights Morill names are all expressly enumerated in the Constitution, some relating to the federal representation, others involving the jurisdiction of the federal courts. Daniel Webster's list was slightly different, but it followed the same principle of constitutional enumeration:

> The obvious meaning therefore of [Article III] is, that the rights derived under the federal Constitution shall be enjoyed by the inhabitants of Louisiana in the same manner as by the citizens of other States. The United States, by the Constitution, are bound to guarantee to every State in the Union a republican form of government; and the inhabitants of Louisiana are entitled, when a State, to this guarantee. Each State has a right to two senators, and

---

[189] *Id.*

[190] Morill, *supra* note 184.

[191] Rufus King, Observations on the Slavery Question (Nov. 22, 1819), *in* CONN. J. (New Haven), Dec. 21, 1819, at 1; *see also* Letter from Rufus King to R. Peters, Jr. (Nov. 30, 1819), *in* 6 THE LIFE AND CORRESPONDENCE OF RUFUS KING 235–38 (Charles R. King ed., Da Capo Press 1971) (1900).

[192] Morill, *supra* note 184.

to representatives according to a certain enumeration of population pointed out in the Constitution. The inhabitants of Louisiana, upon their admission into the Union, are also entitled to these privileges.[193]

Webster and Morill both viewed federal rights and immunities as involving specific guarantees enumerated in the Constitution (thus bestowed "commonly" on all United States citizens), primarily involving the constitutionally express structural guarantees of federalism and access to federal courts. Neither list included any natural or common law liberties beyond those listed in the Federal Constitution, much less rights or immunities derived from state law (such as the right to own slaves).

Pro-slavery advocates did not generally challenge the idea that slavery was a right derived from state law. Nor did they specifically disagree with the idea that Article III of the Louisiana Cession Act protected only federal rights. Instead, their argument sought to tie slavery to ancillary federal guarantees, such as the right to republican self-government or the right of an entering state to equal status with the original states of the Union. As Delaware Congressman Louis McLane argued,

> The most important of the *federal* advantages and immunities, consist in the right of being represented in Congress, as well in the Senate as in this House, the right of participating in the councils by which they are governed. These are emphatically the *"rights, advantages and immunities* of citizens of the U. States. . . . "* Sir, the rights, advantages and immunities of citizens of the United States, and which are their proudest boast, are the rights of self government, first, in their state constitutions, and, secondly, in the government of the Union, in which they have an equal participation.[194]

Notice that McLane's argument echoes the general position of Morill and Webster: federal rights are derived from the Federal Constitution itself (in this case, the Constitution's guarantee of state representation in the federal Congress). The disagreement between these men involved the most relevant source of federal rights and the scope of the federal rights actually conferred.

---

[193] WEBSTER ET AL., *supra* note 180, at 15–16.

[194] Louis McLane, Speech of Mr. McLane, of Delaware, on the Missouri Question (Feb. 7, 1820), *in* AM. WATCHMAN (Wilmington, Del.), Mar. 29, 1820, at 2. McLane argued that the Louisiana Cession Act stipulated that "the inhabitants of the ceded territory shall be incorporated in the union of the United States, and admitted as soon as possible, according to the principles of the Federal Constitution, to the enjoyment of all the rights, advantages and immunities of citizens of the United States." *Id.* (quoting proposed language of Article III of the Act). McLane believed this placed an obligation on Congress to admit a state as soon as it was possible to do so, and that placing conditions on this admission violated the duties and rights secured by Article III.

Free-staters denied that the right to own slaves was a federal right, and they read the Constitution as conferring national power to decide when and under what conditions to admit a new state. Slave-state advocates agreed that slavery was a matter of state law but insisted that the federal right to republican self-government established the right of admitted states to decide the slavery issue for themselves, free from federal interference.

2. Distinguishing Article IV

Both sides in the Missouri debate distinguished the national rights, privileges, and immunities of Article III of the Louisiana Cession Act from the state-conferred rights, privileges, and immunities guarded under Article IV of the Federal Constitution. A key contention of the free-state advocates was that the "rights, advantages and immunities" protected under Article III of the Louisiana Cession Act were legally distinct from the "rights, advantages, and immunities" conferred on individuals as a matter of state law.[195] Article III rights, advantages, and immunities of US citizens, they argued, meant only "those privileges that are common to all the citizens of this republic, not those depending upon state laws. For these are different in different states."[196] As the Delaware Society put it, "[i]n the *character* of citizens of the United States, as members of the federal compact, slaves cannot be held. They can only be held only by citizens of some particular States, deriving their power solely from the State government."[197] The right to slavery involved state, not federal, rights.

---

[195] *See, e.g.,* WEBSTER ET AL., *supra* note 180, at 15 ("The clause cannot be referred to rights, advantages and immunities, derived exclusively from the State governments, for these do not depend upon the federal Constitution. Besides, it would be impossible that all the rights, advantages and immunities of citizens of the different States could be at the same time enjoyed by the same persons. These rights are different in different States; a right exists in one State, which is denied in others, or is repugnant to other rights enjoyed in others.").

At a certain level, of course, Article IV of the Constitution and Article III of the Louisiana Cession Act *did* cover the same territory, at least if one adopted the *Campbell* and *Livingston* reading of the Privileges and Immunities Clause of Article IV. According to this view, the protections of Article IV were, in fact, among the federal rights secured to citizens of the United States. However, that protection did not confer substantive rights but only guaranteed sojourning citizens the same rights as in-state citizens. "If the proposed amendment prevails," Tallmadge explained, "the inhabitants of Louisiana or the citizens of the United States can neither of them take slaves into the state of Missouri. All, therefore, may enjoy *equal* privileges." James Tallmadge, Jr., Speech of the Hon. James Tallmadge, Jun., in the House of Representative of the United States, on the Bill for Authorising the People of the Territory of Missouri To Form a Constitution and State Government, and for the Admission of the Same into the Union, *in* COM. ADVERTISER (N.Y.), Apr. 17, 1819, at 1.

[196] MARCUS, *supra* note 159, at 17–18.

[197] Report of a Committee of the Delaware Society, *supra* note 183, at 25.

"[I]t would therefore be absurd to say, that being admitted to all the rights, advantages, and immunities of citizens of the United States . . . would give to the inhabitants of [Missouri] the right of holding slaves."[198]

This argument presumes an interpretation of Article IV presented in cases like *Campbell* and *Livingston*, at the time the two most influential decisions regarding Article IV.[199] The fact that some states banned slavery did not violate Article IV if the ban applied equally to in-state and visiting out-of-state citizens. As Marcus explained:

> The militia officers of other states, when residing in New-York, are exempt from military duty, except as officers. In some other states this privilege is not granted. It is the privilege, and a great and glorious one, of a citizen of Massachusetts, that his security and comfort cannot be destroyed by a slave population. This privilege is denied to the citizens of Georgia. On this very subject the laws of different states grant different rights.[200]

In his *Memorial*, Daniel Webster agreed that Article IV only "applies to the case of the removal of a citizen of one State to another State; and in such a case it secures to the migrating citizen all the privileges and immunities of citizens *in* the State to which he removes."[201] The alternative, argued Webster, would be a disaster. If Article IV "gives to the citizens of each State all the privileges and immunities of the citizens of every other State, at the same time and under all circumstances," then slaveholding states would be able to force slavery into every state in the Union.

> [I]t would be in the power of that single State, by the admission of the right of its citizens to hold Slaves, to communicate the same right to the citizens of all the other States within their own exclusive limits, in defiance of their own constitutional prohibitions; and to render the absurdity still more apparent, the same construction would communicate the most opposite and irreconcilable rights to the citizens of different States at the same time. It seems therefore to be undeniable, upon any rational interpretation, that this clause of the Constitution communicated no rights in any State, which its own citizens do not enjoy; and that the citizens of Louisiana, upon their admission into the Union, in receiving the benefit of this clause, would not enjoy higher, or more extensive rights than the citizens of Ohio.[202]

---

[198] *Id.* at 25–26.

[199] These cases represented the consensus understanding of the Comity Clause prior to the 1823 decision of *Corfield v. Coryell* – a decision that echoed the same understanding.

[200] MARCUS, *supra* note 159, at 18.

[201] WEBSTER ET AL., *supra* note 180, at 16.

[202] *Id.* at 16–17. According to Pennsylvania Representative Joseph Hemphill:

Although these arguments took place midway between the Founding and Reconstruction, they had a life that extended well beyond the debates over the Missouri Question. Daniel Webster's *Memorial*, for example, was republished in 1854 as part of a pamphlet discussing the Nebraska Question.[203] It was published *again* three years before the Civil War as part of a collection of famous American speeches.[204] That same year, a different collection of speeches reproduced both Rufus King's and John Sergeant's explanations of how the rights, advantages, and immunities of citizens of the United States were those derived from the federal Constitution and were altogether different from the rights, advantages, and immunities of citizens protected under the Comity Clause of Article IV.[205] Ultimately, Webster's distinction between the rights of state citizenship and the rights, advantages, and immunities of citizens of the United States would inform John Bingham's final draft of the Privileges or Immunities Clause.[206]

C. Dred Scott

Although Tallmadge's amendment was never passed (Tallmadge himself voluntarily retired from the House), the resulting compromise presumed that Congress did in fact have power to regulate slavery in the territories, including

> If the right to hold slaves is a federal right and attached merely to citizenship of the United States, it could maintain itself against state authority, and on this principle the owner might take his slaves into any state he pleased, in defiance of the state laws, but this would be contrary to the constitution, and even the broad language that the citizens of each state shall be entitled to all the privileges and immunities of citizens in the several states does not produce this effect, as is plainly manifested by the article which directs that persons escaping from labor shall be delivered up to the party to whom the labor is due, this shows that if slaves are intentionally taken into a state to reside, the state can deny to the master any right to hold them as slaves within its jurisdiction.

Hemphill, *supra* note 182, at 16.

[203] *See* Daniel Webster et al., A Memorial to the Congress of the United States, on the Subject of Restraining the Increase of Slavery in New States to be Admitted Into the Union (1819), *reprinted in* The Nebraska Question 9, 9–12 (N.Y., Redfield 1854). *See also* Horace Greeley, A History of the Struggle for Slavery Extension or Restriction in the United States, from the Declaration of Independence to the Present Day 22, 23 (New York, 1856) (reprinting Webster's speech, including his discussion of the Louisiana Cession Act).

[204] *See* Daniel Webster et al., A Memorial to the Congress of the United States, on the Subject of Restraining the Increase of Slavery in New States to be Admitted Into the Union (1819), *reprinted in* The Political Text-Book, or Encyclopedia 601, 601–04 (M. W. Cluskey ed., Wash., D.C., Wendell 1857).

[205] *See* 2 American Eloquence: A Collection of Speeches and Addresses by the Most Eminent Orators of America: With Biographical Sketches and Illustrative Notes 46, 528–29 (Frank Moore, ed., 1857).

[206] *See infra* Chapter 3.

areas carved out of the former Louisiana territory north of parallel 36°30′.[207] According to the congressional act accompanying the compromise, "in all that territory ceded by France to the United States . . . which lies north of thirty-six degrees and thirty minutes north latitude . . . slavery and involuntary servitude . . . shall be, and is hereby, *forever prohibited.*"[208] By passing this Act, a majority of Congress signaled that they agreed with (or at the very least acquiesced to) the proposition that the federal rights, advantages, and immunities of US citizens under Article III did not include the state-conferred right to own slaves.

Chief Justice Taney, of course, rejected this understanding of federal power in *Dred Scott*. But he did so under the assumption that even though slavery remained a state-conferred property right, Congress had to respect this right in the territories as a matter of due process. Nothing in Taney's opinion challenged the traditional distinction between the local rights of state citizenship and the federal rights of national citizenship. In fact, Taney's conclusion *required* such a distinction: just because one state conferred citizenship upon resident blacks did not make blacks citizens of the United States who could invoke the jurisdiction of federal courts under Article III.[209] Nor did the dissenting justices in *Dred Scott* challenge the distinction between local and national privileges and immunities. Justice John McLean argued that Congress had power to regulate slavery in the territories, and he refused to accept the proposition that slaves were mere property that owners could carry with them into the territories; if this were true, they would have the same

---

[207] *See* Wilentz, *supra* note 169, at 232. A majority of slaveholding states supported the Compromise, even voting on its individual provisions. *See* Graber, *supra* note 135, at 124. As Mark Graber notes, this may have been due in part to a belief that the Compromise was a "boon for slave states" due to the fact that the northern territories were considered uninhabitable. *Id.*

[208] Missouri Enabling Act, ch. 22, § 8, 3 Stat. 545. 548 (1820) (repealed 1854) (emphasis added).

[209] According to Taney:

In discussing this question, we must not confound the rights of citizenship which a State may confer within its own limits, and the rights of citizenship as a member of the Union. It does not by any means follow, because he has all the rights and privileges of a citizen of a State, that he must be a citizen of the United States. He may have all of the rights and privileges of the citizen of a State, and yet not be entitled to the rights and privileges of a citizen in any other State. . . . Nor have the several States surrendered the power of conferring these rights and privileges by adopting the Constitution of the United States. Each State may still confer them upon an alien, or any one it thinks proper, or upon any class or description of persons; yet he would not be a citizen in the sense in which that word is used in the Constitution of the United States, nor entitled to sue as such in one of its courts, nor to the privileges and immunities of a citizen in the other States. The rights which he would acquire would be restricted to the State which gave them.

Dred Scott v. Sanford, 60 U.S. (19 How.) 393 (1856).

right to carry them into free states as well.[210] Justice Benjamin Curtis rejected Taney's argument that one could be a citizen of a state without necessarily being a citizen of the United States.[211] However, Curtis expressly distinguished the privileges that accompany the status of US citizenship from the political and "civil rights" that were wholly dependent on state law.[212] Embracing the consensus *Campbell* reading of Article IV, Justice Curtis explained that the rights of national citizenship were altogether different from the privileges and immunities of citizens in the states, privileges that involved state-conferred rights subject to whatever restrictions the states choose to impose on their own citizens.[213] As controversial as the *Dred Scott* opinion was in regard to the

---

[210] In Justice McLean's words:

> Allowing to my brethren the same right of judgment that I exercise myself, I must be permitted to say that it seems to me the principle laid down will enable the people of a slave State to introduce slavery into a free State, for a longer or shorter time, as may suit their convenience; and by returning the slave to the State whence he was brought, by force or otherwise, the status of slavery attaches, and protects the rights of the master, and defies the sovereignty of the free State.

> *Id.* at 559 (McLean, J., dissenting).

[211] According to Curtis, "my opinion is, that, under the Constitution of the United States, every free person born on the soil of a State, who is a citizen of that State by force of its Constitution or laws, is also a citizen of the United States." *Id.* at 576 (Curtis, J., dissenting). Curtis goes on to argue that Article IV implicitly recognizes that citizens in the states are, thereby, citizens of the United States. *Id.* at 581.

[212] Wrote Curtis,

> The truth is, that citizenship, under the Constitution of the United States, is not dependent on the possession of any particular political or even of all civil rights; and any attempt so to define it must lead to error. To what citizens the elective franchise shall be confided, is a question to be determined by each State, in accordance with its own views of the necessities or expediencies of its condition. What civil rights shall be enjoyed by its citizens, and whether all shall enjoy the same, or how they may be gained or lost, are to be determined in the same way.

> *Dred Scott*, 6 U.S. (19 How.) at 583. Curtis's point was to reject the idea that if blacks were considered citizens of the United States, then, under Article IV, they would necessarily have equal political rights with white citizens in the several states.

[213] According to Curtis:

> Besides, this clause of the Constitution does not confer on the citizens of one State, in all other States, specific and enumerated privileges and immunities. They are entitled to such as belong to citizenship, but not to such as belong to particular citizens attended by other qualifications. Privileges and immunities which belong to certain citizens of a State, by reason of the operation of causes other than mere citizenship, are not conferred. Thus, if the laws of a State require, in addition to citizenship of the State, some qualification for office, or the exercise of the elective franchise, citizens of all other States, coming thither to reside, and not possessing those qualifications, cannot enjoy those privileges, not because they are not to be deemed entitled to the privileges of citizens of the State

citizenship status of blacks and the right to carry slavery into the territories, the case broke no new ground on the accepted meaning of Article IV or the basic legal distinction between state-conferred privileges and immunities and federal privileges or immunities.[214]

D. *The Enumerated Rights of National Citizenship*

In the public debates over the Missouri Compromise and the high-profile opinions in *Dred Scott*, the privileges and immunities of citizens of the United States were treated as altogether distinct from the privileges and immunities of citizens in the several states. Article IV privileges and immunities involved a certain set of state-secured rights that, as a matter of comity, states must equally extend to sojourning citizens from other states. Privileges and immunities of citizens of the United States, on the other hand, involved those rights secured by the national Constitution, which *all* US citizens held *as* citizens of the United States. This was not a common law theory of rights emerging out of an aggregation of state-conferred liberties or an analysis of natural law. Instead, the national rights of US citizens were those conferred by the Federal Constitution itself.[215] Taney's opinion in *Dred Scott* suggested that provisions in the first eight amendments could be considered to be among the privileges and immunities of US citizens. This idea was not unique to Chief Justice Taney's treatment of the Fifth Amendment's Due Process Clause. As other scholars have pointed out, in the years prior to the adoption of the Fourteenth Amendment, a growing number of people began to believe that the Bill of Rights represented privileges belonging to all American citizens.[216]

In an 1835 letter to the secretary of state, Attorney General Benjamin F. Butler discussed the privileges and immunities of citizens of the United States residing in Arkansas Territory. Butler noted that because Arkansas had been

> in which they reside, but because they, in common with the native-born citizens of that State, must have the qualifications prescribed by law for the enjoyment of such privileges, under its Constitution and laws. It rests with the States themselves so to frame their Constitutions and laws as not to attach a particular privilege or immunity to mere naked citizenship. If one of the States will not deny to any of its own citizens a particular privilege or immunity, if it confer it on all of them by reason of mere naked citizenship, then it may be claimed by every citizen of each State by force of the Constitution.

Id. at 583–84.

[214] As far as the particular holding in *Dred Scott* was concerned, Congress simply ignored the Court's decision and, during the Civil War, proceeded to ban slavery in the territories. *See also* Graber, *supra* note 135, at 21 n.40.

[215] In addition to the examples cited, see Editorial, *Union Party in Charleston, in* Alexandria Gazette, page 2, Sept. 3, 1833 (distinguishing between the "rights of freemen" and the "privileges of citizens of the United States").

[216] *See* Amar, *supra* note 167, at 145 (1998).

carved out of the Louisiana Cession, the United States had the "duty of incorporating . . . the inhabitants of the ceded territory into the Union of the United States," and of admitting them "as soon as possible, according to the principles of the Federal constitution, to the enjoyment of all the rights, advantages, and immunities of citizens of the United States."[217] Butler then addressed the content of these national rights:

> They [the inhabitants] undoubtedly possess the ordinary privileges and immunities of citizens of the United States. Among these is the right of the people "peaceably to assemble and to petition the government for the redress of grievances."[218]

Butler's description tracks the approach of Daniel Webster and other antebellum references to the "privileges and immunities of citizens of the United States" that distinguished those rights secured by state law (and granted equal protection under the Comity Clause of Article IV) and those rights of national citizenship that were secured by the federal Constitution and thus were "common to all" US citizens.

E. *Summary*

The antebellum jurisprudence of Article IV was remarkably stable and reflected a broadly held consensus that the Clause protected a limited set of state-conferred rights. This view was expressly adopted by one of the most important anti-slavery state court decisions decided just prior to the Civil War, *Lemmon v. The People*, and was reaffirmed by the Supreme Court in 1868. The privileges and immunities of citizens of the United States had stable jurisprudential roots every bit as deep as Article IV. Beginning with the Louisiana Cession Act of 1803, the phrase "rights, advantages and immunities of citizens of the United States" was read as being no different than a declaration of the "immunities and privileges of citizens of the United States" and was repeatedly defined as referring to a set of national rights conferred by the Constitution itself – rights "common to all" who shared the status of US citizens. Once again, it was the advocates of abolition, men like Rufus King and Daniel Webster, who insisted that these rights were wholly separate and distinct from the state-conferred rights of Article IV.

It is possible, of course, that this longstanding distinction between Article IV privileges and immunities and the privileges and immunities of citizens of the

---

[217] 21 Territorial Papers of the United States 1085 (1829–1836), Papers Relating to the Administration of Governor Fulton, 1835–1836, at p. 1085 (available in Hein online, U.S. Cong. Documents, Territorial Papers of the United States).

[218] *Id.* at 1087.

United States was abandoned at the time of the Civil War. For example, the members of the Thirty-Ninth Congress may have viewed such a distinction as part of the problem they hoped to remedy through the adoption of the Fourteenth Amendment. This seems to be the understanding of a great many Fourteenth Amendment scholars, who argue that the drafters of the Fourteenth Amendment understood the Privileges or Immunities Clause as somehow federalizing Justice Washington's list of "fundamental" rights that he described in *Corfield v. Coryell*.

Whether these previously separate strands of law merged at the time of Reconstruction will be the focus of the next chapter. For now, it is worth pointing out that the man who drafted Section One of the Fourteenth Amendment, John Bingham, insisted that Article IV and Section One of the Fourteenth Amendment protected entirely different sets of "privileges and immunities." As Bingham explained in the years following the adoption of the Amendment:

> Mr. Speaker, that the scope and meaning of the limitations imposed by the first section, fourteenth amendment of the Constitution may be more fully understood, permit me to say that the privileges and immunities of citizens of the United States, *as contradistinguished* from citizens of a State, are chiefly defined in the first eight amendments to the Constitution of the United States.... Mr. Speaker, that decision in the fourth of Washington's Circuit Court Reports [*Corfield*], to which my learned colleague . . . has referred is only a construction of the second section, fourth article of the original Constitution, to wit, "The citizens of each State shall be entitled to all privileges and immunities of citizens in the several States." In that case the court only held that in civil rights the State could not refuse to extend to citizens of other States the same general rights secured to its own.... Is it not clear that *other and different privileges and immunities* than those to which a citizen of a State was entitled are secured by the provision of the fourteenth article, that no State shall abridge the privileges and immunities of citizens of the United States, which are defined in the eight articles of amendment, and which were not limitations on the power of the States before the fourteenth amendment made them limitations?[219]

Over the course of the next two chapters, we will consider whether this 1871 speech by John Bingham represents the original meaning of the Privileges or Immunities Clause of the Fourteenth Amendment.

---

[219] CONG. GLOBE, 42d Cong., 1st Sess. app. 84 (1871) (emphasis added).

3

Framing the Privileges or Immunities Clause

I. BACKGROUND

A. *Reconstruction*

Under the original Constitution, the States and not the federal government held the primary responsibility for both defining and protecting American privileges and immunities. There were but a few absolute national rights that states were bound to respect, and the equal-access rights of the Comity Clause remained largely under the control of state authorities. Whether an American citizen could speak freely, publish his thoughts, practice his religious faith, or decline to financially support a particular church all depended on the substantive content of state law. Most of all, whether a person born in the United States could walk freely without chains and without fear of the lash depended on state law.

As a culture, we know that all this changed in the aftermath of the American Civil War. That war brought an end to American slavery and reconstructed American liberty in a manner that bound both state and national governments to a new set of American privileges and immunities. Those who study law and American history know that this new birth of freedom was painfully slow in coming, but all agree that the key moment in the establishment of truly national American freedom occurred with the adoption of the Thirteenth and Fourteenth Amendments. The Thirteenth abolished slavery. The Fourteenth bound the states to respect the privileges and immunities of citizens of the United States and to provide all persons with the due and equal protection of law. It was through these two amendments that the rights of American citizenship were both fully established and reconstructed.

Historians call this period in American history *Reconstruction*. For constitutional scholars, the term is more than a reference to rebuilding the South.

Although judges and lawyers today focus on the first and fifth sections of the Amendment (rights and powers, respectively), the middle sections of the Fourteenth Amendment involved quite literally the reconstruction of the Union. The struggle over slavery had grievously wounded the structure of American constitutional government and, in 1866, major pieces of that government remained missing. The members of the Thirty-Ninth Congress met in chambers with empty seats, daily reminders that their task was not simply to restore the stability of the national government, but also to restore and repair what slavery and secession had broken apart. In particular, the reconstruction and restoration of America required the reseating of representatives from the southern states. Accomplishing this would require the utmost political skill if Congress hoped to both reunite the country and preserve the individual freedoms bought at such a high price on the battlefield.

With the abolition of slavery, blacks in the southern states now would be counted as full persons for the purposes of determining political representation in the House of Representatives. Before the Civil War, enslaved blacks had counted as only "three-fifths" of persons for the purposes of representation.[1] Thus, as matters stood in early 1866, southern states would enjoy an *increase* in their political power upon their readmission to the Union.[2] Worse, there was every reason to think that the same traitorous officials who held political power in the rebellious states would use their influence to be elected to national office. Nor could one count on the political influence of newly freed blacks to ensure the election of proper candidates – black Americans in 1866 were denied the vote both North and South.[3] The immediate restoration of the southern states would thus threaten any effort to secure civil rights in the South. Even if Republicans acted quickly and enacted a raft of legislation over the veto of an increasingly hostile President Johnson, it remained unclear

---

[1] *See* U.S. Const. art. I, § 2. For a discussion of the "Three-Fifths" Clause and its importance under the original Constitution, and the political implications of its erasure by the Thirteenth Amendment, see Akhil Reed Amar, America's Constitution: A Biography 87–98, 392 (2005).

[2] A point not lost on the Reconstruction Congress. *See* Cong. Globe, 39th Cong., 1st Sess. 2535 (remarks of Mr. Eckley) ("The ratification of the [thirteenth] constitutional amendment changed the condition of representation and rendered an amendment to the constitution necessary in order to equalize the just basis of representation. Under the Constitution as it now stands they would count the entire population in the southern states. Before the Constitution was amended, the counted the entire free population and three fifths of the slaves; but there being now no slaves they would count all. In none of those states do they confer the right of suffrage on the colored population. This presents the anomaly of allowing five million white rebels to represent four million loyal blacks, and makes two white persons – rebels at that – in South Carolina equal to fine white loyalists in Ohio, Pennsylvania or New York.").

[3] Amar, *supra* note 1, at 373–74.

whether the Constitution actually granted the current Congress power to enact and enforce statutes securing American rights, privileges, and immunities in the southern states – or anywhere else. Finally, even fully constitutional civil rights statutes would be subject to reversal by future Democrat-dominated congresses.

Ultimately, the Fourteenth Amendment responded to all of these concerns. The text would define the rights of American citizens and those of all people within the United States, and it would grant Congress power to enforce those rights.[4] Southern states would be readmitted and enjoy political power only to the degree that they opened the door to black suffrage.[5] Even then, no person could participate in national politics if he had joined the rebellion in violation of a previous oath of allegiance to the United States.[6] Finally, once restored, the rebellious states would remain responsible for the financial costs imposed on themselves and the nation by their disastrous decision to secede.[7]

It is easier to perceive the Fourteenth Amendment's theme of reconstruction when the text is viewed in its totality than if one focuses only on Sections One and Five. Understanding the full context of the Amendment allows us to better understand the role of the Privileges or Immunities Clause and appreciate why that Clause received less attention at the time of its enactment than we might give it today. But there is another reason for keeping in mind the entirety of the Fourteenth Amendment as we begin to focus on the meaning of Section One. This Amendment involved the restoration of the states to their proper place as constituent members of the American constitutional system. It was an option, after all, to simply erase the southern states altogether and divide the conquered territory into a small number of nationally regulated provinces.[8] As much as this might have been preferred by some of the more radical members of Congress, both the majority of Congress and the country remained committed to the restoration of the states *as states* and the return of constitutional federalism. Time and again, the Thirty-Ninth Congress considered whether to embrace a form of revolutionary nationalism or maintain the original constitutional structure of federalism and dual sovereignty. Although stretched almost to the breaking point, at every critical fork in the road, a majority held onto the Constitution's dualist structure. It had been the government officials in

---

[4] U.S. Const. amend. XIV, §§ 1 & 5.

[5] *Id.* amend. XIV, § 2.

[6] *Id.* amend. XIV, § 3.

[7] *Id.* amend. XIV, § 4.

[8] For a discussion of the "state suicide" theory forwarded by some radical Republicans during Reconstruction, see Eric L. McKitrick, Andrew Johnson and Reconstruction 110–13 (1960).

the seceding states who had tried to destroy the delicate balance between state and federal power under the original Constitution and, in doing so, they had betrayed their oaths to uphold that Constitution. In setting the terms for their readmission, the members of the Thirty-Ninth Congress would not echo the southern attempt to erase the original constitutional settlement. Their efforts were bent toward repairing and reconstructing that settlement, this time placing it on an even firmer foundation.

In terms of the Fourteenth Amendment, these efforts involved extensive debates over multiple drafts of the Fourteenth Amendment, including two separate and distinct drafts of what became the Privileges or Immunities Clause. Both written by Ohio Congressman John A. Bingham, the first draft used the language of Article IV's Comity Clause. After extensive debate and criticism, this draft was withdrawn by Bingham himself. The second and final draft used the language of national treaties, such as that found in the Louisiana Cession Act of 1803. Why Bingham felt compelled to remove Article IV's protection of the "privileges and immunities of citizens in the several states" and replace it with protection of "the privileges or immunities of citizens of the United States" is the subject of this chapter.

B. *John Bingham*

Despite his key role in drafting Section One of the Fourteenth Amendment, John Bingham remains a frustratingly elusive figure in the search for the original understanding of the Privileges or Immunities Clause.[9] As the author of one of the most important constitutional provisions in our nation's history, Bingham's participation in the Reconstruction debates has been the subject of intense historical study. Despite volumes of work, however, scholars remain hopelessly divided on the simple issue of whether Bingham was a constitutional visionary or a lazy and muddleheaded Representative who cared nothing about constitutional language and lacked sufficient intelligence to understand longstanding constitutional doctrine.[10]

There is good reason for this scholarly divide: John Bingham left a trail of seemingly conflicting statements regarding the meaning of Article IV, the nature of the Bill of Rights, and the relationship of both to the proposed Fourteenth Amendment. For example, at one point, Bingham insisted that his proposed version of the Fourteenth Amendment was based on the text and

---

[9] For a recent and important biography of John Bingham, see GERARD N. MAGLIOCCA, AMERICAN FOUNDING SON: JOHN BINGHAM AND THE INVENTION OF THE FOURTEENTH AMENDMENT (N.Y. Press, 2013).

[10] *See infra* notes [16–18] and accompanying text.

principles of the Privileges and Immunities Clause of Article IV.[11] Later, however, Bingham expressly denied that Article IV had anything to do with the Fourteenth Amendment.[12] Likewise, early in the debates, Bingham insisted that Article IV was part of the federal Bill of Rights; later, however, Bingham expressly limited his definition of the Bill of Rights to just the first eight amendments to the Constitution.[13] Further complicating the picture was Bingham's insistence that Article IV must be read as containing additional, albeit unstated, language – an implied "ellipsis" that Bingham originally believed obligated the states to enforce the federal Bill of Rights despite the Supreme Court's ruling to the contrary in *Barron v. Baltimore*.[14] Later, however, Bingham described *Barron* as "rightfully" decided, and he abandoned his claim that an "ellipsis" reading of Article IV required the states to enforce the first eight amendments.[15]

These seemingly inconsistent and idiosyncratic views have led some scholars to dismiss John Bingham as a trustworthy source of information regarding the original understanding of the Fourteenth Amendment.[16] Those scholars

[11] CONG. GLOBE, 39th Cong., 1st Sess. 1033 (1866).

[12] CONG. GLOBE, 42d Cong., 1st Sess. app. 84 (1871).

[13] *Id.* ("Jefferson well said of the first eight articles of amendments to the Constitution of the United States, they constitute the American Bill of Rights.")

[14] CONG. GLOBE, 39th Cong., 1st Sess. 158 (1866) ("When you come to weigh these words, 'equal and exact justice to all men,' go read, if you please, the words of the Constitution itself: 'The citizens of each State (being *ipso facto* citizens of the United States) shall be entitled to all the privileges and immunities of citizens (applying the ellipsis "of the United States") in the several States.' This guarantee is of the privileges and immunities of citizens of the United States in, not of, the several States.").

[15] CONG. GLOBE, 42d Cong., 1st Sess. app. 84 (1871).

[16] *See* RAOUL BERGER, GOVERNMENT BY JUDICIARY: THE TRANSFORMATION OF THE FOURTEENTH AMENDMENT 145 (1977) (describing Bingham's thinking as "muddled"); CHARLES FAIRMAN, RECONSTRUCTION AND REUNION: 1864–88, pt. 1, at 1288, *in* 6 THE OLIVER WENDELL HOLMES DEVISE HISTORY OF THE SUPREME COURT OF THE UNITED STATES (Paul A. Freund ed., 1971) (describing Bingham's "confused discourse" of May 10, 1866 regarding Section One of the proposed Fourteenth Amendment); CHARLES FAIRMAN, RECONSTRUCTION AND REUNION, 1864–1888, pt. 2, at 133, *in* 7 THE OLIVER WENDELL HOLMES DEVISE HISTORY OF THE SUPREME COURT OF THE UNITED STATES (Paul A. Freund & Stanley N. Katz eds., 1987) (describing Bingham as "distinguished for elocution but not for hard thinking"); Charles Fairman, *Does the Fourteenth Amendment Incorporate the Bill of Rights?*, 2 STAN. L. REV. 5, 26 (1949) [hereinafter Fairman, *Bill of Rights*] (describing Bingham as "befuddled"); John P. Frank & Robert F. Munro, *The Original Understanding of "Equal Protection of the Laws,"* 50 COLUM. L. REV. 131, 164 n.169 (1950) ("[Bingham] had a strong egocentricity and a touch of the windbag. As a legal thinker he was not in the same class with the top notch minds of his time. . . . "); John Harrison, *Reconstructing the Privileges or Immunities Clause*, 101 YALE L. J. 1385, 1404 n.61 (1992) ("Bingham's speeches were highly rhetorical, and his thoughts are hard to follow; he was undoubtedly a gasbag. Whether he was also a gashead is a more difficult and controversial question. My view is that either Bingham's analytical powers were mediocre or he was too lazy to use them.").

who reject the idea that the Fourteenth Amendment "incorporates" the Bill of
Rights against the states, for example, stress the odd views Bingham expressed
early in the 1866 debates regarding Article IV and the Bill of Rights.[17] Pro-
incorporation scholars, on the other hand, either downplay Bingham's idiosyncratic and conflicting statements or instead emphasize Bingham's more traditional comments regarding the Bill of Rights, which he delivered in 1871.[18]
All sides in the incorporation debate, however, assume that Bingham's views
remained consistent throughout the debates: either consistently confusing or
consistently reliable.

An alternative explanation, however, is that Bingham changed his mind as
he listened to hours of constitutional debate in the Thirty-Ninth Congress.
Bingham based his initial draft of the Fourteenth Amendment on an idiosyncratic theory about the Comity Clause of Article IV that Bingham initially
believed obligated the states to enforce the federal Bill of Rights. As the debates
over his proposed amendment proceeded, however, it soon became clear that
his colleagues did not share Bingham's odd reading of Article IV. Where Bingham saw language referring to constitutionally enumerated substantive rights,
his colleagues saw language referring to state-level civil rights – and they cited
copious case law to back up their interpretation. Realizing his efforts were
either doomed to fail or have results he personally opposed, Bingham withdrew his initial draft. When Bingham produced his second and final draft of
the Fourteenth Amendment, he had abandoned the language of Article IV
and instead adopted the language of federal treaties that spoke of the privileges
and immunities of *citizens of the United States*. These rights, Bingham would
explain, were altogether different than the common law rights protected under

---

[17]   *See* FAIRMAN, RECONSTRUCTION AND REUNION: 1864–88, Part One, *supra* note 16, at 1288; Raoul
       Berger, *Incorporation of the Bill of Rights in the Fourteenth Amendment: A Nine-Lived Cat*, 42
       OHIO ST. L.J. 435, 449–52 (1981); Fairman, *Does the Fourteenth Amendment Incorporate the
       Bill of Rights?*, *supra* note 16, at 25–26.
[18]   *See, e.g.*, AKHIL AMAR, THE BILL OF RIGHTS: CREATION AND RECONSTRUCTION 181–83, 183
       n.* (1998); MICHAEL KENT CURTIS, NO STATE SHALL ABRIDGE: FOURTEENTH AMENDMENT
       AND THE BILL OF RIGHTS 121–25 (1986); Richard L. Aynes, *On Misreading John Bingham and
       the Fourteenth Amendment*, 103 YALE L. J. 57, 66–69 (1993); William W. Crosskey, *Charles
       Fairman, "Legislative History," and the Constitutional Limitations on State Authority*, 22
       U. CHI. L. REV. 1 (1954). All of these writers defend Bingham against the most critical asser-
       tions of scholars like Fairman and Berger. None of them identify, much less discuss, any
       degree of inconsistency in Bingham's arguments during the Reconstruction debates. Richard
       Aynes, for example, defends attacks against Bingham for his initial idiosyncratic view of the
       Bill of Rights as including Article IV by suggesting there may have been a transcription
       error in the report of Bingham's speech or that Bingham simply "misspoke." Aynes, *supra*, at
       68 n.61.

Article IV. This second draft protected the Bill of Rights against state abridgement as "privileges or immunities of citizens of the United States," but left common law civil rights in the hands of local government, subject only to the requirements of due process and equal protection.

II. REPUBLICANS AND THE THIRTY-NINTH CONGRESS

Understanding the debates regarding Section One of the Fourteenth Amendment requires some understanding of the legal and political theories that motivated John Bingham and the other members of the Reconstruction Congress. In particular, it is important to understand that the Republicans of the Thirty-Ninth Congress were not monolithic in their approach to constitutional liberty and the proper scope of federal power. Appreciating their differences helps to explain Republicans' varied responses to John Bingham's initial draft of the Fourteenth Amendment, as well as illuminate why that original draft failed to receive a sufficient degree of support from moderate Republicans. Because few, if any, Republicans in the Thirty-Ninth Congress shared John Bingham's peculiar view of Article IV, his initial Article IV-based draft of the Fourteenth Amendment was met with confusion and disagreement. It soon became clear that his proposed language might be understood as vastly expanding the scope of federal power to regulate civil rights in the States – a possibility applauded by radical Republicans but strongly opposed by all conservative Republicans and most moderates, including Bingham himself.

A. *Republican Constitutional Theory at the Time of Reconstruction*

An Ohio Republican well-versed in the language and ideology of Midwestern abolitionist rhetoric, John Bingham shared many of the views that informed moderate Republicans in the Thirty-Ninth Congress.[19] Placing his views in context therefore requires a quick review of the antebellum Constitution and Republican theory at the time of Reconstruction.

The Thirteenth, Fourteenth, and Fifteenth Amendments represent a dramatic restructuring of the dispersion of powers between the federal and states governments. Under the original Constitution, states were generally free to

---

[19] For background on Bingham's roots and abolitionist Republican beliefs, see Richard L. Aynes, *The Antislavery and Abolitionist Background of John A. Bingham*, 37 CATH. U. L. REV. 881 (1988).

regulate local municipal matters free from federal interference.[20] Although Article I, Section Ten imposed some constraints on state activity, most personal rights and civil liberties were left to the control of the states.[21] The Bill of Rights constrained only the federal government (as in "*Congress* shall make no law . . . "),[22] reserving all nondelegated powers and rights to the people in the states under the terms of the Ninth and Tenth Amendments.[23] The federalist language and structure of the Bill of Rights was officially declared by the Supreme Court in *Barron v. Baltimore*, with Chief Justice John Marshall holding that the Fifth Amendment, like the rest of the Bill, bound only the federal government.[24]

In his opinion, Chief Justice Marshall arrived at this state-protective conclusion by comparing the liberties enumerated in the Bill of Rights with the restrictions on federal and state power contained in Article I, Sections Nine and Ten of the original Constitution. Section Nine, which bound the federal government only, used language that sometimes expressly named the federal government as its target and sometimes used passive language in which the government subject to the restriction went unnamed. Section Ten, on the other hand, bound only the states, and began each of its three sections with the language "[n]o state shall . . . " – thus expressly naming the states as the subject of the restriction. To Marshall, the different language in these two sections established a rule of construction: Unless states are expressly named as the subject of a constitutional restriction, constitutional liberties should be construed as running only against the federal government.

---

[20] As James Madison wrote:

> The powers delegated by the proposed Constitution to the federal government are few and defined. Those which are to remain in the State governments are numerous and indefinite. The former will be exercised principally on external objects, [such] as war, peace, negotiation, and foreign commerce. . . . The powers reserved to the several States will extend to all the objects which, in the ordinary course of affairs, concern the lives, liberties, and properties of the people.

THE FEDERALIST NO. 45, at 292–93 (James Madison) (Clinton Rossiter ed., 1961).

[21] According to Earl Maltz: "In the antebellum era, all but the most radical of abolitionists agreed that each state government possessed the exclusive authority to protect the fundamental, natural rights of its own citizens." MALTZ, CIVIL RIGHTS, THE CONSTITUTION, AND CONGRESS, 1863–1869, 32 (1990); *see also* WILLIAM E. NELSON, THE FOURTEENTH AMENDMENT: FROM POLITICAL PRINCIPLE TO JUDICIAL DOCTRINE 27 (1988).

[22] *See* U.S. CONST. amend. I.

[23] *See id.* amend. IX ("The enumeration in the Constitution, of certain rights, shall not be construed to deny or disparage others retained by the people"); *id.* amend. X ("The powers not delegated to the United States by the Constitution, nor prohibited by it to the States, are reserved to the States respectively, or to the people.").

[24] 32 U.S. (7 Pet.) 243, 250–51 (1833).

Because Marshall's reasoning ultimately plays an important role in Bingham's second and final draft of the Privileges or Immunities Clause, it is worth an extended quote. Here are the key portions of Marshall's opinion in *Barron v. Baltimore*:

> If the original Constitution, in the ninth and tenth sections of the first article, draws this plain and marked line of discrimination between the limitations it imposes on the powers of the General Government and on those of the State; if, in every inhibition intended to act on State power, words are employed which directly express that intent; some strong reason must be assigned for departing from this safe and judicious course in framing the amendments before that departure can be assumed. We search in vain for that reason.
>
> Had the framers of these amendments intended them to be limitations on the powers of the State governments, they would have imitated the framers of the original Constitution, and have expressed that intention. Had Congress engaged in the extraordinary occupation of improving the Constitutions of the several States by affording the people additional protection from the exercise of power by their own governments in matters which concerned themselves alone, they would have declared this purpose in plain and intelligible language.
>
> These amendments [the Bill of Rights] contain no expression indicating an intention to apply them to the State governments. This court cannot so apply them.[25]

The long-simmering debate over slavery soon called into question the Founding-era presumption that liberty was best preserved by leaving critical matters of individual rights to state control. Abolitionists railed against chattel slavery, a creature of state law, as a violation of natural law, the principles of the Declaration of Independence, and the preamble to the Constitution.[26] Slavery violated not only the natural rights of slaves in the South, but efforts to preserve slavery affected the rights of individuals in northern states as well. Congress denied individuals the right to petition Congress for the abolition of slavery, the federal mails were purged of abolitionist expression, and the abolitionist press in the North came under assault, with pro-slavery mobs attacking and killing the northern editor of an abolitionist press.[27] By the 1830s, no person within a slaveholding state could expect anything but expulsion or violent

---

[25] Barron v. Mayor & City Council of Baltimore, 32 U.S. (7 Pet.) 243, 249–50 (1833).

[26] ERIC FONER, RECONSTRUCTION: AMERICA'S UNFINISHED REVOLUTION 1863–1877, at 76 (1988).

[27] For a discussion of how slavery affected First amendment rights in the North, see MICHAEL KENT CURTIS, FREE SPEECH, "THE PEOPLE'S DARLING PRIVILEGE": STRUGGLES FOR FREEDOM OF EXPRESSION IN AMERICAN HISTORY (2000).

retribution at the hands of the law or angry mobs if they engaged in open criticism of slavery. In what became one of the most infamous examples of southern state treatment of northern citizens, mobs chased Samuel Hoar (sent to the South as an emissary from Massachusetts) out of South Carolina when he attempted to investigate the imprisonment of free blacks on ships moored in South Carolina harbors.[28]

B. *Abolitionist Thought*

Although united in their opposition to slavery, abolitionists themselves differed significantly on such critical subjects as whether slavery was constitutional, the scope of federal power to limit or ban slavery, and the need to preserve the right to local self-government. Moderates like Salmon P. Chase accepted the legitimacy of the federalist structure, which left the issue of slavery to state determination under the Tenth Amendment.[29] However, Chase also believed that the Due Process Clause of the Fifth Amendment required the federal government to oppose any expansion of slavery beyond the original states and that Congress should refuse to assist in the return of runaway slaves.[30] "Garrisonians," on the other hand, repudiated the Constitution and sought disunion, the secession of the North, and the complete disassociation with slave states.[31] Finally, abolitionists like Lysander Spooner, Alvan Stewart, and William Goodell argued that the Constitution prohibited slavery or, at the very least, empowered Congress to restrict its expansion.[32] Spooner in particular believed that allowing slavery in any area falling within the Louisiana Cession violated the constitutionally protected rights of citizens of the United States. All inhabitants in this territory were "admitted to all the privileges, rights and immunities of the *citizens* of the United States."[33] Therefore, "[t]o allow *any* of the 'inhabitants' included in those treaties, to be held as slaves, or denied the rights of citizenship under the United States constitution, is a plain breach of the treaties."[34] Similarly, according to abolitionist Joel Tiffany, "whenever a state shall by its legislation, attempt to deprive a citizen of the United States

---

[28] *See* William J. Rich, *Why "Privileges or Immunities"? An Explanation of the Framers' Intent,* 42 AKRON L. REV. 1111, 1113–14 (2009) (discussing the expulsion of Samuel Hoar from South Carolina and its impact on the members of the Thirty-Ninth Congress).

[29] FONER, *supra* note 26, at 76.

[30] *Id.*

[31] *Id.* at 138.

[32] *See generally,* Randy Barnett, *Whence Comes Section One?: The Abolitionist Origins of the Fourteenth Amendment,* 3 J. LEG. ANALYSIS 165 (2011).

[33] Lysander Spooner, THE UNCONSTITUTIONALITY OF SLAVERY (Boston, 1845).

[34] *Id.* at 152.

of those rights and privileges which are guaranteed to him by the Federal Constitution, as such citizen, such legislation of the state is void." These "rights and privileges" included "all the guarantys of the Federal Constitution for personal security, personal liberty and private property" including:

> the right of petition, – the right to keep and bear arms, the right to be secure from all unwarrantable seizures and searches, – the right to demand, and have a presentment or indictment found by a grand jury before he shall be held to answer to any criminal charge, – the right to be informed beforehand of the nature and cause of accusation against him, the right to a public and speedy trial by an impartial jury of his peers, – the right to confront those who testify against him, – the right to have compulsory process to bring in his witnesses, – the right to demand and have counsel for his defence, – the right to be exempt from excessive bail, or fines, &c., from cruel and unusual punishments, or from being twice jeopardized for the same offence; and the right to the privileges of the great writ of Liberty, the Habeas Corpus.[35]

C. *The Thirty-Ninth Congress*

Like the abolitionists, the Republican members of the Thirty-Ninth Congress held a variety of positions on natural law, the constitutionality of slavery, and the scope of federal power to eradicate the peculiar institution.[36] There was broad agreement that eradicating slavery and the web of state laws that preserved it required restructuring aspects of the original federalist Constitution. States must no longer be free to shackle any individual except on conviction for a criminal act, and the basic rights of citizens in the states, and citizens moving among the states, must be preserved and protected at a federal level. Beyond this agreed-on set of basic principles, however, Republican unanimity quickly splintered over the *degree* of constitutional restructuring that would be required. Contemporary historians generally divide the Republicans of the Thirty-Ninth Congress into three basic groups: radical, moderate, and conservative.[37] The labels somewhat oversimplify the views of the individuals

---

[35] *See* JOEL TIFFANY, TREATISE ON THE UNCONSTITUTIONALITY OF AMERICAN SLAVERY 57–58, 97, 99 (Cleveland, Ohio: J. Calyer, 1849).

[36] Numerous scholarly works explore the details of Republican theory at the time of Reconstruction. *See generally* MICHAEL LES BENEDICT, A COMPROMISE OF PRINCIPLE: CONGRESSIONAL REPUBLICANS AND RECONSTRUCTION 1863–1869 (1974); FONER, *supra* note 26; NELSON, *supra* note 21; WILLIAM M. WIECEK, THE SOURCES OF ANTISLAVERY CONSTITUTIONALISM IN AMERICA, 1760–1848 (1977).

[37] *See, e.g.*, GARRETT EPPS, DEMOCRACY REBORN: THE FOURTEENTH AMENDMENT AND THE FIGHT FOR EQUAL RIGHTS IN POST-CIVIL WAR AMERICA 101 (2006) (describing Thaddeus Stevens and his "radical faction" as well as the "more cautious" members like William Fessenden and John

involved, some of whom might be radical on some issues but moderate or conservative on others. The distinctions are nevertheless helpful in understanding the basic disagreements among Reconstruction Republicans and important to understanding the arguments and positions of John Bingham. Because the labels were accepted by the members themselves, and because the traditional tripartite characterization continues to be used by most contemporary legal historians, I believe that any attempt at "re-categorizing" would likely cause more confusion than clarification.

Radical Republicans, although disagreeing among themselves about the legal details, generally believed that Congress had full power to protect civil rights in the states even prior to the adoption of the Thirteenth and Fourteenth Amendments. Relying on once-derided theories of federal power adopted by the Supreme Court in cases like *Prigg v. Pennsylvania*, radical Republicans claimed that if Congress had implied power to enforce the fugitive slave provisions of Article IV (the holding of *Prigg*),[38] then Congress also had implied power to enforce the Privileges and Immunities Clause of Article IV.[39] Highlighting Justice Washington's language of "fundamental" rights in the Article IV case *Corfield v. Coryell*,[40] radical Republicans insisted that Congress had full power to nationalize natural and common law civil rights in the states,[41] and they were particularly committed to eradicating state laws prohibiting black suffrage.[42] In general, the radical position rejected the idea of state autonomy in any form and viewed the national government as having general oversight powers over any matter affecting civil liberties in the states.[43]

Bingham); MALTZ, *supra* note 21, at 42. Readers therefore should not equate my use of the term with an effort to disparage its members – indeed, the term was used by members of the Thirty-Ninth Congress themselves. *See* EPPS, *supra*, at 92 (noting Thaddeus Stevens's description of William Fessenden as having "that vile ingredient, called conservatism"). Nor, obviously, is my use of the term an effort to vindicate the views of the now properly discredited "Dunning School" of historical scholarship that portrayed radical Republicans as foolish at best and malevolent at worst. *See also* PAMELA BRANDWEIN, RECONSTRUCTING RECONSTRUCTION: THE SUPREME COURT AND THE PRODUCTION OF HISTORICAL TRUTH 105–06, 115–16 (1999).

[38]   41 U.S. (16 Pet.) 539, 622 (1842).

[39]   *See, e.g.*, CONG. GLOBE, 39th Cong., 1st Sess. 1118 (1866) (remarks of Mr. Wilson).

[40]   6 F. Cas. 546, 550–51 (C.C.E.D. Pa. 1823) (No. 3,320).

[41]   *See, e.g.*, CONG. GLOBE, 39th Cong., 1st Sess. 1072 (remarks of Mr. Nye) (insisting that Congress had "necessary and proper" power to "restrain the respective states from infracting" both enumerated and unenumerated "natural and personal rights").

[42]   *See* MALTZ, *supra* note 21, at 51–52 (discussing Charles Sumner, "the champion of the radical position," and his support for black suffrage).

[43]   *See, e.g.*, CONG. GLOBE, 39th Cong., 1st Sess. 1072 (remarks of Mr. Nye) ("Congress, under the Constitution, has a controlling power to enforce the principle of protection on all the States. Congress is the tribunal of States; and this tribunal of States is the umpire in judging of what is protective republican government in the several States, and what is not; what the form of the state government should be, and what it should not be; what the distribution of power

In this, the radicals in the Thirty-Ninth Congress followed the anti-slavery constitutional arguments of abolitionists like Joel Tiffany, who argued that the Republican Guaranty Clause imposed on the federal government an obligation to intervene in cases where states failed to protect individual "natural and inherent rights."[44]

Moderate Republicans embraced the abolitionist sentiment of their more radical counterparts but insisted that the remedial efforts of the Reconstruction Congress maintain the basic federalist structure of the Constitution.[45] In general, this meant that states ought to retain a degree of quasi-sovereign autonomy over municipal affairs, and federal power must remain limited under the traditional doctrine of enumerated power, with all nondelegated powers remaining under the control of the states under the Tenth Amendment. Although today it might seem surprising that many Republicans embraced aspects of state autonomy even after the Civil War, in fact federalism in antebellum America had served as a useful tool for the opponents of slavery. Antebellum abolitionists, for example, insisted on the autonomy of the states to free slaves who touched the soil of a free state,[46] and they decried nationalist Supreme Court opinions like *Ableman v. Booth* and *Prigg v. Pennsylvania*, which held otherwise.[47] The infamous decision of *Dred Scott*, of course, was anything but a states' rights opinion[48]; its reasoning was expected to ultimately result in denying northern states the right to prohibit slave owners from carrying their slaves in transit across free-state soil.[49] *Lemmon v. The People* (the Lemmon

---

or degree of enfranchisement in order to guard against the despotism of class; and what the machinery to be adopted or tolerated so as to make the State government effective on the side of protection.")

[44] TIFFANY, *supra* 35, at 114; *see also* Randy Barnett, *Whence Comes Section One?, supra* note 32, at 231.

[45] This does not mean that federalism was irrelevant to radicals. As explained earlier, free-state federalism was as important to radicals as to moderates. *See* William E. Nelson, *The Role of History in Interpreting the Fourteenth Amendment*, 25 LOY. L.A. L. REV. 1177, 1177–78 (1992) ("Although the protection of rights and the preservation of federalism strike us as inconsistent goals, I argued that the two goals seemed far more consistent to the Radicals, who had had a long history of using state institutions to protect human rights.").

[46] *See* NELSON, *supra* note 21, at 34–35 (discussing abolitionist use of state law to free slaves brought by their owners to a free state).

[47] *See* Abelman v. Booth, 62 U.S. (21 How.) 506 (1858); Prigg v. Pennsylvania, 41 U.S. (16 Pet.) 539 (1842).

[48] *See* Dred Scott v. Sanford, 60 U.S. (19 How.) 393 (1857).

[49] According to Abraham Lincoln:

[W]hat is necessary to make the institution [of slavery] national? Not war. There is no danger that the people of Kentucky will shoulder their muskets and with a young nigger stuck on every bayonet march into Illinois and force them upon us. There is no danger of our going over there and making war upon them. Then what is necessary for the nationalization of slavery? It is simply the next *Dred Scott* decision. It is merely for the

slave case), conversely, adopted a state-rights reading of the Comity Clause that allowed New York to free any slave being carried in transit within the borders of the state.[50] The nationalist aspirations of the slave power explain why abolitionists like Wendell Philips declared, "I love State Rights; that doctrine is the corner-stone of individual liberty."[51]

Official Republican policy also adhered to a moderate form of federalism. According to the 1860 Republican Platform, "[t]he Federal Constitution, the Rights of the States, and the Union of the States must and shall be preserved."[52] Article 4 of the 1860 Platform specifically addressed Republican fidelity to the original dualist structure of the federal Constitution:

> That the maintenance, inviolate, of the Rights of the States, and especially the right of each State to order and control its own domestic institutions according to its own judgment exclusively, is essential to that balance of powers on which the perfection and endurance of our political fabric depends. . . . [53]

As other historians have noted, moderate Republicans continued to embrace constitutional federalism both during[54] and following the Civil War.[55] "I would say once and for all," announced John Bingham during the debates of the Thirty-Ninth Congress, "that this dual system of national and State government under the American organization is the secret of our strength and power. I do not propose to abandon it."[56] Other moderate Republicans were similarly

Supreme Court to decide that no *State* under the Constitution can exclude it, just as they have already decided that under the Constitution neither Congress nor the Territorial Legislature can do it. When that is decided and acquiesced in, the whole thing is done.

Abraham Lincoln, First Debate, Mr. Lincoln's Reply, *in* 1 Speeches and Writings 1832–1858, at 508, 524 (1989).

[50] *See supra* Chapter 2 at II.C.2.

[51] J. M. W. Yerrington, *Thirty Second Anniversary of the American Anti-Slavery Society*, Nat'l Anti-Slavery Standard (N.Y.), May 15, 1865, at 2.

[52] National Republican Platform, Adopted by the Chicago Convention (1860), *reprinted in* 2 The American Party Battle: Election Campaign Pamphlets, 1828–1876, at 121 (Joel H. Sibley ed., 1999).

[53] *Id.* at 122.

[54] In December of 1860, Lyman Trumbull of Illinois rejected the secessionist idea of absolute sovereignty, but acknowledged that "States are sovereign as to their reserved rights." Cong. Globe, 36th Cong., 2d Sess. 156 (1860).

[55] *See* G. Edward White, *The Origins of Civil Rights in America*, Case W. Res. L. Rev. (2013), available at http://papers.ssrn.com/sol3/papers.cfm?abstract_id=2251425; *see also* Maltz, *supra* note 21, at 30 ("[The task of Reconstruction] was further complicated by the Republicans firm attachment to the basic structure of federalism."); Nelson, *supra* note 21, at 27–39 (discussing the continued commitment to principles of federalism in the Reconstruction Congress).

[56] Cong. Globe, 39th Cong., 2d Sess. 450 (1867).

committed to a "dualist" Constitution.[57] According to Eric Foner, moderates "accepted the enhancement of national power resulting from the Civil War, but they did not believe the legitimate rights of the states had been destroyed, or the traditional principles of federalism eradicated."[58]

In sum, although moderate Republicans obviously rejected the fire-breathing southern arguments of nullification and secession, they continued to believe that a basic separation of power between the national and local governments remained a critical component of American liberty.[59] This moderate commitment to federalism played a key role in the Thirty-Ninth Congress. Without the support of the moderates, congressional initiatives were unlikely to achieve the two-thirds majority required to meet the voting requirements for a proposed amendment or overcome a Presidential veto.[60] As Earl Maltz puts it, "[t]he disposition of the Freedmen's Bureau Bill and the apportionment amendment demonstrated that only those civil rights measures that received virtually unanimous support from mainstream Republicans could be adopted."[61]

D. *The Constitutional Theory of John Bingham*

A native Ohioan and long-time anti-slavery advocate, Representative John A. Bingham's vision of liberty in the post-Civil War Republic went far beyond

---

[57] *See infra* notes 142–43 and accompanying text.

[58] FONER, *supra* note 26, at 242.

[59] NELSON, *supra* note 21, at 114 ("Most Republican supporters of the [Fourteenth] amendment, like the Democrat opponents, feared centralized power and did not want to see state and local power substantially curtailed"). The Republican Party's national platform in 1860 insisted that "the Federal Constitution, the Rights of the States, and the Union of the States, must and shall be preserved." NATIONAL REPUBLICAN PLATFORM, *supra* note 52. The platform went on to guarantee "the maintenance, inviolate, of the Rights of the States, and especially of the right of each State to order and control its own domestic institutions according to its own judgment exclusively." *Id.* at 122. According to Michael Les Benedict, "most Republicans [during Reconstruction] never desired a broad, permanent extension of national legislative power." Michael Les Benedict, *Preserving the Constitution: The Conservative Basis of Radical Reconstruction*, 61 J. AM. HIST. 65, 67 (1974).

[60] *See* U.S. CONST. art. V.

[61] MALTZ, *supra* note 21, at 60. During the debates over the Civil Rights Act of 1866, New York Republican Thomas T. Davis declared: "[T]his Government is one of delegated powers, and . . . every law enacted is circumscribed by the limitation of the Constitution. The states have reserved all sovereignty and power which has not been expressly or impliedly granted to the Federal Government." CONG. GLOBE, 39th Cong., 1st Sess. 1265–66 (1866). Note, however, Republicans generally distinguished the concept of "state sovereignty," which was associated with secession, from "states' rights," which were associated with the more acceptable form of federalism. *See* MALTZ, *supra* note 21, at 33.

the mere abolition of slavery under the Thirteenth Amendment. Bingham was convinced that the original Constitution imposed an obligation on the states to protect the rights listed in the first eight amendments to the Constitution. "[W]henever the Constitution guaranties to its citizens a right," Bingham declared, "such guarantee is in itself a limitation upon the States."[62] During the many months of debate in the Thirty-Ninth Congress regarding the Fourteenth Amendment, Bingham again and again returned to the idea that the Bill of Rights represented privileges and immunities that belonged to all US citizens and that should be guarded against abridgement by both federal and state authorities. In this regard, Bingham's views tracked those of other Republicans who agreed that provisions in the Bill of Rights did or, at the very least, *should* bind the states.[63]

Although John Bingham's reading of particular provisions in the Constitution changed over time, his basic theory of citizenship, natural rights, and constitutional government did not. Like most of his Republican colleagues, John Bingham accepted the concept of natural rights – the idea that some freedoms were so foundational that they belonged to all persons regardless of their status in society. Unlike conventional rights, which were subject to majoritarian political control, natural rights existed independent of the political process.[64] In an 1859 speech, Bingham laid out his dual theory of rights in a manner that strikingly echoes the ultimate structure and content of the Fourteenth Amendment:

> [N]atural or inherent rights . . . are by this constitution guarantied by the broad and comprehensive word "person," as contradistinguished from the limited term citizen – as in the fifth article of amendments, guarding those sacred rights which are as universal and indestructible as the human race, that "no person shall be deprived of life, liberty, or property but by due process of law, nor shall private property be taken without just compensation." And this guarantee applies to all citizens within the United States.[65]

Bingham distinguished the natural rights of *persons* from the more limited and exclusive rights of *citizens*. All persons (including citizens) have the natural right to the procedural protections of due process of law as announced in the Fifth Amendment to the federal Constitution. Bingham also insisted that governments must treat all persons (including citizens) according to "the great

---

[62] CONG. GLOBE, 35th Cong., 2d Sess. 982 (1859).
[63] *See* AMAR, THE BILL OF RIGHTS, *supra* note 18, at 145.
[64] *See* CURTIS, *supra* note 18, at 41–46 (discussing the role of natural rights in Reconstruction Republican political philosophy).
[65] CONG. GLOBE, 35th Cong., 2d Sess. 983 (1859).

principle of EQUALITY."[66] Thus, Bingham objected to the failure of the Civil Rights Act of 1866 to provide equal protection rights to *all persons* and not just citizens.[67]

Bingham's understanding of the rights of American citizenship, however, involved much more than just the procedural protections of due process and equal protection. To begin with, Bingham rejected Taney's theory in *Dred Scott* whereby national citizenship was derivative of state citizenship. "[A]ll free persons born and domiciled with the United States,"[68] or those "naturalized under the laws thereof,"[69] were citizens of the United States. All persons enjoying the status of state citizenship necessarily enjoyed the rights of national citizenship, for "the citizens of each State in the Union are ipso facto citizens of the United States."[70] Finally, Bingham believed that only citizens of the United States could claim to be "the People of the United States," as announced in the Preamble to the federal Constitution.[71]

Like his political hero, Daniel Webster,[72] Bingham believed that the rights of citizens of the United States included the political rights of representation in the national government as expressly enumerated in the

---

[66] *See* CONG. GLOBE, 34th Cong., 3d Sess. app. 139–40 (1857) ("The Constitution is based upon the EQUALITY of the human race. . . . A State formed under the Constitution, and pursuant to its spirit, must rest upon this great principle of EQUALITY. Its primal object must be to protect each human being within its jurisdiction in the free and full enjoyment of his natural rights. Mere *political* or *conventional* rights are subject to the control of the majority; but the rights of human nature belong to each member of the State, and cannot be forfeited but by crime.").

[67] *See infra* note 256.

[68] CONG. GLOBE, 35th Cong., 2d Sess. 984 (1859).

[69] *Id.* at 983.

[70] *Id.* Here Bingham cites "Story on the Constitution, vol. 3, p. 565." *Id.* At that point in his *Commentaries*, Story explained, "[e]very citizen of a state is *ipso facto* a citizen of the United States. And a person, who is a naturalized citizen of the United States, by a like residence in any state in the Union, becomes *ipso facto* a citizen of that state." 3 JOSEPH STORY, COMMENTARIES ON THE CONSTITUTION OF THE UNITED STATES §§ 1687–88, at 565–66 (Fred B. Rothman & Co. 1999) (1833).

[71] According to Bingham:

> The people here referred to are the same community, or body-politic, called, in the preamble of the Federal Constitution, "the people of the United States." They are the citizens of the United States, and no other people whatever. It has always been well understood amongst jurists in this country, that the citizens of each State constitute the body-politic of each community, called the people of the State; and that the citizens of each State in the Union are *ipso facto* citizens of the United States.

CONG. GLOBE, 35th Cong., 2d Sess. 983 (1859).

[72] For one example of Bingham's lionization of Daniel Webster, see CONG. GLOBE, 39th Cong., 1st Sess. 1090 (1866) (referring to the "grand argument" of Daniel Webster, "never to be answered while human language shall be spoken by living man").

Constitution.[73] Bingham also shared the increasingly common view of his contemporaries that the rights of the first eight amendments constituted privileges
and immunities of citizens of the United States.[74] As Bingham's colleague,
Illinois Republican and abolitionist Representative Owen Lovejoy, declared
in 1858, slavery had "claimed the right . . . to hamper a free press, to defile the
pulpit, to corrupt religion, and to stifle free thought and free speech," and
thereby wrongly "denied the rights, privileges and immunities of citizens of
the North or West."[75] Lovejoy demanded, "[l]et those rights be guaranteed and
protected, anywhere and everywhere, 'to the fullest extent, to the fullest extent,
sir.'"[76] Similarly, in January 1865, Ohio Republican James M. Ashley declared
that slavery had not only "forced this terrible civil war upon us" but had "tram-
pled upon the national Constitution," "silenced every free pulpit within its
control," and "made free speech and a free press impossible."[77] As Bingham
himself declared in the debates of early 1866, "I know that the enforcement
of the bill of rights is the want of the Republic."[78] As we shall see, Bingham's
unwavering goal in the debates of the Thirty-Ninth Congress was to secure
to all persons their natural rights of equal protection and due process and to
all citizens of the United States their guaranteed privileges and immunities as
declared in the first eight amendments to the federal Constitution. Like most
moderates, however, Bingham did not believe that admitting blacks to both
natural rights and the rights of national citizenship entitled them to the equal
political rights of suffrage.[79]

---

[73] As Bingham explained:

> I maintain that these powers [of Congress to establish rules for the election of Senators and
> Representatives, as well as the right to judge the election and qualification of members]
> were conferred for the especial protection of the political rights of the citizens of the
> United States. . . . Sir, what are the distinctive political rights of citizens of the United
> States? The great right to choose (under the laws of the States) severally, as I remarked
> before, either directly by ballot or indirectly through their duly-constituted agents, all
> the officers of the Federal Government . . . the right, also, to hold and exercise, upon
> election thereto, the several offices of honor, of power, and of trust, under the Constitution
> and Government of the United States. It is worthy of remark that every political right
> guarantied by the Constitution of the United States is limited by the words people or
> citizen, or by an official oath, to those who owe allegiance to the Constitution.

CONG. GLOBE, 35th Cong., 2d Sess. 983 (1859).

[74] AMAR, THE BILL OF RIGHTS, *supra* note 18, at 181–87.

[75] Cong. Globe, 35th Cong., 1st Sess. 752 (Feb. 18, 1858).

[76] *Id.*

[77] Cong. Globe, 38th Cong., 2d Sess. at 138 (Jan. 6, 1865).

[78] *See* CONG. GLOBE, 39th Cong., 1st Sess. 1291 (1866).

[79] *See* CONG. GLOBE, 37th Cong., 2d Sess. 1639 (1862) (remarks of Rep. Bingham) (arguing that
the rights of citizenship do not include the rights of suffrage).

Bingham's insistence that the states were bound by the Bill of Rights despite the Supreme Court's holding in *Barron v. Baltimore*[80] has led scholars like Akhil Amar to label Bingham a *Barron* "contrarian."[81] Although it is true that Bingham initially believed that states were constitutionally bound to enforce the Bill, he never rejected the reasoning of Chief Justice John Marshall in *Barron*. Bingham simply insisted that, although *Barron* held the Bill unenforceable by federal courts, it nevertheless remained a binding obligation on the states as part of their oath to uphold the Constitution.[82] In fact, when discussing the final version of the Fourteenth Amendment, Bingham expressly declared that the "great" decision of *Barron v. Baltimore* had been "rightfully" decided,[83] and he insisted that a deeper understanding of Marshall's reasoning in *Barron* had convinced him to redraft Section One of the Fourteenth Amendment.[84] This tracks Bingham's general reliance on the reasoning of the famous Chief Justice, particularly when it came to Bingham's understanding of the scope of federal power to enforce the Reconstruction Amendments.[85] Whatever else he was, Bingham was not a *Marshall* contrarian.[86]

III. JOHN BINGHAM'S FIRST DRAFT OF THE FOURTEENTH AMENDMENT

On December 6, 1865, John Bingham, a member of the Joint Committee on Reconstruction, proposed adding a fourteenth amendment to the federal Constitution.[87] The proposed amendment empowered Congress to pass "all necessary and proper laws to secure to all persons in every State of the Union equal protection in their rights of life, liberty, and property."[88] Early the next

---

[80] 32 U.S. (7 Pet.) 243; *see supra* note 24 and accompanying text.

[81] AMAR, THE BILL OF RIGHTS, *supra* note 18, at 185 (Bingham "read the Bill [of Rights] through contrarian lenses").

[82] CONG. GLOBE, 39th Cong., 1st Sess. 1090 (1866).

[83] CONG. GLOBE, 42d Cong., 1st Sess. app. at 84 (1871) ("And yet it was decided [in *Barron*], and rightfully, that these amendments, defining and protecting the rights of men and citizens, were only limitations on the power of Congress, not on the power of the States.").

[84] *Id.*

[85] *See, e.g., id.* at 81 (Bingham citing Marshall's opinion in *Cohens v. Virginia* as a guide to understanding federal power to legislate to enforce "negative limitations of power imposed by the Constitution upon the States").

[86] Professor Richard Aynes believes that Bingham held a "compact" view of the Bill of Rights, whereby states were obligated by oath to enforce the Bill of Rights even in the absence of federal authority to enforce the Bill in the states. *See* Aynes, *supra* note 18, at 71. Although this may have been Bingham's original position, he ultimately came to agree with John Marshall that the Bill was not originally binding upon the states.

[87] CONG. GLOBE, 39th Cong., 1st Sess. 14 (1865).

[88] *Id.*

month, Bingham spoke to the House about the need for the Amendment and, in doing so, provided a sketch of his theory of Article IV and its relationship to the rights of national citizenship.

Pointing to the numerous examples in recent years of states violating "the absolute guarantees of the Constitution," Bingham insisted that "it is time that we take security for the future, so that like occurrences may not again rise to distract our people and finally to dismember the Republic."[89] Referring to the proposed amendment's protection of equal rights, Bingham explained:

> When you come to weigh these words, "equal and exact justice to all men," go read, if you please, the words of the Constitution itself: "The citizens of each State (being *ipso facto* citizens of the United States) shall be entitled to all the privileges and immunities of citizens (applying the ellipsis 'of the United States') in the several States." This guarantee is of the privileges and immunities of citizens of the United States in, not of, the several States. This guarantee of your Constitution applies to every citizen of every State of the Union; there is not a guarantee more sacred, and none more vital in that great instrument. It was utterly disregarded in the past by South Carolina when she drove with indignity and contempt and scorn from her limits the honored representative of Massachusetts, who went thither upon the peaceful mission of asserting in the tribunals of South Carolina the rights of American citizens.
>
> I propose, with the help of this Congress and of the American people, that hereafter there shall not be any disregard of that essential guarantee of your Constitution in any State of the Union. And how? By simply adding an amendment to the Constitution to operate on all the States of this Union alike, giving to Congress the power to pass all laws necessary and proper to secure to all persons – which includes every citizen of every State – their equal personal rights. . . .[90]

As this passage illustrates, Bingham believed the Privileges and Immunities Clause of Article IV reflected an implied understanding about national citizenship that was not expressly included in the Clause but was nevertheless critical to its meaning. Bingham supplied this critical implied language through the addition of what he referred to as an "ellipsis."

> The citizens of each state (being ipso facto citizens of the United States) shall be entitled to all the privileges and immunities of citizens (applying the ellipsis "of the United States") in the several States.

Today, Bingham's addition of the ellipsis might seem odd or strained. In fact, Bingham was relying on analysis supplied by one of the most influential

---

[89] Cong. Globe, 39th Cong., 1st Sess. 158 (1866).
[90] *Id.*

constitutional theorists of his day, Joseph Story. Bingham's ellipsis includes
a quote from Story's 1833 *Commentaries on the Constitution*, in which Story
had written that "[e]very citizen of a state is *ipso facto* a citizen of the United
States."[91] Members of the Thirty-Ninth Congress were familiar with Story's
Commentaries and cited the work repeatedly during the debates of 1866.
Thus, Bingham's use of Story as part of an expanded version of the Comity
Clause would not have appeared odd or controversial at the time, and, in fact,
no one appears to have disagreed with his extended formulation. Including
Story's "ellipsis" allowed Bingham to clarify that the rights protected under
the Comity Clause were those belonging to "citizens of the United States,"
since "citizens in the several States" necessarily *were* citizens of the United
States. Seven years earlier, Bingham had made the same argument in his
1859 speech opposing the admission of Oregon. There, Bingham had quoted
Joseph Story's *Commentaries on the Constitution* for the proposition that "[a]ll
persons enjoying the status of state citizenship necessarily enjoyed the rights
of national citizenship, for 'the citizens of each State in the Union are *ipso
facto* citizens of the United States.'"[92]

Although he relied on Story's ellipsis, Bingham's understanding of the
Comity Clause was quite different from that of Justice Story and other antebellum legal commentators. In his *Commentaries*, Story presented the conventional view of the Comity Clause as merely guaranteeing sojourning citizens
equal access to a limited set of state-secured rights.[93] Bingham, however,
believed that the properly expanded Comity Clause pointed away from state-
secured rights and toward the rights of national citizenship. According to
Bingham in his 1859 speech opposing the admission of Oregon,

> The citizens of each state, all the citizens of each state, being citizens of the
> United States, shall be entitled to "all privileges and immunities of citizens in
> the several states." Not to the rights and immunities of the several States; not
> to those constitutional rights and immunities which result exclusively from
> State authority or State legislation; but to "all privileges and immunities" of

---

[91] 3 STORY, *supra* note 70 at 565–66. Not every antebellum legal commentator agreed with
Story. *See, e.g.*, Caleb Cushing, *Relation of Indians to Citizenship*, 7 OP. ATTY. GEN. 751–52
(1856) ("Some of the commentators, indeed, say that 'every citizen of a state is, *ipso facto*, a
citizen of the United States.' (Story's Commentaries on the Constitution, s. 1693; Rawl on the
Constitution, p. 85.) But they are in this clearly mistaken."). Justice Taney in *Dred Scott* is one
particularly infamous example of someone who rejected the idea that citizens of a state were
necessarily citizens of the United States. *See* Dred Scott v. Sandford, 60 U.S. (19 How.) 393,
405–06 (1857) (Taney, C.J.). Obviously, Bingham would not be criticized for preferring Story
over Taney.

[92] CONG. GLOBE, 35th Cong., 2d Sess. 983 (Feb. 11, 1859) (citing "Story on the Constitution,
vol. 3, p. 565.") (emphasis added).

[93] *See supra* note 70 and accompanying text.

citizens of the United States in the several States. There is an ellipsis employed in the Constitution, but its meaning is self-evident that it is "the privileges and immunities of citizens of the United States in the several States" that it guarantees.[94]

Bingham insisted that these "privileges and immunities of citizens of the United States" included "the rights of life, liberty and property, and their due protection in the enjoyment thereof by law."[95] These were not state-secured privileges; these were federal constitutional rights announced in the Due Process Clause of the federal Constitution.[96] Thus, when Bingham introduced his first draft of the Fourteenth Amendment, he did so with the belief that the Comity Clause bound the states to protect rights announced in the federal Bill of Rights. Indeed, Bingham initially insisted that the Comity Clause was *part* of the federal Bill of Rights. As we shall see, these were not views shared by any other member of the Thirty-Ninth Congress, a fact that doomed the success of his initial draft.

A. *Bingham's Explanation of the First Draft of the Fourteenth Amendment*

Bingham submitted his initial proposal to the Joint Committee on Reconstruction,[97] where he and the other members of the Committee worked

---

[94] CONG. GLOBE, 35th Cong., 2d Sess. 984 (Feb. 11, 1859). For a general discussion of Bingham's speech, see GERARD N. MAGLIOCCA, AMERICA'S FOUNDING SON: JOHN BINGHAM AND THE INVENTION OF THE FOURTEENTH AMENDMENT 62 (2013).

[95] *Id.*

[96] Philip Hamburger argues that Bingham's reference to "due process" in this speech actually involved a reference to state law protections of due process and not to the protections of the Fifth Amendment. *See* Philip Hamburger, *Privileges or Immunities*, 105 Nw. U. L. Rev. 61, 113–14 (2011). This allows Hamburger to argue that Bingham did not believe that the rights protected under Article IV had anything to do with the national rights protected in the first eight amendments. *Id.* It is clear from the full speech, however, that Bingham's reference to "the rights of life, liberty and property, and their due protection in the enjoyment thereof by law" is a reference to the rights of the Fifth Amendment. *See, e.g.*, CONG. GLOBE, 35th Cong., 2d Sess., at 983 ("And in further illustration of my position I invite attention to the significant fact that natural or inherent rights, which belong to all men irrespective of all conventional regulations, are by this constitution guaranteed by the broad and comprehensive term 'person,' as contradistinguished from the limited term citizen – as in the fifth article of amendments, guarding those sacred rights which are as universal and indestructible as the human race, that 'no person shall be deprived of life, liberty, or property but by due process of law, nor shall private property be taken without just compensation.' And this guarantee applies to all citizens within the United States.").

[97] The joint committee included nine members from the House and six from the Senate. The House members were Thaddeus Stevens (R-PA), Elihu Washburne (R-IL), Justin Morrill (R-VT), John A. Bingham (R-OH), Roscoe Conkling (R-NY), George Boutwell (R-MA), Henry Blow (R-MO), Henry Grider (D-KY), and Andrew Jackson Rogers (D-NJ). The Senate

through a number of versions of the Amendment.[98] On February 3, the Committee considered the following draft:

> Congress shall have power to make laws which shall be necessary and proper to secure to all persons in every State full protection in the enjoyment of life, liberty and property; and to citizens of the United States in every State the same immunities, and equal political rights and privileges.[99]

Bingham moved successfully to substitute a different version that relied on the specific language of the Constitution (the parentheticals are in the original):

> The Congress shall have power to make all laws which shall be necessary and proper to secure to the citizens of each state all privileges and immunities of citizens in the several states (Art. 4, Sec. 2); and to all persons in the several States equal protection in the rights of life, liberty, and property (5th Amendment).[100]

The committee adopted Bingham's draft on February 10 and sent the same back to Congress for consideration and debate.[101] In his speech before the House on February 26, Bingham explained what he believed was the meaning and purpose of this initial draft of the Fourteenth Amendment. His speech presents a relatively concise statement of Bingham's constitutional theory at the time, so it is worth an extended excerpt. Of particular importance is Bingham's insistence that the proposed amendment tracked the exact words and ideas of the original Constitution:

> I ask, however, the attention of the House to the fact that the amendment proposed stands in the very words of the Constitution of the United States as it came to us from the hands of its illustrious framers. Every word of the proposed amendment is to-day in the Constitution of our country, save the words conferring the express grant of power upon the Congress of the United States. The residue of the resolution, as the House will see by a reference to the Constitution, is the language of the second section of the fourth article, and of a portion of the fifth amendment adopted by the First Congress in

---

members were William Fessenden (R-ME), James W. Grimes (R-IA), Jacob Howard (R-MI), George Henry Williams (R-OR), Ira Harris (R-NY), and Reverdy Johnson (D-MD).

[98] Bingham introduced his proposed amendment to the Joint Committee on January 16. *See* BENJAMIN B. KENDRICK, JOURNAL OF THE JOINT COMMITTEE OF FIFTEEN ON RECONSTRUCTION: 39TH CONGRESS, 1865–1867, at 51 (1914).

[99] *Id.* at 60 (1914).

[100] *Id.* at 61.

[101] *Id.* at 62–63.

1789, and made part of the Constitution of the country. The language of the second section of the fourth article is –

"The citizens of each State shall be entitled to all privileges and immunities of citizens in the several States."

The fifth article of the amendment provides that – "No person shall be deprived of life, liberty, or property, without due process of law."

Sir, it has been the want of the Republic that there was not an express grant of power in the Constitution to enable the whole people of every State, by congressional enactment, to enforce obedience to these requirements of the Constitution. . . .

I ask the attention of the House to the further consideration that the proposed amendment does not impose upon any State of the Union, or any citizen of any State of the Union, any obligation which is not now enjoined upon them by the very letter of the Constitution. I need not remind gentlemen here that the Constitution, as originally framed, and as adopted by the whole people of this country, provides that –

"This Constitution, and the laws of the United States which shall be made in pursuance thereof, and all treaties made, or which shall be made, under the authority of the United States, shall be the supreme law of the land; and the judges in every State shall be bound thereby, anything in the constitution or laws of any State to the contrary notwithstanding."

Could words be stronger, could words be more forceful, to enjoin upon every officer of every State the obligation to obey these great provisions of the Constitution, in their letter and their spirit? I submit to the judgment of the House, that it is impossible for mortal man to frame a formula of words more obligatory than those already in that instrument, enjoining this great duty upon the several States and the several officers of every State in the Union.

And, sir, it is equally clear by every construction of the Constitution, its contemporaneous construction, its continued construction, legislative, executive and judicial, that these great provisions of the Constitution, this immortal bill of rights embodied in the Constitution, rested for its execution and enforcement hitherto upon the fidelity of the States. The House knows, sir, the country knows, the civilized world knows, that the legislative, executive, and judicial officers of eleven States within this Union within the last five years, in utter disregard of these injunctions of your Constitution, in utter disregard of that official oath which the Constitution required they should severally take and faithfully keep when they entered upon the discharge of their respective duties, have violated in every sense of the word these provisions

of the Constitution of the United States, the enforcement of which are absolutely essential to American nationality.[102]

Bingham's proposal reflects the same view of American liberty he expressed
in his 1859 speech against the admission of Oregon. First, there are certain
natural rights held by all persons that governments must respect regardless
of citizenship. No person should be denied life, liberty, or property without
due process of law. Citizens, on the other hand, are protected in these same
natural rights, but they also receive an additional layer of protection by virtue
of their special relationship to the government.

Notice that Bingham stresses that the words of his proposed amendment
tracked the *exact* language and ideas of the original Constitution. This was a
critical aspect of Bingham's original theory of the Constitution, and he clearly
believed it was an important selling point to the moderates in the Thirty-Ninth
Congress. As noted earlier, Bingham insisted that Article IV of the original
Constitution imposed an obligation on the states to protect liberties listed
in the original Bill of Rights (here, the Fifth Amendment). This meant that
his proposed amendment imposed no new obligations on the states beyond
those that the states already were constitutionally bound to respect. This also
ensured that no power would be granted to the national government beyond
the authority to enforce rights *already* declared in the Constitution. It was
the failure of the states to respect these rights that justified the addition of
an amendment that authorized congressional enforcement of enumerated
constitutional liberty.

On February 28, Bingham delivered a second speech that fleshed out his
ideas in more detail. Only days earlier, Congress had failed to override President Johnson's federalism-based veto of the Freedmen's Bureau Bill.[103] Successful passage of the Fourteenth Amendment would have to satisfy the concerns of moderate Republicans, or the proposal would meet the same fate.
Fully aware of the need to maintain moderate (and moderately conservative)

---

[102] CONG. GLOBE, 39th Cong., 1st Sess. 1034 (1866); *see also Another Amendment to the Constitution*, New York Herald, Feb. 27, 1866, at 1, col. 5 (presenting a slightly different version of
Bingham's speech: "But it was equally clear that by every construction of the Constitution –
its contemporaneous and continuous construction – that great provision contained in the
second section of the fourth article and in a portion of the fifth amendment adopted by the
first congress in 1789, that that immortal bill of rights had hitherto depended on the action of
the several States").

[103] President Johnson vetoed the Bill on February 19. See McKITRICK, *supra* note 8, at 287. The
next day, February 20, the Senate failed to override the veto by two votes, 30–18. *See* CONG.
GLOBE, 39, Cong., 1st Sess. at 943.

support, Bingham began by insisting the Amendment did not "take away from any State any right that belongs to it."[104] The purpose of the Amendment was simply "to arm the Congress of the United States . . . with the power to enforce the bill of rights as it stands in the Constitution today. It 'hath that extent – no more.'"[105] Therefore, "[g]entlemen who oppose this amendment oppose the grant of power to enforce this bill of rights."[106] After quoting the language of Article IV and the Fifth Amendment, Bingham then admonished opponents of the Amendment:

> Gentlemen admit the force of the provisions in the bill of rights, that the citizens of the United States shall be entitled to all the privileges and immunities of citizens of the United States in the several States, and that no person shall be deprived of life, liberty, or property without due process of law; but they say, "We are opposed to its enforcement by act of Congress under an amended Constitution as proposed." That is the sum and substance of all the argument that we have heard on this subject. Why are gentlemen opposed to the enforcement of the bill of rights, as proposed?[107]

Bingham rejected the idea that the Tenth Amendment reserved to the states the right to violate the obligation of the Comity Clause of Article IV – a provision Bingham believed obligated the states to respect the federal Bill of Rights:

> Who ever before heard that any State had reserved to itself the right, under the Constitution of the United States, to withhold from any citizen of the United States within its limits, under any pretext whatever, any of the privileges of a citizen of the United States, or to impose upon him, no matter from what State he may have come, any burden contrary to that provision of the Constitution which declares that the citizen shall be entitled in the several States to all the immunities of a citizen of the United States.[108]

Bingham mocked his colleagues for claiming they were "not opposed to the bill of rights" but only opposed to their federal enforcement.[109] If states had

---

[104] CONG. GLOBE, 39th Cong., 1st Sess. 1088.

[105] *Id.*

[106] *Id.* at 1090.

[107] *Id.* at 1089.

[108] *Id.*

[109] *Id.* ("Ah! Say gentlemen who oppose this amendment, *we are not opposed to the bill of rights* that all shall be protected alike in life, liberty, and property; we are only opposed to enforcing it by national authority, even by the consent of the loyal people of all the States.").

no authority to violate the Bill of Rights, "how can the right of a State be impaired by giving to the people of the United States by constitutional amendment the power by congressional enactment to enforce this provision of their Constitution?"[110] Such enforcement was essential, argued Bingham, in light of Chief Justice Marshall's Supreme Court's ruling in *Barron v. Baltimore*, which held that federal courts could not enforce the Bill of Rights against the states.[111]

Although cases like *Barron* prevented courts from enforcing the Bill against the states, Bingham believed that states nevertheless were constitutionally bound to respect the Bill of Rights. Here, Bingham quoted Daniel Webster regarding the oath taken by all state officials to support the Constitution of the United States.[112] This oath obligated state officials to enforce Article IV and protect what Bingham insisted were its attendant national privileges and immunities.[113] The Supremacy Clause further obligated the states to protect such rights notwithstanding any state law to the contrary.[114] The question thus boiled down to "whether you will give by this amendment to the people of the United States the power, by legislative enactment, to punish officials of States for violation of the oaths enjoined upon them by their Constitution? That is the question, and the whole question."[115] Without such enforcement, the Bill of Rights would stand as "a mere dead letter."[116]

Putting together Bingham's speeches of January and February, it seems clear that he believed that Article IV protected a set of national rights. According to the ellipsis reading of the Comity Clause, the provision protected the "privileges and immunities of citizens (of the United States) in the States."[117] These national rights included rights listed in the Bill of Rights, such as in the Fifth Amendment. Although Supreme Court cases like *Barron v. Baltimore* prevented the federal courts from enforcing these rights against state abridgments, state courts nevertheless remained constitutionally bound to do so according to their oath to uphold the Constitution and the supremacy of federal law.

---

[110] *Id.*
[111] *Id.* at 1089–90.
[112] *Id.* at 1090.
[113] *Id.*
[114] *Id.*
[115] *Id.*
[116] *Id.*
[117] *Id.*

B. *John Bingham's "Bill of Rights"*

One of the major disputes over John Bingham's reliability as an expositor of the Constitution and the Fourteenth Amendment involves statements in which Bingham appears to argue that the Comity Clause of Article IV is part of the Bill of Rights.[118] Legal scholars like Charles Fairman and Raoul Berger who rejected the idea that the Fourteenth Amendment "incorporated" the Bill of Rights point to these references as evidence that Bingham did not mean what we understand as the "Bill of Rights" whenever he used that phrase during the Reconstruction debates.[119] Pro-incorporationist scholars, on the other hand, insist that Bingham meant the first eight amendments to the Constitution when he referred to the Bill of Rights and, as evidence, point to statements Bingham made months (or even years) later.[120]

A close look at the debates suggests that both sides in this debate are partially correct. Bingham originally *did* have an idiosyncratic view of the Bill of Rights that included Article IV. However, as the debates proceeded, Bingham seems to have changed his mind and adopted the more standard understanding of the Bill of Rights as including only the first eight amendments to the Constitution.[121] Trying to force all of Bingham's statements into a single constitutional theory obscures important developments in his thinking that occurred as the debates moved forward.

To begin with, Bingham clearly viewed the Comity Clause of Article IV as part of the Bill of Rights when he defended his initial draft of the Fourteenth Amendment. In his speech of February 13, Bingham quoted both Article IV and the Fifth Amendment and then lamented the lack of congressional power "to enforce obedience to these requirements of the Constitution."[122] Bingham next cited the Supremacy Clause as "enjoin[ing] upon every officer of every State the obligation to obey these great provisions of the Constitution."[123] Bingham's use of the plural for "these requirements" and "these great provisions" indicates that he is referring to both of the provisions he just quoted: the Comity Clause of Article IV and the Fifth Amendment. Bingham then declared that "these

---

[118] John Harrison also notes that Bingham included Article IV as part of the Bill of Rights. Harrison, *supra* note 16, at 1406 & n.72. So did both Fairman and tenBroek. *See* Fairman, *Does the Fourteenth Amendment Incorporate the Bill of Rights?*, *supra* note 16, at 26; Jacobus tenBroek, Equal Under Law 212–15 (Collier Books rev. ed. 1965).

[119] *See, e.g.,* Berger, *supra* note 16, at 160–61; Fairman, *Does the Fourteenth Amendment Incorporate the Bill of Rights? Supra* note 16, at 2526.

[120] *See, e.g.,* Amar, The Bill of Rights, *supra* note 18, at 183.

[121] *See* Chapter 5 notes 81–85 and accompanying text.

[122] Cong. Globe, 39th Cong., 1st Sess. 1034 (1866).

[123] *Id.*

great provisions of the Constitution, this immortal bill of rights embodied in the Constitution, rested for its execution and enforcement hitherto upon the fidelity of the States."[124] Here, Bingham plainly equates "these great provisions" with "this immortal bill of rights."

On February 28, Bingham was even more explicit in his description of Article IV as part of the Bill of Rights:

> Gentlemen admit the force of the provisions in the bill of rights, that the citizens of the United States shall be entitled to all the privileges and immunities of citizens of the United States in the several States, and that no person shall be deprived of life, liberty, or property without due process of law; but they say, "We are opposed to its enforcement by act of Congress under the amended Constitution, as proposed." That is the sum and substance of all the argument that we have heard on this subject. Why are gentlemen opposed to the enforcement of the bill of rights, as proposed? Because they aver it would interfere with the reserved rights of the States! Who ever before heard that any State had reserved to itself the right, under the Constitution of the United States, to withhold from any citizen of the United States within its limits, under any pretext whatever, any of the privileges of a citizen of the United States, or to impose on him, no matter from what State he may have come, any burden contrary to that provision of the Constitution which declares that the citizen shall be entitled in the several States to all the immunities of a citizen of the United States?[125]

John Bingham's statements about the Bill of Rights are a major source of evidence for those who believe the Fourteenth Amendment incorporated the Bill against the states. If Bingham's views were odd or incoherent, this calls into question whether he can be viewed as a reliable source of information about the framers' intent and public understanding of the text. Not surprisingly, pro-incorporation scholars have struggled with the just quoted passages that make it appear that Bingham viewed Article IV as part of the Bill of Rights – a proposition shared by no one else, either in or outside of Congress.[126] William Crosskey, for example, suggested that Bingham might have been holding a copy of the (traditional) Bill of Rights and was gesturing with it when he referred to "this immortal bill of rights."[127] Richard Aynes has raised the possibility of a transcription error, suggesting that the Reporter might have accidently typed

---

[124] *Id.*

[125] *Id.* at 1089.

[126] *See, e.g.,* AMAR, THE BILL OF RIGHTS, *supra* note 18, at 183 n.* (1998); Richard L. Aynes, *The Bill of Rights, The Fourteenth Amendment, and the Seven Deadly Sins of Legal Scholarship,* 8 WM. & MARY BILL RTS. J. 407, 412–13 (2000).

[127] Crosskey, *supra* note 18, at 28.

"*this* bill of rights" (making it appear that Bingham was referring to both the Comity Clause and the first eight amendment) when he should have typed "*the* bill of rights."[128] Most commonly, pro-incorporationist scholars simply ignore these troubling passages and focus instead on the traditional descriptions of the Bill of Rights that Bingham makes much later in the Reconstruction Debates.[129] None of these efforts, I believe, is persuasive. When Bingham described Article IV and the Due Process Clause as "these great provisions" that were part of "this bill of rights," it does not matter whether the reporter failed to write "the" instead of "this" – the result is the same: Bingham was arguing that both Article IV and the Fifth Amendment are part of what he believed were "the Bill of Rights."

On the other hand, it is also true that Bingham later *dropped* his claim that the Bill of Rights included Article IV and instead adopted the common view that the first eight amendments "constituted the American Bill of Rights."[130] A great deal occurred, however, between Bingham's initial and ultimate statements about Article IV and the Bill of Rights. Understanding what occurred, and why Bingham may have changed his mind about Article IV, helps explain why he changed the text of the Fourteenth Amendment.

C. *The Response to Bingham's First Draft of the Fourteenth Amendment*

1. Initial Skirmishes

In January 1866, Congress passed a bill to extend the life of the Bureau of Freedmen, Refugees, and Abandoned Land, a body in which Congress had vested "control of all subjects relating to refugees and freedmen in the rebel states."[131] The new bill not only extended the Freedmen's Bureau Act, but also extended the jurisdiction of the Bureau to freedmen throughout the

---

[128] Aynes, *supra* note 18, at 68 n.61. More seriously, Aynes argues that Bingham may have understood the Fifth Amendment as one of many privileges and immunities of US citizens, but also as one belonging to all persons, citizen or not. *Id.* at 68–69. This reading of the speech has its own problems, including the fact that Bingham goes on to describe both provisions as "absolutely essential to American nationality," indicating that he was not, at that moment at least, discussing anything other than the concerns of American citizenship. But even if correct, this leaves the problem of Bingham's idiosyncratic view that Article IV was part of the Bill of Rights, not to mention Bingham's later *denial* that Section One privileges or immunities included the privileges and immunities of Article IV.

[129] *See, e.g.*, Amar, America's Constitution, *supra* note 1, at 386–87 (2005).

[130] Cong. Globe, 42d Cong., 1st Sess. app. 84 (1871).

[131] 13 Statutes at Large 507 (March 3, 1865); Cong. Globe, 39th Cong., 1st Sess. 688; *see also* McKitrick, *supra* note 8, at 278.

United States and authorized the commissioner to provide freedmen with forty-acre plots of land.[132] On February 19, however, President Johnson vetoed the bill, citing federalism-based concerns about unwarranted intrusion on the reserved powers and rights of the states.[133] The message was persuasive enough to convince eight Republicans who had voted in favor of the bill to now support Johnson's veto. As a result, the vote to override Johnson's veto failed in the Senate by two votes.[134] The failure of the Freedmen's Bureau Bill had immediate implications for the debates on both the Civil Rights Act and the Fourteenth Amendment, signaling to both sides the need to craft their arguments in a manner that would appeal to the moderate vote.

Seeking to build momentum against further intrusion on state autonomy, on February 26, the conservative Democratic Congressman Andrew Jackson Rogers spoke out against Bingham's proposed Fourteenth Amendment. According to Rogers, "[t]he effect of this proposed amendment is to take away the power of the States; to interfere with the internal policy and regulations of the States: to centralize a consolidated power in this Federal Government which our fathers never intended should be exercised by it."[135] Ordinarily, Republicans could ignore firebrand conservative Democrats like Rogers. However, given the failed override of Johnson's veto only days before, Republicans could not afford to be sanguine about Rogers's ability to peel away votes and thus prevent Congress from meeting the two-thirds voting requirement for proposed constitutional amendments. Making matters even more complicated, radical supporters of the proposed amendment relied on *Prigg*-based theories of unenumerated federal power to define and protect any and all common law civil rights in the states[136] – theories that might generate more opposition than support from the more moderate and conservative members of Congress.

---

[132] MALTZ, *supra* note 21, at 48.

[133] CONG. GLOBE, 39th Cong., 1st Sess. 1679 (1866) (President Johnson's veto message).

[134] MALTZ, *supra* note 21, at 49; MCKITRICK, *supra* note 8, at 292.

[135] CONG. GLOBE, 39th Cong. 1st Sess. app. 134 (1866).

[136] According to Pennsylvania Congressman William Kelley, for example, Bingham's proposed amendment should be supported but was unnecessary because congressional power to protect civil rights in the states had already been granted under the Constitution. CONG. GLOBE, 39th Cong. 1st Sess. 1057 (1866). According to Kelley, the powers granted under the Constitution should be liberally construed, as would be a remedial statute, because its purpose was to fix the errors of the Articles of Confederation. *Id.* at 1057–68. Powers were also granted to Congress to guarantee a republican form of government in the states, and in addition, "to enforce every right, privilege, and immunity accorded to the people. . . ." *Id.* at 1058. In the Senate, Senator Nye took an even broader view of congressional power. In addressing congressional power to control the conditions on which the states could be readmitted to the Union, Nye argued that the Constitution provides for broad federal "superintending power of control over the

In response to claims (and complaints) that the proposed amendment would authorize federal takeover of the entire category of common law rights in the states, mainstream Republicans insisted that Bingham's Article IV-based draft would do nothing more than authorize federal enforcement of the Comity Clause of Article IV as *traditionally* understood. According to Republican Congressman William Higby:

> If [Article IV] had been enforced heretofore, how different would have been the condition of the various States of this Union. Had that provision been enforced, a citizen of New York would have been treated as a citizen in the State of South Carolina; a citizen of Massachusetts would have been regarded as a citizen in the State of Mississippi or Louisiana. The man who was a citizen in one State would have been considered and respected as a citizen in every other State of the Union. . . . The intent of this amendment is to give force and effect and vitality to that provision of the Constitution which has been regarded heretofore as nugatory and powerless.[137]

Iowa Republican Congressman Hiram Price held the same view; Bingham's proposed amendment "mean[s] simply this: if a citizen of Iowa or a citizen of Pennsylvania has any business, or if curiosity has induced him to visit the State of South Carolina or Georgia, he shall have the same protection of the laws there that he would have had had he lived there for ten years."[138] Even the radical Republican Frederick Woodbridge of Vermont, a man who otherwise embraced broad theories of natural rights, nevertheless believed that the proposed amendment tracked the traditionally narrow equality reading of Article IV. According to Woodbridge:

> What is the object of the proposed amendment? It merely gives the power to Congress to enact those laws which will give to a citizen of the United States the natural rights which necessarily pertain to citizenship. It is intended to enable Congress by its enactments when necessary to give a citizen of the United States in whatever State he may be, those privileges and immunities which are guaranteed to him under the Constitution of the United States. It is intended to enable Congress to give to all citizens the inalienable rights of life

States." *Id.* at 1072. Nye, like other strong nationalists in the Reconstruction Congress, found such power through a combination of the Republican Guarantee Clause, the Necessary and Proper Clause, and the Supremacy Clause. *Id.* This was not power limited to responding to an emergency like the Civil War, but instead allowed Congress to legislate for the protection of *all* personal and natural rights – a list of unlimited subject matter.

[137] *Id.* at 1054.

[138] CONG. GLOBE, 39th Cong., 1st Sess. 1066 (1866).

and liberty, and to every citizen in whatever State he may be that protection to his property which is extended to the other citizens of the State.[139]

Woodbridge believed that the Comity Clause of Article IV protected "the natural rights which necessarily pertain to citizenship," but interpreted the Clause as doing nothing more than requiring states to guarantee citizens the same rights that were "extended to the other citizens of the State." Wood-bridge, like Price and Higby, defended Bingham's proposal on the assumption that the Amendment would do nothing more than enforce Article IV as traditionally understood. None of them repeated, much less defended, Bingham's claim that the Privileges and Immunities Clause of Article IV was part of the Bill of Rights and that the Amendment would provide substantive protection of the Bill of Rights against state action. Instead, they viewed Bingham's proposal as providing federal power to enforce the Comity Clause as that Clause had been interpreted in cases like *Campbell*, *Livingston*, *Corfield*, and *Abbott* and by treatise writers like Chancellor James Kent and Joseph Story.

2. Federalism: The Concerns of Robert Hale

Conservative Republican Robert Hale of New York was not convinced by the assurances put forward by Woodbridge, Price, and Higby about an amendment of limited scope. On February 27, Congressman Hale delivered a major speech against Bingham's first draft of the Fourteenth Amendment that was reprinted in full a few days later by the *New York Times*.[140] Hale's speech is important because it came from a member who was not opposed to enforcing the Bill of Rights against the states and who did not oppose the second, and significantly

---

[139] *Id.* at 1088 (emphasis added). Woodbridge uses the language of equal protection specifically in regard to the rights of property, but it is clear from his context that he sees the same principles extending to all due process rights. Woodbridge's remarks also make for a good cautionary example regarding references to natural rights in the debates of the Thirty-Ninth Congress. Woodbridge starts with natural rights language but quickly limits the reference to mean only equal protection of state-conferred rights. Thus, although natural rights arguments could be quite broad, the application of natural rights principles was often quite constrained, particularly in light of the political realities facing the Amendment's proponents in the Thirty-Ninth Congress.

[140] *See Amending the Constitution: Federal Power and State Rights*, N.Y. TIMES, Mar. 2, 1866, at 2. On February 28, the *Times*, under its front-page "Washington News" headline, provided a sub-headline, "Debate in the House on the Constitutional Amendment," highlighting the "Clear and Forcible Speech by Mr. Hale Against its Adoption." Washington News, *Debate in the House on the Constitutional Amendment, Clear and Forcible Speech by Mr. Hale Against Its Adoption*, N.Y. TIMES, Feb. 28, 1866, at 1. Earl Maltz credits Hale with delivering the "main critique" of Bingham's proposed amendment. MALTZ, *supra* note 21, at 56.

changed, version of the Fourteenth Amendment.[141] Thus, we can presume that Hale's objections were not driven by a commitment to oppose any effort to require the states to protect substantive rights.

According to the *Times*, Congressman Hale's principal objection was that the proposed amendment threatened to "utterly obliterate State rights and State authority over their own internal affairs."[142] Hale insisted that federalism and states' rights remained a critical component of American constitutional government.[143] Under Bingham's amendment, this dualist system of government would be destroyed by

> a provision under which all State legislation, in its codes of civil and criminal jurisprudence and procedure, affecting the individual citizen, may be over-ridden, may be repealed or abolished, and the law of Congress established instead. I maintain that in this respect it is an utter departure from every principle ever dreamed of by the men who framed our Constitution.[144]

Ignoring the first part of Bingham's amendment, which used the language of Article IV, Hale focused his objections on the language granting federal power "to make all laws which shall be necessary and proper to secure to all persons in the several States equal protection in the rights of life, liberty, and property."[145] Rejecting the limited interpretations of this language offered by defenders of the Amendment, Hale insisted that "[i]t is not a mere provision that when the States undertake to give protection which is unequal Congress may equalize it; it is a grant of power in general terms – a grant of the right to legislate for the protection of life, liberty, and property, simply qualified with

---

[141] Although Hale spoke out against the initial version and voted against it, he did not speak out against Bingham's second version, and he did not vote at all when the House voted 128–37 in support of Bingham's second draft. *See* CONG. GLOBE, 39th Cong., 1st Sess. 2545 (1866) (Hale recorded as not voting); *see* MALTZ, *supra* note 21, at 94.

[142] *Amending the Constitution: Federal Power and State Rights*, N.Y. TIMES, Feb. 27, 1866, at 2 (reporting on Hale's speech).

[143] According to Hale:

> Now, Mr. Speaker, what is the theory of our Constitution? ... In general terms, is it not that all powers relating to the existence and sovereignty of the nation, powers relating to our foreign relations, powers relating to peace and war, to the enforcement of the law of nations and international law, are the powers given to Congress and to the Federal Government by the Constitution, while all powers having reference to the relation of the individual to the municipal government, the powers of local jurisdiction and legislation, are in general reserved to the States?

> CONG. GLOBE, 39th Cong., 1st Sess. at 1063 (1866).

[144] *Id.*

[145] *Id.*

the condition that it shall be equal legislation."[146] To Hale, this altered the nature of the Bill of Rights:

> Now, what are these amendments to the Constitution, numbered from one to ten, one of which is the fifth article in question? What is the nature and object of these articles? They do not contain, from beginning to end, a grant of power anywhere. On the contrary, they are all restrictions of power. They constitute the bill of rights, a bill of rights for the protection of the citizen, and defining and limiting the power of Federal and *State* legislation. They are not matters upon which legislation can be based.[147]

Note that Hale assumed that the Bill of Rights *already* "limit[ed] the power of Federal and State legislation,"[148] thus making the Amendment unnecessary. Immediately challenged on this point by John Bingham,[149] Hale admitted that he knew of no case that expressly supported his claim. Nevertheless, Hale stated that he had always "gone along with the impression that there is that sort of protection thrown over us in some way, whether with or without the sanction of a judicial decision that we were so protected. Of course, I may be entirely mistaken in all this, but I have certainly somehow had that impression."[150]

Returning to his main critique, Hale objected to the "vague and general language" of Bingham's proposed amendment which

> confer[s] upon the Federal Congress powers . . . to legislate upon all matters pertaining to the life, liberty, and property of all the inhabitants of the several States, I put it to the gentleman, whom I know sometimes at least to be disposed to criticise this habit of liberal construction, to state where he apprehends that Congress and the courts will stop in the powers they may arrogate to themselves under this proposed amendment.[151]

It was not that Hale opposed an effort to "protect the liberty of the citizen – the humblest as well as the highest – the negro, the late slave, as well as others. In every such desire on [Bingham's] part I most fully and cordially concur."[152] This initial draft, however, entrenched on "other liberties as important as the liberties of the individual citizen, and those are the liberties and rights of the States." To Hale, preserving the federalist structure of government was essential to the preservation of individual liberty: "I believe that whatever most

[146] *Id.* at 1063–64.
[147] *Id.* at 1064.
[148] *Id.*
[149] *Id.*
[150] *Id.*
[151] *Id.* at 1065.
[152] *Id.*

clearly distinguishes our Government from other Governments in the extent of individual freedom and the protection of personal rights we owe to our decentralized system."[153]

3. John Bingham's Defense of His Initial Draft of the Fourteenth Amendment

Bingham's speech of February 28 was his final attempt to defend the initial draft of the Fourteenth Amendment. Over the previous two days, Bingham had listened to conservative opponents of the Amendment attempt to use the same federalism-based arguments President Johnson had used in vetoing the Freedmen's Bill. The vote on the Amendment would be close; like the veto override, a proposed amendment required a two-thirds majority vote in the House and Senate before qualifying for submission to the states for ratification.

Bingham had to overcome two separate and opposite problems in his effort to shepherd the Amendment to a successful vote. First, he had to counter conservative claims that the proposal authorized broad congressional power to define and enforce the entire subject of civil rights in the states, power that most agreed the original Constitution (with but a few exceptions) had left to the states. To counter these overbreadth arguments, Bingham had to explain how the Amendment had a more limited scope than that claimed by radicals or opposed by the conservatives. A separate problem, however, required an effort in the opposite direction. In their zeal to downplay the scope of the Amendment and win moderate support, some Republican members had claimed that the proposed amendment did nothing more than grant federal power to enforce the equal protection principles of the Comity Clause. If this were the case, then the Amendment would do nothing more than authorize federal power to force the states to provide equal access to state-conferred rights. Bingham, however, had a much broader goal in mind for his proposed amendment, one based on his idiosyncratic understanding of the Comity Clause of Article IV. According to Bingham's "ellipsis" understanding of the Clause, the privileges and immunities of citizens (of the United States) in the several states included federally enumerated rights, especially those listed in the first eight amendments. From Bingham's point of view, Republicans like Higby, Price, and Woodbridge had wrongly narrowed the scope of the proposed amendment when they claimed that it did nothing more than authorize federal enforcement of the equal-access reading Comity Clause.

---

[153] CONG. GLOBE, 39th Cong., 1st Sess. 1065 (1866).

Unfortunately, Bingham's "ellipsis" theory of Article IV was so odd and idiosyncratic that it appears that no other Republican followed his argument. Because his first draft used the exact language of the Comity Clause, members naturally assumed that the proposed amendment referred to the same common law state-protected rights discussed in antebellum cases and treatises. Radical Republicans saw the Comity Clause language in Bingham's proposal as granting federal power to define and protect the "fundamental" common law rights described by Justice Washington in *Corfield v. Coryell*. Mainstream Republicans, on the other hand, saw the language as simply allowing Congress to enforce equal access to state-defined and -conferred civil rights, a reading of the Comity Clause found in antebellum cases like *Corfield*, *Campbell*, *Livingston*, and *Abbott*, as well as in legal treatises like those of Kent and Story.

Bingham, of course, had neither goal in mind. His effort was to protect rights conferred not by state governments but by the federal Constitution, rights that included those listed in the Bill of Rights. Justice Washington's list of state-protected rights in *Corfield v. Coryell* was completely irrelevant to Bingham's effort. This is why Bingham never mentioned *Corfield* or Justice Washington's list at any time during the debates over the framing and adoption of the Fourteenth Amendment – a point that seems to have gone unnoticed in previous historical work on the Fourteenth Amendment.

In his speech of February 28, Bingham needed to explain why protecting the Bill of Rights against state action was necessary (a noncontroversial goal even to conservative Republicans like Robert Hale) while at the same time assuring moderates that the only rights to be protected against state action were those that the Constitution had already placed beyond the proper scope of state power. This limitation was critical because it would rescue Bingham's proposal from the fatal accusation that his amendment would obliterate the properly reserved powers and rights of the states. Bingham began by addressing the most critical problem facing the Amendment's passage, the federalism-based concerns of conservative Republicans:

> I repel the suggestion made here in the heat of debate, that the committee or any of its members who favor this proposition seek in any form to mar the Constitution of the country, or take away from any State any right that belongs to it, or from any citizen of any State any right that belongs to him under that Constitution. The proposition pending before the House is simply a proposition to arm the Congress of the United States, by the consent of the people of the United States, with the power to enforce the bill of rights as it stands in the Constitution today. It "hath that extent – no more."[154]

---

[154] CONG. GLOBE, 39th Cong., 1st Sess. 1088 (1866).

Right out of the gate, Bingham threaded the needle by rejecting both unduly narrow and unduly broad readings of the proposed amendment. The goal was to secure far more than just equal state-conferred rights; he sought nothing less than the enforcement of the Bill of Rights against the states. On the other hand, his amendment had nothing to do with radical efforts to nationalize the countless common law and natural rights traditionally regulated by the states. His proposed amendment sought only "to enforce the Bill of Rights as it stands in the Constitution today. It 'hath that extent – no more.'"[155]

Quoting the Article IV and Fifth Amendment language of his proposal, Bingham challenged his colleagues to join him in supporting federal enforcement of the Bill of Rights:

> What do gentlemen say to these provisions? "Oh, we favor that; we agree with the President that the basis of the American system is the right of every man to life, liberty, and the pursuit of happiness; we agree that the Constitution declares the right of every citizen of the United States to the enjoyment of all privileges and immunities of citizens in the several States, and of all persons to be protected in life, liberty, and property."

> Gentlemen admit the force of the provisions in the bill of rights, that the citizens of the United States shall be entitled to all the privileges and immunities of citizens of the United States in the several States, and that no person shall be deprived of life, liberty, or property without due process of law; but they say, "We are opposed to its enforcement by act of Congress under an amended Constitution, as proposed." That is the sum and substance of all the argument that we have heard on this subject. Why are gentlemen opposed to the enforcement of the bill of rights, as proposed? Because they aver it would interfere with the reserved rights of the States! Who ever before heard that any State had reserved to itself the right, under the Constitution of the United States, to withhold from any citizen of the United States within its limits, under any pretext whatever, any of the privileges of a citizen of the United States, or to impose upon him, no matter from what State he may have come, any burden contrary to that provision of the Constitution which declares that the citizen shall be entitled in the several States to all the immunities of a citizen of the United States?[156]

There are four key moves to Bingham's argument. First, he had based the language of his proposal on the express text of the original Constitution: the Comity Clause and the Fifth Amendment. Second, the privileges and immunities protected against state abridgement by the Comity Clause included

---

[155] *Id.*
[156] *Id.* at 1089.

enumerated rights such as those found in the Bill of Rights. Third, state officials take an oath to uphold the Constitution, including the Comity Clause,
making state enforcement of the Clause obligatory. Fourth, because states are
obliged to enforce the Comity Clause and provisions like the Fifth Amendment under the original Constitution, federal enforcement of these rights
would not intrude on the reserved powers and rights of the states.

Bingham's second move, his assumption that the Comity Clause was part
of the Bill of Rights, was critical to the success of his overall argument. Neither
the Fifth Amendment nor any of the other first eight amendments mentioned
the states. This lack of express language binding the states led the Supreme
Court in *Barron v. Baltimore* to conclude that the Bill of Rights bound only the
federal government.[157] The Comity Clause, however, *does* expressly require
the States to protect the "privileges and immunities of citizens in the several
States."[158] If these privileges and immunities included the rights listed in the
Bill of Rights, then this would provide the textual basis for requiring the states to
enforce the Bill of Rights. This is where Bingham applied his "ellipsis" reading
of the Comity Clause: States shall not violate the "privileges and immunities
of citizens (applying the ellipsis 'of the United States') in the several States."[159]
Since the Bill of Rights clearly involves the rights of citizens of the United
States, the Comity Clause, read with the ellipsis, must include the Bill of
Rights. The result is a Comity Clause that binds the states to protect the Bill of
Rights. Although rather complicated, Bingham's reading of Article IV allowed
him to plausibly claim that his proposed amendment placed no constraint on
the states than that already contained in the original Constitution. As Bingham
put it, the Amendment did not "take away from any State any right that belongs
to it."[160]

Although his reasoning was complicated, his ultimate goal was neither
difficult to grasp nor particularly unpopular. Bingham shared what was then
a widespread idea that states, if not expressly bound to respect the Bill of
Rights, nevertheless ought to protect such fundamental rights of American
citizenship. In many ways, Bingham simply echoed antebellum judicial and
political rhetoric that increasingly interpreted the Bill of Rights as declaring
rights that ought to be respected by all levels of government.[161] Bingham
was so certain that his fellow members agreed with this idea that he made
their assumed acceptance a key part of his argument: "Gentlemen *admit* the

[157] 32 U.S. (7 Pet.) 243, 250–51 (1833).
[158] U.S. Const. art. IV, § 2, cl. 1.
[159] *See supra* notes 140–153 and accompanying text.
[160] Cong. Globe, 39th Cong., 1st Sess. 1088 (1866).
[161] *See* Amar, note 18, at 145.

force of the provisions in the bill of rights. . . . "[162] Although interruptions were common during these debates, and Bingham would be interrupted during this particular speech, there was no interruption here. In fact, despite Bingham's repeated insistence that his effort went toward making the states comply with the Bill of Rights, no member spoke against that effort at any time during the debates. Nor is it likely his effort was misunderstood outside the halls of Congress; in the next chapter, we will learn that public supporters and critics alike understood that Bingham's efforts that spring were focused on requiring the states to protect liberties listed in the first eight amendments.

The objections that *were* raised involved the potential nationalization of common law civil rights, an area of law that most members believed ought to remain under the control of the states. Placing the enumerable subjects of the common law under federal control would destroy the traditional separation of federal and state power. Bingham, of course, believed that the only substantive rights addressed by his proposal were the "privileges and immunities (of citizens of the United States) in the several states," a category Bingham understood to include rights listed in the Constitution and not common law rights in the states. The latter remained under the control of the states, subject only to the requirement that all persons receive the protection of due process before deprivation of life, liberty, or property. Again, because Bingham believed Article IV *already* obligated states to protect the privileges and immunities of citizens of the United States, he insisted that his proposal took away no rights properly belonging to the states under the original Constitution.[163]

Believing that he had established the limited goals of the proposed amendment, Bingham next turned to Hale's argument that states were already bound to enforce the Bill of Rights. Here, Bingham cited Supreme Court cases like *Barron v. Baltimore* and *Livingston v. Moore*, in which the Court had held that

---

[162] CONG. GLOBE, 39th Cong., 1st Sess. 1088 (1866).

[163] According to Bingham:

> It will be noticed, [Mr. Hale of New York] takes care not to utter one single word in opposition to that part of the amendment which seeks the enforcement of the second section of the fourth article of the Constitution of the United States, but by his silence gives his assent to it. But the gentleman reiterates the old cry of State rights, and says, "You are impairing State rights." I would like to know, and when the gentleman comes to make another argument on this subject, I respectfully ask him to inform us whence he derives the authority for supposing, if he does so suppose, that any State has the right to deny to a citizen of any other State any of the privileges or immunities of a citizen of the United States. And if a State has not the right to do that, how can the right of a State be impaired by giving to the people of the United States by constitutional amendment the power by congressional enactment to enforce this provision of their Constitution?

CONG. GLOBE, 39th Cong., 1st Sess. 1089 (1866). In his speech of the previous day, Hale had begged off addressing Article IV when prompted by Bingham. *See supra* note 145 and accompanying text.

the Bill of Rights in general, and the Fifth Amendment in particular, were not applicable to the states.[164] Bingham then quickly pivoted and explained that, although the Bill of Rights was not judicially enforceable against the states, the states nevertheless remained obligated to enforce the Bill of Rights as part of their oath to uphold the Federal Constitution:

> Sir, I stand relieved to-day from entering into any extended argument in answer to these decisions of your courts, that although as ruled the existing amendments are not applicable to and do not bind the States, they are nevertheless to be enforced and observed in States by the grand utterance of that immortal man, who, while he lived, stood alone in intellectual power among the living men of his country.... I refer to that grand argument never yet answered, and never to be answered while human language shall be spoken by living man, wherein Mr. Webster says:... "The Constitution utters its behests in the name and by authority of the people, and it does not exact from States any plighted public faith to maintain it. On the contrary, it makes its own preservation depend on individual duty and individual obliga-tion.... It incapacitates any man to sit in the Legislature of a State who shall not first have taken his solemn oath to support the Constitution of the United States. From the obligation of this no State power can discharge him."[165]

By failing to observe the rights of US citizens guaranteed in the Bill of Rights, state officials had violated their oaths and would continue to do so absent federal compulsion.

> Those oaths have been disregarded; those requirements of our Constitution have been broken; they are disregarded to-day in Oregon; they are disregarded to-day, and have been disregarded for the last five, ten, or twenty years in every one of the eleven States recently in insurrection.

> The question is, simply, whether you will give by this amendment to the people of the United States the power, by legislative enactment, to punish officials of States for violation of the oaths enjoined upon them by their Constitution? That is the question, and the whole question. The adoption of the proposed amendment will take from the States no rights that belong to the States. They elect their Legislatures; they enact their laws.... Is the bill of rights to stand in our Constitution hereafter, as in the past five years within eleven States, a mere dead letter? It is absolutely essential to the safety of the people that it should be enforced.[166]

[164] CONG. GLOBE, 39th Cong., 1st Sess. 1089–90 (1866).

[165] *Id.* at 1090 (quoting Daniel Webster, A Speech Delivered in the Senate of the United States, on the 16th of February, 1833: The Constitution Not a Compact between Sovereign States [Feb. 16, 1833], *in* 3 THE WORKS OF DANIEL WEBSTER 452, 471 [9th ed. 1856]).

[166] CONG. GLOBE, 39th Cong., 1st Sess. 1090 (1866).

In order "to secure the enforcement of these provisions of the bill of rights in every State," Congress must be granted power to force state compliance.[167] Bingham claimed that such power would have been granted in the original Constitution "but for the fact that its insertion in the Constitution would have been utterly incompatible with the existence of slavery in any State; for although slaves might not have been admitted to be citizens they must have been admitted to be persons" – and thus protected by the Due Process Clause of the Fifth Amendment.[168] In short, "gentlemen who oppose this amendment oppose the grant of power to enforce the bill of rights."[169]

Bingham's speech was published in newspapers such as the *New York Times*, and it was also published as a separate pamphlet entitled *"In Support of the Proposed Amendment To Enforce the Bill of Rights."*[170] There seems good reason, therefore, to believe that informed members of Congress and the public were aware of Bingham's arguments. The critical issues, however, involve (1) whether people understood his arguments regarding Article IV and its relationship to his original draft of the Fourteenth Amendment and (2) whether they agreed with his arguments. It appears that neither was the case.

4. Moderate Opposition: The Speech of Giles Hotchkiss

Soon after Bingham finished his defense of his first draft of the Fourteenth Amendment, New York Republican Giles Hotchkiss rose in opposition to the proposed amendment. Hotchkiss's opposition was a body blow to Bingham's effort. As an influential mainstream Republican, Hotchkiss's support of any amendment was critical to its success.[171] In fact, immediately after Hotchkiss spoke in opposition, Bingham moved to postpone further discussion of his

---

[167] *Id.*

[168] *Id.*

[169] *Id.*

[170] *See* John Bingham, One Country, One Constitution, and One People: Speech of Hon. John A. Bingham, of Ohio, in the House of Representatives, February 28, 1866, In Support of the Proposed Amendment To Enforce the Bill of Rights (1866); *Thirty-ninth Congress First Session*, N.Y. Times, Mar. 1, 1866, at 4; *Legislative Acts or Legal Proceedings*, Phila. Inquirer, Mar. 1, 1866, at 8.

[171] According to Earl Maltz, Hotchkiss was a "mainstream Republican." Maltz, *supra* note 21, at 39; *see also id.* at 39–40 ("In the political context of the early Reconstruction era, the position taken by such men [such as Thomas Davis, Roscoe Conkling, Giles W. Hotchkiss and William M. Stewart] was to prove decisive"). According to Michael Kent Curtis, Hotchkiss's speech opposing Bingham's amendment was "particularly influential." Michael Kent Curtis, *The Klan, the Congress and the Court: Congressional Enforcement of the Fourteenth and Fifteenth Amendments & the State Action Syllogism, a Brief Historical Review*, 11 U. Pa. J. Const. L. 1381, 1390 (2009).

proposal.[172] In effect, Hotchkiss's opposition prompted Bingham to withdraw his own proposal and go back to the drawing board, only to emerge weeks later with a completely different draft.

Hotchkiss began by asserting his "desire to secure every privilege and every right to every citizen in the United States that the gentleman who reports this resolution desires to secure."[173] Hotchkiss then stated what he believed was the purpose behind Bingham's amendment:

> As I understand it, [Mr. Bingham's] object in offering this resolution and proposing this amendment is to provide that no State shall discriminate between its citizens and give one class of citizens greater rights than it confers upon another. If this amendment secured that, I should vote very cheerfully for it to-day; but as I do not regard it as permanently securing those rights, I shall vote to postpone its consideration until there can be a further conference between the friends of the measure, and we can devise some means whereby we shall secure those rights beyond a question.[174]

This purportedly "friendly" description of his amendment must have surprised Bingham. Bingham had just spent considerable time on the floor of the House explaining how he wished to accomplish far *more* than simply the equal protection of state-conferred rights. He had explained in detail how the Comity Clause should be read as containing an "ellipsis" that referred to the rights of citizens of the United States – rights that included the substantive protections listed in the Bill of Rights that state officials had taken an oath to enforce. Hotchkiss, however, ignored Bingham's complicated "ellipsis" argument and instead read the proposed amendment as an effort to enforce the Comity Clause as traditionally understood. It was not that Hotchkiss opposed applying the Bill of Rights against the states[175]; he simply saw nothing in the Amendment that *implicated* the federal Bill of Rights. Instead, Hotchkiss presumed the

---

[172] CONG. GLOBE, 39th Cong., 1st Sess. 1095 (1866). The *Congressional Globe* does not specify who made the final successful motion to postpone, but Bingham later reminded his colleagues that he had been the motion's author. *See* CONG. GLOBE, 42d Cong., 1st Sess. app. 115 (1871) (remarks of Rep. Bingham) ("I made the motion myself to postpone and make it an order for that day, but I did not choose to call it up."); *see also id.* (remarks of Rep. Farnsworth) (stating that Bingham's first draft of the Fourteenth Amendment "slept the sleep that knows no waking").

[173] CONG. GLOBE, 39th Cong., 1st Sess. 1095 (1866).

[174] *Id.*

[175] Hotchkiss supported Bingham's second draft of the Fourteenth Amendment that both Bingham and Howard insisted protected rights listed in the first eight amendments. *See* CONG. GLOBE, 39th Cong., 1st Sess. 2545 (May 10, 1866) (listing the House members voting in favor of the second draft of the Fourteenth Amendment).

proposal was nothing more than an effort to authorize federal enforcement of the equal-access principle of the Comity Clause of Article IV.

This led to a second problem for Bingham. As had Higby, Price, Woodridge, and Hale, Hotchkiss also presumed that by using the language of the Comity Clause, the proposed amendment granted federal power to enforce equal protection of those rights that antebellum courts had identified as protected under the Comity Clause. Conservatives opposed such a result because it allowed too great an intrusion into the reserved powers and rights of the States. Hotchkiss agreed, especially because the Republicans might not always be a majority of the federal Congress. As Hotchkiss explained:

> I understand the amendment as now proposed by its terms to authorize Congress to establish uniform laws throughout the United States upon the subject named, the protection of life, liberty, and property. I am unwilling that Congress shall have any such power. Congress already has the power to establish a uniform rule of naturalization and uniform laws upon the subject of bankruptcy. That is as far as I am willing that Congress shall go. The object of a Constitution is not only to confer power upon the majority, but to restrict the power of the majority and to protect the rights of the minority. It is not indulging in imagination to any great stretch to suppose that we may have a Congress here who would establish such rules in my State as I should be unwilling to be governed by. Should the power of this Government, as the gentleman from Ohio fears, pass into the hands of the rebels, I do not want rebel laws to govern and be uniform throughout this Union.[176]

At this point, Bingham interrupted Hotchkiss and gamely repeated his "ellipsis" reading of the Comity Clause and his argument that the proposal would do nothing more than authorize federal enforcement of rights already listed in the Constitution. "The gentleman will pardon me," interjected Bingham:

> The amendment is exactly in the language of the Constitution; that is to say, it secures to the citizen of each of the States all the privileges and immunities of citizens of the several States. It is not to transfer the laws of one State to another State at all. It is to secure to the citizens of each State all the privileges and immunities of citizens of the United States in the several States. If the State laws do not interfere, those immunities follow under the Constitution.[177]

In reply, Hotchkiss ignored Bingham's effort to explain the "ellipsis" reading of the Comity Clause and simply retorted "[c]onstitutions should have their

[176] Cong. Globe, 39th Cong., 1st Sess. 1095 (1866).
[177] *Id.*

provisions so plain that it will be unnecessary for courts to give construction to them; they should be so plain that the common mind can understand them."[178] Apparently defeated, Bingham sat down and had nothing more to say prior to his moving to postpone discussion on his first draft of the Fourteenth Amendment.[179]

Hotchkiss, however, had more to say. He supported the effort "to provide against a discrimination to the injury or exclusion of any class of citizens in any State from the privileges which other classes enjoy, the right should be incorporated into the Constitution."[180] As drafted, however, the nature of these equal rights was left to the control of Congress and subject to federal legislation. This was improper. The goal of the Amendment should be "a constitutional right that cannot be wrested from any class of citizens, or from the citizens of any State by mere legislation." Instead, Bingham had drafted an amendment that "proposes to leave it to the caprice of Congress; and your legislation upon the subject would depend upon the political majority of Congress, and not upon two thirds of Congress and three fourths of the States."[181] Hotchkiss insisted that the Republicans should use their current political numbers and "secure those rights against accidents, against the accidental majority of Congress."[182] Drawing laughter from the other members, Hotchkiss explained:

> Mr. Speaker, I make these remarks because I do not wish to be placed in the wrong upon this question. I think the gentleman from Ohio [Mr. Bingham] is not sufficiently radical in his views upon this subject. I think he is a conservative. [Laughter] I do not make the remark in any offensive sense. But I want him to go to the root of this matter.
>
> His amendment is not as strong as the Constitution now is. The Constitution now gives equal rights to a certain extent to all citizens. This amendment provides that Congress may pass laws to enforce these rights. Why not provide by an amendment to the Constitution that no State shall discriminate against any class of its citizens; and let that amendment stand as part of the organic law of the land, subject only to be defeated by another constitutional amendment. . . .

---

[178] *Id.*

[179] According to Earl Maltz, "[t]he fact that criticisms came from the Republican as well as the Democratic side of the aisle made it clear that the Bingham amendment could not obtain the two-thirds majority necessary for passage. In order to avoid outright defeat, on February 20 Bingham joined in voting to postpone final consideration of his proposal." MALTZ, *supra* note 21, at 59–60.

[180] CONG. GLOBE, 39th Cong., 1st Sess. 1095 (1866).

[181] *Id.*

[182] *Id.*

Let us have a little time to compare our views upon this subject and agree upon an amendment that shall secure beyond question what the gentleman desires to secure. It is with that view, and no other, that I shall vote to postpone this subject for the present.[183]

Hotchkiss's objections revealed the fatal flaw in Bingham's attempt to use the wording of Article IV's Comity Clause to enforce the Bill of Rights. Although his draft had the advantage of using an existing constitutional text (thus reassuring the moderates), it had the disadvantage of calling into play antebellum case law that had construed the Comity Clause as involving equal access to state-conferred civil rights. Bingham believed this language referred to national rights contained in the first eight amendments, but this required one to read an "ellipsis" into the text. Unable or unwilling to embrace Bingham's "ellipsis," however, members ended up debating the merits of federal control of common law civil rights – an outcome moderates and conservatives would never accept and that Bingham himself wanted to avoid. Even Hotchkiss, a man who described himself as a friend of the proposal and the goals Bingham was trying to accomplish, did not read the first section as establishing equal rights among classes within a state, much less as protecting substantive national rights. Hotchkiss believed Bingham sought nothing more than congressional enforcement of Article IV as commonly described in antebellum case law. He did not read any "ellipsis" into the Comity Clause, and he believed the first half of Bingham's proposal "confer[ed] no additional powers" upon Congress beyond those necessary to enforce the equality principle of Article IV.[184] Worse, Hotchkiss read the second section as going far beyond what Bingham and the moderates wanted in terms of federal power to interfere with the states.[185]

---

[183] *Id.* On March 1, the *New York Times* reported that

> Mr. Hotchkiss explained why he should vote in a manner that might be regarded as inconsistent with his usual vote. He did not regard the proposed amendment as permanently securing the rights and privileges of every citizen, and was, therefore, in favor of its postponement until there could be further conference with the friends of the measure and some means devised by which these rights could be secured beyond question.

The *Times* then reported the positive vote for postponement. *Thirty-Ninth Congress, First Session, supra* note 170, at 5.

[184] CONG. GLOBE, 39th Cong., 1st Sess. 1095 (1866).

[185] According to Pamela Brandwein, "Bingham's fellow Republicans balked at the proposal, in part because it would permit Congress to pass municipal codes of civil and criminal law. . . . This was unacceptable to centrist Republicans." PAMELA BRANDWEIN, RETHINKING THE JUDICIAL SETTLEMENT OF RECONSTRUCTION 38 (2011). As the *Springfield Daily Republican* put it, "no sane man supposes that the states would ratify such an amendment. . . . The people will welcome every indication that Congress discards this policy and the leaders who urge it." *Some Hopeful Signs*, SPRINGFIELD DAILY REPUBLICAN, Mar. 2, 1866, at 2.

Realizing his initial effort could not succeed (or, worse, would be mis-construed in the future), Bingham withdrew his own proposal.[186] Although couched in the language of a postponement, Bingham's initial draft was never revived.[187] When Bingham ultimately produced a new draft of the Fourteenth Amendment, the language of Article IV was gone.

IV. INTERMEZZO: THE DEBATE ON THE CIVIL RIGHTS ACT OF 1866

Scholars have long looked to the debates over the Civil Rights Act of 1866 for clues regarding the Thirty-Ninth Congress's intentions for the Fourteenth Amendment. The Act and the Amendment were debated and passed at roughly the same time, and many of the arguments in support of the Act reappeared during the debates over the Fourteenth Amendment. For example, one can find numerous references to Justice Washington's list of fundamental "priv-ileges and immunities" in *Corfield v. Coryell* in both sets of debates. The closeness in time and the seemingly similar references have led a number of scholars to conclude that the Civil Rights Act in general, and *Corfield* in par-ticular, can be used as guides to understanding the meaning of the Privileges or Immunities Clause of the Fourteenth Amendment.[188]

As we shall see, however, one cannot conflate the Act and the Amendment. The texts were proposed by different men and for different purposes: John

---

[186] CONG. GLOBE, 39th Cong., 1st Sess. 1095 (1866). Scholars see Bingham's vote as strategic. MALTZ, *supra* note 21, at 60 (arguing that Bingham agreed to withdraw his amendment "in order to avoid outright defeat."). According to Bingham himself, "I made the motion myself to postpone and make it an order for that day, but I did not choose to call it up." CONG. GLOBE, 42d Cong., 1st Sess. app. at 115 (1871).

[187] See CONG. GLOBE, 42d Cong., 1st Sess. app. 115 (1871) (remarks of Rep. Farnsworth) (stating that Bingham's first draft of the Fourteenth Amendment "slept the sleep that knows no waking").

[188] Most contemporary historical legal scholarship that discusses references to *Corfield* in the Thirty-Ninth Congress cites various instances in which the case was discussed but ignores the deep disagreements between members regarding the proper reading of the case and the antebellum jurisprudence of Article IV. *See, e.g.,* AMAR, THE BILL OF RIGHTS, *supra* note 18 at 177–78 (citing several references to *Corfield* without discussing opposing views); RANDY BARNETT, RESTORING THE LOST CONSTITUTION: THE PRESUMPTION OF LIBERTY 60–68 (2004) (citing several references to *Corfield* in the Reconstruction Congress and concluding that *Corfield* described "natural or inherent rights" and that Congress viewed Article IV and Section One as protecting the same set of rights); JOHN HART ELY, DEMOCRACY AND DISTRUST: A THEORY OF JUDICIAL REVIEW 29 (1980) (noting that the members of the Thirty-Ninth Congress referred "repeatedly" to *Corfield's* interpretation of Article IV as the "key" to what they were writing without discussing opposing views); Erwin Chemerinsky, *The Supreme Court and the Fourteenth Amendment: The Unfulfilled Promise,* 25 LOY. L.A. L. REV. 1143, 1145 (1992) (citing a reference to *Corfield* without discussing opposing views).

Bingham, for example, drafted Section One of the Fourteenth Amendment but he *did not* support the Civil Rights Act. Similarly, although Radical Republicans commonly referred to *Corfield v. Coryell* early in the debates over the Civil Rights Act, John Bingham *never once* referred to *Corfield* during the debates over the Fourteenth Amendment. Finally, and probably most problematically in terms of prior Fourteenth Amendment scholarship, members of the Thirty-Ninth Congress shared radically different views of *Corfield*, so much so that Radical Republican leaders in the Thirty-Ninth Congress ultimately stopped referring to *Corfield* altogether. In short, despite the common assertion to the contrary in Fourteenth Amendment scholarship, there appears to be little evidence that the Fourteenth Amendment represented a consensus attempt to constitutionalize the Civil Rights Act by adopting the language of the Comity Clause and embracing the opinion of Justice Bushrod Washington.

That said, it is not my contention that the clash of competing ideas and ideologies in the Thirty-Ninth Congress produced critically ambiguous texts whose legally operative meaning would have to be later worked out by the courts and the political process. Quite the opposite: It was *because* of the vigorous and extended debates over textual meaning and constitutional policy that we can come to reasonable conclusions about consensus views in the Thirty-Ninth Congress and the likely meaning and scope of provisions like the Privileges or Immunities Clause. Not only do the debates reveal a controlling influence of the moderate Republican balance between protecting rights and preserving federalism, the debates over the Civil Rights Act clarified to the members themselves how certain language was likely to be understood, by both fellow members and by the broader public. The fruits of all this disagreement and debate resulted in a second draft more understandable to the members of the Thirty-Ninth Congress – and to us.

A. *The First Draft of the Civil Rights Bill*

The Civil Rights Bill was introduced by Senator Lyman Trumbull on January 5, 1866.[189] This was early in the first session of the Thirty-Ninth Congress and long before the Republicans realized that, to be successful, their efforts would have to meet the approval of two-thirds of their colleagues. It would not be until after Andrew Johnson's veto of Freedmen's Bureau Act and the failure to attract enough votes for a legislative override that radical Republicans like Trumbull and James Wilson would be forced to trim their efforts and their

---

[189] CONG. GLOBE, 39th Cong., 1st Sess. 129 (1866).

arguments in order to attract the votes of the moderates. In January, however, the Republicans fully expected Johnson to support both the Freedmen's
Bureau and Civil Rights bills.[190]

The initial draft of the Civil Rights Act of 1866 reflected the radical Republican theory of natural rights and federal power to protect the liberty of all
individuals. There was nothing in this first draft relating to the rights of American citizens. Instead, the Act guaranteed equal civil rights to all "inhabitants of
any State or territory of the United States."[191] Presumably its drafters realized
that this would not necessarily guarantee equal rights for the newly freed blacks
if states continue to follow the despised doctrine of *Dred Scott* and refuse to
afford free blacks the status of American citizen. Accordingly, even before the
debates on the Bill began in the House and Senate, its sponsors amended the
proposal.

On January 29, Trumbull moved to add a sentence at the beginning of the
Bill that declared "all persons of African descent born in the United States are
hereby declared to be citizens of the United States."[192] Within days, Trumbull
would further amend the opening clause to read "[t]hat all persons born in
the United States, and not subject to any foreign power, are hereby declared
to be citizens of the United States."[193] By the time the Bill reached its final
form, the first sentence declared "[t]hat all persons born in the United States
and not subject to any foreign power, excluding Indians not taxed, are hereby
declared to be citizens of the United States."[194] According to Earl Maltz, "the
relationship between citizens of the United States and the federal government
became the anchor to which the Civil Rights Bill was attached."[195] In fact,
amending the Bill so that its sole application involved citizens of the United

---

[190] FONER, *supra* note 26, at 247.

[191] The original draft declared:

> [T]here shall be no discrimination in civil rights or immunities among the inhabitants
> of any State or Territory of the United States on account of race, color, or previous
> condition of slavery; but the inhabitants of every race and color . . . shall have the same
> right to make and enforce contracts, to sue, be parties, and give evidence, to inherit,
> purchase, lease, sell, hold, and convey real and personal property, and to full and equal
> benefit of all laws and proceedings for the security of person and property, and shall be
> subject to like punishment, pains, and penalties, and to none other.

See CONG. GLOBE, 39th Cong., 1st Sess. 211 (Jan. 12, 1866).

[192] *Id.* at 474. According to Trumbull, congressional power to confer citizenship could be found
in the power "to establish a uniform rule of naturalization." *See id.* at 475 (in response to a
challenge by Mr. Van Winkle).

[193] *Id.* at 498 (Jan. 30, 1866).

[194] CONG. GLOBE, 39th Cong., 1st Sess. 1366.

[195] EARL M. MALTZ, THE FOURTEENTH AMENDMENT AND THE LAW OF THE CONSTITUTION 58
(2003).

States signaled an emerging focus on the rights of American citizenship that would dominate the debates of both the Civil Rights Bill and the second version of the Fourteenth Amendment.[196]

In his initial remarks on the Bill, Trumbull explained that the purpose of the amended Bill was to secure "the privileges which are essential to freemen" and expressly grounded the statute on congressional power to enforce the Thirteenth Amendment: "Any statute which is not equal to all, and which deprives any citizen of civil rights which are secured to other citizens, is an unjust encroachment of his liberty; and is, in fact, a badge of servitude which, by the Constitution, is prohibited."[197] Trumbull held an expansive view of power to abolish the "badges of servitude," which he insisted included laws that denied blacks the equal right to teach, preach, and bear arms.[198] Trumbull believed that the protections of the Thirteenth Amendment went beyond mere equality, however, and in fact established a baseline set of fundamental rights for all American citizens, which included the list of common law rights described by Justice Washington in the Article IV case *Corfield v. Coryell.*[199]

Such broad interpretations of federal power were unlikely to reassure wavering moderate Republicans. Most members of the Thirty-Ninth Congress were unwilling to embrace either Justice Story's reasoning in *Prigg* or the concept of unenumerated federal power.[200] Delaware's Democratic Senator Willard Saulsbury declared that the Bill was "one of the most dangerous that was ever introduced into the Senate of the United States."[201] Moderates, such as Columbus Delano of Ohio, were also concerned. By claiming congressional power to define and protect the "civil rights" of citizenship, Delano warned, "[y]ou render this Government no longer a Government of limited powers; you concentrate and consolidate here an extent of authority which will swallow up all or nearly all of the rights of the States with respect to the property, the liberties, and the lives of its citizens."[202]

One particular line of argument directly challenged the radical Republican interpretation of the Privileges and Immunities Clause of Article IV. According to Unionist Senator Garrett Davis of Kentucky, supporters of the Bill were

---

[196] Within days, Trumbull would further amend the opening clause to read "That all persons born in the United States, and not subject to any foreign power, are hereby declared to be citizens of the United States, without distinction of color, and there shall be no discrimination in civil rights and immunities. . . . " Cong. Globe, 39th Cong., 1st Sess. 498 (Jan. 30, 1866).

[197] *Id.*

[198] *Id.* at 474.

[199] *Id.* at 474, 475.

[200] Maltz, *supra* note 21, at 64–65.

[201] Cong. Globe, 39th Cong., 1st Sess. 476 (1866).

[202] *Id.* app. at 158.

wrong to rely on Article IV as a source of power to define and enforce national privileges and immunities. The Comity Clause involved nothing more than the right of sojourning citizens to receive the same state-conferred rights as state citizens.[203] In support of this traditional reading of Article IV, Davis spent "an hour of his speech"[204] quoting from and explaining decisions in cases like *Campbell*, *Abbott*, and *Corfield*.[205] After quoting the "fundamental rights" section of Washington's *Corfield* opinion, Davis declared that "[a]ll these rights and privileges are attributed by the decision of the court to the citizens of one State going into another State. . . . The opinions relied on by the honorable Senator do not establish any other proposition."[206] Finally, Davis insisted that Congress lacked the power to confer the status of American citizenship on persons born and living in one of the several states. "Congress has no power to make a citizen," declared Davis, other than by "treaty acquiring territory with inhabitants, or they may be made according to the uniform rule of naturalization which Congress is authorized by the Constitution to establish; and they cannot be made in any other way."[207]

Trumbull responded that Congress had on a number of occasions conferred American citizenship on groups of persons already residing on United States territory. "As long ago as 1802," Trumbull pointed out, "the Congress of the United States declared that the children of persons naturalized in this country, if the children were underage, should become citizens of the United States. Without going through the process of naturalization at all, they were declared by act of Congress to be citizens of the country."[208] Trumbull also quoted the 1843 Act that bestowed the status of American citizenship on the Stockbridge Indian Tribe:

> That the Stockbridge Tribe of Indians, and each and every one of them, shall be deemed to be, and are hereby declared to be, citizens of the United States to all intents and purposes, and shall be entitled to all the rights, privileges and immunities of such citizens, and shall in all respects be subject to the laws of the United States.[209]

Trumbull's precedents were not precisely on point, since none of them involved a group currently residing in particular state. Still, they did count

---

[203] *Id.* at 595 (Feb. 2, 1866).
[204] *Id.* at 600 (remarks of Sen. Trumbull in response to Davis's speech).
[205] *Id.* at 595–97 (remarks of Sen. Davis).
[206] *Id.* at 597.
[207] *Id.*
[208] *Id.*
[209] *Id.* at 600.

as prior examples of Congress declaring a certain group eligible to enjoy "the rights, privileges and immunities" of citizens of the United States. Explaining his use of *Corfield* was more difficult. Davis had been correct in describing those cases as involving not the fundamental rights of citizens of the United States, but only the state-secured rights of citizens in the several states. Confronted with clear and uncontradicted precedent, Trumbull unconvincingly responded that he had "never denied" *Corfield* involved nothing other than state-level privileges and immunities. His point in raising the case, Trumbull explained, was only "for the purpose of ascertaining, if we could, by judicial decision what was meant by the term 'citizen of the United States.'"

> [I]nasmuch as there had been judicial decisions upon this clause of the Constitution, in which it had been held that the rights of the citizen of the United States were certain great fundamental rights, such as the right to life, to liberty, and to avail one's self of all the laws passed for the benefit of the citizen to enable him to enforce his rights; inasmuch as this was the definition given to the term as applied in that part of the Constitution, I reasoned from that, that when the Constitution had been amended and slavery abolished, and we were about to pass a law declaring every person, no matter what color, born in the United States a citizen of the United States, the same rights would then appertain to all persons who were clothed with American citizenship. That was the object for which those cases were introduced. The Senator seems to suppose, and argue to show what no one would controvert, that they were not cases deciding upon the rights of the citizen in the State in which he resided.[210]

Whether or not Trumbull's attempt to walk back his earlier use of *Corfield* was particularly persuasive, it was clear that Trumbull believed Congress *somehow* had power both to bestow the status of national citizenship and to define and protect what Congress perceived to be its attendant rights.[211] Despite the misgivings of a significant minority, on February 2 the Senate passed the Civil Rights Act by a vote of 33 to 12.[212]

---

[210] *Id.*

[211] Trumbull had made a similar point earlier in the debate:

> [A]s a question of power, the Federal government has the power to make every inhabitant of Pennsylvania a citizen. Then could not every inhabitant of Pennsylvania own real estate, and could Pennsylvania deny the right? . . . [T]he Federal Government has authority to make every inhabitant of Pennsylvania a citizen, and clothe him with the authority to inherit and buy real estate, and the State of Pennsylvania cannot help it.

CONG. GLOBE, 39th Cong., 1st Sess. 500 (1866).

[212] *Id.* at 606–07.

B. *Debating in the Shadow of Johnson's Veto of the Freedmen's Bill: The House*

On February 19, just prior to the House debates on the Civil Rights Bill, President Johnson vetoed the Freedmen's Bureau Bill.[213] The impact of the President's veto was enough to convince eight Republican Senators to withdraw their support for the Freedmen's Bill, and the subsequent attempted override failed by two votes.[214] Both the veto and the failed override caught Congress by surprise,[215] and they inaugurated a political reality that would haunt the remainder of that session. To be successful, legislative proposals would have to gain the support of two-thirds of both houses of Congress, the amount necessary to override a veto or pass a proposed constitutional amendment. Republican leaders were well aware of their precarious position and the need to lock in every vote possible, even to the point of removing a Democratic Senator on what historians have described as rather "questionable" grounds.[216] As the debate on the Civil Rights Act continued, it did so under the shadow of Johnson's February veto and with the realization that both the text and its underlying theory would have to command a supermajority of support.[217]

On March 1, House Sponsor James Wilson rose to defend the following version of the Civil Rights Act:

> There shall be no discrimination in civil rights or immunities among citizens of the United States in any State or Territory of the United States on account

---

[213] *See* MCKITRICK, *supra* note 8, at 287.

[214] *See* CONG. GLOBE, 39th Cong., 1st Sess. 943 (1866); *see also* MCKITRICK, *supra* note 8, at 292.

[215] *See* BENEDICT, *supra* note 36, at 156–58.

[216] *See, e.g.*, BRUCE ACKERMAN, WE THE PEOPLE: TRANSFORMATIONS 173 (1998). In his book otherwise critical of President Johnson's veto of the Civil Rights Bill, Carl Schurz writes "the belief grew stronger and stronger in the Northern country that the predominance of the Republican party was – and would be for a few years at least – necessary for the safety and honor of the Republic, and steps taken to ensure that predominance, even such as would, in less critical times, have evoked strong criticism, were now looked upon with seductive leniency of judgment. Mr. Stockton of New Jersey was unseated in the Senate upon grounds which would hardly pass muster in ordinary times, to make room for a Republican successor." CARL SCHURZ, 3 THE REMINISCENCES OF CARL SCHURZ 233 (1908). According to Eric Foner, "[u]nderscoring the intensity of Republican feeling, the Senate expelled Democratic Sen. John P. Stockton shortly before the vote on repassage [of the Civil Rights Bill], on the questionable grounds that the New Jersey legislature in 1865 had illegally altered its rules in order to elect him." FONER, *supra* note 26, at 250. For a detailed account of the Stockton affair, *see* MCKITRICK, *supra* note 8, at 320–23.

[217] As Earl Maltz puts it, "the circumstances of the failure [to override Johnson's veto of the Freedmen's Bureau Bill] demonstrated that only those civil rights measures which could appeal to the most conservative of mainstream Republicans were likely to become law." MALTZ, *supra* note 21, at 49.

of race, color, or previous condition of slavery; and such citizens of every race and color, without regard to any previous condition of slavery or involuntary servitude, except as punishment for crime whereof the party shall have been duly convicted, shall have the same right to make and enforce contracts, to sue, be parties and give evidence, to inherit, purchase, lease, sell, hold, and convey real and personal property, and to full and equal benefit of all laws and proceedings for the security of person and property as is enjoyed by white citizens, and shall be subject to like punishment, pains, and penalties, and to none other, any law, statute, ordinance, regulation, or custom, to the contrary notwithstanding.[218]

Wilson stressed that the Act would leave the "political right" of suffrage "under the control of the several States."[219] Nor would the Act force racial integration of juries and schools because "[t]hese are not civil rights or immunities."[220] The Act's protection of civil rights meant "simply the absolute rights of individuals," which treatise writer James Kent defined as "[t]he right of personal security, the right of personal liberty, and the right to acquire and enjoy property. Right itself, in civil society, is that which any man is entitled to have, or to do, or to require from others, within the limits of prescribed law."[221]

Such civil rights, declared Wilson, were "the natural rights of man; and those are the rights which this bill proposes to protect every citizen in the enjoyment of throughout the entire dominion of the Republic."[222] The term "immunities," on the other hand, "merely secures to citizens of the United States equality in the exemptions from the law. A colored citizen shall not, because he is colored, be subjected to obligations, duties, pains, and penalties from which other citizens are exempted. Whatever exemptions there may be shall apply to all citizens alike."[223]

As expansive as this list of equal civil rights might appear, Wilson insisted that the Act "merely affirms existing law. We are following the Constitution."[224] Co-opting the moderate assurances of John Bingham, Wilson maintained that "[w]e are establishing no new right, declaring no new principle. It is not the object of this bill to establish new rights, but to protect and enforce those which already belong to every citizen."[225] Like Bingham, Wilson grounded the Act

---

[218] Cong. Globe, 39th Cong., 1st Sess. 1117 (1866).
[219] *Id.*
[220] *Id.*
[221] *Id.* (internal quotations omitted).
[222] *Id.*
[223] *Id.*
[224] *Id.*
[225] *Id.*

in the language of the original Constitution. Quoting the Comity Clause of Article IV, Wilson argued that had the states enforced the Comity Clause as interpreted in cases like *Corfield v. Coryell*, "there would be no need for this bill."[226] Here Wilson partially quoted Washington's list of fundamental rights that would be protected under the Act:

> "The right of protection by the Government, the enjoyment of life and liberty, with the right to acquire and possess property of every kind, and to pursue and obtain happiness and safety; to claim the benefit of the writ of *habeas corpus*; to institute and maintain actions of any kind in the courts of the State; to take, hold, and dispose of property either real or personal; to be exempt from higher taxes or impositions than are paid by the other citizens of the State."[227]

Wilson's reading of *Corfield* was quite different from the manner in which Justice Washington's opinion had been understood by antebellum authorities. Instead of guaranteeing out-of-state visitors equal access to a limited set of state-conferred rights, Wilson insisted that "a citizen does not surrender these rights because he may happen to be a citizen of the State that would deprive him of them."[228] Here, Wilson went beyond Article IV's protection of sojourning citizens by treating *Corfield*'s common law rights as if they were substantive national rights that states must provide their own citizens.

Although the Constitution conferred no power on Congress to protect such rights, Wilson did not believe that this posed any barrier to the adoption of the Civil Rights Act. Federal power to "protect a citizen of the United States against a violation of his rights by the law of a single State . . . permeates our whole system, is a part of it, without which the States can run riot over every fundamental right belonging to citizens of the United States."[229] Rejecting the very concept of enumerated federal power, Wilson insisted that

> the right to exercise this power depends upon no express delegation, but runs with the rights it is designed to protect; that we possess the same latitude in respect to the selection of means through which to exercise this power that belongs to us when a power rests upon express delegation; and that the decisions which support the latter maintain the former.[230]

---

[226] *Id.* at 1117–18.
[227] *Id.* (quoting Corfield v. Coryell, 6 F. Cas. 546, 551–52 (C.C.E.D. Pa. 1823) [No. 3,230]).
[228] *Id.* at 1118.
[229] *Id.* at 1119.
[230] *Id.*

This was not the kind of argument likely to reassure wavering moderate Republicans. Conservative Democrats saw their opening and immediately attacked. Radical (as in radically conservative) Democrat Andrew Jackson Rogers pointed out that discussion of the draft version of the Fourteenth Amendment had been postponed until April, but those pushing the Amendment argued that it was necessary in order to pass laws precisely like the Civil Rights Act. Therefore, it appeared that Congress did not, presently, have power to pass the Act.[231]

> [I]s there any member on the other side of the House who, on the honor of a man of conscience and integrity, can make himself believe that this Congress has the right to control the privileges and immunities of every citizen of these States, as contemplated in this bill, without a change in the organic law of the land?[232]

Rogers also turned Wilson's use of *Corfield* against him. Wilson had denied the Act would give black people the political right of suffrage and then had selectively quoted from Washington's opinion for examples of the civil rights that would be protected under the Act.[233] Rogers argued that political rights were but a subcategory of "civil rights" and pointed out that "it has been decided by the circuit court of the United States, in the case of *Corfield v. Coryell* . . . that the elective franchise is included in the words privilege and immunities."[234] Roger's use of *Corfield* against the Civil Rights Act illustrates how the case went from being an asset to a potential liability. At this point in the Reconstruction debates, any bill that opened the door to black suffrage was doomed to fail. Washington's opinion in *Corfield*, however, suggested that suffrage was a privilege or immunity protected under Article IV.[235] If *Corfield* was the standard by which the Civil Rights Act's protections were to be measured, then this now became a reason for mainstream and conservative Republicans to oppose the Act. Accordingly, as the debates went forward, advocates of the Civil Rights Act reduced their reliance on *Corfield* and embraced less pregnant discussions of the Comity Clause found in the treatises of James Kent and Joseph Story and in antebellum cases like *Abbott v. Bayley*.[236]

---

[231] *Id.* at 1120.

[232] *Id.* at 1120–21.

[233] *Id.* at 1117–18.

[234] *Id.* at 1122.

[235] Corfield v. Coryell, 6 F. Cas. 546, 551–52 (C.C.E.D. Pa. 1823) (No. 3,230).

[236] For example, in his next speech, Wilson omitted any reference to *Corfield*. *See* CONG. GLOBE, 39th Cong., 1st Sess. 1294–95 (1866). Likewise, when searching for an antebellum decision representing a consensus view of Article IV, other advocates referred to *Abbott v. Bayley* and the treatises of Kent and Story in their speeches. *See, e.g., id.* at app. 293 (remarks of Rep. Shellabarger) (emphasizing *Abbott v. Bayley* and constitutional treatises in his defense of the Act).

Other members joined Rogers in attacking Wilson's broad view of the rights protected under the Comity Clause and federal enforcement power. According to Indiana Democrat Congressman Michael Kerr, power to pass the Act could not be found in Section Two of the Thirteenth Amendment, because the prohibited discrimination addressed by the Act could be found in both northern free states as well as former Confederate states.[237] This left Article IV as the only plausible source of federal power and as the provision chiefly relied on by its supporters.[238] According to Kerr, however, advocates had badly overread both the Comity Clause and its antebellum case law. The Comity Clause, explained Kerr, "relates to the privileges and immunities which the citizens of *each* State shall enjoy when in any of the *other* States."[239] Thus, its protections involved only those rights that states conferred on their own citizens.

> I understand [Article IV]'s primary object to be to secure equal privileges and immunities to the citizens of *each* State while *temporarily* sojourning in any other State, and its secondary and only other purpose is to prevent any State from discriminating in its laws *in favor of or against* the citizens of any other State *merely because* they are citizens of such other State, or in other words, for mere *sectional* reasons. For example, Indiana cannot form any tacit or express alliance or friendship with Kentucky which shall require or justify Indiana in giving to the citizens of Kentucky who shall settle in Indiana any privileges and immunities it does not equally give to the same *class* of citizens from any other State.[240]

Kerr's argument was amply supported by antebellum treatises and case law, an advantage he pressed at length. Quoting from James Kent's *Commentaries on American Law* and Joseph Story's *Commentaries on the Constitution*, Kerr insisted that the vision of Article IV presented by advocates of the Act was "contrary [to] both the law and the practice throughout the Union."[241] After quoting numerous antebellum cases and legal treatises, Kerr summed up the case against the Act:

> [L]et it be remembered that in all these authorities it is assumed that the privileges and immunities referred to as attainable in the States are required to be attained, if at all, *according to the laws or constitutions of the States*, and never in *defiance* of them. This bill rests upon a theory utterly inconsistent with and in direct hostility to every one of these authorities. It asserts the right

[237] *Id.* at 1268.
[238] *Id.*
[239] *Id.*
[240] *Id.* at 1269.
[241] *Id.*

of Congress to regulate the laws which shall govern in the acquisition and ownership of property in the States, and to determine who may go there and purchase and hold property, and to protect such persons in the enjoyment of it. The right of the State to regulate its own internal and domestic affairs, to select its own local policy, and make and administer its own laws for the protection and welfare of its own citizens, is denied. If Congress can declare what rights and privileges shall be enjoyed in the States by the people of one class, it can by the same kind of reasoning determine what shall be enjoyed by every class.... Congress, in short, may erect a great centralized, consolidated despotism in this capital.[242]

Kerr next addressed the argument, presented by Congressman Thayer of Pennsylvania, that the first eleven amendments are sources of congressional power to enforce rights in the states.

Hitherto, those amendments have been supposed, by lawyers, statesmen, and courts, to contain only *limitations* on the power of Congress.... They were not intended to be, and they are not, limitations on the powers of the States. They are bulwarks of freedom, erected by the people between the States and the Federal Government, and this bill is an attempt to prostrate them. What right has Congress to invade a State, and dictate to it *how* it shall protect its citizens in their right not to be deprived of life, liberty, or property without due process of law?[243]

When challenged by Thayer to explain the value of the Bill of Rights if "there is no power to maintain it," Kerr responded by quoting John Marshall's opinion in *Barron v. Baltimore*:

The Constitution was ordained and established by the people of the United States for themselves, for their own government, and not for the government of the individual States.... Had Congress engaged in the extraordinary occupation of improving the constitutions of the several States by affording the people additional protection from the exercise of power by their own governments in matters which concerned themselves alone they would have declared this purpose in plain and intelligible language.[244]

Finally, Kerr pointed out that, however much the proponents of the Act assured members that the Act would receive only a limited construction, by using the

---

[242] *Id.* at 1270.
[243] *Id.*
[244] *Id.* (quoting Barron v. Mayor & City Council of Baltimore, 32 U.S. (7 Pet.) 243, 247, 250 [1833]).

open-ended term "civil rights and immunities," the Act opened the door to later legislative and judicial adventurism:

> [The Act] does not define the term "civil rights and immunities." What are such rights? One writer says civil rights are those which have no relation to the establishment, support, or management of the Government. Another says they are the rights of a citizen; rights due from one citizen to another, the privation of which is a *civil injury* for which redress may be sought by a *civil action*. Other authors define all these terms in different ways, and assign to them larger or narrower definitions according to their views. Who shall settle these questions? Who shall define these terms? Their definition here by gentlemen on this floor is one thing; their definition after this bill shall have become a law will be quite another thing.[245]

Not only do Kerr's arguments illustrate the deep fissures in the Thirty-Ninth Congress regarding the meaning of decisions like *Corfield v. Coryell*, but his concerns about the broad and undefined category of civil rights signaled a problem that ultimately threatened the passage of the Act.

C. *John Bingham's Opposition to the Civil Rights Act*

Immediately following Kerr's speech, John Bingham rose and moved that the terms "civil rights and immunities" be removed from the Act.[246] The following day, Bingham explained his reasons for doing so in a speech that illustrates his continued goal of protecting the Bill of Rights against state abridgment while maintaining the traditional separation of power between national and state government. Bingham's commitment to federalism – a central part of his opposition to the Civil Rights Act – explains why he must have been particularly troubled by Hotchkiss's claim that his original draft of the Fourteenth Amendment opened the door to federal regulation of civil rights in the states. Bingham opposed the Civil Rights Act for the same reason.

According to Bingham, his proposed removal of the terms "civil rights and immunities" was an effort "to take from the bill what seems to me its oppressive and I might say its unjust provisions."[247] Bingham reminded his colleagues that he did not oppose "any legislation which is authorized by the Constitution of my country to enforce in its letter and its spirit the bill of rights as embodied

[245] *Id.* at 1270–71.
[246] *Id.* at 1271.
[247] *Id.* at 1290–91.

in that Constitution. I know that the enforcement of the bill of rights is the want of the Republic."[248] Under the current Constitution, however,

> the enforcement of the bill of rights, touching the life, liberty, and property of every citizen of the Republic within every organized State of the Union, is of the reserved powers of the States, to be enforced by State tribunals and by State officials acting under the solemn obligations of an oath imposed upon them by the Constitution of the United States.[249]

This reservation of power was made clear by the Tenth Amendment because "[t]he Constitution does not delegate to the United States the power to punish offenses against the life, liberty, or property of the citizen in the States," and "nor does it prohibit that power to the States," this left enforcement of the Act "as the reserved power of the States, to be by them exercised."[250]

Radical Republicans had argued that states should be required to respect all natural rights, including the principles of the Declaration of Independence and the catalogue of common law rights listed in Washington's opinion in *Corfield v. Coryell*. Bingham rejected such a view as destructive of the basic federalist structure of the Constitution. "The prohibitions of power by the Constitution to the States," Bingham explained, "are express prohibitions, as that no State shall enter into any treaty, &c., or emit bills of credit, or pass any bill of attainder, &c. The Constitution does not prohibit States from the enactment of laws for the general government of the people within their respective limits."[251] As much as Bingham shared "an earnest desire to have the bill of rights in your Constitution enforced everywhere," he insisted "that it be enforced in accordance with the Constitution of my country."[252]

Not only did the draft Civil Rights Act purport to regulate rights listed in the Act, such as due process, but the Act also regulated civil rights. This term swept well beyond the subjects specifically listed in the Act and included all manner of rights that properly fell within the control of the states. According to Bingham, "the term civil rights includes every right that pertains to the citizen under the Constitution, laws, and Government of this country," including the political rights of suffrage.[253] The Act would thus prohibit state suffrage laws that discriminated on the basis of race – a fact that would affect almost every

[248] *Id.* at 1291.
[249] *Id.*
[250] *Id.*
[251] *Id.*
[252] *Id.*
[253] *Id.*

state in the Union.[254] Although Bingham desired that "every State should be just [and] should be no respecter of persons," remedying the current situation required a constitutional amendment.[255]

To the extent that the Act was limited to protecting *citizens* from deprivations of life, liberty, and property without due process of law, Bingham believed that this wrongly departed from the language and principles of the Fifth Amendment, which guaranteed the natural rights of due process to *all persons*.[256] Even if based on the Fifth Amendment, however, the Supreme Court had ruled that the Amendment limited only the power of the federal government and not the power of the states.[257] Although the original Freedmen's Bureau Bill had provided similar protections "in the insurrectionary states," that bill had been limited both in its geographic scope (it applied only to rebel states) and in duration (it would no longer apply on "the restoration of those insurrectionary States to their constitutional relations with the United States").[258] "But when peace is restored," Bingham insisted,

> justice is to be administered under the Constitution, according to the Constitution, and within the limitation of the Constitution. What is that limitation, sir? Simply this, that the care of the property, the liberty, and the life of the citizen, under the solemn sanction of an oath imposed by your Federal Constitution, is in the States, and not in the Federal Government. *I have sought to effect no change in that respect in the Constitution of the country.* I have advocated here an amendment which would arm Congress with the power to compel obedience to the oath, and punish all violations by State officers of the bill of rights, but leaving those officers to discharge the duties enjoined upon them as citizens of the United States by that oath and by that Constitution.[259]

Bingham closed his remarks with an extended paean to constitutional virtues of federalism. "To show that I am not mistaken on this subject," Bingham read a passage from Chancellor James Kent, "one of those grand intellects who during life illustrated the jurisprudence of our country, and has left in his works a perpetual monument of his genius, his learning, and his wisdom"[:]

> The judicial power of the United States is necessarily limited to national objects. The vast field of the law of property, the very extensive head of

---

[254] *Id.*
[255] *Id.*
[256] *See id.* at 1292.
[257] *Id.*
[258] *Id.*
[259] *Id.* (emphasis added).

equity jurisdiction, the principal rights and duties which flow from our civil and domestic relations fall within the control, and we might almost say the exclusive cognizance of the State governments. We look essentially to the State courts for protection to all these momentous interests. They touch, in their operation, every chord of human sympathy, and control our best destinies. It is their province to reward and to punish. Their blessings and their terrors will accompany us to the fireside, and be in constant activity before the public eye.[260]

Bingham fully agreed with Kent's praise of federalism:

Sir, I have always so learned our dual system of Government by which our own American nationality and liberty have been established and maintained. I have always believed that the protection in time of peace within the States of all the rights of person and citizen was of the powers reserved to the States. And so I still believe.[261]

The draft Civil Rights Act, however, shattered the idea of limited federal power and the reserved rights of the states. The Act proposed "[t]o reform the whole civil and criminal code of every State government by declaring that there shall be no discrimination between citizens on account of race or color in civil rights or in the penalties prescribed by their laws."[262] Bingham agreed that "there should be no such inequality or discrimination even in the penalties for crime; but what power have you to correct it?"[263]

Bingham's proposed deletion of the terms "civil rights and immunities" would allow Congress to "submit this proposition in the least objectionable form to the final decision of the Federal tribunals of the country."[264] But even if focused on the Fifth Amendment subjects of life, liberty, and property, Congress still lacked the power to enforce the Bill of Rights. Thus, even though Congress adopted Bingham's proposed rescission, Bingham himself refused to support the amended Act.[265]

Bingham's opposition to the Civil Rights Act was premised on the idea that the Constitution places some matters within the control of the federal government while preserving others in the hands of the people in the states. Civil rights in general were matters for state regulation and thus should be

---

[260] *Id.* at 1292–93.

[261] *Id.* at 1293.

[262] *Id.*

[263] *Id.* See also, GERARD N. MAGLIOCCA, AMERICAN FOUNDING SON: JOHN BINGHAM AND THE INVENTION OF THE FOURTEENTH AMENDMENT 120 (2013).

[264] *Id.* at 1291.

[265] *See id.* at 1367 (recording Bingham as voting against the Act). Bingham also did not support the vote to override President Johnson's veto of the Act. *See id.* at 1861 (recording Bingham as not voting on the veto override).

allowed to differ from state to state. This was true under the original Constitution, and Bingham had no desire to alter this arrangement either by statute or amendment. Enumerated rights like those listed in the Due Process Clause of the Fifth Amendment, however, were part of the national Bill of Rights that citizens of the United States had a right to enjoy throughout the United States. Bingham *did* desire national enforcement of the Bill of Rights against the states, but he believed accomplishing this goal required a constitutional amendment. Finally, just as all persons could expect due process from the federal government, so too should all persons in the states equally have expected that their life, liberty, and property would not be deprived without due process of law. Once again, however, enforcing this natural right as a matter of law required an amendment that would extend such a right to all persons and add the power of national enforcement.

As he had done in the past, Bingham spoke of protecting the enumerated liberties in the federal Bill of Rights. There is no call for the nationalization of natural rights, and Bingham says nothing about *Corfield*; instead, he insists that the substance of state-level common law rights were matters *rightfully* left to state control under the Tenth Amendment. This is not a grudging "we'll make do with federalism until we can amend it out of the Constitution" speech. Bingham's entire argument is based on federalist constitutional principles that he clearly valued and that had been praised by prior legal "geniuses" like James Kent. However much states ought to do justice in their administration of law, Bingham believed that it remained an important aspect of the dualist Constitution that states retain control over the various subjects of the common law and civil rights – subject only to the "express" limitations on state action enumerated in the Constitution. As he had attempted to accomplish in his initial draft of the Fourteenth Amendment, Bingham again sought a middle course that protected rights in the states while maintaining a federalist government of limited national power.

D. Defining the Rights of Citizens of the United States: James Wilson's Second Speech Defending the Civil Rights Bill

Bingham's concerns about the term "civil rights and immunities" infringing on the reserved rights of the states was repeated by other members of the House.[266] In light of the defeat of the Freedmen's Bureau Bill, as well as

---

[266] For example, according to George Latham:

> This section provides further "that there shall be no discrimination in civil rights or immunities among the inhabitants of any State or Territory of the United States on account of race, color, or previous condition of slavery." Though by the wording of

the reaction to Bingham's proposed amendment, it was incumbent on the supporters of the Act to respond to claims that the Civil Rights Act exceeded federal power and unjustifiably intruded on the properly reserved rights of the states.

Perhaps sensing that his original remarks had not helped the prospects of the Civil Rights Act, on March 9 James Wilson returned to the floor and delivered an altogether different defense for the Act. This time, Wilson used reasoning that was much more likely to persuade the moderate and conservative Republicans. In his first speech, Wilson had stressed federal power to protect the state-conferred common law rights "of citizens in the several states," such as those protected under Article IV and as discussed in Washington's opinion in *Corfield v. Coryell*.[267] In this second speech, Wilson avoided any mention of *Corfield* or of nationalizing Article IV privileges and immunities of citizens in the several states. Instead, Wilson now claimed that the Act protected only "those rights which belong to men as *citizens of the United States* and none other," such as those rights protected by the Fifth Amendment to the federal Constitution.[268] Wilson's move away from Article IV rights "of citizens in the several states" and toward the constitutionally enumerated rights of "citizens

this clause it might not refer to discriminations by the State or other local law, yet it is very evident from its connections, and from the entire bill, that its reference is to such discriminations. No one, I presume, doubts the power of Congress to place all the inhabitants of the United States upon an equal footing as to all matters within the legitimate scope of congressional legislation, and consequently Congress may provide that there shall be no discrimination on account of race, color, or previous condition of slavery in civil rights or immunities which may be constitutionally defined or regulated by Congress; or in other words, that all may stand upon an equal footing in the Federal courts. But as the right to define and regulate the "civil rights or immunities" of the inhabitants in the several States is not among "the powers delegated to the United States by the Constitution, nor prohibited by it to the States," it is by the tenth amendment "reserved to the States respectively or to the people." My conviction, then, is that Congress has no right under the Constitution to interfere with the internal policy of the several States so as to define and regulate the "civil rights or immunities among the inhabitants" therein. If I am correct in this opinion, this clause is without constitutional warrant, and the balance of the section, being based upon it, necessarily falls with it. . . .

I consider this as one of a series of measures which have been introduced into this Congress, which, if adopted, would change not only the entire policy, but the very form of our Government, by a complete centralization of all power in the national Government, and as most dangerous to the liberties of the people and the reserved rights of the States.

CONG. GLOBE, 39th Cong., 1st Sess. 1295–96 (1866).

[267] *See supra* notes 218–31 and accompanying text.

[268] CONG. GLOBE, 39th Cong., 1st Sess. 1294 (1866) (emphasis added).

of the United States" foreshadows a similar shift in language by John Bingham in his second and final draft of the Fourteenth Amendment.

Recognizing the danger posed by the opposition of moderates like John Bingham, Wilson focused his remarks on Bingham's federalism-based concerns about the Civil Rights Act:

> The gentleman from Ohio tells the House that civil rights involve all the rights that citizens have under the Government; that in the term are embraced those rights which belong to the citizen of the United States as such, and those which belong to a citizen of a State as such; and that this bill is not intended merely to enforce equality of rights, so far as they relate to citizens of the United States, but invades the States to enforce equality of rights in respect to those things which properly and rightfully depend on State regulations and laws. My friend is too sound a lawyer, is too well versed in the Constitution of his country, to indorse that proposition on calm and deliberate consideration. He knows, as every man knows, *that this bill refers to those rights which belong to men as citizens of the United States and none other*; and when he talks of setting aside the school laws and jury laws and franchise laws of the States by the bill now under consideration, he steps beyond what he must know to be the rule of construction which must apply here, and as the result of which this bill can only relate to matters within the control of Congress.[269]

In this passage, Wilson distinguishes "those rights which belong to a citizen of a state as such" and "those rights which belong to men as citizens of the United States."[270] Or, to use the language of the Act, Wilson insisted that there was a difference between the "civil rights and immunities of citizens of the several states" and the "civil rights and immunities of citizens of the United States." Only the latter involved a matter "within the control of Congress."[271] Education laws, jury laws, and the laws of suffrage, conversely, were rights "which properly and rightfully depend on state regulation and laws."[272]

Having limited the Civil Rights Act to the civil rights and immunities of citizens of the United States, Wilson proceeded to define "the great civil rights to which the first section of the bill refers."[273] Abandoning his earlier

---

[269] *Id.* (emphasis added).
[270] *Id.*
[271] *Id.*
[272] *Id.*
[273] *Id.*

invocation of the rights of common law, Wilson now invoked the federal Bill of Rights:

> I find in the bill of rights which [Bingham] desires to have enforced by an amendment to the Constitution that "no person shall be deprived of life, liberty, or property without due process of law." I understand that these constitute the civil rights belonging to the citizens in connection with those which are necessary for the protection and maintenance and perfect enjoyment of the rights thus specifically named, and these are the rights to which this bill relates, having nothing to do with subjects submitted to the control of the several States.[274]

By turning the focus of the Civil Rights Act away from the nationalization of the common law and toward the protection of the Fifth Amendment subjects of life, liberty, and property, Wilson sought to bring his defense of the Act into line with the goals of moderate Republicans. Republicans like Hale believed that the Bill *already* bound the states, and men like Bingham believed that if this were not the case, then the Bill of Rights *ought* to bind the states. Whereas Bingham believed federal enforcement of the Bill required an amendment, Wilson believed such power already existed under the (previously despised) doctrine of *Prigg*.[275]

> Now sir, in relation to the great fundamental rights embraced in the bill of rights, the citizen being possessed of them is entitled to a remedy. That is the doctrine of the law as laid down by the courts. There can be no dispute about this. The possession of the rights by the citizen raises by implication the power in Congress to provide appropriate means for their protection; in other words, to supply the needed remedy.[276]

Wilson's turn toward the Bill of Rights in defense of the Civil Rights Act is important for a number of reasons. To begin with, it illustrates the uncontroversial nature of the idea that states ought to respect the Bill of Rights – an idea that had grown increasingly accepted among northern antebellum legal and political writers. Wilson relied on the assumed support of his

---

[274] *Id.*

[275] Robert Kaczorowski argues that Wilson's view of *Prigg* and *McCulloch v. Maryland* represents the Republican theory of congressional power to enforce the Bill and, therefore, the Fourteenth Amendment. *See* Robert J. Kaczorowsky, *Congress's Power To Enforce Fourteenth Amendment Rights: Lessons from Federal Remedies the Framers Enacted*, 42 HARV. J. LEGIS. 187, 201–03 (2005) (noting that Republican leaders and Wilson saw Congress as having plenary power to protect the civil rights of all Americans based on the "theories of broad implied powers and constitutional delegation" in *Prigg* and *McCulloch*). Kaczorowski's account, however, leaves out the opposing views of John Bingham, the objections to the original draft, the changes in the draft, and Wilson's own concessions regarding the changes.

[276] CONG. GLOBE, 39th Cong., 1st Sess. 1294 (1866).

colleagues for a nationalized bill in his efforts to secure support for the Civil Rights Act. Second, Wilson invoked the antebellum distinction between the rights and immunities "of citizens of the several states" and the rights and immunities "of citizens of the United States." State-secured civil rights such as those covered by Article IV constituted the former, whereas the provisions of the Fifth Amendment and the Bill of Rights constituted the latter. As we shall see, Bingham's second draft of the Fourteenth Amendment abandoned the language of Article IV and invoked the "privileges or immunities of citizens of the United States" – rights that Bingham insisted were altogether different from the state-secured rights protected under Article IV and that included the protections enumerated in the Bill of Rights. Finally, Wilson also adopted the moderate view that there remained a number of matters involving civil rights in the states that were *not* properly a matter of federal cognizance. By doing so, Wilson accepted (as a matter of political reality, if not personal preference) the basic federalist structure of the Constitution – a necessary move if he was to secure the support of the moderate and conservative Republicans.

E. Deleting "Civil Rights and Immunities" from the Civil Rights Act

In his second speech, Wilson insisted that the "civil rights and immunities" language in the Act would receive a narrow interpretation, and he emphasized the relationship between the rights specifically protected in the Act and the Fifth Amendment's protection of life, liberty, and property. This theme of narrow interpretation and emphasis on constitutionally enumerated rights was echoed by later supporters as well.[277] Ohio Representative Samuel Shellabarger, for example, insisted that "if this section did in fact assume to confer or define or regulate these civil rights, which are named by the words contract, sue, testify, inherit, &c., then it would, as seems to me, be an assumption of the reserved rights of the States and the people."[278] Instead, the Act did nothing

---

[277] For example, according to Rep. Hart:

> The Constitution clearly describes that to be a republican form of government for which it was expressly framed. A government which shall "establish justice, insure domestic tranquility, provide for the common defense, promote the general welfare, and secure the blessings of liberty;" a government whose "citizens shall be entitled to all privileges and immunities of other citizens;" where "no law shall be made prohibiting the free exercise of religion;" where "the right of the people to keep and bear arms shall not be infringed;" where "the right of the people to be secure in their persons, houses, papers and effects, against unreasonable searches and seizures, shall not be violated," and where "no person shall be deprived of life, liberty, or property without due process of law."

Id. at 1629.

[278] Id. at 1293.

more than protect "indispensible rights of American citizenship" such as "the right to petition and the right of protection in such property as is lawful for that particular citizen to own."[279] The right to petition is found in the First Amendment to the Constitution, whereas the right of due process in the protection of property is found in the Fifth Amendment. Even here, Shellabarger believed that the substantive content of rights was a matter of state regulation, subject only to the Act's requirement that such rights be equally protected.

Both Wilson's and Shellabarger's arguments presumed a narrow construction of the Act's reference to protecting "civil rights and immunities" in the states. Other members, however, were not so sanguine about such open-ended phrases receiving a narrow construction once the text was enacted. On its face, the Act seemed to presume congressional power to define and protect *all* civil rights, whatever their nature, and regardless of whether such rights were political in nature or were derived from the common law rather than constitutional text. Concerns that such a broad reading would obliterate the reserved powers and rights of the people in the states led proponents of the Act to delete the term "civil rights and immunities" from the first section of the Bill. According to James Wilson:

> When the bill was up before I did offer such an amendment, that nothing in the bill contained should be construed to affect the rights of suffrage in the several States. I will explain. Some members of the House thought, in the general words of the first section in relation to civil rights, it might be held by the courts that the right of suffrage was included in those rights. To obviate that difficulty *and the difficulty growing out of any other construction beyond the specific rights named in the section,* our amendment strikes out all of those general terms and leaves the bill with the rights specified in the section.[280]

Although scholars have noted that the deletion of the "civil rights and immunities" language came in response to concerns about black suffrage,[281] Wilson expressly notes that objection to the term went beyond matters of suffrage and included federalism-based concerns regarding federal power to regulate "other rights" beyond those specific civil rights listed in the Bill.[282]

---

[279] *Id.* (ironically quoting Chief Justice Taney).
[280] *Id.* at 1367 (emphasis added).
[281] *See, e.g.,* Harrison, *supra* note 16, at 1405 n.64.
[282] *See also* GEORGE RUTHERGLEN, CIVIL RIGHTS IN THE SHADOW OF SLAVERY: THE CONSTITUTION, COMMON LAW, AND THE CIVIL RIGHTS ACT OF 1866, at 53 (Oxford, 2013) (also noting the removal of the term "civil rights" due to concerns about "latitudinarian construction" of the term).

F. *Summary*

Both the language and the underlying theory of the Civil Rights Act shifted significantly from the time of its introduction on January 5 to its initial adoption on March 13. Introduced as a Bill to protect the civil rights of all "inhabitants" in the states, its framers amended the language so that it defined and focused solely on citizens of the United States. In the beginning, its supporters claimed to be protecting the natural rights of all men that Justice Washington in *Corfield v. Coryell* claimed were the national rights of American citizens. This theory (and this reading of *Corfield*), however, faced a barrage of objections based on the common antebellum understanding of *Corfield* and Article IV. By the end of the debate, supporters of the Bill had moved away from the radical Republican reading of *Corfield*, deleted the general language of "civil rights," and broadly defended the Bill as a vindication of the constitutionally enumerated rights of citizens of the United States. The theory and constitutional basis of the Bill remained in question (as reflected in the provision providing for review before the Supreme Court), and no single theory of its provisions enjoyed unanimous support. However, the shift in rhetoric is clear and likely reflects the impact of President Johnson's veto of the Freedmen's Bureau Bill and the political reality that successful legislation would have to be couched in language acceptable to moderate Republicans. This meant avoiding any suggestion that Congress held the power to define and protect the substantive content of civil rights in the states.

By the time Congress sent the Civil Rights Act to the desk of President Andrew Johnson for signature, radical Republicans had abandoned their initial claims that the Bill represented an act of federal authority to nationalize the "fundamental" common law rights protected by the Comity Clause and partially listed by Justice Bushrod Washington in *Corfield v. Coryell*. Confronted by uncontradicted antebellum judicial and scholarly precedents that gave a narrow reading of the privileges and immunities of state citizenship, men like Wilson and Trumbull repackaged their efforts as attempts to enforce the rights of *national* citizenship, such as those listed in the Fifth Amendment. Not every radical gave up the broad reading of *Corfield* and Article IV, but the shift in the leadership's justification for the Civil Rights Bill was clear. Instead of *Corfield*, members turned to cases like *Lemmon v. The People* as representing the proper understanding of rights protected under the Comity Clause of Article IV, if only to avoid *Corfield's* reference to the rights of suffrage.

Whether the shift in their public statements reflected a change of heart or simply a political calculation geared to attract the votes of moderates and conservatives, the new focus on the rights of national citizenship seemed well suited, given the language of the statute itself. The Civil Rights Bill began by declaring the rights of national citizenship:

> Be it enacted by the Senate and House of Representatives of the United States of America in Congress assembled, That all persons born in the United States and not subject to any foreign power, excluding Indians not taxed, are hereby declared to be citizens of the United States. . . . [283]

The declaration ignored *Dred Scott*'s holding to the contrary and established the Act's theme of national citizenship: Its provision defined national citizenship and guaranteed the rights attending that citizenship to every person born in the United States and residing in any state in the Union. Although states retained the power to define the general content of local civil rights, when it came to rights associated with life, liberty, and property, citizens of the United States must be treated equally, regardless of the color of their skin. To be a citizen of the United States meant equal access to the rights of citizens of the United States. Such was the theory presented by main sponsors of the Civil Rights Act in the House and Senate.

This was not a theory without problems. Whether Congress had power to confer the rights of national citizenship on persons in the states was not at all clear.[284] Nor was it clear that the rights listed in the Act actually *were* rights of national citizenship. Wilson and others had initially presented the Bill as protecting common law civil rights; it was only later that they attempted to characterize the Act as enforcing rights ancillary to the Fifth Amendment's protection of life, liberty, and property. Even if one accepted the idea that the Act enforced rights ancillary to the Fifth Amendment, nothing in that Amendment conferred enforcement power on the national legislature. Even more problematic was the fact that Supreme Court precedents like *Barron v. Baltimore* clearly held that the Fifth Amendment did not bind the states. As much as Republican moderates like John Bingham wished to require the states to enforce the Bill of Rights, Bingham insisted that doing so required a constitutional amendment. And if John Bingham doubted the Act's constitutionality, how would the Act fare before a Supreme Court whose members were unlikely to have more generous interpretation of congressional power than Bingham?

---

[283] Civil Rights Act of 1866, 14 Stat. 27 (1866).

[284] Justice Taney, for example, had argued in *Dred Scott* that Congress's power of naturalization was "confined to persons born in a foreign country, under a foreign flag" and did not include "a power to raise to the rank of a citizen any one born in the United States, who . . . belongs to an inferior and subordinate class." Dred Scott v. Sandford, 60 U.S. (19 How.) 393, 417 (1857).

Finally, there was the problem of President Andrew Johnson. Johnson had shocked Republicans by his February veto of the Freedmen's Bureau Act. Nevertheless, in early March, there remained hope that he and congressional Republicans might find a way to jointly manage Reconstruction. Johnson's veto of the Civil Rights Act, however, signaled an irreparable breach with the Republicans in the Thirty-Ninth Congress.[285] Ultimately, the competing constitutional visions of Johnson and the Republicans so publicly discussed in the fight over the Civil Rights Act became competing political platforms in the national elections of 1866. The political importance of Johnson's veto was obvious at the time, and historians have since identified this as a key moment in the national struggle over Reconstruction.[286] What has not been recognized, however, is the role Johnson's veto played in the ultimate development of the Fourteenth Amendment.

V. ANDREW JOHNSON'S VETO OF THE CIVIL RIGHTS ACT

President Johnson's February veto of an extension of the Freedmen's Bureau Bill came as a surprise to congressional Republicans.[287] There had been little reason at the time to suspect that Johnson would refuse to work with Congress on a bipartisan approach to Reconstruction. His rejection of the Civil Rights Act, however, amounted to a declaration of political war.[288] On March 27, President Johnson's veto of the Civil Rights Bill exploded across newspaper headlines throughout the United States, with many papers printing his accompanying message in full.[289] Although long considered a key moment in the

---

[285] McKitrick, *supra* note 8, at 315 ("It was thus that key leaders of the Republican Party who had worked for compromise over the past sixteen weeks saw their last ground cut out from under them").

[286] Foner, *supra* note 26, at 251; Michael Les Benedict, A Compromise of Principle: Congressional Republicans and Reconstruction, 1863–1869, at 164 (1974); McKitrick, *supra* note 8, at 314–15.

[287] See Foner, *supra* note 26, at 247; McKitrick, *supra* note 8, at 286–88. Under the original Act, the Freedmen's Bureau was vested with control over every aspect of refugees and freedmen in the southern states until one year following the end of hostilities. The vetoed bill would have both extended the life of the Act and expanded its jurisdiction throughout the country. For a general discussion of the proposed extension of the Freedmen's Bureau Act, see Benedict, *supra* note 286 at 147–50.

[288] According to Eric Foner, "[f]or Republican moderates, the Civil Rights veto ended all hope of cooperation with the President." Foner, *supra* note 26, at 250; *see also id.* (quoting a letter by a member of the Ohio Senate, saying "[i]f the President vetoes the Civil Rights bill, I believe we shall be obliged to draw our swords for a fight and throw away the scabbard").

[289] See, e.g., Albany Evening J., Mar. 28, 1866, at 2 (Albany, N.Y.); Bos. Daily Advertiser, Mar. 28, 1866, at 1; *The Civil Rights Bill and The President's Veto*, N.Y. Times, Mar. 28, 1866, at 1; Daily Nat'l Intelligencer, Mar. 28, 1866, at 1 (Wash., D.C.); The Daily Age, Mar. 28,

story of Reconstruction, the importance of President Johnson's veto in terms of the ultimate draft of the Fourteenth Amendment has been completely missed.

A. *Johnson's Veto Message*

Johnson began his message by distinguishing the rights of national citizenship from the rights of state citizenship and objecting to Congress's effort to confer the former on the freedmen:

> By the first section of the bill, all persons born in the United States, and not subject to any foreign power, excluding Indians not taxed, are declared to be citizens of the United States. This provision comprehends the Chinese of the Pacific States, Indians subject to taxation, the people called Gypsies, as well as the entire race designated as blacks, people of color, negroes, mulattoes, and persons of African blood. Every individual of these races, born in the United States, is by the bill made a citizen of the United States. *It does not purport to declare or confer any other right of citizenship than Federal citizenship.* It does not purport to give these classes of persons any status *as citizens of States*, except that which may result from their status as citizens of the United States. The power to confer the right of State citizenship is just as exclusively with the several States as the power to confer the right of Federal citizenship is with Congress. The right of Federal citizenship thus to be conferred on the several excepted races before mentioned is now for the first time proposed to be given by law.[290]

Having distinguished the rights of national citizenship from that of state citizenship, Johnson then argued that conferring the rights of national citizenship on these "previously excluded groups" was unwise. "Can it be reasonably supposed," Johnson wrote, "that they possess the requisite qualifications to entitle them to *all the privileges and immunities of citizens of the United States?*"[291]

1866, at 1 (Phila., Pa.).; Daily National Republican, Mar. 31 (2d edition), at 1 (publishing excerpt from New Haven Palladium); New Hampshire Sentinel, Apr. 5, 1866, at 1 (Keene, N.H.); N.Y. Trib., Mar. 28, 1866, at 7; Pittsfield Sun, Apr. 5, 1866, at 1(Pittsfield, Mass.); *President's Message Vetoing the Civil Rights Bill*, Cedar Falls Gazette, Apr. 6, 1866, at 1 (Iowa); Salt Lake Daily Telegraph, Mar. 29, 1866, at 2; Semi-Wkly. Telegraph, Apr. 2, 1866, at 1 (Salt Lake City, Utah); Vt. J., Apr. 7, 1866, at 1 (Windsor, Vt.); *Veto of the Civil Rights Bill*, Titusville Morning Herald, Mar. 31, 1866, at 1 (Pa.); Wkly. Patriot & Union, Apr. 5, 1866, at 2 (Harrisburg, Pa.); Wooster Republican, Apr. 5, 1866, at 1 (Wooster, Ohio).
[290] Cong. Globe, 39th Cong., 1st Sess. 1679 (emphasis added).
[291] *Id.* (emphasis added).

[T]he policy of the Government, from its origin to the present time, seems to have been that persons who are strangers to and unfamiliar with our institutions and our laws should pass through a certain probation, at the end of which, before attaining the coveted prize, they must give evidence of their fitness to receive and to exercise the rights of citizens as contemplated by the Constitution of the United States.[292]

Johnson then pivoted and addressed the rights specifically protected in the Civil Rights Act; the right "to make and enforce contracts; to sue, be parties, and give evidence: to inherit, purchase, lease, sell, hold, and convey real and personal property," and to have "full and equal benefit of all laws and proceedings for the security of person and property as is enjoyed by white citizens."[293] According to Johnson, "[h]itherto every subject embraced in the enumeration of rights contained in this bill has been considered as exclusively belonging to the States. They all relate to the internal policy and economy of the respective States."[294] Unlike the "privileges and immunities of citizens of the United States," these "are matters which in each State concern the domestic condition of its people, varying in each according to its own peculiar circumstances, and the safety and well-being of its own citizens."[295] Although the federal Constitution contains some restrictions on state authority in Article I, Section 9, "where can we find a Federal prohibition against the power of any State to discriminate, as do most of them, between aliens and citizens, between artificial persons called corporations and natural persons, in the right to hold real estate?"[296]

> If Congress can declare by law who shall hold lands, who shall testify, who shall have capacity to make a contract in a State, then Congress can by law also declare who, without regard to color or race, shall have the right to sit as a juror or as a judge, to hold any office, and, finally, to vote "in every State and Territory of the United States." As respects the Territories, they come within the power of Congress, for as to them, the law-making power is the Federal power; but as to the States no similar provisions exist vesting in Congress the power "to make rules and regulations" for them.[297]

Johnson believed that, other than those constraints that the Constitution expressly placed on the states, local governments retained the constitutionally

---

[292] *Id.*
[293] *Id.*
[294] *Id.* at 1680.
[295] *Id.*
[296] *Id.*
[297] *Id.*

established right to control the substance of local civil rights. Echoing the same rule announced by the Supreme Court in *Barron v. Baltimore*,[298] Johnson declared, "the Constitution guaranties nothing with certainty, if it does not insure to the several States the right of making and executing laws in regard to all matters arising within their jurisdiction, *subject only to the restriction that in cases of conflict with the Constitution and constitutional laws of the United States* the latter should be held to be the supreme law of the land."[299]

Johnson concluded his objections to the Bill with an appeal to constitutional federalism:

> [The provisions of the Civil Rights Act] interfere with the municipal legislation of the States, with the relations existing exclusively between a State and its citizens, or between inhabitants of the same State – an absorption and assumption of power by the General Government which, if acquiesced in, must sap and destroy our federative system of limited powers, and break down the barriers which preserve the rights of the States. It is another step, or rather stride, toward centralization and the concentration of all legislative power in the national Government.[300]

Johnson's criticism that Congress lacked constitutional authority to confer the status of national citizenship found a response in the addition of the citizenship clause of the Fourteenth Amendment.[301] But even more importantly, Johnson introduced the language of the rights of national citizenship into the legislative and public debate. In one of the most (if not the most) widely publicized speeches of 1866, Johnson announced that Congress had sought to confer the "*privileges and immunities of citizens of the United States*," a category of rights altogether different from the state-conferred rights protected under the Comity Clause.[302] According to Johnson, Congress had no constitutional authority to protect these national privileges or immunities. This particular locution regarding the rights of national citizenship would soon become a part of the Fourteenth Amendment.

---

[298] 32 U.S. 243, 251 (1833) (ruling that the Takings Clause of the Fifth Amendment does not bind the states).

[299] Cong. Globe, 39th Cong., 1st Sess. 1679, 1680 (1866) (emphasis added).

[300] *Id.* at 1681.

[301] U.S. Const., amend. XIV, § 1 ("All persons born or naturalized in the United States, and subject to the jurisdiction thereof, are citizens of the United States and of the State wherein they reside.").

[302] *See supra* notes 290–302 and accompanying text.

B. *Congressional Override: The Speech of Lyman Trumbull*

Following President Johnson's veto of the amended version of the Civil Rights Act, the Senate sponsor of the Bill, Illinois Senator Lyman Trumbull, delivered an extended speech defending the Act against Johnson's objections that the Act expanded federal power beyond the proper subjects of national regulation.[303] The veto and Trumbull's speech signaled the final breach between the President and the Republicans of the Thirty-Ninth Congress. According to Eric McKitrick, when Trumbull spoke on April 4, he "made his case, and that of the Republican Party."[304]

Trumbull began by reassuring any wavering Republicans that although the federal government had power to protect the fundamental civil rights of American citizens, this power would not extend to conferring political rights such as suffrage. "The right to vote and hold office in the States," explained Trumbull, "depends upon the legislation of the various States."[305] Trumbull then carefully cabined the particular rights covered by the Act. Invoking the language of the Fifth Amendment, Trumbull explained that the rights of American citizenship included the equal protection of one's life, liberty, and property.[306] Trumbull also invoked rights covered by the Comity Clause of Article IV, but described these rights as involving the principle of nondiscrimination:

> The bill neither confers nor abridges the rights of any one, but simply declares that in civil rights there shall be an equality among all classes of citizens, and that all alike shall be subject to the same punishment. Each State, so that it does not abridge the great fundamental rights belonging, under the Constitution, to all citizens, may grant or withhold such civil rights as it pleases; all that is required is that, in this respect, its laws shall be impartial.[307]

[303] CONG. GLOBE, 39th Cong., 1st Sess. 1757 (1866).

[304] MCKITRICK, *supra* note 8, at 316.

[305] CONG. GLOBE, 39th Cong., 1st Sess. 1757 (1866).

[306] *Id.* Trumbull's use of the Fifth Amendment as a textual hook for the Act mirrors a similar move by the Act's sponsor in the House, James Wilson, who initially defended the Act by making expansive claims about federal power to protect fundamental rights but eventually moved to an argument based on the enforcement of enumerated rights such as those found in the Fifth Amendment. *Compare* CONG. GLOBE, 39th Cong., 1st Sess. 1117–19 (1866) *with* CONG. GLOBE, 39th Cong., 1st Sess. 1295–96 (1866); *see also* NELSON, *supra* note 21, at 86 (noting the "libertarian scope" became "somewhat narrower" as the Thirty-Ninth Congress crafted specific legislation).

[307] CONG. GLOBE, 39th Cong., 1st Sess. 1760 (1866). Representative Lawrence's speech in the House on April 7 followed this same basic approach: the rights of life, liberty, and property protected under the Fifth Amendment represent inherent rights that no state may abridge. *See id.* at 1833 (Remarks of Mr. Lawrence) (Apr. 7, 1866).

In his veto message to Congress, President Johnson insisted that the Act's attempt to bestow newly freed blacks in the several states with all the privileges and immunities of citizens of the United States was an unprecedented use of congressional power. In response, Trumbull declared, "This is not a misapprehension of the law, but a mistake in fact, as will appear by references to which I shall call the attention of the Senate, and which will show that the President's facts are as bad as his law."[308] Trumbull then repeated his earlier citation of the treaty with the Stockbridge Indians but also added a specific reference to the rights, advantages, and immunities of citizens of the United States guaranteed by the Louisiana Cession Act. Quoting from "Lawrence's Wheaton on International Law," Trumbull recited:

> "[b]y the third article of the first convention of April 30, 1800, with France, for the cession of Louisiana, it is provided that the inhabitants of the ceded territory shall be incorporated into the Union of the United States, and admitted, as soon as possible, according to the principles of the Federal Constitution to the enjoyment of the rights, advantages, and immunities of citizens of the United States."[309]

Trumbull did not disagree with President Johnson that the rights of American citizenship were altogether different from the rights of state citizenship, including the state-level rights specifically named and granted equal protection by the Civil Rights Act. Trumbull simply maintained that Congress had bestowed the rights of national citizenship in the past, citing precedents like the Louisiana Cession Act of 1803 as examples of congressional conferral of the "rights, advantages, and immunities of citizens of the United States."[310]

Trumbull's argument presumes a close link between natural rights and the right to equal protection of the rights of life, liberty, and property. As we shall see, Bingham shared this view and extended such rights to *all persons* in his final version of the Fourteenth Amendment. At this point in the debates, however, advocates of the Civil Rights Act claimed no more than the power to protect US citizens in the exercise of *their* natural rights. In seeking to secure the needed votes, proponents like Trumbull and Wilson narrowed their definition of the rights of American citizenship to rights expressly enumerated

---

[308] *Id.* at 1756.

[309] *Id.* (Apr. 4) (quoting LAWRENCE'S WHEATON ON INTERNATIONAL LAW 897). In his speech to the House supporting an override of Johnson's veto, Representative William Lawrence of Ohio also cited the Louisiana Cession Act as establishing the authority to "declare that classes of people collectively, shall be citizens." *See id.* at 1832.

[310] *Id.* at 1756.

in the Bill of Rights.[311] Even with the assurance of maintaining the principle of limited federal power and the reserved rights of the states, the vote to override Johnson's veto succeeded by only the narrowest of margins.[312] Trumbull's speech was widely reported in the press,[313] as was Congress's successful override of Johnson's veto[314] – the first successful override involving a major piece of legislation in American history.[315]

Although Congress mustered the votes to override Johnson's veto, serious concerns remained regarding whether Congress had power to pass the Act,

[311] Ohio Congressman William Lawrence delivered a speech on April 7, 1866 in which he followed the general theory of Wilson in supporting an override of Johnson's veto, including the arguments that (1) native born persons are citizens; (2) the Privileges and Immunities Clause protects citizens in their fundamental rights in all states, including their own; (3) fundamental rights includes life, liberty, and property; and (4) Congress has implied power to enforce such rights under the court's reading of congressional power in *Prigg* regarding the fugitive slave clause. *Id.* at 1832–37.

[312] The Senate voted on April 6, 1866 to override Johnson's veto, 33 to 15. Cong. Globe, 39th Cong., 1st Sess. 1809 (1866).

[313] As they had with Johnson's veto message, newspapers widely reported Trumbull's speech defending the congressional override, with a number of papers reprinting the entire text of his speech. *See By Telegraph to the Boston Daily Advertiser the Civil Rights Bill Debate in the Senate,* Bos. Daily Advertiser, Apr. 5, 1866, at 1 (providing major excerpts of the speech, including Trumbull's reference to the Louisiana Cession Act); Daily Age (Phila., Pa.), Apr. 5, 1866, at 1 (full speech); N.Y. Herald-Trib., published as N.Y. Trib., Apr. 5, 1866, at 1 (full speech); *Senator Trumbull On The President's Veto,* Hartford Daily Courant, Apr. 7, 1866, at 1 (full speech); *see also* Bos. J., published as Bos. Daily J., Apr. 6, 1866, at 4 (edited version, with text in full until "bad as his law," then paraphrases, "Here Mr. Trumbull read extracts from Wheaton's International Law, showing that by various treaties, resolutions and acts of Congress, Frenchmen and Spaniards, Mexicans and Indians have at various times been made citizens of the United States").

   Trumbull's speech generated responses, both pro and con, regarding whether Congress had the power to grant the rights of national citizenship on persons in the states and whether groups like newly freed blacks were ready to enjoy the rights of American citizenship. *Compare American Citizenship,* Columbian Register (New Haven, Conn.), May 19, 1866 (Vol. LIV; Issue: 2791) (arguing that, although the federal government may make citizens in the territories through treaty or may establish a uniform rule of naturalization for foreign-born immigrants, the Tenth Amendment reserves to the states the power to make citizens of persons born on state soil), *with The Civil Rights Law at the South,* Bos. Daily J., Apr. 24, 1866, at 4 ("While some of the northern democrat organs have been instigating the President not to execute the Civil Rights Act . . . we are glad to observe prominent southern organs taking a much more sensible and becoming course." The *Mobile Register,* for instance, edited by John Forsyth, says that Alabama already has a class of citizens "very similar to what the negroes will be under the Civil Rights Act, namely the colored Creoles, who, being citizens under the Spanish government, were secured the rights of American citizenship by the treaty of 1819. They have proved an exemplary class.").

[314] The Senate voted on April 6, 1866, to override Johnson's veto 33 to 15. Cong. Globe, 39th Cong., 1st Sess. 1809 (1866). The House followed suit on April 9, the override passing on a vote of 122 to 41 (Bingham abstaining). *Id.* at 1861.

[315] McKitrick, *supra* note 8, at 323.

even if the Act was narrowly construed. John Bingham, for example, argued that the Act exceeded Congress's constitutional powers.[316] Bingham not only voted against the Act, he declined to support the congressional override.[317] As Congress took up consideration of a new draft of the Fourteenth Amendment, it did so facing the possibility that the Civil Rights Act might be struck down by the Supreme Court as exceeding federal power. For now, President Johnson had alerted the country to the unconventional effort by Congress to confer on newly freed blacks "the rights *of citizens of the United States*." The people who followed this well-published drama would soon see this phrase again, this time in the second draft of the proposed Fourteenth Amendment.

VI. THE SECOND DRAFT OF THE FOURTEENTH AMENDMENT

A. *Creating the Second Draft*

When John Bingham voted with his colleagues to postpone discussion of his initial draft of the Fourteenth Amendment, the conservative press was pleased, but cautious. Under the headline "Practical Failure of the Constitutional Amendment," the *New York Times* reported Hotchkiss's objection that Bingham's initial draft "was not radical enough" and that Congress had "moved its postponement until the second Tuesday in April."[318] As news emerged that the Committee of Fifteen had completed work on a second draft, so too did warnings in the conservative press. On April 27, the *Richmond Whig* reported:

> After a lull of excitement, it begins to be rumored that the Committee of fifteen is ready to make another report on the subject of reconstruction, which is said to be the suggestion of Robert Dale Owen, and to be more radical than anything that has yet been proposed. The Washington correspondent of the New York World thus describes its provisions: . . . No state shall make or enforce any law which shall abridge the privileges or immunities of citizens of the United States.[319]

When the members of the Joint Committee on Reconstruction renewed their consideration of what would become the Fourteenth Amendment on

---

[316] According to Bingham, "[t]he Constitution does not delegate to the United States the power to punish offenses against the life, liberty, or property of the citizen in the States." Cong. Globe, 39th Cong., 1st Sess. 1291 (1866).

[317] *See* Cong. Globe, 39th Cong., 1st Sess. 1861 (1866).

[318] *Gratifying Triumph of Moderate Counsels*, N.Y. Times, Mar 1, 1866, at 4.

[319] *Congress and its Pet Committee*, Richmond Whig, Apr. 27, 1866, at 1.

April 21,[320] they did so fully aware of their colleagues' objections to national control of common law civil rights. Concerns about federal power doomed the override of the Freedmen's Bureau veto and also contributed to the failure of Bingham's initial draft of the Fourteenth Amendment. Similar concerns forced a change in the language of the Civil Rights Act. Committee members knew that a second draft of the Amendment would have to be attractive to moderate Republicans if it was to have any chance of being passed.

There is no record of the discussions by members of the Joint Committee regarding their views on the various forms of the new draft, but we do know the drafts they considered as well as the votes of individual members. The initial second draft originated as a proposal by former Indiana Congressman Robert Dale Owen[321]:

> Section 1. No discrimination shall be made by any state, nor by the United States, as to the civil rights of persons because of race, color, or previous condition of servitude.[322]

John Bingham immediately moved to amend the proposal by broadening the equal protection principle beyond race and adding a substantive liberty from the Bill of Rights: "[N]or shall any State deny to any person within its jurisdiction the equal protection of the laws, nor take private property for public use without just compensation."[323] After Bingham's motion to amend failed, he joined a majority vote in favor of the original Owen proposal.[324]

Owen's draft closely tracked the earlier criticism of Giles Hotchkiss. Hotchkiss had opposed Bingham's original draft because (1) he presumed Bingham wished simply to force states to equally protect civil rights, but (2) Bingham's proposal left the creation and enforcement of equal civil rights in the politically driven hands of Congress. The Owen proposal remedied these problems by creating a textually defined and judicially enforceable right to equal protection against the states. Although the new draft met Hotchkiss's concerns, Hotchkiss himself had been wrong about Bingham's intentions regarding the Amendment. Although Bingham's original draft used the language of the Comity Clause, Bingham himself wanted to protect the substantive liberties listed in the Bill of Rights. Thus, as drafted, the Owen proposal fell far short of Bingham's goal.

---

[320] KENDRICK, *supra* note 98, at 82.
[321] For a discussion of Robert Dale Owen and his presentment of a draft Fourteenth Amendment to Thaddeus Stevens, see EPPS, *supra* note 37, at 198–99.
[322] KENDRICK, *supra* note 98, at 83.
[323] *Id.* at 85.
[324] *Id.*

Bingham did not give up. Later that day, he succeeded in convincing his fellow committee members to replace Owen's proposal with an entirely different provision:

> [Section] 5. No State shall make or enforce any law which shall abridge the privileges or immunities of citizens of the United States; nor shall any State deprive any person of life, liberty or property without due process of law, nor deny to any person within its jurisdiction the equal protection of the laws.[325]

Bingham's new draft amendment survived a back-and-forth series of votes that first adopted, then rejected, then readopted his proposal.[326] This became the final version of Section One of the Fourteenth Amendment.

Bingham's first draft had used the language of Article IV's Comity Clause and its protection of the rights "of citizens in the several states." Bingham's second draft dropped the language of the Comity Clause and instead protected the rights "of citizens of the United States." Bingham's effort to defend his first draft involved a complicated "ellipsis" reading of Article IV. His speech defending the second and final version of the Privileges or Immunities Clause simply invoked the need to require states to protect rights already declared in the federal Constitution.

B. *Debating the Second Draft*

John Bingham presented the new version of the Fourteenth Amendment to the House of Representatives on May 10, 1866.[327] Although only a few weeks had passed since the failed introduction of his first Article IV-based draft, a great deal had happened. Johnson's veto of the Civil Rights Bill signaled the final breach between the Republicans and the White House on Reconstruction. The elections that fall would be a referendum on presidential and congressional policy regarding American freedom and the readmission of the southern states.

The struggle to secure the support of two-thirds of both houses of Congress to override Johnson's veto of the Freedmen's Bureau Bill (which failed) and the Civil Rights Act of 1866 (which succeeded) illustrated the need to tailor proposals in a manner that maintained the support of moderate Republicans. Speakers who originally pressed for a natural rights reading of *Corfield* and the power of the federal government to oversee all civil rights in the states found

---

[325] *Id.* at 87.
[326] *Id.* For an account of the various votes, see MALTZ, *supra* note 21, at 82.
[327] CONG. GLOBE, 39th Cong., 1st Sess. 2530 (1866).

themselves successfully countered by speakers who held a more traditional reading of *Corfield* and who believed states should be allowed to determine the substantive content of common law civil rights. Finally, Congress had engaged in an extended conversation about the need to extend the national rights of citizenship as it had done under treaties like the Louisiana Cession Act, but do so in a manner that avoided nationalizing the general content of civil rights in the states. Thus, when Bingham introduced an amendment protecting "the privileges or immunities rights of citizens of the United States," he was neither rephrasing the language of Article IV (which he had abandoned) nor introducing a new legal concept. This was the language of national citizenship and antebellum legal treaties recently discussed in widely published presidential statements and congressional speeches.

Partisans in the debates, on the other hand, had an incentive to portray the new draft in exaggerated terms. Accordingly, when the House debated Bingham's new draft on May 10, descriptions of the rights conferred by the Privileges or Immunities Clause varied widely. Opponents of the Amendment, such as Andrew Jackson Rogers, claimed the Privileges or Immunities Clause would nationalize any and every legal and civil right in the country:

> What are privileges and immunities? Why, sir, all the rights we have under the laws of the country are embraced under the definition of privileges and immunities. The right to vote is a privilege. The right to marry is a privilege. The right to contract is a privilege. The right to be a juror is a privilege. The right to be a judge or President of the United States is a privilege. I hold that if that ever becomes a part of the fundamental law of the land it will prevent any State from refusing to allow anything to anybody embraced under this term privileges and immunities.[328]

Immediately following Rogers, Illinois Republican John Farnsworth rose and declared that "[s]o far as this section is concerned, there is but one clause in it which is not already in the Constitution, and it might as well in my opinion read 'No State shall deny to any person within its jurisdiction the equal protection of the laws.' But a reaffirmation of a good principle will do no harm, and I shall not therefore oppose it on account of what I regard as surplussage."[329] Farnsworth and Rogers thus presented polar opposite readings of the text, with Rogers claiming the Amendment nationalized every conceivable right and Farnsworth insisting it added nothing whatsoever to the existing Constitution. Because any proposal that spring could be derailed by swaying only a handful

---

[328] CONG. GLOBE, 39th Cong., 1st Sess. at 2538 (1866).
[329] *Id.* at 2539.

of votes, there was an obvious incentive for opponents and supporters to present unreasonably broad and narrow readings of the text.[330] In this case, neither Farnsworth nor Rogers cared to address what was obviously new text in the second draft: a protection of the privileges or immunities *of citizens of the United States* – a category of rights at once narrower and broader than the visions presented by Rogers and Farnsworth. The afternoon session ended with Farnsworth's speech. The evening session began with Bingham's response to both critics and supporters.

1. John Bingham's Explanation to the House

As a preface to his discussion of the second draft of the Fourteenth Amendment, Bingham briefly noted that the committee had reported two proposed statutory measures in addition to the proposed Fourteenth Amendment. One of these measures barred for life any confederate official from serving in federal office.[331] The proposed amendment also banned anyone who voluntarily joined the Rebellion from voting for federal representatives or federal electors prior to the year 1870.[332] Bingham noted that both the right to serve in federal office and the right to vote for federal representatives were among "the privileges or immunities of citizens of the United States." Congress, however, was within its rights to constrain the exercise of such rights as a condition for readmission to the Union.[333]

The issue of congressional power to impose conditions on readmission was the most hotly debated topics of 1866, and it remains a vexing subject for constitutional scholars today.[334] For our purposes, it is important to focus on Bingham's introductory remarks for what they reveal about the original understanding of privileges and immunities of citizens of the United States. Here is Bingham's full description of the right:

> The franchise of a federal elective office is as clearly one of the privileges of a citizen of the United States as is the elective franchise for choosing Representatives in Congress or Presidential electors. *They are both provided for and guarantied in your Constitution.* Why, then, prohibit rebels from the

---

[330] *See* MALTZ, *supra* note 21, at 93–94.

[331] CONG. GLOBE, 39th Cong., 1st Sess. 2541–42 (1866).

[332] *Id.* at 2542 (quoting Section Three of the proposed amendment).

[333] *Id.*

[334] For competing interpretations of the formal legality of the actions of the Thirty-Ninth Congress, see ACKERMAN, *supra* note 216, at 99–119, 207–34; AMAR, AMERICA'S CONSTITUTION, *supra* note 1, at 364–80; Bruce A. Ackerman, *The Living Constitution*, 120 HARV. L. REV. 1737, 1747 n.25 (2007).

enjoyment of the first for life by an act of Congress and restrict the second for a term of years by a constitutional amendment? To be sure, we all agree, and the great body of the people of this country agree, and the committee thus far in reporting measures of reconstruction agree, that the exercise of the elective franchise, though it be one of the privileges of a citizen of the Republic, is exclusively under the control of the States. But, sir, the committee never intimated and never intended to intimate by any measure they have reported that any State lately in insurrection can exercise either that power or any other until it is restored to its constitutional relation to the Union save by the express or implied consent of the Congress of the United States, nor that after being restored they can exercise that power contrary to the express conditions proscribed by Congress for their restoration. The power to proscribe these conditions is exclusively in Congress. That is the philosophy of every measure of reconstruction now pending before the House.[335]

Bingham's description of "privileges of citizens of the United States" as involving rights "provided for and guarantied by [the] Constitution" was clear and noncontroversial. Southern states and the Democratic Party under the leadership of President Johnson would spent the next several months *insisting* that these were rights of American citizenship that the Republican Congress was wrong to deny.[336] Unlike the state-level civil rights guaranteed equal protection under Article IV, these were rights expressly guaranteed by the Constitution itself. Bingham's reference to the textually granted right of federal representation as a privilege and immunity of citizens of the United States echoes the arguments of Bingham's legal hero, Daniel Webster. During the debates over the admission of Missouri and the application of the Louisiana Cession Act, Webster had insisted that the rights, advantages, and immunities of citizens of the United States were those expressly listed in the federal Constitution, such as the Article I right of the people in each state to elect federal representatives.[337]

---

[335] CONG. GLOBE, 39th Cong., 1st Sess. at 2542.
[336] *See* discussion in Chapter 4.
[337] According to Daniel Webster:

> The obvious meaning therefore of [Article III] is, that the rights derived under the federal Constitution shall be enjoyed by the inhabitants of Louisiana in the same manner as by the citizens of other States. The United States, by the Constitution, are bound to guarantee to every State in the Union a republican form of government; and the inhabitants of Louisiana are entitled, when a State, to this guarantee. Each State has a right to two senators, and to representatives according to a certain enumeration of population pointed out in the Constitution. The inhabitants of Louisiana, upon their admission into the Union, are also entitled to these privileges.

> DANIEL WEBSTER ET AL., A MEMORIAL TO THE CONGRESS OF THE UNITED STATES, ON THE SUBJECT OF RESTRAINING THE INCREASE OF SLAVERY IN NEW STATES TO BE ADMITTED TO THE UNION 15–16 (Boston, Phelps 1819) (Early Am. Imprints, Series 2, no. 47390).

Bingham likewise explained that the privilege of citizens of the United States to vote or run for federal office was "provided for and guarantied *in your Constitution.*"[338]

Bingham then turned to the first section of the proposed amendment:

> The necessity for the first section of this amendment to the Constitution, Mr. Speaker, is one of the lessons that have been taught to your committee and taught to all the people of this country by the history of the past four years of terrible conflict – that history in which God is, and in which He teaches the profoundest lessons to men and nations. There was a want hitherto, and there remains a want now, in the Constitution of our country, which the proposed amendment will supply. What is that? It is the power in the people, the whole people of the United States, by express authority of the Constitution to do that by congressional enactment which hitherto they have not had the power to do, and have never even attempted to do; that is, to protect by national law the privileges and immunities of all the citizens of the Republic and the inborn rights of every person within its jurisdiction whenever the same shall be abridged or denied by the unconstitutional acts of any State.

> Allow me, Mr. Speaker, in passing, to say that this amendment takes from no State any right that ever pertained to it. No State ever had the right, under the forms of law or otherwise, to deny to any freeman the equal protection of the laws or to abridge the privileges or immunities of any citizen of the Republic, although many of them have assumed and exercised the power, and that without remedy. The amendment does not give, as the second section shows, the power of Congress of regulating suffrage in the several States.[339]

In this passage, Bingham continues his longstanding practice of distinguishing the natural rights of all persons from the rights of citizens of the United States. The rights of equal protection are "the inborn rights of every person," whereas "citizens of the Republic" enjoy an additional set of national privileges or immunities. These privileges or immunities are not unlimited; they do not, for example, include a national right of suffrage. In fact, according to Bingham, the Amendment took "from no State any right that ever pertained to it," but simply granted Congress the previously missing power to enforce those national rights states ought to have respected from the beginning.

Weeks earlier, during the debate over the Civil Rights Act, Bingham had declared, "I know that the enforcement of the bill of rights is the want of

---

[338] Cong. Globe, 39th Cong., 1st Sess. 2542 (1866) (emphasis added).

[339] *Id.* at 2542. Bingham here referred to the second section's implied allowance of black dis-enfranchisement by states, so long as the state's representation in Congress was reduced proportionately. *See* U.S. Const. amend. XIV, § 2.

the Republic."[340] At that time, Bingham could not support the Civil Rights Act due to Congress's lack of constitutional authority to enforce national privileges and immunities such as Fifth Amendment right to due process. Bingham now proposes to remedy that situation: "There was a want hitherto, and there remains a want now, in the Constitution of our country, which the proposed amendment will supply." As he had done so often in the past, Bingham described these national privileges and immunities of citizens of the United States in the language of the federal Constitution:

> [M]any instances of State injustice and oppression have already occurred in the State legislation of this Union, of flagrant violations of the guarantied privileges of citizens of the United States, for which the national Government furnished, and could furnish by law no remedy whatsoever. Contrary to the express letter of your Constitution, "cruel and unusual punishment" have been inflicted under State laws within this Union upon citizens, not only for crimes committed, but for sacred duty done, for which and against which the Government of the United States had provided no remedy and could provide none.[341]

Bingham's example of state punishments for "sacred duty done" in violation of the Eighth Amendment involved South Carolina's law requiring "citizens of the United States" to "abjure their allegiance to every other government or authority than that of the State of South Carolina."[342] According to Bingham,

> It was an opprobrium to the Republic that for fidelity to the United States they could not by national law be protected against the degrading punishment inflicted on slaves and felons by State law. That great want of the citizen and stranger, protection by national law from unconstitutional State enactments, is supplied by the first section of this amendment. That is the extent it hath, no more.[343]

---

[340] CONG. GLOBE, 39th Cong., 1st Sess. 1291 (1866).

[341] *Id.* at 2542.

[342] *Id.* Some of Bingham's argument here suggests that he may have continued to personally believe the language of the Comity Clause obligated the states to enforce the Bill of Rights. For example, Bingham states, "Sir, the words of the Constitution that 'the citizens of each State shall be entitled to all the privileges and immunities of citizens in the several states' include, among other privileges, the right to bear true allegiance to the Constitution and the laws of the United States, and to be protected in life liberty and property." *Id.* at 2542. His decision to nevertheless replace the language of the Comity Clause with the language of national treaties reflects his hard-learned knowledge that his colleagues did not have the same understanding of Article IV.

[343] *Id.* at 2543. Bingham's view of allegiance as a national privilege may be part of the definition of US citizenship as the term is used in the federal Constitution. *See, e.g.,* CONG. GLOBE, 39th Cong., 1st Sess. 2884–84 (1866) (Remarks of Mr. Latham) ("Allegiance and protection are

As far as suffrage was concerned, Bingham adopted the moderate position that, once readmitted, the regulation of the federal franchise would be "exclusively under the control of the States."[344] Absent a constitutional amendment, the issue of suffrage remained one of the rights retained by the people in the several states. Unlike radical Republicans, who rejected the very idea of states' rights, republican moderates like Bingham believed the independent sovereignty of the states was a critical aspect of properly functioning constitutional government. Thus, according to Bingham, the purpose of this new draft of the Fourteenth Amendment was "to secure the safety of the Republic, the equality of the States, and the equal rights of all the people under the sanctions of inviolable law."[345] This was not just a statement looking toward the readmission of those southern states that adopted the Amendment; it also reflected the moderate position that states remained an important constituent part of American constitutional government. As Bingham declared a few months later, "I would say once for all, that this dual system of national and State government under the American organization is the secret of our strength and power. I do not propose to abandon it."[346]

Throughout his speech, Bingham insisted that his proposal confirmed to the original federalist vision of the Constitution:

[T]his amendment takes from no State any right that ever pertained to it. No State ever had the right, under the forms of law or otherwise, to deny to any freeman the equal protection of the laws or to abridge the privileges or immunities of any citizen of the Republic, although many of them have assumed and exercised the power, and that without remedy.[347]

reciprocal duties, binding, the one upon the citizen, the other upon the Government; and inseparably connected with the faithful observance of all the obligations of allegiance are all the rights which attach by virtue of citizenship."); *see also* CONG. GLOBE, 35th Cong., 2d Sess. 983 (1859) (remarks of Mr. Bingham) ("Who are the citizens of the United States? Sir, they are those, and those only, who owe allegiance to the government of the United States"); Edward Bates, *Citizenship*, 10 Op. Att'y Gen. 388 (Nov. 29, 1862) ("The Constitution uses the word citizen only to express the political quality of the individual in his relation to the nation; to declare that he is a member of the body politic, and bound to it by the reciprocal obligation of allegiance on the one side, and protection on the other."). On the other hand, Bingham may be referring to the oath Article VI requires of all federal and state officials to uphold the supremacy of the federal Constitution and federal law "any Thing in the Constitution or Laws of any state to the Contrary notwithstanding." U.S. CONST. art. VI, cl. 2. Regardless, Bingham's allegation that South Carolina had violated a privilege of citizens of the United States involved the "cruel and unusual punishment" imposed on persons who refused to violate the oath of allegiance to the United States – a punishment expressly prohibited by the federal Constitution.

[344] CONG. GLOBE, 39th Cong., 1st Sess. 2543 (1866).

[345] *Id.* (emphasis added).

[346] CONG. GLOBE, 39th Cong., 2d Sess. 450 (1867).

[347] CONG. GLOBE, 39th Cong., 1st Sess. 2542 (1866).

It would be an enormous change, of course, if the proposed Amendment nationalized the subject of civil rights and placed the entire matter under federal control. Bingham's claim that the "amendment takes from no State any rights that ever pertained to it" was plausible only if the Amendment limited the privileges and immunities of citizens of the United States to rights that had been listed in the original Constitution – rights "provided for and guarantied *in your Constitution*."[348] The changed text and Bingham's explanation apparently satisfied the conservative side of the House. As Earl Maltz notes, "None of the Republicans who had voiced federalism-based concerns regarding Bingham's initial proposal – Conkling, Hale, congressmen Davis and Hotchkiss, and Senator Stewart – expressed similar objections to the committee's version of section one (although Hale would later claim that he had made such objections)."[349]

Bingham's insistence that the liberties expressly enumerated in the Bill of Rights constituted privileges of citizens of the United States was not new. He had made this claim in defense of his original draft, and he repeated the same in his speech explaining the second draft. What had changed was his use of Article IV. None of his colleagues seemed to understand Bingham's "ellipsis" theory of Article IV's Comity Clause that informed his original draft. Most of the members of the Thirty-Ninth Congress read the Comity Clause in light of antebellum judicial opinions that described the provision as doing nothing more than providing a degree of equal protection for state-conferred rights. With his new draft of the Fourteenth Amendment, Bingham's goal of protecting the Bill of Rights remained the same, but his choice of language to accomplish that goal reflected what he now knew to be the common reading of Article IV. To clarify that the rights to be protected were the constitutionally conferred rights of federal citizens and not the state-conferred civil rights granted a degree of equal protection under the Comity Clause, Bingham abandoned his obscure "ellipsis" argument about Article IV and instead used language expressly declaring that states were bound to protect the "the privileges or immunities *of citizens of the United States*."

Bingham closed his discussion of Section One by repeating his claim that this newly drafted section *only* protected federal privileges and immunities such as those protected under the Eighth Amendment: "That is the extent that it hath, no more."[350] As he had insisted in February, Bingham's purpose was "to arm the Congress of the United States . . . with the power to enforce

---

[348] *Id.* (describing the enumerated right to vote for federal representatives).
[349] MALTZ, *supra* note 21, at 94.
[350] CONG. GLOBE, 39th Cong., 1st Sess. 2542 (emphasis added) (1866).

the bill of rights as it stands in the Constitution today. It 'hath that extent –
no more.'"[351] Bingham refused to join those who sought to nationalize the
substantive content of natural rights or general common law civil rights. As
he had insisted during the debates over the Civil Rights Act, the substance of
such rights was left to state control, subject only to the requirement that they
be protected equally with the procedural rights of due process. Anything more
would not only contradict Bingham's own theory of divided government, but
would doom the Amendment by alienating the votes of moderate and conservative Republicans.[352] Instead, Bingham presented an amendment limited
to those rights actually listed in the Constitution. As Bingham put it in the
midst of the ratification debates, "no state may deny to any person the equal
protection of the laws, including all the limitations for *personal protection of
every article and section of the Constitution.*"[353]

It was possible, of course, to view this as a colossal mistake, and an ignorant one at that. The original Bill of Rights did not bind the states. Treating
provisions like the Eighth Amendment as guaranteeing national privileges
and immunities that states must respect could be viewed either as reflecting
ignorance of the law and judicial precedents like *Barron v. Baltimore* or as a
wicked attempt to constrain the states in matters that the original Constitution left to local control. Conservative critics keeping an eye on events in the
Thirty-Ninth Congress recognized the significance of Bingham's efforts, and
they assailed the idea that states should be bound to follow the Bill of Rights.
As conservative critic S. S. Nicholas wrote not long after Congress passed the
Amendment:

> The bill of rights, or what are termed the guarantees of liberty, contained
> in the Federal Constitution, have none of them any sort of application to or
> bearing upon the State governments, but are solely prohibitions or restrictions
> upon the Federal Government. The recent attempt in Congress to treat
> them as guaranties against the State governments, with an accompanying
> incidental power to enforce the guaranties, is a surprising evidence of stolid
> ignorance of Constitutional law, or of a shameless effort to impose upon the
> ignorant.[354]

---

[351] CONG. GLOBE, 39th Cong., 1st Sess. 1088 (1866).

[352] Note also that Bingham's final draft was supported by conservatives on the Joint Committee
(and opposed by some Radicals). *See* MALTZ, *supra* note 21, at 82. This would make no sense if
those members understood the text as both nationalizing common law civil rights and granting
federal power to regulate the same.

[353] CONG. GLOBE, 39th Cong., 2d Sess. 811 (emphasis added).

[354] S. S. Nicholas, *The Civil Rights Act, in* 3 CONSERVATIVE ESSAYS, LEGAL AND POLITICAL 47,
48–49 (1867).

It is possible that Bingham's critics were (and are) correct and that his efforts reflected a misunderstanding of the original Constitution and a failure to appreciate the Supreme Court's ruling in *Barron v. Baltimore*. As we shall see, the latter criticism is implausible; Bingham well understood *Barron* and its import. For now, it is important to recognize that not only did Bingham clearly announce his intentions inside the halls of Congress, but those intentions seem to have been understood outside the halls as well.

2. Jacob Howard's Explanation to the Senate

Probably the most studied speech of the Thirty-Ninth Congress regarding the Fourteenth Amendment is that of Michigan's Republican Senator Jacob Howard. Howard was a member of the Joint Committee that adopted Bingham's final draft of Section One. Due to an unexpected change in circumstances, it fell on Howard's shoulders to introduce the Amendment to the full Senate. The original plan had been for Senator William Pitt Fessenden to present the amendment, but Fessenden had suddenly fallen ill, leaving Howard to serve as a last-minute stand-in.[355] Despite Howard's own confession that he was not the best person to explain the thinking behind the Joint Committee's proposal, his speech seems to have been considered acceptable to his fellow Senators on the Joint Committee, for it went uninterrupted at the time of its delivery and uncontradicted in the debates and speeches that followed.[356]

Howard began by apologizing for Fessenden's absence; he had hoped that Fessenden "should take the lead, and the prominent lead, in the conduct of this discussion."[357] Nevertheless, Howard promised to present "in a very succinct way, the views and the motives which influenced that committee, so far as I understand those views and motives, in presenting the report which is now before us for consideration, and the ends it aims to accomplish."[358] Turning

---

[355] *See* Cong. Globe, 39th Cong., 1st Sess. 2764–65 (1866) (remarks of Sen. Howard).

[356] According to a *New York Times* editorial, Howard's speech was "frank and satisfactory. His exposition of the considerations which led the Committee to seek the protection, by a Constitutional declaration, of 'the privileges and immunities of the citizens of the several States of the Union,' was clear and cogent. To this, the first section of the amendment, the Union party throughout the country will yield a ready acquiescence, and the South could offer no justifiable resistance." Editorial, *The Reconstruction Committee's Amendment in the Senate*, N.Y. Times, May 25, 1866, at 4. *See also* Bryan H. Wildenthal, *Nationalizing the Bill of Rights: Revisiting the Original Understanding of the Fourteenth Amendment in 1866–67*, 68 Ohio St. L. J. 1509, 1577 (2007).

[357] Cong. Globe, 39th Cong., 1st Sess. 2764–65 (1866).

[358] *Id.* at 2765.

to the text, Howard explained that "[t]he first clause of this section relates to the privileges and immunities of citizens of the United States as such, and as distinguished from all other persons not citizens of the United States."[359] Conceding that "[i]t is not, perhaps, very easy to define with accuracy what is meant by the expression, 'citizen of the United States,'" Howard recounted how the Founders had approached the issue of national citizenship.[360] Because it had been possible that the original states might treat visitors from other "foreign" states as aliens, Howard explained, the Founders had added Article IV to the Constitution

> [w]ith a view to prevent such confusion and disorder, and to put the citizens of the several states on an equality with each other as to all fundamental rights.... The effect of this clause was to constitute *ipso facto* the citizens of each one of the original States citizens of the United States.... They are, by constitutional right, entitled to these privileges and immunities ... and ask for their enforcement whenever they go within the limits of the several States of the Union.[361]

This was not the same "ipso facto" argument regarding Article IV put forth by John Bingham during the debates of the initial draft. Howard, here, was simply echoing the discussion of Article IV found in Joseph Story's *Commentaries on the Constitution*.[362] In fact, Howard declined to analyze the particular content of Article IV privileges and immunities. Such a discussion was not worth the time and, Howard believed, of little current importance to the members of the Thirty-Ninth Congress:

> It would be a curious question to solve what are the privileges and immunities of citizens of each of the States in the several States. I do not propose to go at any length into that question at this time. It would be a somewhat barren discussion. But it is certain the clause was inserted in the Constitution for some good purpose. It has in view some results beneficial to the citizens of the several States, or it would not be found there; yet I am not aware that the Supreme Court have ever undertaken to define either the nature or extent of the privileges and immunities thus guaranteed. Indeed, if my recollection serves me, that court, on a certain occasion not many years since, when this

---

359 *Id.*
360 *Id.*
361 *Id.*
362 3 STORY, *supra* note 70, at 565–66 ("Every citizen of a state is *ipso facto* a citizen of the United States. And a person, who is a naturalized citizen of the United States, by a like residence in any state in the Union, becomes *ipso facto* a citizen of that state.").

question seemed to present itself to them, very modestly declined to go into a definition of them, leaving questions arising under the clause to be discussed and adjudicated when they should happen practically to arise.[363]

If Section One proposed to nationalize the corpus of state-conferred rights covered by Article IV and (under Section Five) authorize congressional regulation of the same, the specific content of Article IV rights would have been a subject of tremendous importance to the Senate. Howard's dismissive treatment of Article IV privileges and immunities (exploring such rights would constitute a "barren" discussion) suggests nothing so momentous was at hand.

Rather than defining Article IV rights, Howard rather weakly suggests that Article IV "has in view *some* results beneficial to the citizens of the several states or it would not be found there."[364] Instead, Howard referred the Senate to Justice Washington's description of Article IV privileges and immunities in *Corfield*, which, he explained, probably represented the approach the Supreme Court would take if it found itself having to define Article IV. After quoting Washington's "fundamental rights" passage in *Corfield*,[365] Howard then turned to the federal Bill of Rights. Because the next passage has played such an important role in Fourteenth Amendment scholarship, it warrants an extended quotation:

> Such is the character of the privileges and immunities spoken of in the second section of the fourth article of the Constitution. To these privileges and immunities, whatever they may be – for they are not and cannot be fully defined in their entire extent and precise nature – to these should be added the personal rights guarantied and secured by the first eight amendments of the Constitution; such as the freedom of speech and of the press; the right of the people peaceably to assemble and petition the Government for a redress of grievances, a right appertaining to each and all the people; the right to keep and to bear arms; the right to be exempted from the quartering of soldiers in a house without the consent of the owner; the right to be exempt from unreasonable searches and seizures, and from any search or seizure except by virtue of a warrant issued upon a formal oath or affidavit; the right of an accused person to be informed of the nature of the accusation against him, and his right to be tried by an impartial jury of the vicinage; and also the right to be secure against excessive bail and against cruel and unusual punishments.

---

[363] Cong. Globe, 39th Cong., 1st Sess. 2765.
[364] Id. (emphasis added).
[365] Id.; *see also* discussion of *Corfield* in Chapter 2.

Now, sir, here is a mass of privileges, immunities, and rights, some of them
secured by the second section of the fourth article of the Constitution, which
I have recited, some by the first eight amendments of the Constitution; and it
is a fact well worthy of attention that the course of decision of our courts and
the present settled doctrine is, that all these immunities, privileges, rights,
thus guarantied by the Constitution or recognized by it, are secured to the
citizen solely as a citizen of the United States and as a party in their courts.
They do not operate in the slightest degree as a restraint of prohibition upon
State legislation. States are not affected by them, and it has been repeatedly
held that the restriction contained in the Constitution against the taking of
private property for public use without just compensation is not a restriction
upon State legislation, but applies only to the legislation of Congress.[366]

Howard read the Privileges or Immunities Clause as protecting rights listed
both in the Comity Clause of Article IV and in the first eight amendments
to the Constitution. Here, though, one must be careful not to read Howard
as advocating the radical Republican view that matters granted equal protection under the Comity Clause must be transformed into substantive national
rights. If you look closely at the quote, you will see that Howard's reference to
privileges and immunities that "are not and cannot be fully defined in their
entire extent and precise nature" was a reference to rights "secured by the
second section of the fourth article of the Constitution," the Comity Clause.
According to standard antebellum cases like *Corfield*, it was in fact the case that
the rights granted equal protection under the Comity Clause could never be
exhaustively listed, if only because states remained free to alter and adjust the
privileges and immunities they granted to their own citizens. There is nothing
in Howard's speech, however, that suggests Howard believed the Privileges or
Immunities Clause transformed the equally protected state-secured rights of
the Comity Clause into substantive nonenumerated rights of national citizenship. Instead, it appears that Howard simply included the equally protected
"privileges and immunities" of the Comity Clause as part of the constitutionally secured rights protected under the Privileges or Immunities Clause,
along with the other enumerated rights of the first eight amendments. Or, put
another way, Howard believed that the privileges and immunities of citizens
of the United States included all the personal guarantees enumerated in the
Constitution, from the equal rights of Article IV to the substantive rights of the
first eight amendments.

   This view fits with the antebellum understanding of "privileges and immunities of citizens of the United States." Daniel Webster and other antebellum

---

[366] CONG. GLOBE, 39th Cong., 1st Sess. 2765 (1866).

abolitionist writers had insisted that federal rights and immunities were those listed in the Constitution, including the rights of representation in Article I and the right to access federal courts listed in Article III.[367] According to such a view, Article IV rights, as traditionally understood, also would be considered among the privileges and immunities of national citizenship. In his commentaries, for example, Joseph Story described Article IV rights as belonging to "citizens of the United States," as had antebellum courts.[368] Again, this reading did not treat Article IV rights as substantive national rights. Instead, it simply reflected that citizens of the United States had a right of equal access to a limited set of state-conferred rights when traveling to a state other than their home state. Treating the equal protection principle of Article IV as one of the constitutionally enumerated privileges and immunities of citizens of the United States also fits with Bingham's speech introducing Section One to the House, particularly Bingham's assertion that the Amendment threatened none of the reserved rights and powers of the States. Finally, and most importantly, federal enforcement of this traditional reading of Article IV would not have threatened the successful passage of the Amendment. Indeed, it would explain Howard's nonchalant treatment of the issue.

Nor would it have been redundant for the Privileges or Immunities Clause to cover rights already announced in the federal Constitution. As Bingham and other advocates repeatedly insisted, the problem was not so much a failure of the original Constitution to list federal privileges and immunities as it was a failure to provide congressional power to *enforce* constitutionally enumerated rights. As Howard explained to his colleagues:

> Now, sir, there is no power given in the Constitution to enforce and to carry out any of these guarantees. They are not powers granted by the Constitution to Congress, and of course do not come within the sweeping clause of the Constitution authorizing Congress to pass all laws necessary and proper for carrying out the foregoing or granted powers, but they stand simply as a bill of rights in the Constitution, without power on the part of Congress to give them full effect;[369] while at the same time the States are not restrained from violating the principles embraced in them except by their own local constitutions, which may be altered from year to year. The great object of the first section of this amendment is, therefore, to restrain the power of

---

[367] *See* discussion in Chapter 2.

[368] *Id.*

[369] Although it is not clear, Howard may have adopted (or was explaining) Bingham's view that Article IV and the first eight amendments collectively constituted the "Bill of Rights."

the States and compel them at all times to respect these great fundamental guarantees.[370]

Howard's later speeches in the Thirty-Ninth Congress strongly support a conclusion that Howard's reference to Article IV involved the enumerated rights of equal protection and not unenumerated substantive rights. Only a few months after Howard delivered his speech on the Fourteenth Amendment, the same Thirty-Ninth Congress debated what conditions ought to be placed on the admission of Nebraska to the Union, in particular whether the state should be required to grant blacks the right to vote. In support of such a condition, some members argued that Congress had the power to place any condition it wished on the admission of a new states and that the condition could not be thereafter altered without the consent of Congress. Howard was appalled by such arguments, for they suggested that Congress could regulate all manner of subjects that the Constitution reserved to the people in the states. According to Howard, if Congress could require a state to provide equal voting rights for a black man, it could also require equal voting rights for women.[371] The same power would allow Congress to control state regulation of how real estate can be distributed among a decedent's heirs and the legal proceedings in regard to the collection of debt.[372] "Indeed," objected Howard,

> we may go through all the details of State policy, State legislation, and *individual* rights, as regulated by the constitutions of the States.... What, then, becomes of State rights?... It denies to the people of the States almost all, yes, all, substantially, of those original and immemorial rights which have been exercised by the people of the States ever since the dissolution of our connection with Great Britain.[373]

Such a states-rights objection would be odd if Howard believed that his committee had already proposed an amendment to the Constitution that transformed all natural and common law rights in the states into substantive national liberties, with additional federal power to enforce the same. More likely, Howard understood the proposed Fourteenth Amendment as leaving the general regulation of unenumerated individual rights to the discretion of the people in the states, subject only to the equal access requirements of Article IV and the general Fourteenth Amendment requirements of due process and equal protection.

---

[370] CONG. GLOBE, 39th Cong., 1st Sess. 2765–66 (1866).
[371] CONG. GLOBE, 39th Cong., 2d Sess. 219 (1866).
[372] *Id.*
[373] *Id.* (emphasis added).

3. The First Eight Amendments

Notice also that Howard omitted the Ninth Amendment from his list of enumerated "privileges or immunities of citizens of the United States." Instead, he listed only the first eight amendments to the Constitution. Given that the proposed amendment was about enhancing federal power to protect personal rights in the states, it makes sense that Howard would have little to say about the Tenth Amendment.[374] But why omit the Ninth?

The Ninth Amendment declares that "the enumeration in the Constitution, of certain rights, shall not be construed to deny or disparage others retained by the people."[375] If this provision was understood as a reference to an unenumerated category of "privileges and immunities of citizens of the United States," then the adoption of the Fourteenth Amendment would open the door to federal identification and enforcement of an unlimited list of federally defined rights. Not only would such a proposal conflict with Howard's own views of matters best left to state control, we also know that any such proposal in the Thirty-Ninth Congress would have met with immediate, and likely successful, resistance. It is possible, of course, that Howard omitted the Amendment in a disingenuous effort to avoid the more controversial aspects of the proposed Amendment. More likely, though, Howard simply shared the common view that distinguished the individual rights listed in the first eight amendments from the federalism-based protections of the Ninth and Tenth Amendments.

Although today it is common to view the Ninth Amendment as a rather enigmatic reference to "other" individual rights,"[376] in the period between the Founding and the Civil War, the Ninth Amendment was understood as working in tandem with the Tenth Amendment to preserve the people's retained rights of local self-government.[377] Every court and legal commentator who addressed the Ninth Amendment during this period treated the provision as preserving rights and powers to state-level control. Defenders of the seceding states, for example, cited the Ninth Amendment as preserving the right of the people in the states to secede from the Union.[378] Howard's omission of the

---

[374] It is possible to view both the Ninth and Tenth Amendments as protecting individual liberty. *See* Kurt T. Lash, The Lost History of the Ninth Amendment (2009); *see also infra* Chapter 6. Given the context in which the amendment was enacted, however, it makes sense that Howard would focus on the personal guarantees of the first eight amendments.

[375] U.S. Const. amend. IX.

[376] *See, e.g.,* Griswold v. Connecticut, 381 U.S. 479, 488 (1965) (Goldberg, J., concurring).

[377] *See* Lash, *supra* note 374.

[378] *See id.* at 241; *see also* Cong. Globe, 39th Cong., 1st Sess. 2467 (1866) (Representative Boyer) (arguing that the Ninth and Tenth Amendments prohibit the Federal government from "trampl[ing] upon" the southern States by disenfranchising the large majority of their voting population).

Ninth Amendment likely reflected the consensus antebellum understanding of the clause.[379] As we shall see, John Bingham also focused his attention on the first eight amendments.[380]

4. Normalizing *Corfield v. Coryell*

In Chapter 2, I discussed Justice Washington's opinion in *Corfield v. Coryell*[381] and its commonly accepted meaning in antebellum jurisprudence.[382] As the reader will have noticed, the case played a prominent and repeated role in the debates of the Thirty-Ninth Congress. *Corfield* came up during the debates over Bingham's first and second drafts of the Fourteenth Amendment and during the debates over the Civil Rights Act. The case is cited in the *Congressional Globe* for 1866 so often that scholars have long assumed Justice Washington's discussion of Comity Clause privileges and immunities somehow holds the key to the original understanding of the Privileges or Immunities Clause of Section One. Some scholars, for example, believe that members of the Thirty-Ninth Congress intended to transform Justice Washington's list of "fundamental rights" into substantive national rights, including natural and civil rights previously left to state control.[383]

---

[379] One can find scattered examples of non-federalist interpretations of the Ninth Amendment. For example, early in the debates of the Thirty-Ninth Congress, Senator James Nye declared:

> In the enumeration of natural and personal rights to be protected, the framers of the Constitution apparently specified everything they could think of – "life," "liberty," "property," "freedom of speech," "freedom of the press," "freedom in the exercise of religion," "security of person," &c.; and then, lest something essential in the specifications should have been overlooked, it was provided in the ninth amendment that "the enumeration in the Constitution of certain rights should not be construed to deny or disparage other rights not enumerated." This amendment completed the document. It left no personal or natural right to be invaded or impaired by construction. All these rights are established by the fundamental law.

Cong. Globe, 39th Cong., 1st Sess. 1072 (1866). Nye was a Radical Republican who also believed that Congress had full supervisory authority over civil rights in the states. *See supra* note 136. As was true for other radical Republicans, his views represented a minority position.

[380] Cong. Globe, 42d Cong., 1st Sess., app. 84. In the next chapter, I take a closer look at John Bingham's discussion of the Privileges or Immunities Clause in the Forty-Second Congress.

[381] *See* Corfield v. Coryell, 6. F. Cas. 546, 551–52 (C.C.E.D. Pa. 1823) (No. 3,320).

[382] *See* Chapter 2 at III.E.

[383] *See, e.g.,* Barnett, Restoring the Lost Constitution, *supra* note 188, at 62–68 (presenting statements made by members of the Thirty-Ninth Congress as evidence that members of Congress sought to transform *Corfield's* fundamental rights into substantive national rights).

Having now canvassed both antebellum law and the actual debates in the Thirty-Ninth Congress, we can see why such assertions are, at least as a historical matter, deeply problematic. The antebellum understanding of *Corfield* was no different from the understanding of other antebellum Comity Clause cases like *Abbott v. Baily* and *Lemmon v. The People*. The case did not represent a list of substantive "fundamental" national rights; its accepted meaning involved the rights of equal access to a limited set of state-conferred rights. Radical Republicans in the Thirty-Ninth Congress who initially pressed for a broad natural rights reading of *Corfield* were immediately challenged by colleagues who cited antebellum case law that interpreted both *Corfield* and the Comity Clause of Article IV in a far more limited fashion. It is not surprising, therefore, that proponents of the Civil Rights Act and Section One increasingly avoided references to *Corfield* as the debates progressed and it became clear that the passage of both required the support of moderates and conservative Republicans, who resisted any calls for the nationalization of natural or common law civil rights. By the end of the debates, even radical Republicans began to embrace the more limited view of *Corfield*.

A good illustration of the "normalization" of *Corfield* involves an effort by Ohio Republican Representative Samuel Shellabarger to pass a civil rights bill that would enforce the rights covered by the Comity Clause.[384] First

---

[384] Philip Hamburger contends that Bingham may have based his second draft of the Fourteenth Amendment on Samuel Shellabarger's Bill. *See* Philip Hamburger, *Privileges or Immunities*, 105 Nw. U. L. Rev. 61, 124 (2011). Hamburger believes that Bingham may have been so struck by the title and content of the Bill that he decided to copy Shellabarger's language and approach in his second draft of the Fourteenth Amendment. *Id.* This would mean that the final language of the Privileges or Immunities Clause, like Shellabarger's bill, protected nothing other than the equal protection rights of the Comity Clause. *Id.* at 124–25.

There are a number of problems with this theory. To begin with, although Hamburger describes Shellabarger as giving a speech to his fellow members regarding the meaning of his proposed bill (*see id.* at 120), this never in fact happened. Following Shellabarger's initial submission on April 2, 1866, the bill was sent to committee without comment. *See* Cong. Globe, 39th Cong., 1st Sess. at 1719 (1866). Days later, James F. Wilson proposed amending the Bill to clarify "[t]hat the enumeration of the privileges and immunities of citizenship in this act contained shall not be deemed a denial or abridgment of *any other* rights, privileges, or immunities which appertain to citizenship under the Constitution." *See* 39th Cong., 1st Sess. H.R. 437 (May 7, 1866) (Wilson's amended version of Shellabarger's Bill) (emphasis added). Wilson's amended version was reported back to the House on July 25, long after the debates on the Fourteenth Amendment. *See* Cong. Globe, 39th Cong. 1st Sess. at 4148 (1866). However, the House had more pressing matters to attend to, and Wilson successfully suggested that the Bill be tabled until the next session. Shellabarger had no objection to Wilson's amendment and he agreed with the postponement. *Id.* Because this denied Shellabarger the chance to make a speech explaining the bill, he asked that his remarks be added to the official record in the appendix of the *Congressional Globe*. *See* Cong. Globe, 39th Cong., 1st Sess. 4148 (July 25, 1866). Wilson brought the bill forward the next session with the same amendment but,

introduced in April, Shellabarger explained his "Bill to Declare and Protect All the Privileges and Immunities of Citizens of the United States," in a speech submitted for entry into the congressional record in July.[385] In the submitted text of his speech, Shellabarger distinguished his proposed bill from the original Civil Rights Act on the grounds that the latter "insures equality in *certain* civil rights," whereas his newly proposed bill "protects *all* the fundamental rights of the citizen of one State who seeks to enjoy them in another State."[386]

Like other radical Republicans,[387] Shellabarger believed that the "fundamental rights" guaranteed to sojourning citizens under Article IV were the substantive rights of "national citizenship" that a state could no more deny its own citizens than it could deny them to visitors from other states.[388] Shellabarger conceded, however, that Article IV as traditionally interpreted by antebellum courts and treatise writers did not protect substantive rights. Because his bill proposed to do nothing more than enforce the privileges and immunities of

---

again, no action was taken and the bill apparently died. *See* Cong. Globe, 39th Cong., 2d Sess., H.R. 1037 (Jan. 23, 1867) (Wilson of the Judiciary Committee reporting Shellabarger's Bill.)

In the end, Shellabarger's bill was never discussed in either house of Congress, was repeatedly put off, and ultimately died. This is not the kind of history that suggests that Shellabarger's Bill had much, or even any, impact on anyone's thinking in the Thirty-Ninth Congress. Nor would anyone have found the mere *title* of Shellabarger's Bill to be at all unique. Rights covered by the Comity Clause had been described as the privileges "of citizens of the United States" as far back as Joseph Story's *Commentaries*. Bingham himself had repeatedly used the same language in an "ellipsis" to describe the rights protected under Article IV. Thus, Bingham would have had no reason to be impressed by the mere title of Shellabarger's undiscussed and ultimately ignored bill. In fact, Shellabarger may have intentionally used language he had heard Bingham use earlier in the debates in an effort to attract the votes of moderate Republicans.

By the time Shellabarger's Bill got out of committee, Bingham's second draft of Section One was already on the table and had been presented as protecting much more than just the rights of the Comity Clause – thus the need for Wilson's amendment clarifying that Shellabarger's bill should *not* be read as an exclusive list of national privileges or immunities. In fact, Wilson proposed his clarifying amendment to Shellabarger's Bill within days of the Joint Committee's final vote on Bingham's proposed second draft of Section One. *See* Kendrick, *supra* note 98, at 106 (April 28, 1866) (adopting Bingham's draft), and Bills and Resolutions, House of Representatives, 39th Cong., 1st Sess. May 7, 1866 (Ordered to be printed. Amendment in the nature of a substitute to bill H.R. 437, proposed by Mr. J. F. Wilson) ["H.R. 437" was Shellabarger's Bill].

[385] Cong. Globe, 39th Cong., 1st Sess. app. 293 (1866).

[386] *Id.* (emphasis added).

[387] *See* Maltz, *supra* note 21, at 39 (describing Shellabarger as a "Radical Republican"); *see also* Benedict, *supra* note 36, at 175 (listing Shellabarger as one of the radical Republican leaders in the House of Representatives).

[388] *See* Cong. Globe, 39th Cong., 1st Sess. app. 293 (discussing how the rights protected by the bill were "fundamental" rights that states could not rightfully deny to their own citizens).

Article IV as traditionally understood,[389] its scope was limited to guaranteeing sojourning citizens equal access to a limited set of state-conferred rights.

No doubt aware that he would have to carefully circumscribe the scope of the bill if it was to have any chance of passage, Shellabarger engaged in an extended examination of antebellum case law and commentary regarding the Comity Clause of Article IV as a limited provision providing nothing more than equal access to a limited set of state-conferred rights. Instead of relying on Justice Washington's opinion in *Corfield*, Shellabarger instead relied on *Lemmon v. The People* as his primary example of the proper meaning of Article IV:

> This clause, therefore, enacts that all "the privileges and immunities" of a "general" or "national" citizenship shall be enjoyed in every State by the citizens of the United States. Again, it was the design of this clause, as is expressed by the court of appeals of New York, in *Lemmon v. The People* (6 Smith's Reports, 626, 627) to secure to the citizens of every State within every other State the "privileges and immunities (whatever they might be) accorded in each to its own citizens."[390]

As discussed earlier, *Lemmon* represents an important example of the traditional antebellum reading of the Comity Clause as providing no more than equal access to state-conferred rights. Shellabarger relies on this same interpretation, citing *Lemmon* and the commentaries of Joseph Story and Chancellor Kent. Tying all these sources together for the same proposition, Shellebarger explained, "[t]he same thing is decided in *Livingston v. Van Ingen* (9 John. R., 507) and in numerous other cases."[391]

As far as the specific content of Article IV privileges and immunities, Shellabarger quoted Justice Washington's listing of "the rights of protection of life and liberty, and to acquire and enjoy property, and to pay no higher impositions than other citizens, and to pass through or to reside in the State at pleasure; and to enjoy the elective franchise according to the regulations of

---

[389] Although the states had yet to ratify the Fourteenth Amendment, Shellabarger believed that Congress had implied power to enforce any right listed in the Constitution. *See id.* ("[A]s these rights grow out of and belong to national citizenship and not out of state citizenship, and as the Constitution expressly enjoins that every citizen of the United States 'shall be entitled' to them 'in the several states,' therefore it is within the power and duty of the United States to secure by appropriate legislation these fundamental rights."); *see also id.* at 295 (citing the Supreme Court's decision in *Prigg*, among other cases, as precedent for unenumerated federal power to enforce enumerated rights). Although this view of federal power was embraced by a number of radical Republicans, it was not shared by a majority in the Thirty-Ninth Congress. It is not surprising, therefore, that this particular bill was never passed (or even discussed).

[390] *Id.* at 293.

[391] CONG. GLOBE, 39th Cong., 1st Sess. app. 293 (1866).

the laws of each State."[392] However, to make sure that his use of *Corfield* was not construed as an attempt to nationalize a set of substantive natural rights, Shellabarger assured the House that "[t]o this enumeration of fundamental rights [from *Corfield*] Story adds what I have already noted, to wit: 'all such as citizens of the same State would be entitled to under like circumstances.'"[393]

For his own part, Shellabarger believed that the rights that Chancellor Kent and others described as fundamental "cannot be taken away from any citizen of the United States by the laws of any State, neither from its own citizens nor from those coming in from another State" and that these rights were ones "which every citizen of the United States holds as the gift of his national Government, and which neither any individual nor any State can rightfully deprive him of."[394] This was not, however, a reading that Shellabarger derived from the Privileges and Immunities Clause of Article IV.[395] Shellabarger conceded that *that* particular Clause protected nothing more than equal access to a limited set of "fundamental" state-conferred rights. Thus, in order "to avoid any doubtful exercise of power by the United States, and not to assume or trench upon the powers of the States," Shellabarger limited his bill to federal enforcement of Article IV, as that clause had been traditionally understood:

> [The Bill] protects no one except such as seek to or are attempting to go either temporarily or for abode from their own State into some other. It does not attempt to enforce the enjoyment of the rights of a citizen within his own State, against the wrongs of his fellow-citizens of his own State after the injured party has become or when he is a citizen of the State where the

---

[392] CONG. GLOBE, 39th Cong., 1st Sess. app. 293 (1866) (internal quotations omitted). According to Shellabarger:

> This I copy from Chancellor Kent's enumeration. (2 Kent, s. p. 710.) He takes this enumeration of rights from the opinion of Judge Washington, in the case of *Corfield v. Coryell* (4 Washington's Circuit Court Reports, 371,) in which case Chancellor Kent says:
>
> > "It was decided that the privileges and immunities conceded by the Constitution of the United States to citizens in the several States were to be confined to those which were fundamental, and which belonged of right to the citizens of all free Governments. Such are the rights of protection of life, liberty, and to acquire and enjoy property, and to pay no higher impositions than other citizens, and to pass through or reside in the State at pleasure, and to enjoy the elective franchise according to the regulation of the law of the State."

> *Id.* The inclusion of the rights of suffrage probably doomed Shellabarger's proposal. The bill was put over to the next session, where it apparently died.

[393] *Id.*

[394] *Id.*

[395] Shellabarger likely derived such a right from his reading of the Republican Guarantee Clause.

injury is done. This is because the bill is confined to the enforcement of this single clause of the Constitution. Without determining what further powers the Government may have in enforcing rights of "national citizenship" in favor of all its citizens, without regard to the fact of their passing from one State into another, it was thought best to make this act single and compact in its scope and structure, and to that end to confine its provisions to the single object of seeing that this clause of the Constitution was executed throughout the Republic. In *Abbott v. Bailey* (6 Pick. R. 92) it is decided "that the privileges and immunities of 'the citizens in each State,' in every other State can, by virtue of this clause, only be applied in case of a removal from one State into another." To conform the bill to this view of this constitutional provision, it was deemed best to limit it in accordance with that decision, and to make it secure to all the people those great international rights which are embraced in unrestrained and secure inter-State commerce, intercourse, travel, sojourn, and acquisition of abode.[396]

This description of *Corfield* is completely different from the reading Radical Republicans had pressed in the early months of 1866. At that time, men like James F. Wilson had insisted that *Corfield* presented a listed of substantive national rights that Congress could force states to respect under the doctrine of *Prigg v. Pennsylvania*.[397] As a fellow radical Republican, Shellabarger would be expected to take the same broad view of national privileges and immunities and federal power to enforce the same.[398] But perhaps reflecting the same calculation that led Wilson to abandon his initial reliance on a radical reading of *Corfield*, here Shellabarger expressly adopts the standard antebellum reading of the Comity Clause as protecting nothing more than equal access to state-conferred rights. Shellbarger placed *Corfield* alongside traditional interpretations of the Privileges and Immunities Clause in cases like *Lemmon* and *Livingston*, and similar discussions of the Clause in works by Joseph Story and Chancellor Kent. Most tellingly, in choosing a case that best represented the consensus view of the Comity Clause among his colleagues in the Thirty-Ninth Congress, Shellbarger passed over *Corfield* and chose *Abbott v. Bayley* – the quintessential "equal access to state-conferred rights" opinion.[399]

---

[396] *Id.*

[397] *See supra* note 384 and accompanying text (discussing Wilson's speech of March 1).

[398] And he would do so in the future. *See infra* Chapter 5 note 34 and accompanying text (discussing Shellabarger's arguments regarding the 1871 Ku Klux Klan Act).

[399] By the end of the Thirty-Ninth Congress, John Bingham also seems to have adopted the conventional view of the Comity Clause. A few months after his introduction of the final version of the Fourteenth Amendment, Bingham delivered a speech supporting the admission of Nebraska as the thirty-seventh state. Addressing those who insisted that Nebraska be admitted on the condition that no nonresident be taxed at a higher rate than a citizen "or be denied

The repeated references to *Corfield v. Coryell* in the debates of the Thirty-Ninth Congress can create a kind of illusion. Members cited the case so often that it can appear that there must have been some kind of agreed-upon reading of the case that made Justice Washington's opinion central to the proper understanding of the Civil Rights Act and the Fourteenth Amendment. What citation rates do not disclose, however, is the battle over the proper understanding of *Corfield* that occurred in the first session of the Thirty-Ninth Congress. Although radical Republicans initially pushed for a broad fundamental rights reading of the case, their efforts were successfully rebutted by fellow members. Although some members continued to press for a broad reading of the case, it is clear that the vast majority of the Thirty-Ninth Congress maintained the traditional antebellum view of the case, a view ultimately conceded even by radical Republicans like Samuel Shellabarger.[400]

---

the immunities or privileges of citizens therein," Bingham pointed out that such a condition was unnecessary – protection from this form of discrimination against *nonresidents* was already guaranteed by Article IV. According to Bingham:

> It is urged also that States have been admitted upon the condition that non-resident citizens of the United States should be subject to no other or higher rate of tax than resident citizens or be denied the immunities or privileges of citizens therein. But this is simply a carrying out of that provision of the Constitution which declares that "the citizens of each State shall be entitled to all privileges and immunities of citizens [of the United States] (supplying the ellipsis) in the several States."

CONG. GLOBE, 39th Cong., 2d Sess. 450 (1867). This is a wholly conventional reading of Article IV's protection of sojourning citizens along the same lines as that expressed in cases like *Livingston v. Van Ingen, Abbott v. Bayley, Lemmon v. The People*, and the commentaries of Story and Kent. Bingham reads Article IV as guaranteeing nonresident citizens the same rights as those provided by a state to its own resident citizens. Although Bingham once again refers to an unstated "ellipsis" in Article IV, he does so not to prove the existence of substantive national rights, but only to point out that the equal protection guarantees of Article IV are bestowed on all US citizens. This approach tracked the commonly cited views of Joseph Story who, in his *Commentaries*, wrote that Article IV's "citizens in the several states" were "ipso facto" citizens of the United States. It also tracks the same use of the "ipso facto" expression in Jacob Howard's speech introducing the second draft of the Fourteenth Amendment.

[400] Some scholars have suggested that post-Civil War cases like *Paul v. Virginia* rejected an earlier fundamental rights reading of the Clause and replaced it with an altogether new equal-state-conferred rights reading of Article IV and that this affected later discussion of Article IV in the Reconstruction Congress. *See, e.g.,* MICHAEL KENT CURTIS, NO STATE SHALL ABRIDGE: THE FOURTEENTH AMENDMENT AND THE BILL OF RIGHTS 161 (1986) (noting that Bingham's ultimate reading of Article IV came after *Paul v. Virginia*). As this analysis has shown, however, long before the Court decided *Paul*, most members of the Thirty-Ninth Congress accepted the consensus antebellum construction of the Privileges and Immunities Clause and viewed *Corfield* as simply one of a number of cases that viewed Article IV as an equal state rights provision. *Paul v. Virginia* had no effect whatsoever on the consensus view of Article IV either inside or outside of Congress.

C. *The Citizenship Clause*

1. The Remaining Gap in Bingham's Second Draft

Two problems were repeatedly invoked by those calling for a constitutional amendment protecting the privileges and immunities of citizens of the United States. First, states had failed to respect those rights listed in the first eight amendments that members like John Bingham, Jacob Howard, and others viewed as fundamental national rights of national citizenship. Second, states had also failed to extend equal access to the rights of state citizenship as required by the Comity Clause of Article IV. Neither of these dual injuries to the body politic could be remedied because Congress lacked power to enforce the enumerated rights of American citizenship.

Adding the privileges or immunities clause of Section One and the enforcement powers of Section Five would go a long way toward protecting the substantive and equality rights of citizens of the United States. The problem was that states could continue to evade their responsibilities by maintaining restrictive definitions of state and national citizenship. In *Dred Scott*, the Supreme Court had declared that blacks, free or otherwise, could not be considered citizens of the United States and therefore were not entitled to the rights of American citizens. The Civil Rights Act had attempted to reverse this ruling by declaring that "all persons born in the United States and not subject to any foreign power, excluding Indians not taxed, are hereby declared to be citizens of the United States." Serious questions remained, however, regarding Congress's power to confer the rights of national citizenship on individuals born and residing in the existing states. President Johnson insisted that Congress lacked such power, as did some members of Congress.[401] Even

---

[401] For example, in debating whether to override Johnson's veto of the Civil Rights Act, Mr. Johnson had insisted:

> This bill, in its first section, makes all who were born in the United States at any time, and who are now living, citizens of the United States, and, as such, citizens of the States in which they may respectively reside, and confers upon them all the rights belonging to those who have heretofore been considered citizens of the States wherein they reside.... [But] [t]here is not a single word in the Constitution which gives to this department of the Government, or to any other department of the Government, any power to declare who shall be a citizen of the United States.... The design of the power [of naturalization] is to remove the disabilities arising from the fact of alienage, and nothing else.... Standing, therefore, as well upon the nature of the Government itself, as a Government of enumerated powers specifically designated,

moderates like John Bingham refused to support the Civil Rights Act, in part because of a lack of constitutional authority. It was quite possible that the Act would be invalidated by the Supreme Court or, even if upheld, repealed by a later (possibly Democratic) Congress.

There were even more problems: Even if the Louisiana Cession Act represented a valid precedent for congressional power to confer *national* citizenship, the equal protection rights of Article IV involved the rights of *state citizenship* – a status Congress had never before attempted to confer or control. Blacks from Massachusetts visiting Mississippi might be denied equal civil rights if Mississippi refused to give its own black residents the status of state citizenship. In such a case, Mississippi might plausibly claim that Article IV allowed it to "equally deny" the rights of state citizenship to any black American, regardless of out-of-state citizenship. Even if a state granted a form of citizenship to its black residents, the state might grant only some, but not all of the rights conferred on residents of the most favored race. Adding a new statute demanding that states confer *full* state citizenship on all persons residing in the state would be subject to the same vulnerabilities as the Civil Rights Act: It might be struck down by the Supreme Court as beyond the powers of Congress or repealed by a later Congress.

If Congress wished to safely and permanently guarantee the privileges and immunities of both national *and* state citizenship, it would have to do more than pass an amendment protecting the rights of citizenship. It would have to pass an amendment defining and protecting the *status* of federal and state citizenship as well. As originally proposed, the second version of the Fourteenth Amendment did not solve – or even address – the potential constitutional problems of the Civil Rights Act. Bingham's second draft addressed substantive national "privileges or immunities," including the Comity Clause rights of visiting out-of-state citizens. The Civil Rights Act, on the other hand, addressed equality rights that residents could assert against their *own* state. The Equal Protection Clause of Bingham's new draft might cover the provisions of the

as upon the express provision that everything not granted was to be considered as remaining with the States unless the Constitution contained some particular prohibition of any power before belonging to the States, what doubt can there be that if a State possessed the power to declare who should be her citizen before the Constitution was adopted that power remains as absolute and as conclusive as it was when the Constitution was adopted? The bill, therefore, changes the whole theory of the Government.

Cong. Globe, 39th Cong., 1st Sess. 1776–77 (1866).

Civil Rights Act but that Clause spoke of equal *protection* of laws, not equal laws.[402] This might require "equal laws," but perhaps not.[403]

This illustrates how Bingham's second draft of Section One of the Fourteenth Amendment, as originally proposed, did not easily map onto the Civil Rights Act. Having seen how the draft emerged, this should come as no surprise. As much as scholars often claim that Section One was intended to constitutionalize the Civil Rights Act, Bingham's particular efforts had nothing to do with the Civil Rights Act. His two drafts of the Fourteenth Amendment were introduced wholly apart from the Civil Rights Act and for wholly different purposes.

But Bingham did not draft all of Section One of the Fourteenth Amendment. Before being submitted to the states, members of the Thirty-Ninth Congress recognized the gaps in Bingham's proposal and added a provision that forever closed the door on *Dred Scott* and guaranteed the rights of state citizenship to all persons born in the United States and residing in a state. This would be the text that constitutionalized the Civil Rights Act of 1866.

2. Debating the Citizenship Clause

On May 30, Senator Jacob Howard proposed adding an opening sentence to Section One of the Fourteenth Amendment that declared "all persons born in the United States, and subject to the jurisdiction thereof, are citizens of the United States and of the states wherein they reside."[404] According to Howard, the additional sentence was "declaratory of what I regard as the law of the land already" and "settles the great question of citizenship and removes all doubt as to what persons are or are not citizens of the United States."[405] There followed a discussion regarding why the proposed addition did not use the language of the Civil Rights Act and exclude "Indians not taxed." Wisconsin Republican Senator James Doolittle pointed out that conferring citizenship

---

[402] For a discussion of the difference and its potential importance, see Christopher R. Green, *The Original Sense of the (Equal) Protection Clause: Pre-enactment History*, 19 GEO. MASON U. CIV. RTS. L. J. 1 (2008); Christopher R. Green, *The Original Sense of the (Equal) Protection Clause: Subsequent Interpretation and Application*, 19 GEO. MASON U. CIV. RTS. L. J. 219 (2009).

[403] States could plausibly claim that every member of a class was equally protected, but that different classes had different rights; men might have rights different from women, and blacks might have rights different from whites. Whether or not this is the best reading, the text itself is ambiguous.

[404] CONG. GLOBE, 39th Cong., 1st Sess. 2890 (1866).

[405] *Id.*

necessarily meant conferring the privileges and immunities attached to such citizenship:

> Mr. President, citizenship, if conferred, carries with it, as a matter of course, the rights, the responsibilities, the duties, the immunities, the privileges of citizens, for that is the very object of this constitutional amendment to extend.[406]

Doolittle argued that the proposed sentence, which included all persons born in the United States and subject to its jurisdiction, seemed to include "the wild Indian of the plains" living on federal reservations.[407] The Civil Rights Act had excluded this group by excluding "Indians not taxed" from its definition of citizenship, and Doolittle wanted to know why the same language was not to be included in Section One of the Fourteenth Amendment. After all, Doolittle insisted, wasn't Section One specifically drafted to constitutionalize the Civil Rights Act?

> Mr. President, the celebrated civil rights bill which has been passed during the present congress, which was the forerunner of this constitutional amendment, and to give validity to which this constitutional amendment is brought forward, and which without this constitutional amendment to enforce it has not validity so far as this question is concerned, uses the following language:
>
> "That all persons born in the United States and not subject to any foreign power, excluding Indians not taxed, are hereby declared to be citizens of the United States."
>
> Why should this language be criticized any more now, when it is brought forward here in this constitutional amendment than when it was in the civil rights bill?[408]

Doolittle's assertion that the Fourteenth Amendment was meant to constitutionalize the Civil Rights Bill triggered an immediate objection by Maine's Republican Senator William Pitt Fessenden:

> I want to say to the honorable Senator, who has a great regard for the truth, that he is drawing entirely upon his imagination. There is not one word of correctness in all that he is saying, not a particle, not a scintilla, not the beginning of truth.[409]

[406] *Id.* at 2893.
[407] *Id.* at 2892.
[408] *Id.* at 2896.
[409] *Id.*

Fessenden first pointed out that the "citizenship clause" now under discussion had not been discussed at all by the Committee of Fifteen, much less had they proposed it as part of the proposed amendment.[410] Doolittle acknowledged this, but nevertheless insisted that the Amendment had been proposed to ensure the validity of the Civil Rights Act.

> As I understand, a member from Ohio, Mr. Bingham, who in a very able speech in the House maintained that the civil rights bill was without authority in the Constitution, brought forward a proposition in the House of Representatives to amend the Constitution so as to enable Congress to declare the civil rights of all persons, and that constitutional amendment, Mr. Bingham being himself one of the committee of fifteen, was referred by the House to that committee, and from the committee it has been reported. I say I have a right to infer that it was because Mr. Bingham and others of the House of Representatives and other person upon the committee had doubts, at least, as to the constitutionality of the civil rights bill that the proposition to amend the Constitution now appears to give it vitality and force. It is not an imputation upon anyone.

This led to a colloquy between Doolittle and other members regarding the relationship of the Fourteenth Amendment to the Civil Rights Act:

> Mr. Grimes. [Doolittle's remarks are] an imputation upon every member who voted for the bill, the inference being legitimate and logical that they violated their oaths and knew they did so when they voted for the civil rights bill.

> Mr. Doolittle. The Senator goes too far. What I say is that they had doubts.

> Mr. Fessenden. I will say to the Senator one thing: whatever may have been Mr. Bingham's motives in bringing it forward, he brought it forward some time before the civil rights bill was considered at all and had it referred to the committee, and it was discussed in the committee long before the civil rights bill was passed. Then I will say to him further, that during all the discussion in the committee that I heard nothing was ever said about the civil rights bill in connection with that. It was placed on entirely different grounds.

> Mr. Doolittle: [If Congress already has the power to confer citizenship then] what is the necessity of amending the constitution at all on this subject?

> Mr. Doolittle: I said the committee of fifteen brought it forward because they had doubts as to the constitutional power of Congress to pass the civil rights bill.

[410] *Id.* ("[T]his was not brought forward by the committee of fifteen at all.").

Mr. Fessenden: Exactly; and I say, in reply, that if they had doubts, no such doubts were stated in the committee of fifteen, and the matter was not put on that ground at all. There was no question raised about the civil rights bill.

Mr. Howard. I was a member of the same committee, and the Senator's observations apply to me equally with the Senator from Maine. We desired to put this question of citizenship, and the rights of citizens and freedmen under the civil rights bill beyond the legislative power of such gentlemen as the Senator from Wisconsin, who would pull the whole system up by the roots and destroy it, and expose the freedmen again to the oppression of their old masters.[411]

There is no reason to think Fessenden and Howard were not telling the truth. The second draft of the Fourteenth Amendment as drafted by John Bingham and put forward by the committee aimed at an entirely different (and far more difficult) target than the Civil Rights Act. The Amendment's provisions not only sought to protect substantive national rights, but its internal sections dealt with the hotly contested issue of readmission of the southern states. Its drafting and debate followed parallel, but entirely different, tracks from those of the Civil Rights Act. It was only after the Amendment had been essentially completed that the goals of the Amendment and the Civil Rights Act converged. Absent a definition of national and state citizenship, neither the equal rights of the Civil Rights Bill nor the substantive rights of the Fourteenth Amendment could be assured. If the addition of a citizenship clause to the Fourteenth Amendment had the additional effect of making ironclad the validity of the Civil Rights Act, so much the better. The addition of the citizenship clause was quickly agreed to by both houses of Congress, and the Amendment was sent on to the States for ratification.[412]

D. *Summary*

John Bingham believed the ability to enforce the Bill of Rights against the states was "the want of the republic." Filling that need required finding the right language. Following a failed attempt to impose an alien theory on the text of the Comity Clause, Bingham found the language he was looking for in a phrase with roots going back to the Louisiana Cession Act of 1803. By protecting the

---

[411] *Id.* at 2896.
[412] Cong. Globe, 39th Cong., 1st Sess. 2545, 3042, 3149 (1866); *see* Richard L. Aynes, *The 39th Congress (1865–1867) and the Fourteenth Amendment: Some Preliminary Perspectives*, 42 Akron L. Rev. 1019, 1041–42 (2009).

"privileges or immunities of citizens of the United States," Bingham simultaneously expanded and limited federal enforcement of national liberty in the states. Neither he nor any other moderate Republican wished to federalize the entire subject of civil rights in the states. Instead, Bingham never wavered from the purpose that he announced early in the session: "To arm the Congress of the United States, by the consent of the people of the United States, with the power to enforce the bill of rights as it stands in the Constitution today." His efforts "hath that extent – no more."[413] Jacob Howard explained how the final draft of the Privileges or Immunities Clause accomplished Bingham's goal. The privileges and immunities of citizens of the United States involved those rights announced in the federal Constitution. This included not just the first eight amendments, but also the traditional protections of the Comity Clause. Prior to the Fourteenth Amendment, Congress had no express power to protect constitutionally enumerated rights, and the Constitution contained no language expressly requiring the states to respect the enumerated rights of the first eight amendments. Both omissions would be remedied with the ratification of the Fourteenth Amendment.

But ratification would be a battle. Whatever John Bingham's or Jacob Howard's understanding of legal terms like "privileges and immunities of citizens of the United States," it was now up to the people in the states to consider the meaning of the Privileges or Immunities Clause and decide whether it, along with the rest of the Fourteenth Amendment, ought to be added to the federal Constitution.

---

[413] CONG. GLOBE, 39th Cong., 1st Sess. 1088 (1866).

4

The Public Debate

Introduction: The Amendment and the Public

For the ratification of the federal Constitution, the key votes occurred on different days in separate state ratifying conventions.[1] For the ratification of the Fourteenth Amendment, the key vote arguably took place on a single day: November 6, 1866. On that day, congressional Republicans secured a landslide victory in the national congressional elections.[2] Both Republicans and Democrats had made the election of 1866 a referendum on the Fourteenth Amendment.[3] Had the Republicans lost a congressional majority, this would have doomed any hope for passing the Amendment and may well have triggered a new civil war.[4] Instead, the Republicans received a national mandate to move forward in their effort to secure the Amendment's

---

[1] The debates in and around the state ratifying conventions for the federal Constitution can be found exhaustively presented in the multivolume work THE DOCUMENTARY HISTORY OF THE RATIFICATION OF THE CONSTITUTION (Merrill Jensen et al. eds.).

[2] *See* BRUCE A. ACKERMAN, WE THE PEOPLE: TRANSFORMATIONS 182 (1998) [hereinafter 2 ACKERMAN] (describing the results of the Republican's "landslide" victory).

[3] According to Eric Foner, "More than anything else, the election became a referendum on the Fourteenth Amendment. Seldom, declared the *New York Times*, had a political contest been conducted 'with so exclusive reference to a single issue.'" ERIC FONER, RECONSTRUCTION: AMERICA'S UNFINISHED REVOLUTION, 1863–1877, at 267 (1988); *see also* 2 ACKERMAN, *supra* note 2, at 180–82 (1998) (describing how the Fourteenth Amendment became the campaign focus for the 1866 election); ERIC L. MCKITRICK, ANDREW JOHNSON AND RECONSTRUCTION 449 (1960) (noting "the positive function of the election [of 1866] as a referendum on the Fourteenth Amendment").

[4] According to Michael Les Benedict, "A Johnsonian gain of only twenty or thirty seats would bring on the crisis [of an 'alternate congress'].... Republicans urged northern voters to 'secure the all-important point, the election of at least 122 Republicans to the next House of Representatives, the only way ... by which the country can be saved from an outbreak of violence.'" MICHAEL LES BENEDICT, A COMPROMISE OF PRINCIPLE: CONGRESSIONAL REPUBLICANS AND RECONSTRUCTION 1863–1869, at 207 (1974) (emphasis omitted) (quoting 3 *Nation* 221, 230

ratification and protect the rights of American citizens in the southern states.[5]

The conjunction of a proposed constitutional amendment and a major national election created a political dynamic quite different from that which existed at the time of the Founding. In 1787, the voters who needed to be persuaded were the members of the individual state ratifying conventions.[6] Pamphlets and newspaper editorials were generally regional,[7] and the conventions themselves often included days of detailed analysis and debate on the proposed Constitution.[8] In 1866, by contrast, the relevant voters were the national electorate. Newspapers and pamphlets enjoyed far greater circulation and national penetration[9] and were put to use by two dominant political parties

[1866]); *see also* 2 ACKERMAN, *supra* note 3, at 178 (discussing the crisis of an alternate congress). According to Congressman Ben Butler at Johnson's Impeachment Trial:

> Does anyone doubt that if the intentions of the respondent [Johnson] could have been carried out, and his denunciations had weakened the Congress in the affections of the people, so that those who had in the North sympathized with the rebellion could have elected such a minority even of the Representatives to Congress as, together with those sent up from the governments organized by Johnson in the rebellious States, should have formed a majority of both or either House of Congress, that the President would have recognized such body as the legitimate Congress, and attempted to carry out its decrees by the aid of the Army and Navy and the Treasury of the United States . . . and thus lighted the torch of civil war?

PROCEEDINGS IN THE TRIAL OF ANDREW JOHNSON, PRESIDENT OF THE UNITED STATES, BEFORE THE UNITED STATES SENATE, ON ARTICLES OF IMPEACHMENT EXHIBITED BY THE HOUSE OF REPRESENTATIVES, WITH AN APPENDIX 77 (1868) [hereinafter JOHNSON IMPEACHMENT TRIAL].

[5] *See, e.g.*, MCKITRICK, *supra* note 3, at 450 ("The people had spoken and the primary decision on reconstruction had thus been placed beyond dispute for the first time since the end of the war. The Union was to be restored, but there would have to be terms."); *see also The Election, Final Repudiation of the Democratic Party*, N.Y. TIMES, Nov. 7, 1866, at 1 (reporting election results).

[6] For accounts of the ratification debates in the several states, see THE DOCUMENTARY HISTORY OF THE RATIFICATION OF THE CONSTITUTION, *supra* note 1.

[7] *See* PAULINE MAIER, RATIFICATION: THE PEOPLE DEBATE THE CONSTITUTION, 1787–1788, at 83–85 (2010).

[8] See *id.* for the best and most accessible introduction to the ratification debates.

[9] There were twenty-four daily newspapers at the time of the Founding. By the time of the Civil War, there were more than 250. Taking advantage of technological developments like the telegraph and railroads, newspapers vastly increased their circulation and penetration. James Gordon Bennett's *New York Herald*, for example, had a circulation of "77,000 on the eve of the Civil War, the largest daily circulation in the world." Thomas C. Leonard, *Magazines and Newspapers, in* THE READER'S COMPANION TO AMERICAN HISTORY (Eric Foner & John A. Garraty eds. 1991). Horace Greeley's *New York Tribune* had a weekly circulation of 200,000. *Id.* According to Eric McKitrick, "The fact is that by the summer of 1866 the American people

with the ability to coordinate and widely disseminate their positions on the proposed Fourteenth Amendment.[10] Relatively little debate on the Amendment took place in the state assemblies.[11] A great deal of debate took place on the national campaign trail.[12] This different dynamic has important implications for those seeking to determine the original meaning of the Amendment.

Fourteenth Amendment scholars have long lamented the "silence" of the state ratifying conventions regarding their understanding of the Fourteenth Amendment.[13] When combined with the coercive measures Congress used to secure ratification by the southern states,[14] this silence makes determining the original meaning of the Fourteenth Amendment seem doubly problematic: There seems to be little we can glean from ratification assemblies in the states, and the ratification of those assemblies seems to lack the same kind of democratic legitimacy as those that met at the time of the Founding.[15] The result

actually had at their disposal an extraordinary amount of information upon which to make up their minds about any political issue, probably as much as would ever be the case in comparable circumstances." McKitrick, *supra* note 3, at 439.

[10] For a discussion of the political parties' use of American newspapers during the Civil War, see McKitrick, *supra* note 3, at 439–42.

[11] According to Michael Kent Curtis, "Most of the state legislatures that considered the Fourteenth Amendment either kept no record of their debates, or their discussion was so perfunctory that it shed little light on their understanding of its meaning." Michael Kent Curtis, No State Shall Abridge: The Fourteenth Amendment and the Bill of Rights 145 (1986).

[12] Both parties tied their fortunes to the electorate's conclusion regarding the need to pass the Fourteenth Amendment. *See* Foner, *supra* note 3, at 267. This guaranteed that the Amendment would play a role in every major campaign speech right up to the November elections.

[13] Charles Fairman first articulated the "argument from silence" against an incorporationist reading of the Fourteenth Amendment. *See* Charles Fairman, *Does the Fourteenth Amendment Incorporate the Bill of Rights?*, 2 Stan. L. Rev. 5, 81–132 (1949). For responses to Fairman that concede the problem of relative "silence," see Curtis, *supra* note 11, at 131–53; Akhil Reed Amar, The Bill of Rights: Creation and Reconstruction 197–206 (1998); *see also* William E. Nelson, The Fourteenth Amendment: From Political Principle to Judicial Doctrine 110 (1998) ("The debates examined so far in Congress, in the state legislatures, in the columns of newspapers, and in the correspondence of congressmen contained little analysis of the issues that would come to plague the Supreme Court once section one of the Fourteenth Amendment became part of the Constitution.").

[14] *See* Military Reconstruction Act of Mar. 2, 1867, ch. 153, 14 Stat. 428 (requiring states to ratify the Fourteenth Amendment as a condition for readmission to the Union). For a discussion of the revolutionary nature of the First Reconstruction Act, see 2 Ackerman, *supra* note 2, at 198–200.

[15] For a modern discussion of the Fourteenth Amendment and political legitimacy, *compare* Amar, *supra* note 13, *with* 2 Ackerman, *supra* note 2. *See also* Akhil Reed Amar, America's Constitution: A Biography 364–80 (2005) (discussing how the Fourteenth Amendment was legitimately adopted against "within the general Article V framework"); Bruce Ackerman, 2006 *Oliver Wendell Holmes Lectures: The Living Constitution*, 120 Harv. L. Rev. 1737, 1747 n.25 (2007) (discussing belief that the Fourteenth Amendment was adopted against an unconstitutional background).

has been a far thinner historical account of the original understanding of the Fourteenth Amendment than that which exists for the original Constitution.

Once we understand that the key debates took place as part of a national election and not in individual state ratifying conventions, however, much of the presumed methodological difficulty regarding originalist study of the Fourteenth Amendment disappears. There was a deep and robust public discussion of the Amendment in 1866, one that culminated in a landslide national election in favor of adding the text to the Constitution. As had been the case at the time of the Founding, supporters and opponents of the proposed constitutional text developed sophisticated and specific arguments regarding the meaning of the text. The Democratic Party and men like President Andrew Johnson, O. H. Browning, and S. S. Nicholas played the roles once played by Anti-Federalists like Patrick Henry, Melancton Smith, and "Brutus." The Republican Party and men like John Bingham, Jacob Howard, and George W. Paschal stepped into roles once played by Federalists like James Wilson, Alexander Hamilton, and James Madison. Republicans even had their own "Publius," the pseudonymous "Madison" who published essays in the *New York Times* that explained and defended the need for the proposed Fourteenth Amendment.[16]

Because originalist accounts of the Fourteenth Amendment have tended to focus on the framing debates in the Thirty-Ninth Congress, they have both undervalued and underexplored the public political debates of 1866. Most critically, they have completely missed President Johnson's important role as leader of the Anti-Amendment Party in the drama of the Fourteenth Amendment. As the de facto national head of the Democratic Party, Johnson took the lead in crafting arguments against the proposed Amendment. Through what Bruce Ackerman has coined the "paradox of resistance,"[17] Johnson's sustained attempt to defeat the Amendment both deepened and helped shape public understanding of the proposed text and its impact on the autonomy of the states. It was President Johnson, for example, who first declared that congressional efforts to protect the "privileges and immunities of citizens of the United States" required a constitutional amendment.[18] When Congress submitted a

---

[16] *See, e.g.*, Madison, *The National Question: The Constitutional Amendments – National Citizenship*, N.Y. TIMES, Nov. 10, 1866, at 2.

[17] 2 ACKERMAN, *supra* note 2, at 164. According to Ackerman, Andrew Johnson's fight against the Fourteenth Amendment had the ironic result of "increas[ing] the legitimacy of the decision by the People to embrace revolutionary reform." *Id.* Ackerman describes how Johnson's long fight "gave the turbulent debate a pragmatic anchor in reality," rather than involving a "heady" discussion of "constitutional abstractions." *Id.*

[18] See Chapter 3.

proposed amendment that adopted the President's own locution, Johnson responded by challenging the very legitimacy of the Republican Congress and making opposition to the Amendment the focus of the Democratic platform in the fall elections. The subsequent national debate between Johnsonian Democrats and congressional Republicans clarified the choice facing the country: Either accept President Johnson's assurance that the southern states could be trusted to protect the national rights of American citizens, such as freedom of speech and assembly, or adopt the Fourteenth Amendment and empower the national government to protect the privileges and immunities of citizens of the United States.

Viewing ratification of the Fourteenth Amendment through the lens of a national election allows us to see how politically salient events during the summer of 1866 transformed a dry theoretical discussion of the Amendment's merits into an argument over what was literally a matter of life and death in the southern states. The July 30 massacre of freedmen meeting in convention in New Orleans became a national scandal, particularly when it became clear that state officials had led the attack. Republicans used the New Orleans riot as a stark example of the need to adopt the Fourteenth Amendment to protect the rights of speech and assembly against state abridgement. President Johnson's feckless response to the massacre only heightened public concern that the Administration had no intention of securing the rights of national citizenship in the southern states. This political blunder became a disaster when Johnson had his Secretary of the Interior, O. H. Browning, publish a letter representing the Administration's position that the Fourteenth Amendment was unnecessary in light of existing protections in state Constitutions. Republicans around the country excoriated the letter and pointed to the blood-stained hands of Louisiana officials as evidence that southern states could not be trusted to protect the national rights of speech and assembly. Only weeks after the publication of Browning's letter, Republicans enjoyed a landslide victory at the polls and a popular mandate to secure the ratification of the Fourteenth Amendment.

Despite the Democrats' political defeat, President Andrew Johnson had one final act to play in the drama of the Fourteenth Amendment. With ratification at an impasse due to the southern-state policy of "masterly inactivity,"[19]

---

[19] The idea was that the passing of time would wear down northern support for Reconstruction. As Benjamin Wood published in a contemporary essay for the *New York Daily News*:

> We answer, let them do nothing, so far as political action is concerned. Let them simply watch and wait. A masterly inactivity is the best policy they can adopt. Time, that will gradually teach the masses of the North the necessity of redeeming the republicanism

President Johnson met with conservative advisors and drafted an alternative amendment that he hoped would attract the support of northern and southern conservatives. Unlike the proposed Fourteenth Amendment, which declared that "no state shall" henceforth violate the rights of citizens of the United States, Johnson's alternate version erased the proposed Privileges or Immunities Clause and replaced it with a passive reaffirmation of the Comity Clause. Instead of requiring states to enforce substantive rights like speech and assembly, Johnson's alternative would merely require that states provide equal access to a limited set of state-conferred rights. The proposal went nowhere, and Congress proceeded to pass a series of legislative acts that ultimately secured the ratification of the Amendment.

The 1866 national political struggle between Johnson and congressional Republicans opens a historical window on the original meaning and public understanding of Section One of the Fourteenth Amendment. By making the proposed Amendment the focus of the dispute between contending political parties, Johnson triggered a sustained national public debate regarding the nature and importance of the privileges and immunities of citizens of the United States. The events of the summer of 1866 further deepened the national debate by focusing on the particular enumerated rights of speech and assembly – rights that were widely accepted examples of the privileges or immunities of citizens of the United States.[20]

In the preceding chapter, I examined the actions in the Thirty-Ninth Congress that led to the drafting and passage of the Fourteenth Amendment's Privileges or Immunities Clause. My focus was on the men who framed and debated the Clause. This is a common focus in legal histories of the Fourteenth Amendment, but my purpose in doing so is different from that of most prior histories. The effort is not to somehow recreate the aggregate "intentions of the framers" or even the intentions of *the* framer, John Bingham. Instead, my overall effort is to identify the likely public understanding of the Privileges or Immunities Clause. Doing so requires understanding the antebellum

---

of the country, will work out the problem in the interests of the South. The Radicals demand negro suffrage and the ratification of the Constitutional Amendment. They can get neither except by the consent of the Southern States and the suffrages of the Southern people.

"*Masterly Inactivity the Policy of the South,*" N.Y. DAILY NEWS, Dec. 1, 1866, *reprinted in* Charles Fairman, RECONSTRUCTION AND REUNION 1864–1888, PART ONE, at 256 (2010) (internal footnotes omitted).

[20] Michael Curtis has done extremely valuable work highlighting concerns about speech and press both before and after the adoption of the Fourteenth Amendment. *See, e.g.,* MICHAEL KENT CURTIS, FREE SPEECH: "THE PEOPLE'S DARLING PRIVILEGE": STRUGGLES FOR FREEDOM OF EXPRESSION IN AMERICAN HISTORY (2000); CURTIS, NO STATE SHALL, *supra* note 11.

conception of the term "privileges and immunities of citizens of the United States" (Chapter 1) and determining whether this antebellum understanding, or some form of it, informed the debates that led to the drafting of the Clause (Chapter 2). The latter inquiry is important because it provides evidence of the likely public understanding of these terms in 1868 – the time of the ratification of the Fourteenth Amendment. But the debates only get us so far. Whatever the framers may have thought they were doing by choosing certain terms and phrases, the Amendment itself may have been understood quite differently by the public that debated and ultimately ratified the Amendment. We would expect there to be some overlap, even significant overlap, between the two. But not only is this not necessarily the case, the basic theory of the Constitution as an expression of the people's will suggests that the understanding of those who ultimately ratified the document is the understanding that brings democratic legitimacy to the judicial enforcement of the text. In short, our story of the original meaning of the Privileges or Immunities Clause is critically incomplete without an understanding of how the text was viewed outside the halls of Congress.

The story of public understanding, however, requires revisiting some of the events described in the prior chapter. The public did not remain in the dark about the Fourteenth Amendment until Congress adopted the proposal and sent the text to the states for ratification on June 13, 1866.[21] Newspapers and political commentaries provided a constant flow of information about the activities of the Thirty-Ninth Congress, including full accounts of Bingham's two drafts of the Fourteenth Amendment. Our exploration of public understanding therefore begins with the initial efforts of the Thirty-Ninth Congress in early 1866.

I. THE EARLY MONTHS OF 1866

As the Thirty-Ninth Congress began its discussion of what would become the Fourteenth Amendment, conservative critics outside the halls of Congress could only watch in frustration. Instead of following President Andrew Johnson's lead and moving to normalize relations with the southern states,[22]

---

[21] CONG. GLOBE, 39th Cong., 1st Sess. 3148.

[22] Johnson had already signaled his intent to normalize relations with the southern states by issuing a broad pardon in May of 1865 and by having his Secretary of State William Seward count the votes of southern states for the purposes of ratifying the Thirteenth Amendment that December. *See* MCKITRICK, *supra* note 3, at 49 (discussing the Amnesty Proclamation of May 29, 1866); 2 ACKERMAN, *supra* note 2, at 153 (discussing Seward's "provocative" proclamation regarding the ratification votes of the southern states).

Congress seemed intent on imposing conditions on the readmission of the rebel governments.[23] The delay did not sit well with the conservatives. In an essay published on January 10, 1866, Unionist Kentucky Judge Samuel Smith (S. S.) Nicholas essentially echoed the views of the Johnson Administration. "The only proper pending issue," Nicholas wrote, "is how speedily to restore national concord. . . . The speedy restoration of the desired amity indispensably requires, that the South should be promptly invited to a participation in the legislation of Congress."[24] Recognizing that Congress intended to bestow the rights of citizenship on newly freed blacks, Nicholas questioned whether such an effort was possible absent a constitutional amendment reversing *Dred Scott*:

> If the object of the exclusion experiment is to obtain for freed negroes a change from their mere denizenship to full citizenship, then the effort is to coerce the eleven States into doing what it is very doubtful whether they have power to do. According to the express decision of the Supreme Court, and the concurring legislative and judicial action of nearly every State, a negro never was and never can become a full citizen by reason of any mere State action. Indeed, it is doubtful whether he ever can be made such, except by an amendment of the Constitution.[25]

In fact, the Thirty-Ninth Congress was engaged in multiple efforts intended to secure the rights of freedmen. In addition to preparing a reauthorization of the Freedmen's Bureau Act,[26] Congress was drafting a Civil Rights Act that would both define and confer the status of citizenship on newly freed blacks while also guaranteeing a certain degree of equal civil rights in the states.[27] On a separate but parallel track, John Bingham was spearheading an effort to pass an amendment to the federal Constitution that would require states to protect the constitutionally enumerated rights of citizens and the natural rights of all

---

[23] Radical Republicans like Thaddeus Stevens held to a "Dead States" theory whereby the rebel states had committed "political suicide" and could be excluded from participating in the national government until such time as the "living" states were satisfied they had restored a proper form of republican government. *See* Garrett Epps, Democracy Reborn: The Fourteenth Amendment and the Fight for Equal Rights in Post-Civil War America 101–02 (2006). Not all members of the Thirty-Ninth Congress subscribed to the Dead States theory, but the majority agreed that the southern states ought not to be readmitted until Congress could be assured of the proper protection of individual liberty.

[24] 3 S. S. Nicholas, *Power and Policy of Exclusion, in* Conservative Essays, Legal and Political 5, 7 (1867).

[25] *Id.* at 14.

[26] *See* Earl M. Maltz, Civil Rights, the Constitution, and Congress, 1863–1869, at 48 (1990).

[27] *Id.* at 61.

persons to due process and equal protection.[28] None of this was being done in secret: The Press reported major speeches in the House and Senate, and the country received a steady stream of newspaper editorials commenting on the policies of the Thirty-Ninth Congress.[29]

A. *Reporting the First Draft of the Fourteenth Amendment*

The *New York Times* and the *New York Herald* (the most widely distributed newspaper in the country at the time[30]) both reported Bingham's speech of January 26, in which he declared that states ought to be bound to protect the "immortal Bill of Rights."[31] By February 1, observers deep in the heartland knew that Congress was moving toward nationalizing constitutionally enumerated rights. According to the *Fort Wayne Daily Democrat*, the Senate had instructed the Joint Committee on Reconstruction to "enquire into [the] expediency of amending the Constitution of the United States so as to declare with greater certainty the power of Congress to enforce and determine by appropriate legislation *all the guarantees contained in that instrument.*"[32] On February 3, 1866, the Joint Committee on Reconstruction adopted Ohio Congressman John Bingham's initial draft of the Fourteenth Amendment, and newspapers began their coverage of the debates. On February 14, the *Daily Milwaukee News* reported both Bingham's first draft and his explanation that "the object of the amendment was to *extend universally* the guarantee of constitutional protection."[33] The Illinois *Alton Telegraph* also reported Bingham's proposed amendment and his explanation that "[t]he proposed amendment placed no obligation on any State or citizen not now enjoined by the letter of the Constitution."[34]

Newspaper reportage covered the arguments of both supporters and critics of Bingham's initial draft of the Fourteenth Amendment. The *New York Times*,

---

[28] See Chapter 3.

[29] For a discussion of the significant depth of reporting on political issues during 1866, see McKitrick, *supra* note 3, at 439.

[30] Amar, The Bill of Rights, *supra* note 13, at 187; McKitrick, *supra* note 3, at 441.

[31] N.Y. Times, Feb 27, 1866, at 8 (reprinting Bingham's speech and its reference to "this immortal Bill of rights"); *see also Another Amendment to the Constitution*, N.Y. Herald, Feb. 27, 1866, at 1 ("But it was equally clear that by every construction of the Constitution – its contemporaneous and continuous construction – that great provision contained in the second section of the fourth article and in a portion of the fifth amendment adopted by the first congress in 1789, that that immortal bill of rights had hitherto depended on the action of the several States.").

[32] *The Nigger Congress!*, Fort Wayne Daily Democrat, Feb. 1, 1866, at 2 (emphasis added).

[33] Daily Milwaukee News, Feb. 14, 1866, at 1 (emphasis added).

[34] Alton Telegraph, Mar. 2, 1866, at 2.

for example, reported Congressman Robert Hale's objection that Bingham's effort would "utterly obliterate State rights and State authority over their own internal affairs."[35] On March 1, the *New York Times* published John Bingham's speech of February 28, in which Bingham declared that his proposal did not "take from any State rights that belonged to it under the Constitution" and that "[t]his was simply a proposition to arm the Congress of the United States, by the consent of the people, with power to enforce the Bill of Rights as it stood in the Constitution. It had that extent – no more."[36] The *Times* then reported Robert Hale's "clear and forcible speech"[37] opposing Bingham's amendment in part because Hale believed that the states already were constrained by the federal Bill of Rights.[38] That same day, the *Times* also printed an editorial on "Amending the Constitution," which noted Hale's "able and interesting speech" and warned that Bingham's "amendment seem[ed] to be only another of the steps proposed by the Radicals in Congress, for the consolidation of the central power, and the complete overthrow of State authority."[39] Almost in confirmation of the *Times*'s warning, the *Congressional Globe* published Bingham's speech of February 28 as a pamphlet titled, *"One Country, One Constitution, and One People": In Support of the Proposed Amendment To Enforce the Bill of Rights*.[40] Finally, on March 10, the *Times* reported Bingham's declaration that "the enforcement of the Bill of Rights in the Constitution was the want of the republic."[41]

Despite the widespread coverage, it is difficult to gauge the degree of public awareness of the content of the proposal, much less public understanding of Bingham's particular theory of the Constitution (his colleagues, after all, failed to grasp Bingham's convoluted "ellipsis" argument). However, anyone following the debate in the *New York Times* and the widely circulated *Herald*

---

[35] *Amending the Constitution: Federal Power and State Rights*, N.Y. TIMES, Feb. 27, 1866, at 2 (reporting on Hale's speech).

[36] N.Y. TIMES, Mar 1, 1866, at 4.

[37] *Debate in the House on the Constitutional Amendment, Clear and Forcible Speech by Mr. Hale Against Its Adoption*, N.Y. TIMES, Feb. 28, 1866, at 1.

[38] The *Times* reported that Hale described the first ten amendments as "a bill of rights for the protection of the citizen, and defining and limiting of power of Federal and *State* legislation" and also reported Hale's colloquy with Bingham, in which Hale noted that he had always "gone along with the impression" that the Bill of Rights bound the states "in some way, whether with or without the sanction of a judicial decision that we are so protected." *Amending the Constitution: Federal Power and State Rights*, N.Y. TIMES, Mar. 2, 1866, at 2 (emphasis added).

[39] Editorial, *Amending the Constitution*, N.Y. TIMES, Mar. 2, 1866, at 4.

[40] See John Bingham, Representative from Ohio, *One Country, One Constitution, and One People: In Support of the Proposed Amendment To Enforce the Bill of Rights* (Feb. 28, 1866) (pamphlet printed by CONG. GLOBE).

[41] *Thirty-ninth Congress: First Session. Senate*, N.Y. TIMES, Mar. 10, 1866, at 1.

would have known that Bingham was attempting to nationalize the Bill of Rights. At this point, however, there was little reason for the general public to focus its attention on the debates of the Thirty-Ninth Congress. That would change as the fall elections approached and both national parties made the proposed amendment the focus of their campaigns. At this point, by clarifying the purposes of his Amendment, Bingham had alerted the political opposition, both in Washington, DC, and around the country, that a proposal was now on the table that could dramatically alter the autonomy of the states.

The partisan divide, and newspaper reporting of the same, deepened with President Johnson's March 27 veto of the Civil Rights Acts. As discussed in Chapter 3, Johnson's veto was widely reported (and reprinted) throughout the United States.[42] For the first time in 1866, the public was alerted to a congressional effort to protect "the privileges and immunities of citizens of the United States" and claims that doing so required a constitutional amendment. Lyman Trumbull's response to Johnson's veto also received significant newspaper coverage, including Trumbull's claim that Congress had bestowed the rights of national citizenship in the past through treaties like the Louisiana Cession Act of 1803.[43] Although Congress overrode Johnson's veto, his

[42] ALBANY EVENING J. (Albany, N.Y.), Mar. 28, 1866, at 2; BOS. DAILY ADVERTISER, Mar. 28, 1866, at 1; *The Civil Rights Bill and The President's Veto*, N.Y. TIMES, Mar. 28, 1866, at 1; DAILY NAT'L INTELLIGENCER (Wash., D.C.), Mar. 28, 1866, at 1; THE DAILY AGE (Phila., Pa.), Mar. 28, 1866, at 1; DAILY NATIONAL REPUBLICAN, Mar. 31 (2d edition), at 1; NEW HAMPSHIRE SENTINEL (Keene, N.H.), Apr. 5, 1866, at 1; N.Y. TRIB., Mar. 28, 1866, at 7; PITTSFIELD SUN (Pittsfield, Mass.), Apr. 5, 1866, at 1; *President's Message Vetoing the Civil Rights Bill*, CEDAR FALLS GAZETTE (Iowa), Apr. 6, 1866, at 1; SALT LAKE DAILY TELEGRAPH, Mar. 29, 1866, at 2; SEMI-WKLY. TELEGRAPH (Salt Lake City, Utah), Apr. 2, 1866, at 1; VT. J. (Windsor, Vt.), Apr. 7, 1866, at 1; *Veto of the Civil Rights Bill*, TITUSVILLE MORNING HERALD (Pa.), Mar. 31, 1866, at 1; WKLY. PATRIOT & UNION (Harrisburg, Pa.), Apr. 5, 1866, at 2; WOOSTER REPUBLICAN (Wooster, Ohio), Apr. 5, 1866, at 1.

[43] *See By Telegraph to the Boston Daily Advertiser the Civil Rights Bill Debate in the Senate*, BOS. DAILY ADVERTISER, Apr. 5, 1866, at 1 (providing major excerpts of the speech, including Trumbull's reference to the Louisiana Cession Act); THE DAILY AGE (Phila., Pa.), Apr. 5, 1866, at 1 (full speech); N.Y. HERALD-TRIB., published as N.Y. TRIB., Apr. 5, 1866, at 1 (full speech); *Senator Trumbull On The President's Veto*, HARTFORD DAILY COURANT, Apr. 7, 1866, at 1 (full speech); *see also* BOS. DAILY J., Apr. 6, 1866, at 4 (edited version, with text in full until "bad as his law," then paraphrases, "Here Mr. Trumbull read extracts from Wheaton's International Law, showing that by various treaties, resolutions and acts of Congress, Frenchmen and Spaniards, Mexicans and Indians have at various times been made citizens of the United States"). Trumbull's speech generated responses, both pro and con, regarding whether Congress had the power to grant the rights of national citizenship on persons in the states and whether groups like newly freed blacks were ready to enjoy the rights of American citizenship. *Compare American Citizenship*, COLUMBIAN REGISTER (New Haven, Conn.), May 19, 1866 (Vol. LIV; Issue: 2791) (arguing that, although the federal government may make citizens in the territories through treaty, or may establish a uniform rule of naturalization for foreign-born immigrants, the Tenth Amendment reserves to the states the power to make

objections alerted the country to the congressional efforts to confer on newly freed blacks "the rights *of citizens of the United States.*" The people who followed this well-published drama would soon see this phrase again, this time in the text of the proposed Fourteenth Amendment.

B. *Reporting the Second Draft of the Fourteenth Amendment*

When John Bingham voted with his colleagues to postpone discussion of his initial draft of the Fourteenth Amendment, the conservative press was pleased but cautious. Under the headline, "Practical Failure of the Constitutional Amendment," the *New York Times* reported Hotchkiss's objection that Bingham's initial draft "was not radical enough" and that Congress had "moved its postponement until the second Tuesday in April."[44] As news emerged that the Committee of Fifteen had completed work on a second draft, so too did warnings in the conservative press. On April 27, the *Richmond Whig* reported:

> After a lull of excitement, it begins to be rumored that the Committee of fifteen is ready to make another report on the subject of reconstruction, which is said to be the suggestion of Robert Dale Owen, and to be more radical than anything that has yet been proposed. The Washington correspondent of the New York World thus describes its provisions: . . . No state shall make or enforce any law which shall abridge the privileges or immunities of citizens of the United States.[45]

Once adopted and reported to Congress, newspapers around the country quickly reported John Bingham's second draft of the Privileges and Immunities Clause and its adoption by the House.[46] Although newspaper coverage of the final House debates was relatively slight,[47] the coverage of Jacob Howard's

citizens of persons born on state soil), *with The Civil Rights Law at the South*, Bos. Daily J., Apr. 24, 1866, at 4 ("While some of the northern democrat organs have been instigating the President not to execute the Civil Rights Act . . . we are glad to observe prominent southern organs taking a much more sensible and becoming course." The Mobile Register, for instance, edited by John Forsyth, says that Alabama already has a class of citizens "very similar to what the negroes will be under the Civil Rights Act, namely the colored Creoles, who, being citizens under the Spanish government, were secured the rights of American citizenship by the treaty of 1819. They have proved an exemplary class.").

[44] *Gratifying Triumph of Moderate Counsels*, N.Y. Times, Mar 1, 1866, at 4.

[45] *Congress and its Pet Committee*, Richmond Whig, Apr. 27, 1866, at 1.

[46] *Amendment of the Constitution – Proposition of the Reconstruction Committee*, S.F. Bull., published as Evening Bull., May 1, 1866, at 2 (reporting the new draft); *Passage in the House of the Constitutional Amendment of the Committee of Fifteen*, N.Y. Herald, May 11, 1866, at 6; Burlington Daily Hawkeye (Iowa), May 12, 1866, at 2.

[47] *See, e.g., From Washington*, Janesville Gazette, May 2, 1866, at 1 (noting that "Mr. Bingham of Ohio" would present an amendment "next Tuesday morning"); *see also Closing A Debate:*

presentation to the Senate of the final draft of the Fourteenth Amendment was
wide and deep. At least four major papers reprinted Howard's discussion of
Section One: the *New York Times*, the *Philadelphia Inquirer*, the Washington,
DC *National Intelligencer*, and the *New York Herald*.[48] The public dissemi-
nation of Howard's speech is important for a number of reasons. Not only did
Howard present the official understanding of the Committee of Fifteen, but
he also presented the public with a detailed account of the meaning of "privileges or immunities of citizens of the United States" including its protection
of "the personal rights guarantied and secured by the first eight amendments
of the Constitution."[49] Even those papers with a conservative bias appreciated
Howard's clarity and good faith explanation of the Amendment. The *New York
Times*[50] devoted a major editorial to Howard's "frank and satisfactory" speech
and praised his detailed description of the Privileges or Immunities Clause as
"clear and cogent."[51] In fact, from this point forward, public discussion of the
Fourteenth Amendment commonly referred to the proposal as the "Howard
Amendment."[52]

Speech of Hon. Thaddeus Stevens on Closing Debate on the Reconstruction Amendments, N.Y.
TIMES, May 14, 1866, at 8 (recording Stevens's final comments on the amendment).

[48] *See Senator Howard's Speech*, PHILA. INQUIRER, May 24, 1866, at 8; N.Y. TIMES, May 24, 1866,
at 1; NAT'L INTELLIGENCER, May 24, 1866, at 3; N.Y. HERALD, May 24, 1866, at 1. According to
Eric Foner, at that time the Herald was the nation's most widely circulated paper. *See* FONER,
supra note 3, at 260–61. Regional papers also printed the relevant portions of Howard's speech.
See Speech of Hon. J. M. Howard in the Senate, May 25, HILLSDALE STANDARD (Mich.),
June 5, 1866. Thomas Hardy has identified a few transcription errors and slight differences in
the newspaper reporting of Howard's speech, but none affecting the substantive content or
any critical passage. *See* Thomas T. Hardy, *Original Popular Understanding of the Fourteenth
Amendment as Reflected in the Print Media of 1866–68*, 30 WHITTIER L. REV. 695, 715–16 (2009).
Hardy's helpful article primarily focuses on the published speeches of Bingham and Howard
and does not discuss the general political debates regarding the Fourteenth Amendment in
1866. *See id.*

[49] CONG. GLOBE, 39th Cong., 1st Sess. 2765 (1866).

[50] According to Michael Les Benedict, the *New York Times* "was the conservative organ of the
Seward–Weed faction of the New York Republican Party." BENEDICT, *supra* note 4, at 111.

[51] Editorial, *The Reconstruction Committee's Amendment in the Senate*, N.Y. TIMES, May 25,
1866, at 4.

[52] *See* N.Y. DAILY HERALD, June 29, 1866, at 4 ("The Raleigh N.C. Standard says of Reconstruction
and the Constitutional Amendment: 'We prefer the President's plan. We are for that plan
against all others. But if we cannot get it, we will take the Howard amendment, because we
know that if we reject it the terms thereafter imposed will be much harder than any we have
yet feared. Is this view not reasonable? Who says nay to it?'"); FLAKE'S BULL., July 8, 1866, at 4
(Galveston, Texas) (same); CINCINNATI DAILY ENQUIRER, Sept. 21, 1866, at 3 ("[Gubernatorial
candidate] Hon. W. Fred Dockery stands boldly on the Howard amendment and the whole
basis, which Governor Holden says will give him a large majority in the western part of the
State, and with the vote of the rest of the State, may elect him."); N.Y. TRIB., Sept. 21, 1866, at
5 (also reporting Dockery's support of the "Howard Amendment"); BOS. DAILY ADVERTISER,

Not every paper printed Howard's entire speech, and at least one report emphasized the link to the Comity Clause.[53] Still, whether by way of Bingham's long-reported effort to nationalize the Bill of Rights, President Johnson's warnings, or the substantial reporting of Howard's description of national "privileges or immunities," the general idea of the Amendment seemed to be getting through. As conservative commentator S. S. Nicholas ruefully wrote not long after Congress adopted the proposed Fourteenth Amendment: "The bill of rights, or what are termed the guaranties of liberty, contained in the Federal Constitution, have none of them any sort of application to or bearing upon the State governments, but are solely prohibitions or restrictions upon the Federal Government. The recent attempt in Congress to treat them as guaranties against the State governments, with an accompanying incidental power to enforce the guaranties, is a surprising evidence of stolid ignorance of Constitutional law, or of a shameless effort to impose upon the ignorant."[54]

II. PRESIDENTIAL OPPOSITION

A. *Andrew Johnson's Challenge to the Legitimacy of the Thirty-Ninth Congress*

On June 13, 1866, Congress sent the proposed Fourteenth Amendment to the Secretary of State for forwarding to the states for ratification.[55] Nine days later, President Johnson sent a message to Congress in which he refused to support the Amendment and, instead, challenged the very legitimacy of the sitting Congress. "Thirty-six States which constitute the Union, eleven are excluded from representation in either House of Congress," Johnson wrote. This despite

---

Sept. 22, 1866, at 1 (same as above); Bos. DAILY J., Nov. 21, 1866, at 4 (noting Governor Worth's publicly declared opposition to the "Howard Amendment"); N.Y. HERALD, Nov. 30, 1866, at 3 ("Unconditional Union man" Mr. Logan of Rutherford County submitted the following resolve: "that it is the sense of this House that the article proposed by the Congress of the United States as an amendment to the constitution of the same, known as the Howard Amendment and Article 14, should be ratified by the General Assembly of North Carolina, now in session."), *The Howard Amendment*, TIMES-PICAYUNE, published as DAILY PICAYUNE, Mar. 9, 1867, at 9 (New Orleans, La.) (presenting a tally of states that had ratified or rejected "The Howard Amendment"); *see also* JOSEPH B. JAMES, THE RATIFICATION OF THE FOURTEENTH AMENDMENT 100 (1984) (noting that the "Howard Amendment" was "a name often given to the Fourteenth Amendment").

[53] *See Reconstruction the Debate in the Senate*, Bos. DAILY ADVERTISER, May 24, 1866, at 1 (paraphrasing Howard's speech as referring only to the rights of the Comity Clause).

[54] 3 S. S. Nicholas, *The Civil Rights Act*, *in* CONSERVATIVE ESSAYS, LEGAL AND POLITICAL, *supra* note 24, at 47, 48–49.

[55] *See* CONG. GLOBE, 39th Cong., 1st Sess. at 3135 (1866).

the fact that "they have been entirely restored to all their functions as States in conformity with the organic law of the land, and have appeared at the national capital by Senators and Representatives, who have applied for and have been refused admission to the vacant seats."[56] Nodding toward the fall elections, Johnson added,

> Nor have the sovereign people of the nation been afforded an opportunity of expressing their views upon the important questions which the amendment involves. Grave doubts, therefore, may naturally and justly arise as to whether the action of Congress is in harmony with the sentiments of the people, and whether State legislatures, elected without reference to such an issue, should be called upon by Congress to decide respecting the ratification of the proposed amendment.[57]

Johnson's meaning was clear: The current Congress lacked the legal and political legitimacy to propose an amendment. Both the "letter and spirit of the Constitution . . . suggest[ed] a doubt whether any amendment to the Constitution ought to be proposed by Congress and pressed upon the Legislatures of the several States for final decision until after the admission of . . . loyal Senators and Representatives of the now unrepresented States."[58] Reconstruction should not go forward until first readmitting the excluded states.

Johnson's assault on the legitimacy of the sitting Congress profoundly raised the stakes for the coming election. If the Republicans ended up with less than 122 seats in the House (a loss of twenty to thirty seats), Johnson could cobble together a coalition of conservative northern and currently excluded southern representatives and set up a "true" Congress in opposition to the Republicans.[59] What would happen at that point was anyone's guess, but a new civil war was not beyond imagining.[60] The potential stakes made both defending and challenging the Amendment a delicate proposition. Democrats

---

[56] CONG. GLOBE, 39th Cong., 1st Sess. 3349 (1866).

[57] *Id.*

[58] *Id.*

[59] For a study of the constitutional issues raised in the standoff between President Johnson and the Republicans, see 2 ACKERMAN, *supra* note 2. For the particular point about the Republican need to maintain 122 seats (or avoid a loss of twenty to thirty seats), see *id.* at 178.

[60] According to Congressman Ben Butler at Johnson's Impeachment Trial:

> Does any one doubt that if the intentions of the respondent [Johnson] could have been carried out, and his denunciations had weakened the Congress in the affections of the people, so that those who had in the North sympathized with the rebellion could have elected such a minority even of the Representatives to Congress as, together with those sent up from the governments organized by Johnson in the rebellious States, should have formed a majority of both or either House of Congress, that the President would

initially avoided challenging the Amendment on its merits, focusing instead on the timing and necessity of the proposal. Most of all, Democrats portrayed the Amendment as an attempt to give blacks the rights of suffrage.

Republicans responded that the Amendment did nothing more than constitutionalize the same rights of national citizenship first announced in the Civil Rights Act. President Johnson himself had suggested that federal enforcement of these rights required a constitutional amendment. Nor would the Amendment confer the rights of suffrage; citizenship involved personal rights, not political rights. In fact, throughout the early summer of 1866, Republicans tended to downplay the potential scope of the Amendment in order to avoid alienating the votes of wavering Republicans in the upcoming elections. A bloody riot in New Orleans that summer, however, would change that calculation. By fall, Republicans would engage in a full-throated defense of an amendment that would bind the states to protect the constitutionally enumerated rights of speech, petition, and assembly.

B. *Initial Conservative Criticism*

Even before Johnson delivered his message, critics of the proposed amendment and of Congressional Reconstruction picked up on the idea that the exclusion of the South violated the "letter and spirit" of the Constitution. To supporters of the South, the current Republican policy of exclusion violated the constitutional privileges of citizens of the United States. In his June 14 essay discussing the Joint Committee on Reconstruction, S. S. Nicholas insisted that "as citizens of the United States, [loyal southerners] are secured many rights and privileges with which the public law has nothing to do, and which can not be taken from them except by a usurpation and violation of the Constitution as morally and treasonably base as rebellion."[61] President Johnson's pardon of the previous summer had:

> embraced at least nineteen-twentieths of all the Southern people. When this was done, all those pardoned, some five or six millions, stood where they did as to all rights belonging to citizens before the war. The Constitution tells us

> > have recognized such body as the legitimate Congress, and attempted to carry out its decrees by aid of the Army and Navy and the Treasury of the United States . . . and thus lighted the torch of civil war?

> JOHNSON IMPEACHMENT TRIAL, *supra* note 4, at 77; *see also* 2 ACKERMAN, *supra* note 2, at 179.

[61] 3 S. S. Nicholas, *Report of Joint Congressional Committee, in* CONSERVATIVE ESSAYS, LEGAL AND POLITICAL, *supra* note 24, at 22, 29–30.

what those rights are. Among them is the important right to be represented in Congress. It says that the people of every State shall have two Senators and at least one Representative.[62]

As far as the proposed Fourteenth Amendment was concerned, Nicholas had little criticism beyond objecting the nationalization of matters best left to the states.

> The first section is uncalled for, and comparatively inoperative except as to the citizenizing of the negro, and except for the after clause [Section Five] giving Congress the power to enforce the article by appropriate legislation, or, in other words, to harass the States by Congressional intrusion within what should be exclusive State jurisdiction, according to the original theory of the Constitution. The other matters are already well provided for in the State constitutions, where they appropriately belong, and need no aid from the Federal Government.[63]

Nicholas, who understood the Amendment as an effort to impose the national Bill of Rights on the States,[64] viewed the enterprise as entirely unnecessary. State Constitutions contained their own declarations of rights covering the essential rights of person and property.[65] Nationalizing these rights would merely afford Congress an excuse to interfere with matters that under "the original theory of the Constitution" had been left to the control of the states. Most of all, the *real* constitutional privileges being violated were those of loyal (or pardoned) Southerners who were denied their rightful seats in Congress. As Thomas Ewing wrote to O. H. Browning that summer, "the exclusion of the States, as States, for any reason, supposed or alleged, is a violation of their constitutional privileges."[66] In light of the wrongful exclusion of the southern

---

[62] *Id.* at 30.

[63] *Id.* at 31–32.

[64] *Id.* at 48–49.

[65] *See also Speech of the Hon. Montgomery Blair, in* Speeches of the Campaign of 1866 in the States of Ohio, Indiana and Kentucky 4 (Cincinnati Com. 1866) ("No state shall impair the privileges and immunities of citizens of the United States. What are these privileges and immunities? Where are they defined? Where written? The Constitution has already put each citizen of each State upon the same footing as citizens of the several States") [hereinafter Speeches of the Campaign of 1866].

[66] *Thomas Ewing's Letter to Hon. O. H. Browning, Read at the Democratic Convention at Columbus, Aug. 7, in* Speeches of the Campaign of 1866, *supra* note 65, at 10; *see also* Macon Daily Telegraph, June 15, 1866, at 2 (arguing that since "the highest authority in the government has declared that the southern states are still members of the Union [for the purposes of counting votes for the Thirteenth Amendment], Article V requires the participation of the currently excluded states. And, if the southern states are not part of the Union, it would be unconstitutional under Article V to count their votes for ratification").

states, Congress could not legitimately propose an amendment to the federal Constitution.[67]

Other critics of Section One generally echoed Nicholas's federalism-based objections, with some pointing out that rejecting the "Howard amendment" might actually lead to more onerous demands in the future.[68] It was not so much the content of rights that triggered conservative opposition as it was the idea that Congress intended to extend these rights to black as well as white citizens.[69]

C. *The First Phase of Public Republican Advocacy*

Republican advocates of the Fourteenth Amendment that summer generally dealt in vague generalities. John Bingham, for example, maintained his general theory that Section One did nothing more than bind states to follow previously announced constitutional norms, but he pitched at the high level of generality:

> That amendment consists of five sections, the first of which provides [quoting the section in full]. It is the spirit of Christianity embodied in your legislation. It is a simple, strong, plain declaration that equal laws and equal and exact justice shall hereafter be secured within every State of this Union by the combined power of all the people of every State. It takes from no State any right which hitherto pertained to the several States of the Union, but it imposes a limitation upon the States to correct their abuses of power, which hitherto did not exist within the letter of your Constitution, and which is essential to the nation's life. Look at that simple proposition. No State shall deny to any person, no matter whence he comes, or how poor, how weak, how simple – no matter how friendless – no State shall deny to any person within its jurisdiction the equal protection of the laws.[70]

---

[67] *See* NELSON, *supra* note 13, at 93.

[68] *See* Opinion, N.Y. HERALD-TRIB., *published as* N.Y. DAILY HERALD, June 29, 1866, at 4 ("The Raleigh N.C. Standard says of Reconstruction and the Constitutional Amendment: 'We prefer the President's plan. We are for that plan against all others. But if we cannot get it, we will take the Howard amendment, because we know that if we reject it the terms thereafter imposed will be much harder than any we have yet feared. Is this view not reasonable? Who says nay to it?'").

[69] NELSON, *supra* note 13, at 96–97.

[70] John Bingham, Aug. 24, 1866, *Speech at Bowerston, Ohio*, *in* SPEECHES OF THE CAMPAIGN OF 1866, *supra* note 65, at 19. The quote is quintessential Bingham. As Garrett Epps writes, "Bingham absorbed an old-style Protestantism that equated republicanism with God's will, and the United States with His kingdom on earth." EPPS, *supra* note 23, at 97.

A number of Republicans expressly tied Section One of the Fourteenth Amendment to the Civil Rights Act of 1866,[71] a reference rendered ambiguous in light of President Johnson's objection that, by conferring the status of citizenship on freedmen, the Act had not only granted certain equal rights, but had also necessarily conferred *all* the substantive rights of citizens of the United States.[72] The same was true of speeches that described the Clause as guaranteeing equal rights of citizens in the states, since both nationalizing the Bill of Rights and enforcing the Comity Clause would have had that effect.[73] Others, however, focused solely on the equal rights of

---

[71] *See, e.g., Speech of John Sherman, Cincinnati, Sept. 28, in* SPEECHES OF THE CAMPAIGN OF 1866, *supra* note 65, at 39 ("[President Johnson's] objection to the Civil Rights Bill is that we had no power to pass it; but, my friends, we took it out of his way. We proposed to appeal to the people of the United States to give Congress the power to pass it – [great cheers and laughter] and we *did*. . . . What are the features of that amendment? Everything that was radical that he objected to – I believe the President does not like that name – was stricken out. The first section was an embodiment of the Civil Rights Bill, namely; that every body – man, woman and child – without regard to color, should have equal rights before the law; that is all there is in it."); *see also* Bryan H. Wildenthal, *Nationalizing the Bill of Rights: Revisiting the Original Understanding of the Fourteenth Amendment in 1866–67*, 68 OHIO ST. L.J. 1509, 1575 n.223 (2007) (arguing that there is nothing inconsistent with this speech and the principle of incorporation and pointing out that Sherman later gave a speech that clearly does envision the Bill of Rights as the rights of American citizenship).

[72] Speakers often focused on the Bill's grant of citizenship without exploring the implications or addressing Johnson's objection that doing so necessarily conferred all the rights of citizens of the United States. *See, e.g., Speech of Indiana Republican Senator Lane, Aug. 18, 1866 (Indianapolis), in* SPEECHES OF THE CAMPAIGN OF 1866, *supra* note 65, at 14 ("The first clause in that Constitutional Amendment is simply a re-affirment of the first clause of the Civil Rights Bill, declaring the citizenship of all men born in the United States without regard to race or color. Then there is another provision, and a most important one, namely, basing representation on population, excluding such as are excluded by the local law from the suffrage on account of race or color."); *Speech of Lyman Trumbull, Aug. 2, 1866, Chicago Tribune, in* SPEECHES OF THE CAMPAIGN OF 1866, *supra* note 65, at 6 ("[The Civil Rights Bill's] great feature was to confer upon every person born upon American soil the right of American citizenship, and every thing belonging to the free citizen of the Republic. . . . The first [section of the proposed Fourteenth Amendment], and it is all one, article declares the rights of the American citizen. It is a reiteration of the rights as set forth by the Civil Rights Bill. An unnecessary declaration, perhaps, because all the rights belong to the citizen, but it was thought proper to put in the fundamental law the declaration that all good citizens were entitled alike to equal rights in this Republic, and that all who were born here, or who came here from foreign lands, and were naturalized, were to be deemed citizens of the United States in every State where they happen to dwell.")

[73] As an example of this kind of ambiguity, see *Speech of General Butler, Gloucester (Boston Advertiser, Aug. 27), in* SPEECHES OF THE CAMPAIGN OF 1866, *supra* note 65, at 20 ("The first section [of the proposed amendment] (and I thought it was in the Constitution already) is that every citizen of every State shall have the right of every citizen of every State – in other words, that any one here shall walk in peace in South Carolina the same as a citizen of South Carolina can now walk in Massachusetts.").

citizenship.[74] Although a promise of "equal rights" was a common theme, Republicans in this first phase of advocacy avoided exploring the precise content of those "equal" rights.

Although generally playing it safe in regard to the precise content of the rights covered by Section One of the Amendment, Republicans were explicit in denying that the Amendment would enfranchise blacks.[75] General Robert

[74] *See Speech of Governor Morton, Anderson Indiana, Sept. 22, in* SPEECHES OF THE CAMPAIGN OF 1866, *supra* note 65, at 35 ("This amendment consists of four sections, the first section declares that every man born in the United States, without regard to color, or naturalized according to the laws of the land, shall be a citizen of the United States and of the State in which he lives. What is the object of this? It is to give every man, without regard to color, the equal protection of the laws, and to protect him in his life, liberty and property. . . . We say that the colored man has the same right to enjoy his life and property, to have his family protected, that any other man has. We propose that, without regard to color, all these rights shall be enjoyed, and to this end we have declared that every man born upon the soil of the United States shall be regarded a citizen of the United States."); *see also Speech of Gen. Benjamin Butler, Toledo Ohio, Oct. 3, in* SPEECHES OF THE CAMPAIGN OF 1866, *supra* note 65, at 41 ("[The first condition for readmission] was that every citizen of the United States should have equal rights with every other citizen of the United States, in every State. Why was this necessary? It was because the President, in vetoing the Civil Rights Bill, said that it was unconstitutional to pass a law that every citizen of the United States should have equal rights with every other citizen in every State of the Union. To render that certain, which we all supposed up to that hour was certain, Congress said: 'Well, we'll put it in the Constitution so it shall be there forever.'"); *Speech of Michigan Senator Zachariah Chandler, Mount Clemons, Mich., Oct. 22, in* SPEECHES OF THE CAMPAIGN OF 1866, *supra* note 65, at 56 ("[The first clause] simply gives equal civil rights, before the law, to all persons, white or black, or naturalized. Every man, under this, has a right to sue and be sued, to make contracts and enforce them, and to enjoy all civil rights; but not the right to vote. That is left with the States. Had I had my way, I would have gone further.").

[75] For example, in his speech of July 27, Indiana Governor Oliver P. Morton focused on the Privileges or Immunities Clause only to refute Democrat claims that it would grant blacks the right of suffrage:

> It is from the first part of the second clause of the section, which says "that no State shall make or enforce any law that shall abridge the privileges or immunities of citizens of the United States," that it is pretended that to extract negro suffrage. Now if the right of suffrage is a privilege or immunity belonging to citizens of the United States, as such, then these gentlemen are right: but if, on the other hand, the right of suffrage is conferred, regulated, bestowed or withheld, by the several States, then it is not a privilege or immunity of citizens of the United States, as such, but is conferred upon such citizens of a State as the Constitution and laws thereof prescribe. Women and children are citizens of the State, but have not the right of suffrage. If the right of suffrage is a privilege or immunity of citizens of the United States, as such, then it has always been so, for the amendment only defines who shall be citizens of the United States, but does not confer new privileges or immunities, and in that case would always have been under the control of Congress, and not the States.

> *Speech of Governor Morton, New Albany Indiana, July 27, in* SPEECHES OF THE CAMPAIGN OF 1866, *supra* note 65, at 3.

Schenck, for example, read the first section of the proposed Amendment and then declared to his audience:

> Is there any Democrat here who will dare to stand up and say that this is not right and just? It is putting into the organic law of the land a declaration of those principles of liberty and equality that were understood to be in the Constitution without any such amendment, by those who framed it. It is the removal of doubt upon that question, as we sought also to remove it by the corresponding Civil Rights Bill, passed by two-thirds of each House of Congress over the head of the President. But they are afraid that it may have some concealed purpose of elevating negroes; that if you make them, as you do women and children born here or naturalized, citizens of the United States, you necessarily make them voters.... But it does no such thing; it simply puts all men throughout the land upon the same footing of equality before the law, in order to prevent unequal legislation.[76]

In general, Republican speakers in this first phase of the election season avoided specifics in regard to the Privileges or Immunities Clause, preferring instead to stress the general rights of due process and equality under law. Neither Republicans nor Democrats said anything that contradicted Jacob Howard's description of the rights of national citizenship, but neither did anyone attempt to present a fully developed theory of Section One. In this initial phase of speeches and commentary, the most consistent theme among the Republicans was an assurance that the proposed amendment would not confer the rights of suffrage. This reflected the most consistent criticism of the

---

[76] *Speech of General Robert C. Schenck, Aug. 18, 1866 (Dayton Ohio), in* SPEECHES OF THE CAMPAIGN OF 1866, *supra* note 65, at 13. On August 7, Speaker of the House Shuyler Colfax gave a speech in Indianapolis that followed this same approach:

> [The first section of the Fourteenth Amendment] is the Declaration of Independence placed immutably and forever in the Constitution.... It declares that every person – every man, every woman, every child, born under our flag, or naturalized under our laws, shall have a birthright in this land of ours.... We passed a Bill on the ninth of April last, over the President's veto, known as the Civil Rights Bill, that specifically and directly declares what the rights of a citizen of the United States are – that they may make and enforce contracts, sue and be parties, give evidence, purchase, lease, and sell property, and be subject to like punishments. That is the last law on the subject. Democrats haven't found that out yet. They have been hunting up a new edition of Webster's dictionary to find the meaning of the word citizen.... I grant that a man who votes has a right to be called a citizen, but it don't follow that every citizen has a right to vote.

Speech of Shuyler Colfax, Speaker of the House of Representatives, Aug. 7th, Indianapolis, in SPEECHES OF THE CAMPAIGN OF 1866, *supra* note 65, at 14. *See generally* SPEECHES OF THE CAMPAIGN OF 1866, *supra* note 65 (recording many similar examples).

Democrats, who repeatedly warned that the Amendment either expressly or implicitly enfranchised blacks.

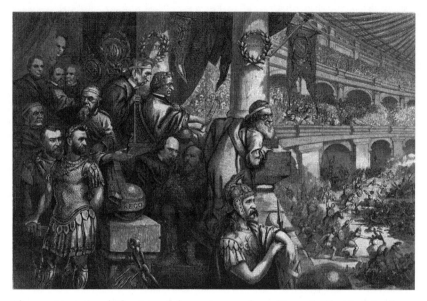

Thomas Nast. Amphitheatrum Johnsonianum; from *Harper's Weekly*, March 30, 1867.

D. *The Debate Turns to Rights: Speech and Assembly in the Southern States*

No single event in 1866 more clearly illustrated the states' continued failure to protect the constitutionally enumerated rights of American citizens than the New Orleans Riot of July 30, 1866. The riot left scores dead and wounded, many of them blacks who had fought for the Union in the Civil War.[77] To Republicans, the violence in New Orleans exemplified everything that was wrong with President Johnson's approach to Reconstruction and starkly illustrated the need to require states to protect the rights of speech, press, assembly, and due process.

1. The Memphis Riot and the Call for a Southern Loyalist Convention

Major rioting in 1866 actually began in Tennessee. In May, three days of police-led rioting in Memphis left at least forty-eight dead.[78] According to

---

[77] McKITRICK, *supra* note 3, at 421.
[78] *See* H.R. REP. No. 101, at 34 (1866); *see also Scenes in Memphis*, HARPER'S WKLY., http:// blackhistory.harpweek.com/7Illustrations/Reconstruction/ScenesInMemphis.htm (last visited

the official House Report, "[t]he whole evidence discloses the killing of men, women, and children – the innocent, unarmed, and defenceless pleading for their lives . . . ; . . . the burning of dwellings, the attempts to burn up whole families in their houses, and the brutal and revolting ravishings of defenceless and terror-stricken women."[79] The Report concluded,

> [T]he fact that the chosen guardians of the public peace, the sworn executors of the law for the protection of the lives, liberty, and property of the people, and the reliance of the weak and defenceless in time of danger, were found the foremost in the work of murder and pillage, gives a character of infamy to the whole proceeding which is almost without a parallel in all the annals of history.[80]

The rising tide of violence and the not-coincidental political resurgence of former rebels in the southern states inspired southern loyalists to band together in their pursuit of political reform. On July 4, 1866, a call went out for a Convention of Southern Loyalists to be held in Philadelphia that fall (any site in the southern states being too dangerous for such an assembly). Widely published in newspapers throughout the South and North,[81] the Call emphasized both the failure of the southern states and the current Administration to protect the constitutional rights of citizens of the United States:

> The great issue is upon us! The majority in Congress and its supporters firmly declare that the rights of the citizen enumerated in the Constitution and established by supreme law, must remain inviolate. Rebels and rebel sympathizers assert that the rights of the citizen must belong to the states alone, and under such regulations as the respective States choose voluntarily to prescribe. We have seen this doctrine of State sovereignty carried out in its practical results, until all authority in Congress was denied, the Union

---

Aug. 6, 2013) (illustrating scenes from the riot, including the burning of a schoolhouse and the murder of African Americans).

[79] H.R. REP. No. 101, at 5 (1866).

[80] *Id.* at 34.

[81] *See* Bos. DAILY ADVERTISER, July 12, 1866, at 1; Bos. POST, July 12, 1866, at 2; *Call for the Southern Unionists' Convention,* EVENING POST (N.Y.C.), July 12, 1866, at 1; *Call for a National Convention by Southern Radicals,* MACON TELEGRAPH, July 17, 1866, at 3; *Call for a National Convention by Southern Radicals,* MACON WKLY. TELEGRAPH, July 23, 1866, at 6; *Convention of Loyal Southerners,* ALBANY EVENING J., July 12, 1866, at 2; *Convention of Loyal Southerners,* DAILY ALBANY ARGUS, July 13, 1866, at 2; *Convention of Loyal Southerners,* WASH. REPORTER (Wash., Pa.), July 18, 1866, at 2; *The Southern Radicals,* ALEXANDRIA GAZETTE (Alexandria, Va.), July 12, 1866, at 2; TITUSVILLE HERALD (Titusville, Pa.), July 14, 1866, at 1; *see also The Philadelphia National Convention,* N. Y. TIMES, July 12, 1866, at 1 ("The indications are that this Convention will be one of the most imposing and important assemblages ever held in this country.").

temporarily destroyed, the constitutional rights of the citizens in the South nearly annihilated, and the land desolated by civil war.

The time has come when the structure of Southern States' Governments must be laid on constitutional principles, or the despotism grown up under an atrocious leadership be permitted to remain. We know of no other plan than that Congress, under its constitutional powers, shall now exercise its authority to establish the principle whereby protection is made coextensive with citizenship. We maintain that no State, either by its organic law or legislation, can make transgression on the rights of the citizen legitimate. We demand, and ask you to concur in demanding, protection to every citizen of the great Republic on the basis of equality before the law, and further, that no State government should be recognized as legitimate under the Constitution in so far as it does not by its organic law make impartial protection full and complete. Under the doctrine of State Sovereignty, with Rebels in the foreground controlling Southern legislatures, and embittered by disappointment in their schemes to destroy the Union, there will be no safety for the loyal element of the South. Our reliance for protection is now on Congress, and the great Union party that has stood, and is standing by the nationality, by the constitutional rights of the citizen, and by the beneficent principles of free government.

For the purposes of bringing the loyal Unionists of the South into conjunctive action with the true friends of Republican government of the North, we invite you to send delegates in goodly numbers from all Southern States, including Missouri, Kentucky, West Virginia, Maryland, and Delaware, to meet at Independence Hall, in the city of Philadelphia, on the first Monday of September next. It is proposed that we should meet at that time to recommend measures for the establishment of such government in the South as accords with and protects the rights of all citizens.

We trust this call will be responded to by numerous delegations of such as represent the true loyalty of the South – that kind of Government which gives full protection to all the rights of the citizen, such as our fathers intended, and we claim as our birthright. Either the lovers of constitutional liberty must rule the nation, or rebels and their sympathizers be permitted to misrule it. Shall loyalty or disloyalty have the keeping of the destinies of the nation?[82]

Accompanying the Call was a circular signed by the provisional governor of Texas, A. J. Hamilton, along with Alabama Judge M. J. Saffold and Tennessee Congressman William B. Stokes. The circular expanded on the need for a

---

[82] Alexandria Gazette, July 12, 1866, at 2.

Convention to address the southern states' failure to protect the rights of due process, speech, and press against the violence of the mob:

> We had all hoped that when treason was beaten in the field, and her armed traitors captive to the Government which they had wickedly sought to destroy, we of the South who, through four long years of untold suffering and horrors, adhered to her fortunes and her banner amidst all the changes and vicissitudes of war, would at least receive protection to all the constitutional rights of American citizens. We relied too, as we had a right to rely, on the earnest and efficient co-operation of the Executive of the Nation. . . .

> We confidently expected his hearty co-operation with the political department of the Government in providing such governments in the States lately in rebellion as would protect the country from conspirators in official positions against its peace; and secure to loyal citizens life, liberty and property, together with the inestimable privilege of impressing upon the minds of others his conscientious convictions of truth, by speech and through the medium of the press. We also had reason to hope that the freedman as well as the loyal white man in the South would find ample protection for all his rights as an *American citizen*, by actual military force if necessary, until equal laws and corrected public sentiment would place them on a firm and enduring basis. In these hopes, predicated on the oft-repeated declarations of the President, we have been grievously disappointed – cruelly deceived. . . .

> Let us act boldly as becomes free men; and if we thereby incur danger, the country will understand and appreciate the shameless hypocrisy of those who prate of their loyalty and right to readmission into the Union in one breath, and, in the next, excite a brutalized mob to violence upon a citizen for exercising the constitutional right of meeting with his fellow-citizens to petition the political power of the nation for a redress of grievances.[83]

The circular proved prescient. Only weeks later, one of the Call's signers would lie among the dead in the riot of New Orleans.

2. The Riot of New Orleans

The specific events of July 30 unfolded against a background of resurgent rebel power in the state of Louisiana.[84] In an effort to regain control of the

---

[83] *Circular signed by A. J. Hamilton, M. J. Saffold, Wm. B. Stokes*, TRIB. TRACTS NO. 2, July 10, 1866, at 3–4.

[84] For an account of the riot, see JAMES G. HOLLANDSWORTH, JR., AN ABSOLUTE MASSACRE: THE NEW ORLEANS RACE RIOT OF JULY 30, 1866 (2001). *See also* CURTIS, NO STATE SHALL ABRIDGE, *supra* note 11, at 136–37.

state legislature, a coalition of conservative Unionists and radical Republicans attempted to reconvene the state's 1864 constitutional convention.[85] The idea was to draft a new state constitution that would enfranchise blacks and disenfranchise former rebels and then submit the new constitution for ratification by the people of Louisiana.[86] The newly appointed presiding officer of the convention, Judge Rufus K. Howell, published a call for the return of delegates. In the portion of the call quoted here, note the self-conscious reference back to the same convention that led to the adoption of the federal Constitution:

> Whereas, by the wise, just and patriotic policy developed by the Congress now in session, it is essential that the organic law of the State of Louisiana should be revised and amended, so as to form a civil government in this State in harmony with the general government, establish impartial justice, insure domestic tranquility, secure the blessings of liberty to all citizens alike . . . and whereas, further, it is important that the proposed amendments to the Constitution of the United States should be acted on in this State with the shortest delay practicable. . . .
>
> Now, therefore, I, Rufus K. Howell, President *pro tem*, of the Convention [of 1864], as aforesaid, by virtue of the power and authority thus conferred on me and in pursuance of the aforesaid resolutions of adjournment, do issue this my proclamation reconvoking the said "Convention for the Revision and Amendment of the Constitution of Louisiana," and I do hereby notify and request all the delegates to said Convention to assemble in the Hall of the House of Representatives, Mechanics Institute Building, in the City of New Orleans, on the fifth Monday (thirtieth day) of July 1866.[87]

Although the sitting Governor J. Madison Wells endorsed the convention,[88] anti-conventionists contacted the local military authority, General Absalom Baird, seeking to have the convention leaders arrested for planning an unlawful assembly.[89] Baird refused on the grounds that it was no crime to convene the assembly and that its legal validity would have to be challenged in the courts.[90] Desperate to stop the convention from taking place, the leader of anti-conventionists, Lieutenant Governor Albert Voorhies, contacted President Johnson, informing him of a proposed plan to arrest the conventioners under a warrant issued by a local court. In such a case, Voorhies asked Johnson,

---

[85] For discussions of the political situation in New Orleans and the riot itself, see Benedict, *supra* note 4, at 206; Foner, *supra* note 3, at 263; McKitrick, *supra* note 3, at 421.

[86] Benedict, *supra* note 4, at 204.

[87] Reprinted in Albany Evening J., Aug. 1, 1866, at 2.

[88] See Foner, *supra* note 3, at 204.

[89] See id.

[90] See id.; see also McKitrick, *supra* note 3, at 423.

would the federal military "interfere to prevent a process of [the state] court?"[91] Johnson immediately responded, "[t]he military will be expected to sustain, not obstruct or interfere with, the proceedings of the courts."[92] This was all the encouragement local police needed. What happened next, according to General Sheridan's subsequent report, was "an absolute massacre."[93] The police and white Louisianans attacked the convention hall, shooting down delegates as they fled despite their raising a white flag. Altogether, about forty delegates and supporters were killed, with hundreds more wounded.[94]

3. Reportage and Johnson's Response

Apart from the federal election, the New Orleans riot was one of the most heavily covered events of 1866 (the coverage of the two often intertwined).[95] Newspapers reported General Sheridan's report of "an absolute massacre" and that "at least nine-tenths of the casualties were perpetrated by the police and citizens by stabbing and smashing in the heads of many who had been already wounded or killed by policemen."[96] Instead of moving to hold the rioters accountable, President Johnson encouraged local officials to continue to suppress "all illegal or unlawful assemblies," including those that "assume to exercise any power or authority without first having obtained the consent of the people of the State."[97] In essence, Johnson took the position that

---

[91] McKITRICK, *supra* note 3, at 423.

[92] *Id.*

[93] *The New Orleans Riot*, COM. ADVERTISER, Aug. 31, 1866, at 2 (N.Y.C.). Sheridan had determined that state and local officials were responsible for the massacre. *See* MICHAEL LES BENEDICT, THE IMPEACHMENT AND TRIAL OF ANDREW JOHNSON 53 (1973). Johnson "suppressed the section of General Philip H. Sheridan's report that called it a massacre by the police." GLENNA R. SCHROEDER-LEIN & RICHARD ZUCZEC, ANDREW JOHNSON: A BIOGRAPHICAL COMPANION 96 (2001). In a letter sent to General Grant on August 2, Sheridan wrote, "The more information I obtain of the affair of the 30th, in this city, the more revolting it becomes. It was no riot; it was an absolute massacre by the police. . . . It was a murder which the Mayor and police of the city perpetrated without the shadow of a necessity. . . . " Letter from P. H. Sheridan, Major-General Commanding, to U.S. Grant, General (Aug. 2, 1866), *reprinted in* 6 THE AMERICAN ANNUAL CYCLOPEDIA AND REGISTER OF IMPORTANT EVENTS OF THE YEAR 1866, at 456 (1867).

[94] HOLLANDSWORTH, *supra* note 84, at 143.

[95] The references are so numerous they are impossible to list. In a search of the precise phrase "New Orleans riot" in one historical newspaper database, Evans, for example, returns 448 references to the event in 1866 alone. Reporting continued for months after the riots. *See, e.g., The New Orleans Riot, Report of the Military Commission*, NEW YORK TIMES, Oct. 4, 1866.

[96] *The New Orleans Riot*, COM. ADVERTISER (N.Y.C.), Aug. 31, 1866, at 2.

[97] Here are Johnson's instructions sent to local military officials and published in northern newspapers:

citizens seeking to exercise their right to assemble for the purposes of amending either state or federal law could do so only with the permission of state authorities.

Only a few weeks later, during his famous campaign "Swing Around the Circle,"[98] President Johnson laid the blame for the riots not on state officials in Louisiana who, it was now clear, had perpetrated the assault, but on the Republicans in Congress.[99] In a speech reported by the *Missouri Democrat*, Johnson insisted that the conventioners intended to "supersed[e] and upturn the civil government which had been recognized by the government of the United States," and that everyone who participated in the convention "was a traitor to the Constitution of the United States."[100] Ultimate responsibility for the traitorous assembly, however, lay with the "Radical Congress" who had "determine[d] that a government established by negro votes was to be the government of Louisiana."[101]

Johnson's failure to defend the rights of speech and assembly in New Orleans and his exoneration of the local authorities proved politically disastrous.[102] According to Eric McKitrick, "Johnson's belligerent defense of those authorities had the worst possible effect on Northern public opinion"[103] and would help seal the fate of Democrats that November.[104] Most importantly, the riots of Memphis and New Orleans became a living lesson to the public regarding the meaning and necessity of Section One of the Fourteenth Amendment.

> To Andrew S. Herron, Attorney General of Louisiana:
>
> You will call on General Sheridan, or whoever may be in command, for sufficient force to aid the civil authorities in suppressing all illegal or unlawful assemblies, who usurp or assume to exercise any power or authority without first having obtained the consent of the people of the State. If there is to be a Convention, let it be composed of delegates chosen from the people of the whole State. The people must be first consulted in changing the organic laws of the State. Usurpation will not be tolerated. The laws and the Constitution must be sustained, and thereby peace and order maintained.

See *The New Orleans Riot. The President Forbids "Unlawful Assemblies." Thirty Negroes and Several Whites Killed*, ALBANY EVENING J., Aug. 8, 1866, at 2.

[98] For an account of Johnson's politically disastrous "Swing Around the Circle," see MCKITRICK, *supra* note 3, at 428.

[99] *See* FONER, *supra* note 3, at 265.

[100] Mo. DEMOCRAT, Sept. 10, 1866, *reported in* 1 TRIAL OF ANDREW JOHNSON: PRESIDENT OF THE UNITED STATES, BEFORE THE SENATE 341 (1868).

[101] *Id.*

[102] His speech laying blame for the riot on Congress became part of the evidence used against him in his impeachment trial. *See id.*; *see also* THE POLITICAL HISTORY OF THE UNITED STATES OF AMERICA DURING THE PERIOD OF RECONSTRUCTION 269 (1875).

[103] *See* MCKITRICK, *supra* note 3, at 427.

[104] *Id.* at 421.

III. THE FALL CAMPAIGN

A. *The Rising Call to Protect the Rights of Speech and Assembly against State Abridgment*

When John Bingham and Jacob Howard described the Privileges or Immunities Clause of Section One of the Fourteenth Amendment as protecting substantive rights enumerated in the first eight amendments, they did so as a matter of abstract theory. In the aftermath of state-sponsored murder of Americans participating in a constitutional convention, Howard's theory now had immediate and practical application. Southern Loyalists increasingly called for the adoption of the Fourteenth Amendment to protect their rights as American citizens against state-directed (or consciously permitted) violence.

In August, one of the signers of the Call for the Loyalist Convention, Alabama Judge M. J. Saffold, sent to the *Montgomery Mail* a letter (which he also published as a pamphlet) mocking the newspaper's attempt to frighten him into silence by labeling Saffold a "Radical Orator."[105] As much as the newspaper's reference to "radicalism" was meant to terrorize "the great nonslaveholding peoples of the South," to "free, unfettered intellects" the term "extends the great guarantees of the our Constitution, of 'free speech,' 'free press,' the 'immunities and privileges' of citizens of the different States."[106] That kind of "radicalism," Safford exclaimed, "I accept as the greatest *political virtue!*"[107] Safford applauded the demands of the so-called radical Congress that southern rebels "banish your proscriptive public sentiment, manufactured for despotic purposes, and let in democratic principles" as well as their demand "[t]hat the constitutional guarantees of free speech, free press, constitutional comity between the states, must prevail."[108] Finally, Safford goaded his critics on the subject of black suffrage by pointing to the riots of Memphis and New Orleans as examples of southern "representation" of black citizens:

> But you say, we represent our women and children, why cannot we represent our negroes? Simply because *representation* means *protection*, and the Congress does not believe you are disposed to *protect* them. You have given them no reason to believe so. Representation is not for the benefit of the

---

[105] Letter from M. J. Saffold of Ala. to the Editors of Montgomery "Mail" (Aug. 13, 1866), *in* SOUTHERN ARISTOCRATIC REPUBLIC! VS. SOUTHERN DEMOCRATIC REPUBLIC!: "IRREPRESSIBLE CONFLICT!", WASH. DAILY CHRON. 1, 4, 10, 11 (1866), *available at* http://www.archive.org/stream/southernaristocroosaff#page/10/mode/2up.

[106] *Id.*

[107] *Id.*

[108] *Id.*

representative, it is for that of the *represented*. The negroes do not wish you to represent them. They prefer to be unrepresented, so long as you massacre them as you did at New Orleans and Memphis.[109]

B. *The Southern Loyalists' Convention*

After a long summer, on September 3, 1866, supporters of the Union from southern and border states gathered in Philadelphia for a five-day convention. Participants included Frederick Douglass, Texas judge and legal scholar George W. Paschal, provisional Texas Governor A. J. Hamilton, and Alabama Judge M. J. Saffold. One of the original signers of the Call for convention who would not attend, Anthony Paul Dostie, perished in the New Orleans riot.[110]

Although the convention split on the subject of black suffrage,[111] members "readily endorsed" the proposed Fourteenth Amendment.[112] Speech after speech condemned the riots of Memphis and New Orleans[113] and called for the adoption of the proposed amendment to prevent states from further abridging the rights of American citizens of free speech, free press, and equal protection of the laws.[114] The fact that border-state delegates would not support any radical measure that might hurt their prospects in the fall election[115] makes it all the

---

[109] *Id.* at 11.

[110] *See The Southern Loyalists' Convention, in* THE TRIBUNE TRACTS No. 2, at 62 (1866), *reprinted in* GALE ARCHIVAL EDITIONS ON DEMAND (recording resolution adopted regarding "Respect for the Memory of Dr. Dostie").

[111] *See* FREDERICK DOUGLASS, THE LIFE AND TIMES OF FREDERICK DOUGLASS: FROM 1817–1882, at 348–49 (John Lobb ed., 1882). Suffrage was not discussed until the second half of the convention, after border-state members had voted in support of the Fourteenth Amendment and returned home. *See The Southern Loyalists' Convention, supra* note 110, at 52.

[112] *See* FONER, *supra* note 3, at 270.

[113] One of the first items on the convention agenda was a motion by Mr. E. Heistand of Louisiana "[t]hat we, as the representatives of the loyal State lately in rebellion against the Government, demand of the President of the United States, the publication of the testimony taken before the Military Commission appointed by Brevet Major-General Baird, commanding the Department of Louisiana, to examine into the causes of the massacre of loyal men in the city of New Orleans, on the 30th day of July last, as well as the report made by the said commission in order that the people of the United States may see the manner in which said massacre was resolved upon and deliberately executed by the reconstructed Rebels of the South." *See The Southern Loyalists' Convention, supra* note 110, at 12. On the convention's fifth day, the assembly adopted a report with a detailed and damning report of the New Orleans riot and the egregious actions of the Johnson Administration. *See id.* at 48–51; *see also id.* at 20 (recording speech of Mr. Moss asking, "How long would it take, with a few more examples besides New Orleans – how easy would it be to see the whole south in flame?").

[114] *See, e.g., id.* at 54 (recording Mr. Bott's resolution); *id. passim.*

[115] Douglass reports that, on the train to the convention, some members tried to persuade him not to attend in order to avoid public controversy. *See* DOUGLASS, *supra* note 111, at 341–42.

more significant that the entire convention repeatedly declared that the south-
ern states had violated the enumerated constitutional rights of citizens of the
United States – rights that would be protected under the proposed Fourteenth
Amendment.

1. The "Appeal"

Midway through the convention, the assembly adopted an "Appeal of the
Loyal Men of the South to their Fellow-Citizens of the United States."[116]
Drafted by a committee chaired by judge and scholar George W. Paschal, the
"Appeal" was both an account of the abridgment of constitutional rights by
the governments in the southern states and a call to support the policies of
the Thirty-Ninth Congress, including the adoption of the Fourteenth Amendment. The Appeal opened by lamenting President Johnson's betrayal of loyal
southerners: "Unexpected perfidy in the highest places of Government, accidently filled by one who adds cruelty to ingratitude, and forgives the guilty as
he proscribes the innocent," had encouraged rebels to renew their hopes for
revenge against supporters of the Union. "Where we expected a benefactor,
we find a persecutor."[117] Johnson's lenient treatment of former rebels, and
his obstruction of Republican Reconstruction policy, had made outbreaks of
southern violence inevitable. By turning a blind eye, Johnson had "allowed
the Rebel soldiery to persecute the teachers of colored schools, and to burn
the churches in which the freedmen have worshipped the living God."[118]

> That a system so barbarous should have culminated in the frightful riot at
> Memphis, and the still more appalling massacre at New Orleans, was as
> natural as that a bloody war should flow from the teachings of John C.
> Calhoun and Jefferson Davis. Andrew Johnson is responsible for all these
> unspeakable cruelties. . . . [119]

Turning to the southern states' longstanding failure to protect the rights of
American citizens, the Appeal declared, "The hand of the government was
stayed for eighty years. The principles of constitutional liberty languished for
want of government support."[120] Here, the Appeal specifically pointed to the
states' abridgment of the privileges and immunities of citizens of the United
States, such as the rights of speech and press:

[116] *See The Southern Loyalists' Convention, supra* note 110, at 22.
[117] *Id.*
[118] *Id.* at 23.
[119] *Id.*
[120] *Id.*

Statute books groaned under despotic laws against unlawful and insurrectionary assemblies aimed at the constitutional guaranties of the right to peaceably assemble and petition for redress of grievances. It proscribed democratic literature as incendiary, nullified constitutional guaranties of freedom and free speech and a free press. It deprived citizens of the other States of their privileges and immunities in the States. . . . [121]

The Appeal concluded by announcing its support of the Republican Congress in the forthcoming elections and for the adoption of the Fourteenth Amendment. Although the Amendment might be more lenient to the southern states regarding their readmission than the Loyalists might prefer, ratification "would be the commencement of a complete and lasting protection to all our people."[122]

2. Sherwood's Address

At the same time the convention considered approving the Appeal, it also considered a proposed alternative address authored by Texas Judge Lorenzo Sherwood. Sherwood assured the assembly that he "agree[d] with the address" proposed by Judge Paschal, and thought it should be "printed and circulated through the land." Nevertheless, he thought it "a little too short" and asked permission to read what he considered to be an address that "cover[ed] the whole case." To applause and cries of "read it from the stand," Sherwood offered his extended version.[123]

Sherwood's address began by noting that the Loyalists had presented a platform that sought to "avoid all things that might excite cavil or affect the sensibilities of any lover of Free Government." Here were the principles the convention considered unassailable:

We stand on the Constitutional rights of the citizen; those rights specified and enumerated in the great charter of American liberty in the following form –

Security to Life, Person and Property; Freedom of the Press; Freedom of Opinion; and Freedom in the exercise of Religion. Fair and impartial Trial by Jury under such regulations as to make the administration of justice

---

[121] Id.; see also Convention of, "Appeal of the Loyal Men of the South to Their Fellow Citizens," N.Y. HERALD-TRIB., published as N.Y. DAILY TRIB., Sept. 7, 1866, at 1; Address of the Southern Loyalists: Appeal of the Loyal Men of the South to Their Fellow Citizens, NEWARK DAILY ADVERTISER, Sept. 7, 1866, at 1.

[122] The Southern Loyalists' Convention, supra note 110, at 24.

[123] Id. at 25.

complete. Unobstructed commerce between the States, and the right of the citizens of each State to pass into and sojourn in any other State, and to enjoy the immunities and privileges of the citizens of such other State. Exemption from any order of nobility or government through privileged class: The Guaranty of Republican Government in every State and, all the People thereof, making the preservation and maintenance of the above enumerated rights, *unless forfeited by crime*, the constitutional test and definition of what is Republican Government.[124]

According to Sherwood, "[t]hese natural, cardinal, fundamental rights of the citizen were established in political form by the Constitution of the United States." Because these rights were "established by the supreme law of the land, there is no power, legislative, executive or judicial, State or National, that has authority to transgress or invade them; and protection of these rights must be made co-extensive with American citizenship."[125] Indeed, declared Sherwood, "[t]he constitutional rights of the citizens throughout the Union must be maintained inviolate!"[126]

The proceedings of the convention were published in pamphlet form, and at least one newspaper published the Appeal and Sherwood's extended Address.[127] Regardless of the degree to which the country read the particular speeches and resolutions, the proceedings themselves illustrate the common conception of the proposed Fourteenth Amendment as guarding against state-sponsored abridgment of constitutionally enumerated rights such as speech and assembly. Proponents of the Fourteenth Amendment had been making this same point since May. The violence of that summer, however, gave the issue an importance and immediacy otherwise lacking in a theoretical debate about rights of American citizenship.

C. *The Second Phase of Republican Advocacy*

Soon after the Convention of Southern Loyalists, the Republican activist and future Missouri senator Carl Schurz delivered a speech in Philadelphia echoing many of the Convention's themes. Republicans, Schurz explained, sought to restore "a Union based upon universal liberty, impartial justice and equal rights," "on every square foot of which free thought may shine out in free utterance." President Johnson, on the other hand, would restore "a Union

---

[124] *Id.*
[125] *Id.* at 33.
[126] *Id.* at 31.
[127] *See* N.Y. DAILY TRIB., Sept. 9, 1866, at 1.

in a part of which the rules of speech will be prescribed by the terrorism of the mob, and free thought silenced by the policeman's club and the knife of the assassin."[128] Less than a week later, the *Wooster Republican* challenged claims by President Johnson and conservative Democrats that the southern states were "in an attitude of loyalty toward the Government, and of sworn allegiance to the Constitution of the United States. In no one of them is there the slightest indication of resistance to this authority":

> *"Loyal to the Constitution,"* these men who prohibit the circulation of papers that do not suit them, threaten the lives of loyal men who desire to live among them, and mob peaceable assemblages of citizens! The whole conduct of the South today is as boldly defiant of the Constitution and of the lawmaking power of the Government as it ever was in 1861.[129]

A few weeks later, in Carthage, Ohio, General Benjamin Butler spoke about how the Fourteenth Amendment would protect citizens of the United States in their rights of free expression. "Before the war," Butler reminded the crowd,

> You know that you did not dare to go to any of the Southern States and there express your opinions freely upon the great questions that were dividing the American people: because, my friends, we knew that, we say now that we will have inserted in the Constitution of the United States, in the form of the proposed Amendment, a clause securing to every citizen a right to go where he pleases within the limits of the United States, and then and there assert his high and noble rights and dignity as an American citizen.[130]

Similarly, Ohio Republican congressman Columbus Delano reminded his listeners of the longstanding problem of mob violence against free expression in the South:

> I know very well that the citizens of the South and of the North going South have not hitherto been safe in the South, for want of constitutional power to protect them. I know that white men have for a series of years been driven out of the South, when their *opinions* did not concur with the "chivalry" of the Southern slaveholders. I know that you remember when an able lawyer from Massachusetts was expelled from South Carolina by a Southern mob. And I know that we determined that these privileges and immunities of citizenship by this amendment of the Constitution ought to be protected, and I know

---

[128] Carl Schurz, Speech delivered in Phila., Pa. (Sept. 8, 1866), *in* Speeches, Correspondence and Political Papers of Carl Schurz 412–413 (Frederic Bancroft ed., 1913).

[129] *Issues of Fact. Spirit of the South*, Wooster Republican (Wooster, Ohio), Sept. 13, 1866, at 1.

[130] Gen. B. F. Butler, Speech at Carthage Ohio (Oct. 6, 1866) *in* Speeches of the Campaign of 1866, *supra* note 65, at 44.

you have lost your reason, every man of you, who denies the propriety of their protection.[131]

It was clear that Republicans had struck a popular chord by using well-known Southern suppression of speech and assembly in their efforts to gain reelection and ratify the Fourteenth Amendment. It was universally accepted in the North that the rights of speech and assembly of citizens of the United States ought to be protected against any abridgment by state or federal authorities.[132] The repeated and uncontradicted Republican claim that such protection would be achieved by ratifying the Fourteenth Amendment reflected the Republicans' calculation that such claims increased support for both the Party and the proposed amendment.

D. *The Democrat Counter-Offensive*

Prior to the fall of 1866, Democrats had by and large avoided addressing the specific substance of the Fourteenth Amendment, preferring instead to stress issues of unconditional readmission, state autonomy, and the dangers of black suffrage.[133] The Republican strategy of emphasizing the need to protect the specific rights of speech, assembly, and due process, however, made Democrat avoidance of the Amendment's merits impossible. According to an October 6 editorial in *Harper's Weekly* titled "A Clear Issue":

> The Address of the National Union Committee states briefly, precisely, and forcibly the exact issue. It is sharply defined, and there can be no misapprehension. It is the issue set forth at Syracuse, at the Loyal Southern Convention in Philadelphia, and by every Union orator and journal in the country. The foolish cry that nobody but the President and the Democrats know what they want has already died away. Vermont and Maine know distinctly what they wish. Illinois and Pennsylvania and Ohio and New York are not in the least doubt. The present issue is that the Constitutional Amendment, which the President himself formerly warmly favored, shall be adopted by any late insurgent State before it resumes its place in Congress. This Amendment

---

[131] Representative Columbus Delano, Republican, Speech at Coshocton, Ohio (Aug. 28, 1866), *in* SPEECHES OF THE CAMPAIGN OF 1866, *supra* note 65, at 23.

[132] For an exhaustive treatment of widespread support for freedom of speech in the North prior to and during Reconstruction, *see* CURTIS, *supra* note 20.

[133] For example, not one of the ten principles of the National Union Platform adopted in August 1866 at the Philadelphia National Union Convention (the so-called Arm-in-Arm Convention) addressed the merits of the Fourteenth Amendment. *See Declaration of Principles*, National Union Convention, *in* THE POLITICAL HISTORY OF THE UNITED STATES OF AMERICA DURING THE PERIOD OF RECONSTRUCTION, *supra* note 102, at 240, 240–41.

simply fixes in the organic law the legitimate results of the war. . . . It defines and defends citizenship in the United States and its rights.[134]

Ultimately, President Johnson decided to meet the Republican arguments head-on and challenge the necessity and the merits of Section One of the Fourteenth Amendment.

1. The Letter of Interior Secretary O. H. Browning

In late October, President Johnson arranged to have his Secretary of the Interior, O. H. Browning, publish a letter laying out the Administration's position on the Fourteenth Amendment.[135] Newspapers throughout the country published Browning's letter, which was "generally taken as the official statement of the Administration's position."[136] Instead of echoing the standard Democratic objections to the timing of the Amendment, Browning launched a frontal assault on Section One, characterizing it as a Republican effort to destroy the autonomy of the States:

> The first section of the proposed article contains, among other things, the following provision:
>
> "Nor shall any State deprive any person life liberty or property without due process of law."
>
> Why insert such a provision in the Federal Constitution? It already contains [the Fifth Amendment] . . . [M]ost of the State constitutions, I believe all of them, contain a similar provision, as a limitation upon the powers of the States respectively. . . . The object and purpose are manifest. It is to subordinate the State judiciaries, in all things, to Federal supervision and control – to annihilate totally the independence and sovereignty of State judiciaries in the administration of State laws, and the authority and control of the States over matters of purely domestic and local concern. . . .

---

[134] HARPER'S WKLY., Oct. 6, 1866, at 627.

[135] Letter from O. H. Browning to Colonel W. H. Benneson and Major H. V. Sullivan (Oct. 13, 1866) (published in N.Y. papers on Oct. 24, 1866; CINCINNATI COM., Oct. 26, 1866). According to Eric L. McKitrick, "[t]he letter had been read by Browning to Johnson on Oct. 20 and the President was especially anxious that it be published." McKITRICK, *supra* note 3, at 469 n.55 (citing 2 DIARY OF ORVILLE HICKMAN BROWNING 101 (James G. Randall ed. 1933); *see also* JAMES, *supra* note 52, at 74.

[136] McKITRICK, *supra* note 3, at 469. McKitrick notes that the letter was "a campaign document" for President Johnson and was "discussed with great animation in the Democratic press both North and South," with southern newspapers in particular viewing the letter as representing the President's "sweeping repudiation of the [Fourteenth] Amendment." *Id.* at 469 & n.55.

The Federal judiciary has jurisdiction over all questions arising under the
Constitution and laws of the United States, and by virtue of this new provision,
if adopted, every matter of judicial investigation, civil or criminal, however
insignificant, may be drawn into the vortex of the Federal judiciary. . . . [I]f
a murderer be arrested, tried, convicted and sentenced to be hung, he may
claim the protection of the new constitutional provision, allege that a State is
about to deprive him of life without due process of law, and arrest all further
proceedings until the Federal Government shall have inquired whether a
State has a right to punish its own citizens for an infraction of its own laws,
and have granted permission to the State tribunals to proceed.[137]

By highlighting the fact that most southern state constitutions already contained analogues to the federal Due Process Clause, Browning hoped to generate suspicion that the Republicans were attempting to use a needless amendment as a tool for federal domination of state civil and criminal procedure.[138]
The Johnson Administration presumably hoped to attract the support of conservatives who continued to believe in constitutional federalism. But however
successful such an argument might have been had it been made in the spring,
after the summer riot in New Orleans it was no longer plausible to claim
that the southern states had any interest in providing the rights of due process to loyal southern Unionists. Instead of shoring up conservative support,
Browning's letter proved to be a political disaster.

2. "A Huge Political Blunder"

The first wave of criticism came from papers traditionally disposed to support
the President. According to an editorial published in the *Evening Post*,[139] if the
letter represented the position of the Administration (which the *Post* assured

---

[137] *Secretary Browning's Letter*, COLUMBUS DAILY ENQUIRER, Oct. 30, 1866, at 2 (Columbus,
    Ga.); *see also The Constitutional Amendment. Letter From Hon. O. H. Browning*, DAILY NAT'L
    INTELLIGENCER (Wash., D.C.), Oct. 24, 1866, at 2; N.Y. TIMES, Oct. 24, 1866.

[138] In his effort to prove the Fourteenth Amendment was not understood as incorporating the Bill
    of Rights against the states, Charles Fairman points to O. H. Browning's speech at the Illinois
    constitutional convention of 1869–70. There, Browning urged the state's retention of the grand
    jury but "never so much as suggested that the Fourteenth Amendment incorporated the federal
    Bill of Rights and thus had fastened the grand jury upon the several states." Charles Fairman,
    Does the Fourteenth Amendment Incorporate the Bill of Rights?: The Original Understanding,
    2 STAN. L. REV. 5, 99 (1949). Putting aside whether Browning's above-quoted letter suggests he
    was fully aware of the possible implications of the ratified Fourteenth Amendment, Browning
    himself would have been one of the last persons to encourage an understanding of the *ratified*
    Fourteenth Amendment as binding the states to enforce the Bill of Rights.

[139] According to Michael Les Benedict, "Johnson's activity in the Louisiana crisis was probably
    the most important factor in his abandonment by the states-rights-oriented Democratic wing
    of the Republican party represented by the editors of the N.Y. *Evening Post*." BENEDICT, *supra*
    note 4, at 206.

its readers it doubted), then it had to be regarded as "a political blunder."[140] It simply was not plausible to believe that the southern states could be trusted to protect individual liberty:

> If Mr. Browning had contended himself with saying "This is not the proper time to discuss or adopt constitutional amendments; all the states ought to be represented in Congress when so important a measure as a change in the organic law is considered" – he would have stood on different ground. But to oppose an amendment which appeals most strongly to the justice and self-respect of the people, to set himself against this reform at any time, is a huge political blunder. . . .
>
> Mr. Browning objects to the provision of the first article of the Amendment: "Nor shall any state deprive any person of life, liberty or property without due process of law." – that it interferes with the right of a state. What right? To oppress its citizens? Is that a right? But he adds that the states already have guarantees to the same effect. Alas, it is too true, both that they have, and that these guarantees have been openly, constantly, flagrantly violated in the late slave states, for many years past. Out of this arises the necessity for an amendment which shall protect the low and weak everywhere. But the purpose is not to "subject the state judiciaries" but to arouse them to the performance of duties which they have neglected; to make lawful liberty, the security of life, person and property, a reality and not a mere sham, all over the land.[141]

The editorial concluded, "If a state refuses to do justice, it obliges the general government to do it."[142]

Other papers echoed the *Post's* view that the letter was a mistake. The *New Orleans Times*, for example, predicted that "the document will operate mischievously, and its publication is a mistake that will add to the difficulties of the President's policy."[143] Papers less friendly to the Administration were more blunt. According to the *Sparta Eagle*, "[t]he most foolish and ill-timed document that has emanated from any of the departments at Washington since Andy Johnson's 22 of February speech is Secretary Browning's letter."[144]

> Even the leading Democratic journal in the North, the New York *World* is disgusted at its sophistry and the false premises which it assumes. . . . This letter is received as an authorization document from the White House evincing

---

[140] *Secretary Browning's Letter*, Evening Post (N.Y.C), Oct. 24, 1866, at 2.
[141] *Id.*
[142] *Id.*
[143] New Orleans Times, Oct. 31, 1866, at 4.
[144] Sparta Eagle, Oct. 31, 1866, at 2.

Andy's deadly hostility to the ratification of the amendment. . . . No Democratic speaker has yet during this campaign descended to the infamy of
attacking this amendment on its merits. The Democratic press, too, have
avoided this issue. . . . The people accept the issue made by the renegade
Secretary, and will render their verdict in November.[145]

Republicans quickly responded to Browning's letter, using it as both an example of the President's feckless policies and an opportunity to remind the public
of the state-driven violence in the southern states. "[The President's] secretary
has done him the kindness to revive the almost forgotten roll of pro-slavery
arguments in defense of [the President's] obstinacy," wrote the *Massachusetts
Spy*.[146]

The first clause declaring that no state "shall deprive any person of life, liberty
or property without due process of law," provokes Mr. Browning into the
absurdity of saying that it will be used "to annihilate the state judiciary," and
"gradually but surely revolutionize the whole structure of our government."
Gen. Tillson, who is not a radical, and was sent to administer the Freedmen's
Bureau in Georgia because he was not a radical, relates in a letter, which
we refer to elsewhere, how innocent persons are deprived of life, liberty
and property in that state without due process of law, and how the Georgia
judiciary, though appealed to again and again to stop the carnival of cruelty,
remains cold as a stone, and as cruel in its indifference as the mob in its
crimes. This liberty of the mob to trample upon the weak and helpless, and
of the courts to complacently hold their hands while persons entitled to their
protection are lawlessly doomed to death or to a living despair, is what Mr.
Browning classes as among the reserved rights of the states, to interfere with
which is to annihilate the state judiciary and change the entire structure of
our government![147]

Most of all, Browning's letter clarified the difference between the Reconstruction policies of the President and those of the Republican Congress. Where
the President would leave the protection of free speech and equal protection of the laws to the states, Republicans insisted that recent history – both
before the War and that summer – amply demonstrated the necessity of adding
an amendment that would permanently nationalize these essential rights of
national citizenship. This was a message repeated north and south, from the
east coast to the interior.

---

[145] *Id.*
[146] *Mr. Browning's Letter*, Mass. Spy, Nov. 2, 1866, at 1.
[147] *Id.*

In Vermont, Governor Paul Dillingham declared that "the riots at Memphis and New Orleans have furnished the most complete and startling evidence of the inherent error of the executive scheme, and have written its condemnation in characters of blood."[148] According to the *Semi-Weekly Wisconsin*,

> Secretary Browning, like most of the rebel and Copperhead leaders through-out the land, regards the Amendments *as positively evil*.... He insists that [Section One of the Amendment] will be a dangerous limitation of State authority and State courts. But if Mr. Browning had the large patriotism of a true national man, he would better appreciate the grand nobility of an ordi-nance in a Republic, which may eventually cover the Continent, declaring that a citizen of Maine or a citizen of Wisconsin should enjoy the same civil rights in Louisiana or in Texas, as the citizens who are born or reside in those States. Mr. Browning must remember the case of Mr. Hoar, of Massachusetts, who was sent to South Carolina for the purpose of persuading the haughty Legislature of that State to relax some of its barbarous laws for the imprison-ment of colored seamen. Mr. Hoar was absolutely driven out of that State, and not permitted the right of domicile or the *right of free speech*, though he was a citizen of the United States, and had been a member of the National Congress.

> That outrage, and hundreds like it, was performed under [the] laws of a sovereign State. That outrage was committed under the Constitution, as it was, because there were many lawyers who held that South Carolina had a constitutional right so to act. But under the present amendments, it is manifest that such an outrage could not be committed.[149]

E. *The Election*

On November 6, the Republicans won a landslide victory against their Demo-cratic opponents.[150] The Republicans had needed to maintain at least 122 seats in the House. They won 144.[151] Republicans also carried every state legislature in the North and won every contested governorship.[152] "Republicans could barely believe the election returns," writes Michael Les Benedict, "a victory as great as that of 1864, a majority of over three quarters of each branch of Congress."[153]

---

[148] *See* JOURNAL OF THE SENATE OF THE STATE OF VERMONT, 1866, at 26.
[149] SEMI-WKLY. WIS., Oct. 31, 1866.
[150] Note the various dates of separate elections in the states.
[151] 2 ACKERMAN, *supra* note 2, at 182.
[152] MCKITRICK, *supra* note 3, at 447; *see also* 2 ACKERMAN, *supra* note 2, at 182.
[153] BENEDICT, *supra* note 4, at 208.

A week after the election, the *New York Times* published the first of what would be a series of articles by the pseudonymous "Madison." In "The National Question," Madison explained the importance of the Republican victory:

> The elections are now over. The country has decided between the policy of the President and Congress. . . . The one great issue really settled is, that the people will not lose the fruits of the victory won in the suppression of the rebellion. They demand and will have protection for every citizen of the United States, everywhere within the national jurisdiction – *full and complete protection* in the enjoyment of life, liberty and property, the pursuit of happiness, the right to speak and write his sentiments, regardless of localities; to keep and bear arms in his own defence, to be tried and sustained in every way as an equal, without the distinction to race, condition or color. These are the demands; these the securities required. In addition to these rights of the citizen, it is demanded that the life of the nation shall be sustained, and the Union perpetuated.[154]

Despite the Republican victory, the struggle for ratification would continue for two more years. It was not that the Amendment and its implications for the southern states remained unclear. It would have been difficult for anyone following the debates between the Republicans and the Johnson Administration not to have recognized that the issue involved binding the states to protect both substantive and procedural rights of American citizens. The issue was one of southern intransigence and continued doubts in the North regarding whether states ought to be so bound.

That winter, supporters of the Republican Congress continued to stress the need to protect the enumerated constitutional rights of American citizens against abridgment by the states. In the January 1867 issue of the *Atlantic Monthly*, Frederick Douglass reminded readers of how the South had suppressed free speech, free press, and the free exercise of religion:

> Freedom of speech and of the press it slowly but successfully banished from the South, dictated its own code of honor and manners to the nation, brandished the bludgeon and the bowie-knife over Congressional debate, sapped the foundations of loyalty, dried up the springs of patriotism, blotted out the testimonies of the fathers against oppression, padlocked the pulpit, expelled liberty from its literature, invented nonsensical theories about master-races and slave-races of men, and in due season produced a Rebellion fierce, foul, and bloody.[155]

---

[154] *The National Question. The Constitutional Amendment – National Citizenship*, N.Y. TIMES, Nov. 10, 1866, at 2.

[155] Frederick Douglass, *An Appeal to Congress for Impartial Suffrage*, ATLANTIC MONTHLY, Jan. 1867, at 112, 117.

In an essay published in the *New York Times*, the pseudonymous "Madison" continued his discussion of Fourteenth Amendment privileges and immunities and stressed the need to require states to protect the rights of free speech and the Fifth Amendment. According to Madison, this protection must be "coextensive with the whole Bill of Rights in its reason and spirit."[156] In a follow-up essay, "Madison" explained that the delay in ratifying the Fourteenth Amendment was due to southern resistance to the idea of being bound to follow the Bill of Rights – resistance exemplified by the violence of southern mobs:

> The positions heretofore illustrated have been that there exists a necessity of defining national citizenship, growing out of the fact that one-eighth part of the whole population of the United States is not generally admitted to have any legal *status* whatever; and that there also exists a necessity of more clearly defining the privileges, immunities, and rights of the citizen, and of securing his protection everywhere against mob violence and unjust State and municipal legislation. . . .
>
> Both the Senate and the House Reports of the Legislature of Texas base the strongest opposition to the Constitutional Amendment, upon the ground that it assumes to define national citizenship; and they distinctly claim that no one is a citizen of the United States except in and through his citizenship of a State. Most of the States refuse to declare their secession ordinances void; on the contrary insist that they have only been repealed, and everywhere among them it is objected that to Congress is given the power to enforce the Bill of Rights.[157]

Again, the idea that the Amendment would bind the states to enforce personal liberties enumerated in the Bill of Rights was no longer (if it ever was) a disputed proposition. The debate involved whether this was a good idea. In South Carolina, Governor Benjamin Franklin (B. F.) Perry opposed the Amendment on the grounds that it "ma[de] citizens of all negroes in the Southern States and invest[ed] them with all the rights of citizenship, without regard to their fitness or moral character. . . . The last section of the amendment utterly wipe[d] out all the rights of the States and centralize[d] all power in Congress."[158] In his address to the Ohio legislature, Governor Jacob D. Cox

---

[156] *The Proposed Constitutional Amendment – What it Provides*, N. Y. TIMES, Nov. 15, 1866, at 2.

[157] Madison, *The National Question – National Citizenship*, N.Y. TIMES, Nov. 28, 1866.

[158] Governor B. F. Perry, *Governor Perry on the Constitutional [Illegible] to the Editor of the Herald*, N.Y. HERALD, Nov. 22, 1866, at 5.

recommended ratification of the Amendment for similar reasons cited by Governor Perry:

> The first section [of the Fourteenth Amendment]... was necessary long before the war, when it was notorious that any attempt to exercise freedom of discussion in regard to the system which was then hurrying on the rebellion, was not tolerated in the Southern States; and the State laws gave no real protection to immunities of this kind, which are the very essence of free government.... If these rights are in good faith protected by State laws and State authorities, there will be no need for federal legislation on the subject, and the power will remain in abeyance; but if they are systematically violated, those who violate them will be themselves responsible for all the necessary interference of the central government.[159]

In January, while discussing a proposed anti-whipping bill, John Bingham reminded his colleagues that Congress remained without power to enforce the Bill of Rights, but that this would change with the adoption of the Fourteenth Amendment:

> One word further about the gentlemen's statement that the provision of the eighth amendment has relation to personal rights. Admit it, sir; but the same is true of many others of the first ten articles of amendment. For example, by the fifth of the amendments it is provided that private property shall not be taken for public use without just compensation. Of this, as also of the other amendments for the protection of personal rights, it has always been decided that they are limitations upon the powers of Congress, but not such limitations upon the States as can be enforced by Congress and the judgments of the United States courts.

> On the contrary, the Supreme Court, when presided over by men who never were suspected of mere partisan judgments, whose ability and integrity were acknowledged by all and challenged by none, ruled invariably as I have stated. If these limitations upon your power confer power to legislate over the States, why not enforce them all by penal enactment?...

> So far as we can constitutionally do anything to prevent the infliction of cruel punishments by State laws I wish to see it done. I trust the day is not distant when by solemn act of the Legislatures of three fourths of the States of the Union now represented in Congress the pending constitutional amendment will become part of the supreme law of the land, by which no State may deny to any person the equal protection of the laws, including all the limitations for personal protection of every article and section of the Constitution.... "[160]

---

[159] JAMES, *supra* note 52, at 162 (emphasis added) (quoting CINCINNATI COM., Jan. 3, 1867).
[160] CONG. GLOBE, 39th Cong., 2d Sess. 811 (1867).

One year after John Bingham first spoke of an amendment requiring the states to enforce the Bill of Rights, the only issue involved whether such an amendment would be ratified. Throughout the summer and fall of 1866, governors and state legislative assemblies considered the proposed amendment, although they left little in terms of a historical record for later generations to consult.[161] Governors generally drafted messages to their respective assemblies introducing the Amendment in vague and general terms.[162] Occasionally, these messages referred to the particular rights secured by Section One. Governor Paul Dillingham of Vermont, for example, pointed to the riots of Memphis and New Orleans as evidence of the need to go beyond the Reconstruction policy of President Johnson and enact an amendment to protect "the property, liberty and lives of all the people of the United States."[163] Ohio Governor Jacob Cox was more specific:

> The [sections of the Amendment] consist, first, of the grant of power to the National government to protect the citizens of the whole country in their legal privileges and immunities, should any State attempt to oppress classes or individuals, or to deprive them of equal protection of the laws.... A simple statement of these propositions is their complete justification. The first was proven necessary long before the war, when it was notorious that any attempt to exercise freedom of discussion in regard to the system which was then hurrying on the rebellion, was not tolerated in the Southern States; and the State laws gave no real protection to immunities of their kind, which are the very essence of free government.[164]

---

[161] According to Michael Curtis, "[m]ost of the state legislatures that considered the Fourteenth Amendment either kept no record of their debates, or their discussion was so perfunctory that it shed little light on their understanding of its meaning." CURTIS, *supra* note 11, at 145.

[162] *See, e.g.,* MAINE SENATE JOURNAL, 20–21 (1867) (Governor's Message) ("the providential and inevitable results of the war as affecting the rights of American citizenship should be recognized in good faith, and practically embodied in enactment and institution"); SENATE JOURNAL OF THE STATE OF NEBRASKA, 1st, 2d, and 3d Sess., May 17, 1867, 57–58 (1867) (Governor's Message) ("[Section One] accepts fully and forever vindicates . . . the idea that was the corner stone of American Independence, but has been for a time rejected by the builders of the national superstructure."); 4 THE MESSAGES AND PROCLAMATIONS OF THE GOVERNORS OF THE STATE OF MISSOURI 81 (1924) (Message of Governor Thomas C. Fletcher) ("The first section of the proposed amendment secures to every person, born or naturalized in the United States, the rights of a citizen thereof in any of the States. It prevents a State from depriving any citizen of the United States any of the rights conferred on him by the laws of Congress, and secures to all persons equality of protection in life, liberty and property, under the laws of the State."); JOURNAL OF THE SENATE OF THE STATE OF CONN. (1866), at 44 (1866) (Message of Governor Hawley) ("[The proposed amendment would establish the] full protection, safety and honor everywhere for the rights of all loyal citizens everywhere, without distinction of race or color.").

[163] JOURNAL OF VERMONT SENATE 1866, at 24–25 (1866).

[164] OHIO EXEC. DOC., Part I, 282 (1867). *Reported in* Fairman, *supra* note 138, at 96.

In the few recorded state legislative debates, there is clear evidence that at least some of the assemblies were well aware of the substantive nature of the rights protected under Section One, as well as of the textualist nature of the "privileges or immunities of citizens of the United States." In Pennsylvania, Republican Representative Mann responded to arguments that the Amendment was unnecessary by reminding the assembly that, under slavery, the South had "denounced the Tribune as an abolitionist paper, and they only had to say that any paper was an abolition paper to justify the rifling and burning of mails. And from 1838 down to the surrender of Lee, there was an entire suppression of freedom of speech in those States."[165] Pennsylvania Representative M'Camant likewise insisted that the Amendment was "necessary to secure to us the blessings of peace and the freedom of every man, woman and child in the country – that freedom of speech and action which before the war was denied and even now is denied to every man who has not been a rebel or rebel sympathizer; a secessionist, or a traitor."[166] M'Camant asked that Democrats be "as true to the Constitution as has been the Republican organization. Stand by us in demanding from the South that our citizens and loyal men everywhere be protected by their laws in the enjoyment of *all their constitutional rights. . . .* We demand the freedom of speech and of the press."[167] Representative Allan supported the Amendment because he desired to give blacks "all the rights which the Constitution provides for men – all the rights which this amendment indicates – in full."[168]

Opposition to the Amendment ranged from radical criticism that the Amendment was too conservative to conservative criticism that the Amendment would destroy the autonomy of the states. In Massachusetts, radical Republicans opposed the Amendment for failing to provide suffrage for blacks and because its protections were superfluous: Citizens of the United States were already protected against state abridgement of liberties listed in the Bill of Rights, thus rendering Section One "at best, mere surplusage."[169] In New Hampshire, opponents claimed the Amendment constituted "a dangerous infringement upon the rights and independence of the States."[170] The Texas legislature considered the proposal as effectively repealing the Tenth Amendment.[171]

---

[165] Pa. Leg. Rec. Appendix XLV (1867).

[166] *Id.* at LV.

[167] *Id.* at LVI.

[168] *Id.* at XCIX.

[169] H.H. Doc. No. 149, Mass. Gen. Ct., at 1–4 (1867).

[170] James, *supra* at 52.

[171] *Id.* at 60.

In short, there is nothing in the historical record that contradicts Jacob Howard's description of the Privileges or Immunities Clause as protecting constitutionally enumerated rights and some evidence that echoes the substantive enumerated rights reading of the Clause. None of its supporters described the Amendment as nationalizing the subject of civil rights in the states, and many described the Amendment as requiring the states to protect rights listed in the Bill of Rights, especially speech and assembly. For some, the limited scope of the Amendment elicited support, for others opposition. Unfortunately, the combination of radical Republican hopes for something greater, Democratic hopes for something less, and southern resistance to any amendment whatsoever resulted in painfully slow movement toward ratification.

IV. WINTER 1866–1867: SECURING THE FOURTEENTH AMENDMENT

A. *President Johnson's Alternative "Fourteenth Amendment"*

By the end of 1866, only six states had ratified the Fourteenth Amendment[172] with an equal number voting to reject the proposal – four of those rejections coming in December alone.[173] By the beginning of 1867, writes Joseph James, "[t]he situation had now reached a stage in which even its advocates believed the amendment would not pass."[174]

Sensing an opportunity to move momentum away from ratification, in December 1866 President Johnson met with a number of provisional southern governors and like-minded conservative politicians to begin forging a North–South alliance that would craft a new approach to Reconstruction.[175] As a result of those meetings, Johnson and his associates began drafting a "counter-Fourteenth Amendment."[176] In January 1867, Senator James R. Doolittle of Wisconsin, "a conservative leader and close associate of the President,"[177] met with cabinet members and presidential advisors to discuss a proposed alternative to the Howard Amendment.[178] The next day, a second meeting

---

[172] Connecticut (June 25, 1866), New Hampshire (July 6, 1866), Tennessee (July 19, 1866), New Jersey (Sept. 11, 1866), Oregon (Sept. 19, 1866), Vermont (Oct. 30, 1866).

[173] Texas (Oct. 22, 1866), Georgia (Nov. 9, 1866), Florida (Dec. 6, 1866), North Carolina (Dec. 14, 1866), Arkansas (Dec. 17, 1866), South Carolina (Dec. 20, 1866).

[174] JAMES, *supra* note 52, at 131.

[175] *Id.* at 134, 138.

[176] *Id.* at 134–35.

[177] *Id.*

[178] *Id.* at 137.

took place with President Johnson's approval (and likely participation) in order to frame a specific "counter-amendment."[179] The third section of the final version erased the Privileges or Immunities Clause and replaced it with a passive restatement of Article IV's Comity Clause:

> Sect. 3. All persons born or naturalized in the United States and subject to the jurisdiction thereof, are citizens of the United States, and of the State in which they may reside, and the citizens of each State shall be entitled to all the privileges and immunities of citizens of the several States. No state shall deprive any person of life, liberty or property without due process of law; nor deny to any person within its jurisdiction the equal protection of the laws.[180]

Johnson's counter-amendment had little chance of success. The Republicans were committed to ratifying the Fourteenth Amendment, and the southern states were equally committed to doing nothing, the so-called policy of masterly inactivity.[181] What is important about Johnson's proposal is what it tells us about the common understanding of the Privileges or Immunities Clause.

The only change in Johnson's counter-version of Section One of the Fourteenth Amendment involves the Privileges or Immunities Clause. After months of opposing the Amendment due to its intrusion into matters Johnson believed ought to be left to state control, Johnson was not seeking to place greater constraints on the states than those in the proposed Amendment. This might seem an obvious point, but numerous scholars have argued that the Fourteenth Amendment should be read to reflect the radical Republican reading of the Comity Clause. James Wilson and Lyman Trumbull, for example, occasionally insisted that the Comity Clause should be read in conjunction with a broad reading of *Corfield v. Coryell*[182] as authorizing federal protection of unenumerated natural rights.[183] If this was the 1867 public understanding of the Comity Clause, then it is wholly implausible to think that Johnson would have introduced such language into his counter-amendment.

More likely, Johnson and his advisors viewed the language of the Comity Clause in the same manner as did antebellum courts and treatise writers who

---

[179] *Id.* at 137–38.

[180] *Id.* at 140 (citing WALTER L. FLEMING, DOCUMENTARY HISTORY OF RECONSTRUCTION, 1:238 [1907]).

[181] MCKITRICK, *supra* note 3, at 472; *see also* JAMES, *supra* note 52, at 143–46 ("Most reaction [in the South] was in terms of continued inactivity rather than activity for or against any plan.").

[182] 6 F. Cas. 546 (C.C.E.D. Pa. 1823) (No. 3,230).

[183] *See* discussion in Chapter 3.

interpreted the Clause as doing nothing more than guaranteeing sojourning citizens equal access to a limited set of state-secured rights. By replacing Bingham's Privileges or Immunities Clause with a passive restatement of the Comity Clause, Johnson would ensure that the Amendment would not be read as applying the Bill of Rights against the states. Indeed, Johnson's reworded provision would do nothing at all, because his counter-amendment omitted both the "no state shall" language and a final section granting Congress power to enforce the Amendment. In other words, just as one would expect, Johnson's counter-amendment was an effort to lessen the proposed restrictions on the state governments. Johnson recognized the distinction between "privileges and immunities of citizens in the several states" and "privileges or immunities of citizens of the United States" and preferred the former over the latter.

B. *The End Game*

In the final days of their session, the Thirty-Ninth Congress enacted the First Reconstruction Act over the veto of President Johnson.[184] The Act divided the southern states into districts and instructed the military commanders of each district to "suppress insurrection, disorder and violence."[185] Acting under that protection, states were to elect delegates regardless of "race, color or previous condition" (excluding former rebels) to a convention for drafting a new state constitution.[186] These constitutions would then be submitted to the people of the states, black and white, for ratification and, if approved by a majority, submitted to Congress "for examination and approval."[187] Finally, and most importantly, even if their proposed state constitution was approved, no former member of the Confederacy would be allowed to rejoin the Union until after three-fourths of the states, north and south, had voted to ratify the Fourteenth Amendment.[188] Only a few days after the Thirty-Ninth Congress passed the first Reconstruction Act, the Fortieth Congress met and immediately passed the Second Reconstruction Act.[189] This second Act instructed

---

[184] See Edward McPherson, *Reconstruction Act of the Thirty-ninth Congress, in* THE POLITICAL HISTORY OF THE UNITED STATES OF AMERICA DURING THE PERIOD OF RECONSTRUCTION, *supra* note 102, at 191–92 (1875).

[185] *See id.* at 191–92.

[186] *Id.*

[187] *Id.*

[188] *See id.; see also* 2 ACKERMAN, *supra* note 2, at 197–98 ("Even then [if the southern states ratified the Fourteenth Amendment], they would have to wait until the Amendment received the approval of three-fourths of the states. . . . ").

[189] 2 ACKERMAN, *supra* note 2, at 202.

the military district commanders to register eligible black and white voters for the state constitutional convention, oversee the election of convention delegates, and also oversee the vote to ratify the convention's proposed state constitution.[190]

The passage of the two Reconstruction Acts signaled the beginning of the end game for the Fourteenth Amendment, a final phase that would include a presidential impeachment.[191] As important as these later events were to the ultimate successful ratification of the Amendment, they did not involve substantive debate regarding the meaning of the Fourteenth Amendment. After March 2, 1867, the future of the Amendment turned on a strategy of political pressure, not one of debate and persuasion.

The process by which Congress secured ratification raises important and difficult questions of political legitimacy. It does not, however, involve issues of original textual meaning. The debates of 1866 forced a deep and prolonged discussion of the meaning of the Amendment and the content of the rights of citizens of the United States. These debates not only provided the Union an opportunity to signal its collective approval of the Amendment in the elections of 1866, they also have left behind a substantial corpus of material from which we can draw reasonable conclusions about the public meaning of texts like the Privileges or Immunities Clause. This is particularly true if we can cross-check these conclusions against the framing debates and consensus antebellum understanding of phrases like "privileges and immunities of citizens of the United States."

C. Ratification and Closure

On July 21, 1868, both houses of Congress issued a concurrent resolution "declaring the ratification of the Fourteenth Amendment."[192] One week later, Secretary of State William Seward signaled Andrew Johnson's acquiescence by issuing the Executive Branch's own proclamation of ratification.[193] On the eve of the President's surrender, Judge George W. Paschal delivered a speech in the Texas House of the Representatives. Paschal was a Texas judge, legal scholar, political activist, and one of the first professors of jurisprudence in the law department of Georgetown University – a department he helped

---

[190] See Edward McPherson, *Reconstruction Act of the Fortieth Congress*, in THE POLITICAL HISTORY OF THE UNITED STATES OF AMERICAN DURING THE PERIOD OF RECONSTRUCTION, *supra* note 102, at 192–93.

[191] See McKITRICK, *supra* note 3, at 486.

[192] See *Telegraph Washington, July 21, 1868*, Bos. DAILY ADVERTISER, July 22, 1868, at 1.

[193] 15 Stat. 710 (1868); *see also* 2 ACKERMAN, *supra* note 2, at 234.

found.[194] Paschal had been a member of the Southern Loyalists' Convention, where he joined Frederick Douglass in calling for the passage of the Fourteenth Amendment and the protection of "the right to peaceably assemble" and the "constitutional guarantees of freedom and free speech and a free press."[195] On this day, Paschal celebrated the passage of an amendment that conferred the rights of citizenship in the tradition of Congress's bestowal of the rights through American treaties like the Louisiana Cession Act of 1803:

> The nation was obliged to define citizenship according to the rules of com-
> mon sense. And not only to define citizenship according to an universal
> standard, but to add the guarantee that "No state shall make or enforce
> any law abridging the privileges or immunities of citizens of the United
> States".... The purchase of Louisiana and Florida, the conquest of Califor-
> nia, and the purchase of Arizona and Alaska have all involved nice questions
> of the transfer of allegiance and the rights of citizenship. It is time that these
> things were settled upon an enduring basis.[196]

One week later, Paschal published a letter in the *New York Herald-Tribune* explaining that, with the passage of the Fourteenth Amendment, the guarantees of the Bill of Rights were now protected against abridgment by state-sanctioned mobs who might otherwise be emboldened by the failed policies of Andrew Johnson:

> The lines defining American citizenship will no longer be matter of doubt.
> Nor is the remaining guarantee in this clause less important. "No state shall
> make or enforce any law abridging the privileges or immunities of citizens
> of the United States; nor shall any State deprive any person of life, liberty

---

[194] See Richard Aynes, *George Washington Paschal*, 17 AMERICAN NATIONAL BIOGRAPHY 107 (John A. Garraty & Mark C. Carnes eds., Oxford Univ. Press, 24 vols., 1999). Paschal also authored an influential treatise on the Constitution of the United States that Congress ordered at the same time it finalized the framing of the Fourteenth Amendment. *See Thirty-Ninth Congress, First Session, Senate House of Representatives*, N.Y. TIMES, May 15, 1866, at 1 (reporting "Mr. Cooke offered a resolution, which was adopted, instructing the judiciary committee to inquire into the expediency of purchasing from GEORGE W. PASCHAL his copyright of the Constitution of the United States, with his notes of judicial and legislative decisions thereon, together with the copious index thereto"); *see also* GEORGE W. PASCHAL, THE CONSTITUTION OF THE UNITED STATES DEFINED AND CAREFULLY ANNOTATED (1868).

[195] See PASCHAL, *supra* note 195, at 263; *see also Appeal of the Loyal Men of the South to Their Fellow Citizens*, N.Y. DAILY TRIB., Sept. 7, 1866, at 1; *Address of the Southern Loyalists: Appeal of the Loyal Men of the South to Their Fellow Citizens*, NEWARK DAILY ADVERTISER, Sept. 7, 1866, at 1.

[196] See George W. Paschal, Speech in the Hall of the House of Representatives (July 27, 1868), in *On the 14th Article of Amendment to the Constitution of the United States*, DAILY AUSTIN REPUBLICAN, July 30, 1868, at 4.

or property without due process of law, nor deny to any person within its jurisdiction the equal protection of the laws."

Law readers are so accustomed to see similar provisions in the State Constitutions, that they underrate this national guaranty. They should have lived in the South, where there was always a class of "persons" for whom there was a summary and barbarous code; they should know that the national bill of rights has, by a common error, been construed not to apply to or control the States; they should have seen and felt that for 30 years there was even half the area of the Union where no man could speak, write, or think against the institution of Slavery; they should know that even now to be called a "Radical" is to endanger life; they should know that all the laws passed under Mr. Johnson's new governments reestablish slavery in a more onerous form to the blacks than the rule of buying and selling and scourging.[197]

V. SUMMARY

A standard theme in Fourteenth Amendment historical scholarship is the relative "silence" regarding the public understanding of "privileges and immunities," a theme driven by the lack of recorded discussion of the subject in the state ratifying conventions. An investigation of the public political debates, however, reveals a surprisingly rich discussion of the meaning and scope of the privileges and immunities of citizens of the United States. Although there were continued disputes regarding the full scope of the clause, much of the debate was driven by a common agreement that ratifying the Clause would bind the states to protect certain substantive national rights. To Republicans, this was a necessary precondition for readmission to the Union. To Democrats, this was an unconstitutional effort to marginalize and ultimately destroy the autonomy of the states.

The picture that emerges from the historical record is one of escalating public awareness that adopting the Privileges or Immunities Clause would bind the states to protect substantive rights such as those listed in the first eight amendments to the Constitution. John Bingham publicly announced this as his intention right out of the gate in the early months of 1866, a fact reported by newspapers and expressly lamented by political critics. While Bingham struggled to find the right language for his amendment, the country experienced a political earthquake, with Andrew Johnson formally breaking with the Republican Congress and accusing them of unconstitutionally seeking

---

[197] *The Fourteenth Article*, N.Y. HERALD-TRIB., *published as* N.Y. DAILY TRIB., Aug. 6, 1868, at 2 (printing letter by George W. Paschal, Austin, Tex., July 24, 1868).

to protect the national "privileges and immunities of citizens of the United States." Johnson's veto of the Civil Rights Act dramatically raised the political stakes in the stand-off between the congressional and presidential visions for Reconstruction, and the resulting newspaper coverage and political mobilization would have raised public awareness of the competing visions at the same time. Jacob Howard's widely published presentation of the second draft of the Fourteenth Amendment took place during this period of heightened public awareness, a fact that probably explains why Howard's role was indelibly linked to the proposal – the "Howard Amendment" – as the public debates moved forward. This made Howard's explanation of the Clause as protecting the personal rights listed in the first eight amendments to the Constitution an essential part of an informed public understanding of the proposal.

Viewing the Amendment in light of the modern judicial protection of individual rights, it is possible to miss the fact that Section One was, literally, a moderate proposal. The text did not federalize common law civil rights, and it avoided nationalizing the rights of suffrage. Advocates presented the Privileges or Immunities Clause as doing nothing more than securing those rights already announced in the federal Constitution. This reading of "privileges and immunities of citizens of the United States" had a history stretching back into statutes and treaties of the early nineteenth century, such as the Louisiana Cession Act of 1803. The key proponents of the Fourteenth Amendment brought this antebellum understanding of national privileges or immunities into the public consciousness through their explanations of the Privileges or Immunities Clause.

In 1866, the idea of holding the states accountable for rights listed in the first eight amendments was not particularly controversial (indeed, some members of Congress thought this was already the case), and it allowed the Republicans to make the claim that they were attempting nothing other than requiring the southern states to follow the existing federal Constitution. A far more radical proposal would have been to federalize the list of "fundamental" rights described by Justice Bushrod Washington in *Corfield v. Coryell*. As much as this might have been the preference of radical Republications, such a proposal had no chance of passage in the Thirty-Ninth Congress and would have significantly undermined Republican efforts in the elections of 1866.

The moderate nature of the Fourteenth Amendment and its embrace by Republicans hamstrung Democratic efforts in the election of 1866. Opposing state protection of the rights of speech and assembly would have been politically foolhardy. Instead, Democrats focused on the nature by which the Amendment was proposed, in particular the failure to forestall consideration of a constitutional amendment until the readmission of the southern states. As far as substantive national privileges and immunities were concerned, the best Democrats could do was argue that these rights, as valuable as they were, were nevertheless already protected under the constitutions of individual states. The summer riots of New Orleans exploded this argument and allowed Republicans to make the adoption of an Amendment protecting free speech and assembly a key part of their case for reelection that fall. Their success amounted to a public vindication of the Amendment and policies of congressional Reconstruction. As if to underline a broad public understanding of the Privileges and Immunities Clause as protecting substantive constitutional rights, President Johnson and the Democrats made one final effort to erase the Amendment's protection of the "privileges or immunities of citizens of the United States" and replace it with Comity Clause language protecting the "privileges and immunities of citizens in the several states." It is not Johnson's failure that is significant so much as the fact that his effort reflects a broadly shared understanding that the protections of the Privileges or Immunities Clause went beyond those afforded by the Comity Clause of Article IV.

In fact, Andrew Johnson ultimately played a critical, if ironic, role in the public understanding of the proposed Amendment. His opposition greatly advanced the depth of penetration in terms of the public understanding of the text, and it greatly increased the opportunity for counter-readings to have their day in the sun. Republicans could have disavowed Howard's claims about the Amendment protecting enumerated constitutional rights and, in so doing, undermined Johnson's claims that the Amendment intruded on matters best left to the states. Instead, Republicans embraced the substantive rights meaning. Likewise, Johnson could have joined the ratification effort, but with the caveat that he understood the Amendment as doing nothing more than requiring equal protection of state-level civil rights. Instead, both Democrats and Republicans accepted the substantive rights understanding of the Amendment and made that reading the basis of their advocacy or their opposition.

Whatever might have been achieved through the judicial enforcement of the Privileges or Immunities Clause, the Supreme Court quickly nullified the entire effort by reading the Clause as having no effect whatsoever on the power of the states to abridge speech, infringe the right to bear arms, or violate any other personal right listed in the first eight amendments. For years, scholars have assumed this evisceration of the Privileges or Immunities Clause occurred in the so-called *Slaughter-House Cases*. In fact, the Court in

Slaughter-House adopted a reading of the Privileges or Immunities Clause remarkably close to that held by Bingham himself. It was *United States v. Cruikshank* that slammed the door on Bingham's dream, and did so in a case cruelly echoing the same murderous riot that helped convince the country to embrace the Fourteenth Amendment in the first place.

5

Post-Adoption Commentary on the Privileges or Immunities Clause

Post-ratification discussions and commentary are of questionable help in determining the original meaning of constitutional text. Prior to ratification, the proposed text must be framed in terms that meet supermajoritarian approval, and proponents must explain the proposed text in terms that reflect commonly held interpretations of the terms and phrases. Failure to do so risks immediate objection by anyone not otherwise disposed to support the proposal and, in the context of the Thirty-Ninth Congress, losing the support of key constituencies.[1] Following ratification, however, the incentives change. Partisans on all sides are now free to press interpretations that further their legal and political objectives, regardless of whether the interpretation reflects a broadly accepted textual meaning. Success now requires only a single majoritarian vote – of a legislature or a court – rather than surviving the two-round supermajoritarian procedure of Article V. For that reason, at least as a matter

---

[1] It is possible, of course, that proponents might purposefully use ambiguous terms in the hopes of avoiding immediate opposition while at the same time laying the textual groundwork for a more controversial political or judicial interpretation later on. But to be successful, this tactic seems to require either an inattentive or naïve assembly unaware that they are adopting a text whose meaning might later be applied in a manner contrary to their actual preferences. Or, at the very least, it presumes an assembly willing to roll the dice on an ambiguous text in the hope that later interpretation will roll in their favor. None of the above seems to describe the members of the Thirty-Ninth Congress. Members constantly raised the possibility of future problematic interpretations, and they repeatedly forced textual changes to avoid precisely this problem. (See the demanded changes to the Civil Rights Act and Bingham's redrafting of the Privileges and Immunities Clause.) This does not mean that the final text was free of ambiguity. It does mean that proponents drafted and argued with the knowledge that their efforts would be closely scrutinized and ambiguity politically punished by a critically important handful of moderate Republicans. The framers of the Amendment also knew the proposal would go through a second round of voting in the public arena, where opponents would have a second opportunity to exploit problems or ambiguities in the text. In sum, prior to ratification, there existed a political context that rewarded broadly understood and broadly acceptable texts and arguments.

of theory, scholars generally give post-adoption evidence relatively little weight in determining the historical meaning of the Privileges or Immunities Clause.

Despite the problematic nature of post-ratification evidence as a source for determining original understanding, post-adoption events have played a relatively large role in scholarly discussion of the historical understanding of the Fourteenth Amendment. The Supreme Court's 1873 decision in the *Slaughter-House Cases* and the failed Blaine Amendment of 1875, for example, have played disproportionately large roles in discussions of the historical meaning of the Privileges or Immunities Clause. This is probably due in large part to the assumed lack of pre-ratification evidence: Against a presumed background of pre-ratification "silence," the significance of post-ratification discussion takes on a larger role, if only by default. Now that we know there is a rich historical record of pre-ratification discussion, this greatly reduces the need to rely on post-adoption commentary as evidence of original meaning.

In fact, instead of viewing later discussions and events as casting light backward, it is now possible to view pre-ratification discussions as casting light forward, better enabling us to understand the nature of post-ratification debates over the meaning of the Privileges or Immunities Clause. In particular, it is now clear that far from contradicting John Bingham's explanation of the Privileges or Immunities Clause, Justice Miller's majority opinion in the *Slaughter-House Cases* closely tracked Bingham's understanding of the distinction between Article IV's "privileges and immunities of citizens in the several states" and the Fourteenth Amendment's "privileges or immunities of citizens of the United States." Rather than representing an unduly narrow reading of Bingham's work, Justice Miller presented a moderate understanding of the text that rejected post-ratification efforts by both radicals and conservatives to link the Privileges or Immunities Clause to Article IV. But if not the end of the Privileges or Immunities Clause, *Slaughter-House* was prelude to the end. The Court would soon enough close the door on any meaningful application of the Clause, and the idea of national privileges and immunities would quickly fade from our collective memory.

This chapter recounts the early debates over the meaning of the Privileges or Immunities Clause. In doing so, I address events and judicial rulings that, if not significant at the time, have come to be treated as significant by modern histories of the Privileges or Immunities Clause. For example, scholars commonly view Miller's opinion in *Slaughter-House* as contradicting John Bingham's vision of the Privileges or Immunities Clause, and a number of scholars have pointed to the so-called Blaine Amendment of 1875 as evidence the Fourteenth Amendment did not incorporate the Bill of Rights. As we shall see, neither of these claims is meaningfully supported the historical record.

Although it seems proper to address post-adoption events that have played such a large role in prior histories of the Privileges or Immunities Clause, in the end we are left with Jacob Howard's public explanation of the Clause as protecting the constitutionally enumerated rights of citizens of the United States as the most likely original meaning of the text.

I. EARLY DEBATE ON THE PRIVILEGES OR IMMUNITIES CLAUSE

A. *Early Judicial Decisions*

In one of the first judicial opinions addressing the meaning of the Privileges or Immunities Clause, the Ohio Supreme Court adopted the moderate reading of the Clause presented by John Bingham and Jacob Howard. According to Judge Luther Day:

> This [case] involves the equity as to what privileges or immunities are embraced in the inhibition of this clause. We are not aware that this has been as yet judicially settled. The language of the clause, however, taken in connection with other provisions of the amendment, and of the constitution of which it forms a part, affords strong reasons for believing that it includes only such privileges or immunities as are derived from, or recognized by, the constitution of the United States. A broader interpretation opens into a field of conjecture limitless as the range of speculative theories, and might work such limitations of the power of the States to manage and regulate their local institutions and affairs as were never contemplated by the amendment.[2]

Echoing John Bingham, Judge Day defines the privileges or immunities of United States citizens to include "only such privileges or immunities as are derived from, or recognized by, the constitution of the United States," and he rejects the effort to interpret the Clause as protecting unenumerated rights.[3]

Other judges took a more expansive approach. In his circuit court opinion striking down the same Louisiana slaughter-house monopoly later upheld in *The Slaughter-House Cases*,[4] Justice Joseph P. Bradley insisted the newly enacted Clause protected the "sacred rights of labor." In the *Live Stock Dealers*

---

[2] Garnes v. McCann, 21 Ohio St. 198 (Ohio Sup. Ct. 1871).

[3] In *Garnes*, the Ohio Supreme Court rejected a claim that the Fourteenth Amendment forbids segregated public schools. *Id.* at 211–12. For an argument that the Equal Protection Clause, properly interpreted, *does* forbid de jure racial segregation, *see* Michael McConnell, *Originalism and the Desegregation Decisions*, 81 Va. L. Rev. 947 (1995).

[4] Live-Stock Dealers' & Butchers' Ass'n v. Crescent City Live-Stock Landing & Slaughter-House Co., 15 F.Cas. 649 (C.C.La. 1870).

case, Bradley began by distinguishing the Comity Clause of Article IV from the Privileges or Immunities Clause:

> The new prohibition that "no state shall make or enforce any law which shall abridge the privileges or immunities of citizens of the United States" is not identical with the clause in the constitution which declared that "the citizens of each state shall be entitled to all privileges and immunities of citizens in the several states." It embraces much more.

> The "privileges and immunities" secured by the original constitution, were only such as each state gave to its own citizens. Each was prohibited from discriminating in favor of its own citizens, and against the citizens of other states.

> But the fourteenth amendment prohibits any state from abridging the privileges or immunities of the citizens of the United States, whether its own citizens or any others. It not merely requires equality of privileges; but it demands that the privileges and immunities of all citizens shall be absolutely unabridged, unimpaired.

These absolute privileges and immunities, according to Bradley, included rights that may not have been intended or anticipated by those who debated and adopted the Amendment:

> It is possible that those who framed the article were not themselves aware of the far reaching character of its terms. They may have had in mind but one particular phase of social and political wrong which they desired to redress. Yet, if the amendment, as framed and expressed, does in fact bear a broader meaning, and does extend its protecting shield over those who were never thought of when it was conceived and put in form, and does reach social evils which were never before prohibited by constitutional enactment, it is to be presumed that the American people, in giving it their imprimatur, understood what they were doing, and meant to decree what has in fact been decreed.[5]

One of these unanticipated yet fully protected rights involved the "privilege . . . of every American citizen to adopt and follow such lawful industrial pursuit – not injurious to the community – as he may see fit, without unreasonable regulation or molestation, and without being restricted by any of those unjust, oppressive, and odious monopolies or exclusive privileges which have been condemned by all free governments." This, wrote Bradley, involved "nothing more nor less than the sacred right of labor."[6]

---

[5] *Id.* at 652.
[6] *Id.*

Bradley's opinion is based entirely on the text of the Amendment and his analysis of the inherent requirements of a free republican government.[7] He concedes his reading has nothing to do with the explanations provided by the framers of the Amendment, and he ignores entirely the public debate. Bradley does not cite *Corfield v. Coryell*; in fact, he cites no judicial precedent at all other than noting that the Supreme Court had previously declined to define "privileges and immunities."[8] As would the majority in *Slaughter-House*, Bradley distinguishes Article IV "privileges and immunities" from Fourteenth Amendment "privileges or immunities." Bradley does this to emphasize the different kinds of protection afforded by the different clauses, with the Comity Clause providing equal protection and the Fourteenth Amendment providing absolute rights. This tracks the common understanding of the Comity Clause and it probably explains why Bradley did not believe *Corfield* supported his opinion. Other advocates of a broad reading of the Privileges or Immunities Clause, however, would find the pregnant language of *Corfield* irresistible, in particular Justice Washington's reference to the privilege of suffrage.

B. *Women's Suffrage*

1. The Memorial of Victoria Woodhull

On December 21, 1870, women's rights advocate Victoria C. Woodhull submitted a memorial to the United States Senate and House of Representatives calling for legislation guaranteeing women the equal right to vote in the states.[9] According to the memorial, the Fifteenth Amendment prohibits the states from "pass[ing] any law to deny or abridge the right of any citizens of the United States the right to vote . . . neither on account of sex nor otherwise."[10] Woodhull insisted that laws denying women the right to vote violated the command

---

[7] According to Bradley: "These privileges cannot be invaded without sapping the very foundations of republican government. A republican government is not merely a government of the people, but it is a free government. Without being free, it is republican only in name, and not republican in truth, and any government which deprives its citizens of the right to engage in any lawful pursuit, subject only to reasonable restrictions, or at least subject only to such restrictions as are reasonably within the power of government to impose, – is tyrannical and unrepublican. And if to enforce arbitrary restrictions made for the benefit of a favored few, it takes away and destroys the citizen's property without trial or condemnation, it is guilty of violating all the fundamental privileges to which I have referred, and one of the fundamental principles of free government."

    Live-Stock Dealers', 15 F. Cas. at 652.

[8] *Id.* (citing Connor v. Elliot, 18 How. [59 U.S.] 591 [1855]).

[9] *See* 41st Cong., 3d Sess., Senate, Mis. Doc. No. 16.

[10] *Id.*

of the Fourteenth Amendment that "'no State shall make or enforce any law which shall abridge the privileges or immunities of citizens of the United States' nor deny to any person within its jurisdiction the equal protection of the laws.'"[11]

Woodhull presented her memorial before the House Committee on the Judiciary on January 11, 1871.[12] Also appearing before the Committee in support of Woodhull's memorial was Washington lawyer and radical Republican Albert G. Riddle. According to Riddle, passage of the Privileges or Immunities Clause had the effect of constitutionalizing the right to vote for all citizens of the United States.[13] Repeating his argument that evening before a convention of the National Woman Suffrage Association, Riddle insisted that Bushrod Washington's opinion in *Corfield v. Coryell* held the key to understanding the Privileges or Immunities Clause, in particular Washington's inclusion of "the right to exercise the elective franchise" as one of the protected privileges and immunities of citizens of the United States.[14] In support of this expansive reading of the Privileges or Immunities Clause, Riddle cited Justice Bradley's recent Article IV-based circuit court opinion in the "The Crescent City Livestock Company," including Bradley's concession that "[i]t is possible that those who framed the article were not themselves aware of the far-reaching character of its terms," but that the text could "bear a broader meaning."[15]

Riddle later expanded on his argument before the Supreme Court of the District of Columbia in a challenge to the municipality's refusal to register women to vote.[16] According to Riddle, the Fourteenth Amendment's grant of American citizenship to all persons born in the United States had the effect of bestowing all the rights of American citizenship on such persons, including the right to vote. "[T]he right to vote is a natural right," and one of citizens' "privileges and immunities" recognized by Justice Bushrod Washington in *Corfield v. Coryell*.[17] Although "we know as a matter of fact that women were

---

[11] *Id.*

[12] 2 HISTORY OF WOMEN'S SUFFRAGE, 1861–1876, at 444 (Elizabeth Cady Stanton, Susan B. Anthony, Matilda Joslyn Gage eds., 1882).

[13] Riddle's comments about his testimony are reproduced in 2 HISTORY OF WOMEN'S SUFFRAGE, *supra* note 12, at 448.

[14] *Id.* at 453.

[15] *Id.* at 457. *See also* Reva B. Siegel, *She the People: The Nineteenth Amendment, Sex Equality, Federalism and the Family*, 115 HARV. L. REV. 947, 972–74 (2002).

[16] *See* ARGUMENTS OF COUNSEL AND OPINION IN THE SUPREME COURT OF THE DISTRICT OF COLUMBIA ON THE WOMEN'S SUFFRAGE QUESTION (Judd & Detweiler, 1871) (Sara J. Spencer v. Board of Registration and Sarah E. Webster v. The Judges of Election) (available at Library of Congress: American Memory website.

[17] *Id.* at 6, 26–27.

not at all in the minds of the framers and adopters of this amendment," as Justice Bradley explained in the "Live Stock Dealers" case, "if it is possible that those who framed the article were not themselves aware of the far-reaching character of its terms," "if the amendment, as framed and expressed, does, in fact, bear a broader meaning . . . it is to be presumed that the American people, in giving it their imprimatur, understood what they were doing."[18]

2. The Woodhull Report

On January 30, the House Committee on the Judiciary delivered its response.[19] Chaired by John Bingham, the eight-member committee divided 6 to 2 against women's suffrage, with Representatives William Loughridge and Benjamin F. Butler dissenting.[20] Although John Bingham chaired the Committee and submitted the Report, the Report seems to contradict some of Bingham's express personal statements about the Privileges or Immunities Clause. Because he agreed with the bottom line, Bingham may have simply acquiesced to the reasoning of his fellows. This is not clearly the case, however, given some of the odd aspects of the Report (more on this later). In fact, the Report seems to represent a rather garbled combination of conflicting theories, Bingham's included, all of which agreed that the Privileges or Immunities Clause did not grant women the right to vote.

Here is the Report's key section regarding the Privileges or Immunities Clause:

> The clause of the Fourteenth Amendment, "No state shall make or enforce any law which shall abridge the privileges or immunities of citizens of the United States," does not, in the opinion of the committee, refer to privileges and immunities of citizens of the United States other than those privileges and immunities embraced in the original text of the Constitution, article 4, section 2. The fourteenth amendment, it is believed, did not add to the privileges or immunities before mentioned, but was deemed necessary for their enforcement as an express limitation upon the powers of the States. It had been judicially determined that the first eight articles of amendment of the Constitution were not limitations on the power of the States, and it

---

[18] *Id.* at 29.
[19] House of Representatives, Committee on the Judiciary, *Victoria C. Woodhull. Report*, 41st Cong., 3d sess., January 30, 1871, H. Rept. 22. The members of the Committee were John Bingham (Chair), Burton C. Cook, Charles A. Eldridge, Giles W. Hotchkiss, Stephen W. Kellogg, Michael C. Kerr, Ulysses Mercur, John A. Peters, William Loughridge, and Benjamin F. Butler.
[20] *Id.*

was apprehended that the same might be held of the provision of the second section, fourth article.

To remedy this defect of the Constitution, the express limitations upon the States contained in the first section of the Fourteenth Amendment, together with the grant of power in Congress to enforce them by legislation, were incorporated in the Constitution. The words "citizens of the United States," and "citizens of the states," as employed in the Fourteenth Amendment, did not change or modify the relations of citizens of the State and nation as they existed under the original Constitution.[21]

According to the Report, the right of suffrage involved the relationship between a citizen and his or her respective state. Although Justice Washington listed the right to vote as a privilege and immunity of citizens in the several states, he specified the "elective franchise, *as regulated and established by the laws or Constitution of the State in which it is to be exercised.*"[22] Finally, even if the Committee were wrong about the Constitution, Woodhull's claimed right "can be established in the courts without further legislation."[23]

In general, the Woodhull Report majority appears to reduce the Privileges or Immunities Clause to a mere restatement of the Comity Clause of Article IV, guaranteeing nothing other than equal enforcement of state-secured rights and privileges. This would contradict Bingham's earlier claim that the Clause covered constitutionally enumerated rights such as those listed in the Bill of Rights. In fact, only a few weeks later, Bingham would expressly define the Privileges or Immunities Clause as protecting liberties listed in the first eight amendments and emphatically declare that the Clause was not a restatement of Article IV.[24] Again, there is no reason to think that the Report reflected Bingham's personal theory of the Privileges or Immunities Clause; the Report was a summation of the views of a multimember majority. Perhaps, because the bottom line was one with which he agreed (the Clause did not nationalize unenumerated rights in general, much less political rights), Bingham may have been content to acquiesce to the views of other members. It also is possible that Bingham might have agreed with the Report insofar as he continued to believe that Article IV, properly read, secured all constitutionally enumerated rights and did not understand the Report as claiming otherwise. This is the problem with committee reports: One cannot know whether the reasoning of the report reflects the unanimously held constitutional theory of every member

---

[21] *Id.*

[22] *Id.*

[23] *Id.* at 4.

[24] *See infra at* notes 81–85.

of the majority, just the theory of the drafter, or a compromise explanation that represents no one member's particular views.

In fact, there is reason to think the Report actually represents a garbled account of the combined views of the Committee majority. Consider again the Report's odd rationale for the adoption of the Privileges or Immunities Clause:

> The fourteenth amendment, it is believed, did not add to the privileges or immunities before mentioned, but was deemed necessary for their enforcement as an express limitation upon the powers of the States. It had been judicially determined that the first eight articles of amendment of the Constitution were not limitations on the power of the States, and it was apprehended that the same might be held of the provision of the second section, fourth article.[25]

Purporting to explain Congress's rationale for proposing the Privileges or Immunities Clause, this paragraph begins with a legally correct account of the Supreme Court's treatment of the Bill of Rights. Because the Bill lacked language expressly binding the states, it "had been judicially determined" as not binding on the states. This is a reference, of course, to Chief Justice Marshall's opinion in *Barron v. Baltimore*, which declined to apply the Bill of Rights against the states due to the lack of language expressly limiting the powers of the states. So far, so good. But then the paragraph veers away from the Bill of Rights and addresses the Comity Clause of Article IV: "it was apprehended that the same might be held of the provision of the second section, fourth article." This is neither an argument raised in the debates of the Thirty-Ninth Congress nor a correct statement of law. Antebellum courts had consistently interpreted the Comity Clause as "limiting the powers of the States," a fact members of the Thirty-Ninth Congress repeatedly reminded the assembly in their numerous references to Comity Clauses cases like *Abbott v. Bayley* and *Corfield v. Coryell*. Not only is the Report wrong on this obvious point, the argument borders on incoherency. The majority appears to argue that, because the courts refused to apply the Bill of Rights against the states due to the lack of language expressly requiring them to do so, instead of fixing *that* problem, Congress added a provision that would ensure courts would enforce the Comity Clause against the states – which they were already doing. The argument is so odd (both legally and historically) that it raises the possibility of a garbled transmission of the Committee's actual views.

[25] 41st Cong., 3d Sess., January 30, 1871, H. Rept. 22.

The majority might have been trying to say that, due to the lack of a provision expressly granting Congress power to enforce enumerated liberties, there was a concern that the courts might rule that Congress had no power to pass enforcement legislation like the Civil Rights Act of 1866. Although the Supreme Court had found implied power to enforce Article IV in *Prigg*, the current Supreme Court might not follow that approach in the future. Although this reconstruction of the Report would make more sense legally, it is in tension with the sentence's opening reference to a need for constitutional language expressly *binding the states* and not the need for language granting *congressional power*.

A second possible explanation is that the Committee majority actually identified two problems, each of which required a different remedy. Consider these consecutive sentences in the Report:

> It had been judicially determined that the first eight articles of amendment of the Constitution were not limitations on the power of the States, and it was apprehended that the same might be held of the provision of the second section, fourth article. To remedy this defect of the Constitution, the express limitations upon the States contained in the first section of the Fourteenth Amendment, together with the grant of power in Congress to enforce them by legislation, were incorporated in the Constitution.

The first sentence refers to two problems, one involving a judicial construction of "the first eight articles of amendment" (the Bill of Rights) and a possible judicial construction of "the second section, fourth article" (the Comity Clause). The second sentence refers to two remedies, one involving the addition of language expressly binding the states and the other involving an express grant of congressional enforcement power. As written, the reference to Article IV in the first sentence makes no sense: Courts *had* interpreted the Comity Clause as binding the states. Also, as written, the second sentence contains a remedy without a problem: Nothing in the first sentence says anything about a perceived lack of congressional enforcement power.

Suppose, however, that the Report either misstates or garbles the actual views of the Committee. The Committee may have actually believed that past judicial construction of the Bill of Rights and possible future judicial construction of Article IV represented two separate problems requiring two separate remedies. Courts in the past had refused to apply the personal rights listed in the Bill of Rights against the states due to a lack of language expressly requiring them to do so (see *Barron*). Thus, the need for an Amendment with language expressly binding the states. Also, courts in the future might refuse to follow *Prigg* and rule that Congress had no power to enforce the equal protection principles of the Comity Clause (a concern repeatedly raised in the Thirty-Ninth Congress). Thus, the additional need for language expressly granting Congress enforcement power. Here is how the key paragraph could be easily reconstructed to reflect this idea (with the replacement language in italics):

> It had been judicially determined that the first eight articles of amendment of the Constitution were not limitations on the power of the States, and it was apprehended ~~that the same might be held of the provision of the second section, fourth article~~ *that courts might also hold the second section, fourth article cannot be enforced by Congress.* To remedy this defect of the Constitution, the express limitations upon the States contained in the first section of the Fourteenth Amendment, together with the grant of power in Congress to enforce them by legislation, were incorporated in the Constitution.

This reconstruction fits with the Committee's refusal to read the Privileges or Immunities Clause as protecting "fundamental" unenumerated rights like the rights of suffrage. Moderates like Bingham believed that the addition of express language binding the states involved only those substantive rights listed in the Constitution, and both moderates and conservatives believed that the equal protection principles of the Comity Clause left states free to determine the qualifications for suffrage. Finally, if this reconstruction represents a clearer view of what the Committee was trying to say, then this explains why Bingham felt comfortable delivering a speech only weeks later that seems to directly conflict with the actual language of the Report; nothing in the Report was intended to conflict with the Bingham-Howard reading of the Privileges or Immunities Clause.

This, of course, is pure conjecture, and one that readers may find rather unconvincing. As written, the Report claims that the rationale for drafting the Privileges or Immunities Clause involved a concern that the courts might interpret the Comity Clause as not binding the states. Read literally, this would have been understood *at that time* as nonsense, both as a matter of well-known law and recent history. Nevertheless, perhaps it is safer to simply accept what was written rather than try to reconstruct a more plausible paragraph. If so, we are left with nothing more than a historical oddity that tells us more about sloppy committee work than the original understanding of the Privileges or Immunities Clause.[26] For their part, the minority members of the Committee

---

[26]   Anti-incorporationist scholars have attempted to use the Report as evidence that the Privileges or Immunities Clause was not understood as incorporating the Bill of Rights. The Report, of course, says nothing at all about whether the Privileges or Immunities Clause protects

ignored the problematic sentence altogether. Instead, they concentrated on the Report's attempt to equate the privileges or immunities *of citizens of the United States* with the *privileges and immunities of citizens in the several states.*

3. The Views of the Minority

In their "Views of the Minority," Loughridge and Butler insisted that the Privileges or Immunities of citizens of the United States "are inherent... they belong to the citizen as such, for they are not therein specified or enumerated."[27] Therefore, the majority was wrong to suggest that the privileges guaranteed by the Fourteenth Amendment "do not refer to any other than the privileges embraced in section 2, of article 4, of the original text."[28] Drawing a clear distinction between the two texts, the minority report explained,

> Section 2, of article 4, provides for the privileges of "citizens of the *States,*" while the first section of the fourteenth amendment protects the privileges of "*citizens of the United States.*" The terms citizens of the *States* and citizens of the *United States* are by no means convertible.[29]

In support of maintaining a distinction between Section One and Article IV, the minority cited Justice Bradley's recent opinion in *The Live Stock Dealers* case, in which Bradley insisted that the Privileges or Immunities Clause "is not identical" with the Comity Clause but in fact "embraces much more."[30] His opinion "seems to intimate very strongly that the amendment was intended to secure the natural rights of citizens, as well as their equal capacities before the law."[31] Even if the majority were right to reduce the clause to the privileges covered by the Comity Clause, it was still the case "that the right of suffrage is a fundamental right of citizenship" granted equal protection under both the Comity Clause of Article IV and the Privileges or Immunities Clause of the

substantive national rights. The only issue before the Committee was whether the Clause protected *unenumerated* natural rights like the rights of suffrage. Although the Report equates the rights protected under the Privileges or Immunities Clause with the rights protected by the Comity Clause, this assertion is ambiguous. As we already know, it was possible to understand Article IV as protecting all constitutionally enumerated rights. Finally, no previous scholar has noticed that the Report's assertion about the debates in the Thirty-Ninth Congress and the courts' treatment of Article IV are demonstrably false.

[27] House of Representatives, Committee on the Judiciary, *Victoria C. Woodhull. Report*, 41st Cong., 3d sess., January 30, 1871, H. Rept. 22, Part 2, 4 (Views of the Minority).

[28] *Id.*

[29] *Id.* at 5.

[30] *Id.*

[31] *Id.*

Fourteenth Amendment.[32] Most of all, the majority was wrong to imply that the only rights protected by the Privileges or Immunities Clause were those expressly protected by Constitution:

> These privileges of the citizen exist independent of the Constitution. They are not derived from the Constitution or the laws, but are the means of asserting and protecting rights that existed before any civil governments were formed – the right to life, liberty, and property.[33]

If the minority understood the majority as claiming that Congress adopted the Privileges or Immunities Clause due to a concern that courts would not apply the Comity Clause against the states, they make no mention of it. Nor does the minority consider whether the majority Report closes the door on the protection of enumerated rights, such as those listed in the first eight amendments. Instead, the minority focuses on the Report's clear rejection of the unenumerated rights of suffrage and puts forward a reading of the Privileges or Immunities Clause as protecting all fundamental natural rights.

In the end, it is unclear what role, if any, the Woodhull Report can play in helping us understand the original meaning of the Privileges or Immunities Clause. The claims of the majority Report, if taken literally, are demonstrably false. For that reason alone, one would be justified in dismissing the Report as a sloppy committee product reflecting the commonly held view that the Fourteenth Amendment did not nationalize the rights of suffrage, and, beyond that, saying nothing illuminating about the Privileges or Immunities Clause. Whatever one makes of the Report, we are not left in the dark regarding Bingham's personal view of the Privileges or Immunities Clause: Only a few weeks later, Bingham took to the floor of the House of Representatives and offered the most detailed analysis of the ratified Privileges or Immunities Clause presented by any member during the Reconstruction Congress.

II. JOHN BINGHAM'S FINAL WORD ON AMERICAN PRIVILEGES OR IMMUNITIES

A. *The Ku Klux Klan Act*

John Bingham's speech in defense of the proposed Ku Klux Klan Act of 1871 includes a detailed explanation of his decision to abandon his initial draft of the Fourteenth Amendment and replace it with a clause protecting the

---

[32] *Id.* at 6.
[33] *Id.* at 10.

rights "of citizens of the United States." The proposed Act went much further than the Civil Rights Act of 1866. As introduced by Samuel Shellabarger, the Act criminalized private conspiracies to violate the "rights, privileges, or immunities of another person."[34] Shellabarger's bill listed a number of specific actions covered by the proposal, including "murder, manslaughter, mayhem, robbery, assault and battery, perjury and subornation of perjury."[35] According to Eric Foner, "[t]he Ku Klux Klan Act pushed Republicans to the outer limits of constitutional change."[36]

The proposal triggered immediate objections by states' rights advocates, who insisted that Congress had no power to regulate ordinary criminal activity in the states.[37] The exercise of such power, they claimed, would destroy the independent existence of the states and create a federal government of general police powers.[38] Moreover, it was not at all clear that Congress's Section Five power to enforce Section One of the Fourteenth Amendment authorized Congress to regulate private interference with constitutional rights; the text of Section One forbade *states* from abridging privileges or immunities, due process, or the equal protection of the law.

In his speech presenting the Ku Klux Klan Act to the House of Representatives, Shellabarger insisted that Congress had power to enact the law under Section Two of the Thirteenth Amendment and Section Five of the Fourteenth Amendment.[39] Although the specific actions regulated by the Act were not expressly mentioned under either amendment, Shellabarger argued that the proper "rule of interpretation" of those amendments should not be one of "strict construction," but should instead follow the common law maxim that remedial statutes ought to be "liberally and beneficently construed."[40] Abandoning the limited reading of *Corfield* and Article IV that he had adopted in the summer of 1866,[41] Shellabarger now insisted that Justice Washington's opinion in *Corfield* listed the "fundamental rights of citizenship" that Congress had power to protect under the Privileges or Immunities Clause of Section One.[42]

In prior speeches, Shellabarger had referred to the long line of antebellum cases and commentary describing the Clause as an equal protection

---

[34] *Id.* at 68 (remarks of Rep. Shellabarger). For the final version, see 17 Stat. 13 (1873).
[35] CONG. GLOBE, 42d Cong., 1st Sess. app. 68 (1871).
[36] ERIC FONER, RECONSTRUCTION: AMERICA'S UNFINISHED REVOLUTION 1863–1877, at 455 (1988).
[37] *See id.*
[38] *Id.* at 456.
[39] CONG. GLOBE, 42d Cong., 1st Sess. app. 68 (1871).
[40] *Id.*
[41] *See* supra, Chapter 3, notes 381–400 and accompanying text.
[42] CONG. GLOBE, 42d Cong., 1st Sess. app. 69 (1871).

principle.[43] Now, however, Shellabarger omitted any mention of antebellum case law other than *Corfield v. Coryell*. Shellabarger particularly stressed Justice Washington's statement that the privileges and immunities of citizens included the rights of *protection*, rights that impliedly authorized government enforcement.[44] Protection against common crimes, Shellabarger explained, was an essential aspect of citizenship "in every free Government."[45] To the degree that members still questioned whether there was express authority to pass the Ku Klux Klan Act, Shellabarger reminded them of the Supreme Court's decision in *Prigg v. Pennsylvania*, which held that Congress had implied power to enforce the provisions of Article IV regarding runaway slaves.[46]

> I appeal to [the ruling in *Prigg*] as fixing the interpretation of the Constitution in this regard and as authorizing affirmative legislation in protection of the rights of citizenship under Federal law, since now these rights of citizenship are brought by the fourteenth amendment, under the care of the Constitution itself, as to all citizens, just as the old Constitution, protected such of them as went from one State to another, by the clause as to their rights in the several States. . . . [47]

Shellabarger's attempt to equate the privileges and immunities of Article IV with the privileges or immunities of Section One met with an immediate challenge. According to Indiana Representative Michael Kerr (who, like Bingham, joined the Woodhull Report), pointed out that the language of the Privileges or Immunities Clause "does not distinctly refer to the 'privileges or immunities' of citizens of the States."[48]

> The privileges or immunities which are to be enjoyed under this provision are those alone which inhere in and attach to the very idea of citizenship of the United States. . . . Observe that the privileges and immunities of citizens of the States, in the relations of the States to each other, are protected to them by the second section of the fourth article of the Constitution, and not by anything in the fourteenth article of amendments.[49]

---

[43] *See* Chapter 3 at note 384.
[44] *Id.*
[45] *Id.*
[46] *Id.* at 70; *see also* Prigg v. Pennsylvania, 41 U.S. (16 Pet.) 539, 622 (1842).
[47] Cong. Globe, 42d Cong., 1st Sess. app. 70 (1871).
[48] *Id* at 47.
[49] *Id.*

Republican Representative John F. Farnsworth of Illinois (described by Michael Curtis as having views that ranged from radical to conservative[50]) objected to Shellabarger's attempt to transform the equal protection principles of Article IV into a set of substantive national rights. Farnsworth had supported the original Fourteenth Amendment with the understanding that it did nothing more than protect *equal rights* in the states,[51] and he voiced his astonishment to hear the amendment he had so recently supported being cited in support of a law that Farnsworth believed would destroy the reserved rights of the people in the states.[52] He reminded those members who had served with him in the Thirty-Ninth Congress that John Bingham's first draft of the Fourteenth Amendment threatened to empower Congress to regulate civil rights in the states. This initial draft, Farnsworth pointed out, had been roundly criticized as undermining the principles of limited federal power and ultimately rejected.[53] When Bingham rose to object that his original draft had not been rejected but only withdrawn and recomposed, Farnsworth cuttingly responded, "Why was it put in another form? Did the gentleman put it in another form to deceive somebody?"[54] Although Bingham promised to explain why he redrafted the Fourteenth Amendment, Farnsworth ignored him and declared what he believed to be the original understanding of Section One:

> Why, sir, we all know, and especially those of us who were members of Congress at that time, that the reason for the adoption of this amendment was because of the partial, discriminating, and unjust legislation of those States under governments set up by Andrew Johnson, by which they were punishing and oppressing one class of men under different laws from another class.[55]

In support of this "equal rights" reading of Section One, Farnsworth quoted Congressman Poland's statement that Section One "secures nothing beyond what was intended by the original provisions in the Constitution, that the citizens of each State shall be entitled to all the privileges and immunities of

---

[50] Michael Kent Curtis, No State Shall Abridge: The Fourteenth Amendment and the Bill of Rights 38–39 (1986).

[51] Cong. Globe, 39th Cong., 1st Sess. 2539 ("So far as this section [Section One] is concerned, there is but one clause in it which is not already in the Constitution, and it might as well in my opinion read, 'No State shall deny to any person within its jurisdiction the equal protection of the laws.'").

[52] Cong. Globe, 42d Cong., 1st Sess. app. 115 (1871).

[53] *Id.*

[54] *Id.*

[55] *Id.* at 116.

citizens in the several States."[56] "The gentleman from Vermont," Farnsworth assured the House, "did not dream that the provision went any further than that."[57]

B. *John Bingham's Explanation of the Second Draft of the Privileges or Immunities Clause*

Bingham faced a delicate task when he rose in defense of the proposed Ku Klux Klan Act. He supported Shellabarger's efforts to pass the Act, but Shellabarger's argument conflicted with Bingham's views of the Constitution in several ways. Shellabarger's effort to read Justice Washington's list of privileges and immunities in *Corfield* and Article IV mirrored similar efforts by James Wilson and other radical Republicans in the Thirty-Ninth Congress, efforts that had been easily turned aside by members who simply quoted antebellum case law and legal treatises.[58] Not only was Shellabarger wrong as a matter of law, Bingham and the other moderate Republicans opposed any attempt to portray Congress as having broad supervisory power over the states in any matter relating to civil rights (including the right to happiness, according to Justice Washington's list in *Corfield*). Bingham had expressly rejected such broad assertions of federal power during the debates over the Civil Rights Act of 1866, not only because Congress lacked the power, but also because the very idea conflicted with what Bingham believed was the essential federalist division of power between state and national governments.

Even worse, Shellabarger's attempt to use the Comity Clause as a guide to understanding the Privileges or Immunities Clause could backfire. Farnsworth was right about the standard equal protection reading of the Comity Clause. If Shellabarger managed to convince his colleagues that Article IV Privileges and Immunities were the same as Fourteenth Amendment Privileges or Immunities, then Farnsworth's equal protection readings of the Fourteenth Amendment would likely win the day. This would not only result in a rejection of the proposed Bill, but would also undermine Bingham's long-declared goal of securing an amendment that required the States to follow the federal Bill of Rights.

Bingham was thus faced with the task of delivering a speech that supported the proposed Ku Klux Klan Act but also explained the errors of both the Act's supporters (such as Shellabarger) and its opponents (such as Farnsworth).

[56] *Id.*
[57] *Id.*
[58] *See* discussion in Chapter 3.

Bingham's speech of 1871 is well known among Fourteenth Amendment scholars because of its invocation of the theory of incorporation of the Bill of Rights. What has gone unaddressed, however, is the purpose of Bingham's speech – the need to counter both unduly broad and unduly narrow readings of the Privileges or Immunities Clause.

Bingham's main argument in support of the Act was that it represented a justified use of Section Five powers to enforce the "express negative limitation" placed on the states by the Equal Protection Clause of the Fourteenth Amendment.[59] Providing equal protection included the power to ensure the equal protection of "life, liberty and property as provided in the supreme law of the land, the Constitution of the United States."[60] Congressional power to enforce the Equal Protection Clause through legislation, Bingham insisted, "is as full as any other grant of power to Congress."[61]

Bingham then addressed the claim that the First and Fifth Sections of the Fourteenth Amendment did nothing more than empower Congress to enforce the Comity Clause of Article IV. Here, Bingham explained why the debate between Shellabarger and Farnsworth regarding the proper reading of Article IV was wholly irrelevant to determining the meaning of Section One. The Privileges or Immunities Clause of the Fourteenth Amendment protected a completely different set of rights than those protected under Article IV. The key to understanding the Clause was not to be found in Justice Washington's list, but in the enumerated rights of the Constitution.

Taking up Farnsworth's challenge to explain why he had abandoned his original draft of the Fourteenth Amendment, Bingham explained that he had reread "the great decision of Marshall" in *Barron v. Baltimore* and realized that his original draft would not accomplish his desired goal of protecting the Bill of Rights against infringement by the States.[62] In *Barron v. Baltimore*, Bingham explained,

[I]t was decided, and rightfully, that these [first eight] amendments, defining and protecting the rights of men and citizens, were only limitations on the power of Congress, not on the power of the States.

In reexamining that case of *Barron*, Mr. Speaker, after my struggle in the House in February, 1866, to which the gentleman has alluded, I noted and apprehended as I never did before, certain words in that opinion of Marshall. Referring to the first eight articles of amendments to the Constitution of the

[59] *See id.* at 81.
[60] *See id.* at 83.
[61] *Id.*
[62] *See id.* at 84.

United States, the Chief Justice said: "Had the framers of these amendments intended them to be limitations on the power of State governments they would have imitated the framers of the original Constitution, and have expressed that intention."

Acting upon this suggestion I did imitate the framers of the original constitution. As they had said "no State shall emit bills of credit, pass any bill of attainder, *ex post facto* law, or law impairing the obligations of contracts;" imitating their example and imitating it to the letter, I prepared the provision of the first section of the fourteenth amendment as it stands in the Constitution, as follows:

"No state shall. . . . "[63]

Bingham's original view of the Bill of Rights in the Thirty-Ninth Congress was that states were obligated to enforce the Bill, due to a combination of Article IV's declaration of the "Privileges and Immunities of Citizens [with the ellipsis "of the United States"] in the several States," and the constitutional requirements that state officials take an oath to uphold the federal Constitution as the supreme law of the land.[64] In the first round of debates over the Fourteenth Amendment, both friend and foe rejected this reading of Article IV – thus Bingham's reference to his "struggle" of February 1866. Once he removed the language of the Comity Clause from the second draft, Bingham stopped referring to Article IV. There is nothing about the Comity Clause (much less references to *Corfield*) in either Bingham's defense of the second version in May 1866 or in his 1871 discussion of the Privileges or Immunities Clause.

Bingham apparently continued to believe that states had no actual right to violate the first eight amendments, and he still apparently believed that the states had at least a moral duty to respect the Bill of Rights as part of their oath to uphold the federal Constitution.[65] However, Bingham expressly accepted Marshall's decision in *Barron*, describing it as a "great decision" "rightfully" decided.[66] Whatever their moral obligations, states had the legal authority to ignore the Bill of Rights under the original Constitution if they chose to

---

[63] CONG. GLOBE, 42d Cong., 1st Sess. app. 84 (1871).

[64] CONG. GLOBE, 39th Cong., 1st Sess. 1089 (1866).

[65] *See* CONG. GLOBE, 42d Cong., 1st Sess. app. 85 (1871) ("The States never had the right, though they had the power, to inflict wrongs upon free citizens by a denial of the full protection of the laws; because all state officials are by the Constitution required to be bound by oath or affirmation to support the Constitution."). Bingham's belief that states had a moral obligation to respect the Bill of Rights makes sense given his belief that such rights were, in fact, essential aspects of American citizenship, even if not enforceable (prior to the Fourteenth Amendment) as a matter of constitutional law.

[66] CONG. GLOBE, 42d Cong., 1st Sess. app. 84 (1871).

do so. But if *Barron* was rightfully decided and the original Constitution did not bind the states to enforce the Bill of Rights, then Bingham had erred in using the language of Article IV in his initial draft of the Fourteenth Amendment. His newfound appreciation of Marshall's reasoning in *Barron* convinced him that not only did he need to draft a clause that expressly bound the states, he also needed to use language that pointed away from the state-conferred rights of Article IV and toward the essential *federal* rights of American citizenship.

In the early years of the Fourteenth Amendment, however, the proper interpretation of the Privileges or Immunities Clause remained a matter of some dispute. Shellabarger linked the Clause to Article IV and insisted the Clause nationalized the subject of civil rights in the States. Conservatives insisted the Clause did nothing more than allow Congress to enforce the equal protection principles of the Comity Clause. While chairing the House Judiciary Committee during the Woodhull hearing, Bingham heard about Justice Bradley's opinion in *The Live-Stock Dealers'* case, which read the Privileges or Immunities Clause as nationalizing the unenumerated "sacred right of labor."[67] Given that Bradley's opinion and the meaning of the Privileges or Immunities Clause were destined to land before the Supreme Court, Bingham may have believed it was important to set the record straight and clearly explain the distinction between the Privileges and Immunities Clause of Article IV and the Privileges or Immunities Clause of Section One.

> Mr. Speaker, that the scope and meaning of the limitations imposed by the first section, fourteenth amendment of the Constitution may be more fully understood, permit me to say that the privileges and immunities of citizens of the United States, *as contradistinguished from citizens of a State* [the language of Article IV], are chiefly defined in the first eight amendments to the Constitution of the United States. Those eight amendments are as follows. . . .[68]

Bingham then quoted, word for word, the first eight amendments to the federal Constitution.[69] His rendition takes up almost an entire column in the *Congressional Globe*.[70] These substantive rights, Bingham explained, were altogether different from the privileges and immunities protected under

---

[67] *See* Live-Stock Dealers' & Butchers' Ass'n v. Crescent City Live-Stock Landing & Slaughter-House Co., 15 F. Cas. 649 (C.C.D. La. 1870) (No. 8408) (Bradley, Circuit Justice).

[68] CONG. GLOBE, 42d Cong., 1st Sess. app. 84 (1871) (emphasis added).

[69] *Id.*

[70] *See id.*

Article IV.[71] As Bingham put it, the substantive privileges or immunities "of citizens of the United States" such as those listed in the federal Bill of Rights must be "contradistinguished from" the privileges and immunities of *citizens of a state*,[72] which under Article IV received only a degree of equal protection.[73]

Having established why Farnsworth was wrong to treat the Privileges or Immunities Clause as nothing more than an equal rights provision, Bingham now turned to Samuel Shellabarger's suggestion that Section One transformed Justice Washington's list of civil rights in *Corfield* into substantive national rights:

> Mr. Speaker, that decision in the fourth of Washington's Circuit Court Reports, to which my learned colleague [Mr. Shellabarger] has referred is only a construction of the second section, fourth article of the original Constitution, to wit, "The citizens of each State shall be entitled to all privileges and immunities of citizens in the several States." In that case the court only held that in civil rights the State could not refuse to extend to citizens of other States the same general rights secured to its own.[74]

This is the traditional antebellum reading of the Privileges and Immunities Clause as an equal rights provision. After quoting the legal arguments of Daniel Webster, as well as Story's *Commentaries on the Constitution*, Bingham concluded:

> Is it not clear *that other and different privileges and immunities* than those to which a citizen of a State was entitled are secured by the provision of the fourteenth article, that no State shall abridge the privileges and immunities of citizens of the United States, which are defined in the eight articles of amendment, and which were not limitations on the power of the States before the fourteenth amendment made them limitations?[75]

Although Bingham delivered his speech a few years after the adoption of the Fourteenth Amendment, there seems little reason to doubt the sincerity of Bingham's explanation for the altered language of the Privileges or Immunities Clause. Nothing in his speech of 1871 contradicts any of the goals and principles Bingham declared during the Thirty-Ninth Congress. In all of his efforts to secure the Fourteenth Amendment, Bingham never once relied on *Corfield*,

---

[71] *Id.*

[72] *Id.*

[73] *See id.* ("State[s] could not refuse to extend to citizens of other States the same general rights secured to [their] own.").

[74] *Id.*

[75] *See* Cong. Globe, 42d Cong., 1st Sess. app. 84 (1871) (emphasis added).

much less natural rights interpretations of *Corfield*. It was radical Republicans like Shellabarger who tried to overread Justice Washington's opinion in the Thirty-Ninth and Forty-Second Congresses – only to be rebuffed both times.[76]

Finally, it is important to recognize the textualism of John Bingham's theory of federal privileges or immunities. Over and over again, Bingham refers to the privileges and immunities of citizens of the United States in a manner that references the express enumerated rights of the Constitution. The enumerated rights of the Bill of Rights "secured ... all the rights dear to the American citizen."[77] These enumerated rights were the "essential rights of person" that the founding generation had enshrined in the Constitution.[78] According to Bingham, Congress "may safely follow the example of the makers of the Constitution and the builders of the Republic, by passing laws for enforcing all the privileges and immunities of citizens of the United States, as guarantied by the amended Constitution and *expressly enumerated in the Constitution*."[79] Congress had full power "to make laws to enforce [the citizen's] guarantied 'privileges' under the Constitution, *as defined therein* and assured by the fourteenth amendment." "[W]hat would this government be worth if it must rely upon States to execute its grants of power, its limitations of power upon States, and *its express guarantees of rights to the people*."[80] After reading the first eight amendments, Bingham concluded "these are the rights of citizens of the United States *defined in the Constitution* and guaranteed by the Fourteenth Amendment."[81]

This text-based understanding of the privileges or immunities of US citizens fits with Bingham's rejection of arguments by members like Samuel Shellabarger and James Wilson who insisted on federal power to generally regulate the substance of civil rights in the States.[82] Such a nationalization

---

[76] See also CONG. GLOBE, 42 Cong., 2d sess., app. 26 (1871) (speech of Ohio Sen. John Sherman) (linking the Privileges or Immunities Clause to the common law and the "other rights" of the Ninth Amendment and calling for judicial identification and enforcement of the same); RANDY BARNETT, RESTORING THE LOST CONSTITUTION: THE PRESUMPTION OF LIBERTY 66–67 (2004). Prof. Barnett uses Sherman's post-adoption speech, among other things, as evidence of the original meaning of the Privileges or Immunities Clause. Even if Sherman had spoken prior to the adoption of the Amendment, instead of years later, his views would represent a decided minority. *See* Chapters 3 and 4.

[77] CONG. GLOBE, 42d Cong., 1st Sess. app. 84 (1871).

[78] *Id.*

[79] *Id.*

[80] *Id.* at 85 (emphasis added).

[81] *Id.* (emphasis added).

[82] *See* Bryan H. Wildenthal, *Nationalizing the Bill of Rights: Revisiting the Original Understanding of the Fourteenth Amendment in 1866–67*, 68 OHIO ST. L.J. 1509, 1618–19 (2007).

of common law civil liberties was anathema to Bingham's belief in "our dual system of government" that was "essential to our national existence."[83] Bingham thus occupied a middle ground between radicals like Shellabarger and conservatives like Farnsworth. The Fourteenth Amendment did in fact protect a category of substantive national rights, but only those rights listed in the Constitution itself. Following the lead of Jacob Howard's influential presentation of the proposed Fourteenth Amendment, Bingham noted that these federal privileges and immunities rights were "chiefly defined in the first eight amendments," but also included others expressly defined in the Constitution, such as the limitations on state power listed in Article I, section 10,[84] or the equal protection principles of the Comity Clause.

Although Bingham's speech illustrates the continuity in his thinking from 1866 to 1871,[85] it also reveals a serious dispute over the proper interpretation of the newly ratified Privilege or Immunities Clause. The Supreme Court would resolve this dispute as a matter of operative law when they heard the appeal in the *Live-Stock Dealers'* case. But rather than "eviscerating" the Privileges or Immunities Clause, as so many legal scholars maintain, the Court adopted Bingham's middle ground.

III. THE SUPREME COURT AND THE PRIVILEGES OR IMMUNITIES CLAUSE: THE *SLAUGHTER-HOUSE CASES* AND *UNITED STATES V. CRUIKSHANK*

A. *The* Slaughter-House Cases

The *Slaughter-House Cases* involved a Louisiana monopoly that had the effect of shuttering the plaintiffs' businesses. Supreme Court Justice Samuel Miller led a majority of the Court in rejecting, among other things, the plaintiffs' claim that the monopoly violated their Fourteenth Amendment "privilege or immunity" to pursue a trade.[86] Post-New Deal legal academics have subjected Justice Miller's opinion in the *Slaughter-House Cases* to excoriating criticism. According to Laurence Tribe, Miller "incorrectly gutted the Privileges

---

[83] *See* CONG. GLOBE, 42d Cong., 1st Sess. app. 84 (1871).

[84] *Id.* (remarks of Rep. Bingham) (discussing his imitating of the language of Article I, Section Ten in the language of Section One of the Fourteenth Amendment and detailing the first eight amendments as the privileges and immunities of citizens of the United States).

[85] A fact that should help rehabilitate Bingham in the eyes of constitutional scholars who too often have unfairly dismissed this key figure in American constitutional history as confused and inept.

[86] *The Slaughter-House Cases*, 83 U.S. 36 (1873).

or Immunities Clause."[87] Sanford Levinson calls the opinion "shoddily justified."[88] According to Leonard Levy, Miller's opinion is "one of the most tragically wrong opinions ever given by the Court."[89] Charles L. Black described *Slaughter-House* as "probably the worst holding, in its effect on human rights, ever uttered by the Supreme Court."[90] The list goes on.

In some ways, such widespread criticism is surprising. Few scholars, for example, disagree with Miller's specific conclusion that the Privileges or Immunities Clause does not protect what Justice Bradley called the "sacred rights of labor."[91] Instead, the bulk of scholarly criticism is aimed at what scholars believed Miller implied: that the Privileges or Immunities Clause did not incorporate the Bill of Rights.[92] The criticism, it turns out, is unfounded. The issue of incorporation was not before the Court in *Slaughter-House*, and Justice Miller said nothing in his opinion that could be viewed as closing the door on viewing the Privileges or Immunities Clause as protecting enumerated constitutional rights. To the contrary, Miller specifically named the rights of the First Amendment as "privileges or immunities of citizens of the United States."[93] Most recently, a number of scholars have challenged the oft-repeated claim that Miller rejected incorporation of the Bill of Rights.[94] In fact, a close examination of Miller's opinion reveals an understanding of the Clause that

[87] Laurence H. Tribe, *Taking Text and Structure Seriously: Reflections on Free-Form Method in Constitutional Interpretation*, 108 HARV. L. REV. 1221, 1297 n.247 (1995).

[88] Sanford Levinson, *Some Reflections on the Rehabilitation of the Privileges or Immunities Clause of the Fourteenth Amendment*, 12 HARV. J.L. & PUB. POL'Y 71, 73 (1989).

[89] Leonard W. Levy, *The Fourteenth Amendment and the Bill of Rights, in* JUDGMENTS: ESSAYS ON AMERICAN CONSTITUTIONAL HISTORY 64, 69 (1972).

[90] CHARLES L. BLACK, A NEW BIRTH OF FREEDOM 55 (1997).

[91] *But see* BARNETT, *supra* note 76, 203, 211–14 (arguing that the dissent properly "understood the liberty to pursue an occupation [was] a fundamental right closely related to 'free labor'" and defending the recognition of such a right in *Lochner v. New York*).

[92] *See, e.g.*, PAMELA BRANDWEIN, RECONSTRUCTING RECONSTRUCTION: THE SUPREME COURT AND THE PRODUCTION OF HISTORICAL TRUTH 61, 67–68 (1999); CURTIS, NO STATE SHALL ABRIDGE, *supra* note 50, at 175; Richard L. Aynes, *Constricting the Law of Freedom: Justice Miller, the Fourteenth Amendment, and the Slaughter-House Cases*, 70 CHI-KENT L. REV. 627, 653–55 (1994); John Harrison, *Reconstructing the Privileges or Immunities Clause*, 101 YALE L. J. 1385, 1415 (1992); Michael Kent Curtis, *Resurrecting the Privileges or Immunities Clause and Revising the Slaughter-House Cases Without Exhuming Lochner: Individual Rights and the Fourteenth Amendment*, 38 B.C. L. REV. 1, 71 n.249, 86 (1996).

[93] *The Slaughter-House Cases*, 83 U.S. 36, 79 (1873) ("The right to peaceably assemble and petition for redress of grievances, the privilege of the writ of *habeas corpus*, are rights of the citizen guaranteed by the Federal Constitution.").

[94] *See* Bryan H. Wildenthal, *The Lost Compromise: Reassessing the Early Understanding in Court and Congress on Incorporation of the Bill of Rights in the Fourteenth Amendment*, 61 OHIO ST. L. J. 1051 (2000); Kevin Newsom, *Setting Incorporation Straight: A Reinterpretation of the Slaughter-House Cases*, 109 YALE L. J. 643, 666 (2000).

closely tracks the Bingham-Howard understanding of American privileges and immunities.

The literature on *Slaughter-House* is broad and deep. There are important investigations of the legal and factual background of the case,[95] as well as political science investigations involving possible motivations behind the various opinions.[96] For the purposes of this chapter, I want only to consider whether the Court's legal analysis of the Privileges or Immunities Clause conforms to how that clause was presented by those who framed the Fourteenth Amendment and advocated its ratification.

B. *Miller's Opinion*

Justice Samuel Miller began his analysis of Section One by examining the citizenship clause: "All persons born or naturalized in the United States, and subject to the jurisdiction thereof, are citizens of the United States and of the State wherein they reside." As have all constitutional scholars to this day, Miller explains that this sentence "overturns the Dred Scott decision by making *all persons* born within the United States and subject to its jurisdiction citizens of the United States."[97] Miller then notes how the opening sentence clearly distinguishes between "citizenship of the United States and citizenship of a State":

> Not only may a man be a citizen of the United States without being a citizen of a State, but an important element is necessary to convert the former into the latter. He must reside within the State to make him a citizen of it, but it is only necessary that he should be born or naturalized in the United States to be a citizen of the Union.[98]

The fact that the opening sentence of the Fourteenth Amendment established a distinction between national and state citizenship was, to Miller, "of great weight in this argument," since the provision relied on by the plaintiffs in the case "speaks only of privileges and immunities of citizens of the United States, and does not speak of those of citizens of the several States."[99]

---

[95] *See, e.g.,* Charles Fairman, Reconstruction and Reunion, 1864–88, Part One (Macmillan, 1971) (The Oliver Wendell Holmes Devise History of the Supreme Court of the United States, vol. 6).

[96] *See, e.g.,* Pamela Brandwein, Rethinking the Judicial Settlement of Reconstruction (2011).

[97] *Slaughter-House Cases*, 83 U.S. at 73.

[98] *Id.* at 73–74.

[99] *Id.* at 74.

The argument, however, in favor of the plaintiffs rests wholly on the assumption that the citizenship is the same, and the privileges and immunities guaranteed by the clause are the same.

The language is, "No State shall make or enforce any law which shall abridge the privileges or immunities of citizens of *the United States.*" It is a little remarkable, if this clause was intended as a protection to the citizen of a State against the legislative power of his own State, that the word citizen of the State should be left out when it is so carefully used, and used in contradistinction to citizens of the United States, in the very sentence which precedes it. It is too clear for argument that the change in phraseology was adopted understandingly and with a purpose.

If, then, there is a difference between the privileges and immunities belonging to a citizen of the United States as such, and those belonging to the citizen of the State as such the latter must rest for their security and protection where they have heretofore rested; for they are not embraced by this paragraph of the amendment.[100]

To this point, Miller's argument seems wholly unobjectionable. Antebellum law and political rhetoric recognized a distinction between the privileges and immunities of state citizenship and privileges and immunities of national citizenship. John Bingham impliedly recognized the distinction when he withdrew his Article IV-based draft and replaced it with the final version of the Clause, and Bingham expressly distinguished the two sets of privileges and immunities in his speech of 1871. Moreover, Justice Joseph Bradley also noted the distinction in his circuit court opinion in the *Live-Stock Dealers'* case. History, text, and judicial precedent all support Miller's opening distinction between Article IV privileges and immunities and Fourteenth Amendment privileges and immunities.

Miller then proceeds to analyze Article IV privileges and immunities. Here, Miller embraced Justice Washington's definition in *Corfield* that such rights were those deemed "*fundamental;* which belong of right to the citizens of all free governments, and which have at all times been enjoyed by citizens of the several States which compose this Union, from the time of their becoming free, independent, and sovereign," and included "the right to acquire and possess property of every kind, and to pursue and obtain happiness and safety, subject, nevertheless, to such restraints as the government may prescribe for the general good of the whole."[101] Unlike federal rights, however, these were "rights belonging to the individual as a citizen of a State. They are so spoken

---

[100] *Id.* at 74–75.
[101] *Id.* at 76 (quoting *Corfield v. Coryell*).

of in the constitutional provision which [Justice Washington] was construing. And they have always been held to be the class of rights which the State governments were created to establish and secure."[102] Article IV did not create these rights, nor did it guarantee such right to citizens of a particular state. "Its sole purpose," Miller explained, "was to declare to the several States, that whatever those rights, as you grant or establish them to your own citizens, or as you limit or qualify, or impose restrictions on their exercise, the same, neither more nor less, shall be the measure of the rights of citizens of other States within your jurisdiction."[103]

Miller's treatment of Article IV reflects the antebellum jurisprudence of Article IV's Comity Clause. This is how every court and legal treatise writer described the clause prior to the Civil War, and this was the court's approach in the critically important case of *Lemmon v. The People*, in which the New York court rejected an attempt to make the right to carry slaves into a free state a protected privilege and immunity of citizens in the several states. Although radical Republicans in the Thirty-Ninth Congress attempted to read *Corfield* and the Comity Clause as protecting a set of substantive national rights, these attempts were short-lived and easily turned aside by members who knew the actual law. In a sharply worded sentence, Justice Miller gives such attempts the back of his hand:

> It would be the vainest show of learning to attempt to prove by citations of authority, that up to the adoption of the recent amendments, no claim or pretence was set up that those rights depended on the Federal government for their existence or protection, beyond the very few express limitations which the Federal Constitution imposed upon the States – such, for instance, as the prohibition against ex post facto laws, bills of attainder, and laws impairing the obligation of contracts. But with the exception of these and a few other restrictions, the entire domain of the privileges and immunities of citizens of the States, as above defined, lay within the constitutional and legislative power of the States, and without that of the Federal government.[104]

Having established the consensus antebellum reading of the Comity Clause, Miller then moves to the central issue: whether the innumerable state-secured civil rights granted equal protection under *Corfield* and Article IV had been transformed into innumerable substantive national rights through the adoption of the Privileges or Immunities Clause. To ask the question was to answer it:

---

[102] *Id.*
[103] *Id.* at 77.
[104] *Id.*

Was it the purpose of the fourteenth amendment, by the simple declaration that no State should make or enforce any law which shall abridge the privileges and immunities of *citizens of the United States,* to transfer the security and protection of all the civil rights which we have mentioned, from the States to the Federal government? And where it is declared that Congress shall have the power to enforce that article, was it intended to bring within the power of Congress the entire domain of civil rights heretofore belonging exclusively to the States?

All this and more must follow, if the proposition of the plaintiffs in error be sound. For not only are these rights subject to the control of Congress whenever in its discretion any of them are supposed to be abridged by State legislation, but that body may also pass laws in advance, limiting and restricting the exercise of legislative power by the States, in their most ordinary and usual functions, as in its judgment it may think proper on all such subjects. And still further, such a construction followed by the reversal of the judgments of the Supreme Court of Louisiana in these cases, would constitute this court a perpetual censor upon all legislation of the States, on the civil rights of their own citizens, with authority to nullify such as it did not approve as consistent with those rights, as they existed at the time of the adoption of this amendment. The argument we admit is not always the most conclusive which is drawn from the consequences urged against the adoption of a particular construction of an instrument. But when, as in the case before us, these consequences are so serious, so far-reaching and pervading, so great a departure from the structure and spirit of our institutions; when the effect is to fetter and degrade the State governments by subjecting them to the control of Congress, in the exercise of powers heretofore universally conceded to them of the most ordinary and fundamental character; when in fact it radically changes the whole theory of the relations of the State and Federal governments to each other and of both these governments to the people; the argument has a force that is irresistible, in the absence of language which expresses such a purpose too clearly to admit of doubt.

We are convinced that no such results were intended by the Congress which proposed these amendments, nor by the legislatures of the States which ratified them.[105]

From a modern perspective, Miller's use of the background principles of federalism as a guide to interpreting the Fourteenth Amendment seems almost perverse. Modern scholars tend to portray the adoption of the Reconstruction Amendments as representing the enshrinement of constitutional nationalism, and our legal culture has long embraced judicial oversight of "fundamental"

---

[105] *Id.* at 77–78.

rights[106] and congressional regulatory control of once "ordinary" matters of state control, such as growing wheat in one's backyard.[107] From the perspective of a country seeking to reconstruct the Union, however, Miller's refusal to read the Fourteenth Amendment as eradicating constitutional federalism makes more sense. In fact, the evidence presented in prior chapters strongly suggests that Justice Miller was absolutely right. Efforts in the Thirty-Ninth Congress to nationalize *Corfieldian* civil rights were consistently defeated, and defeated expressly on the grounds that control over the substance of such rights ought to be left to the people in the individual states. No such proposal would have made it out of Congress. The proposal that Congress did adopt was presented to the public as doing nothing more than securing those rights already enshrined in the federal Constitution. Not even Justice Bradley in the *Live-Stock Dealers'* case could bring himself to argue that framers of the Fourteenth Amendment intended to constitutionalize the rights of *Corfield,* much less that the public understood that this would be the result of ratifying the Amendment. Anyone who participated in the framing of the Amendment, or who followed the political debates of 1866, would know that this was not the case. Miller's point about the continued viability of constitutional federalism mirrors a common consensus among those who framed and ratified the Fourteenth Amendment: that the substantive content of nonconstitutionally enumerated civil rights ought to be left to the control of the people in the several states, subject only to the requirements of due process and equal protection.[108]

Had Miller ended his analysis of the Privileges or Immunities Clause at this point, his opinion likely would never have become a lightning rod of contemporary criticism. Instead, Miller embarked on a wholly unnecessary examination of what *might* be recognized as national privileges or immunities should the proper case come before the Court:

> But lest it should be said that no such privileges and immunities are to be found if those we have been considering are excluded, we venture to suggest some which own their existence to the Federal government, its National character, its Constitution, or its laws.

> One of these is well described in the case of *Crandall* v. *Nevada.* It is said to be the right of the citizen of this great country, protected by implied guarantees of its Constitution, "to come to the seat of government to assert any claim

---

[106] *See* Griswold v. Connecticut, 381 U.S. 479 (1965) (Supreme Court recognizing a fundamental right of privacy).

[107] *See* Wickard v. Filburn, 317 U.S. 111 (1942) (Supreme Court upholding federal regulation of home-grown and home-consumed wheat).

[108] Following the same reasoning, the Supreme Court rejected the women suffrage advocate's reading of the Privileges or Immunities Clause in *Bradwell v. Illinois,* 83 U.S. 130 (1873), a decision handed down the same day as *Slaughter-House.*

he may have upon that government, to transact any business he may have with it, to seek its protection, to share its offices, to engage in administering its functions. He has the right of free access to its seaports, through which all operations of foreign commerce are conducted, to the subtreasuries, land offices, and courts of justice in the several States."

Another privilege of a citizen of the United States is to demand the care and protection of the Federal government over his life, liberty, and property when on the high seas or within the jurisdiction of a foreign government. Of this there can be no doubt, nor that the right depends upon his character as a citizen of the United States. The right to peaceably assemble and petition for redress of grievances, the privilege of the writ of *habeas corpus*, are rights of the citizen guaranteed by the Federal Constitution. The right to use the navigable waters of the United States, however they may penetrate the territory of the several States, all rights secured to our citizens by treaties with foreign nations, are dependent upon citizenship of the United States, and not citizenship of a State. One of these privileges is conferred by the very article under consideration. It is that a citizen of the United States can, of his own volition, become a citizen of any State of the Union by a *bonâ fide* residence therein, with the same rights as other citizens of that State. To these may be added the rights secured by the thirteenth and fifteenth articles of amendment, and by the other clause of the fourteenth, next to be considered.

But it is useless to pursue this branch of the inquiry, since we are of opinion that the rights claimed by these plaintiffs in error, if they have any existence, are not privileges and immunities of citizens of the United States within the meaning of the clause of the fourteenth amendment under consideration.[109]

Miller's list of rights falls into two broad categories. First, Miller describes those rights provided by the federal government by way of its enumerated powers and which are triggered by one's status as an American citizen.[110]

---

[109] *Id.* at 79–80

[110] In this first half of his list of the rights of national citizenship, Miller is largely quoting himself from *Crandall v. State of Nevada*, 73 U.S. 35 (1867). In *Crandall*, Miller stated:

But if the government has these rights on her own account, the citizen also has correlative rights. He has the right to come to the seat of government to assert any claim he may have upon that government or to transact any business he may have with it. To seek its protection, to share its offices, to engage in administering its functions. He has a right to free access to its seaports, through which all the operations of foreign trade and commerce are conducted, to the subtreasuries, the land offices, the revenue offices, and the courts of justice in the several states, and this right is in its nature independent of the will of any state over whose soil he must pass in the exercise of it.

The views here advanced are neither novel nor unsupported by authority. The question of the taxing power of the states, as its exercise has affected the functions of the federal government, has been repeatedly considered by this Court, and the right of the states in

These include the rights of access to federal institutions and rights of protection established by laws or treaties. Second, Miller lists those rights enumerated in the Constitution itself. This second group includes "[t]he right to peaceably assemble and petition for redress of grievances" (rights enumerated in the First Amendment), the privilege of the writ of habeas corpus (rights enumerated in Article I, section Nine), the right of citizenship "conferred by the very article under consideration" by which "a citizen of the United States can, of his own volition, become a citizen of any State of the Union by a *bonâ fide* residence therein, with the same rights as other citizens of that State,"[111] and the other "rights secured by the thirteenth and fifteenth articles of amendment, and by the other clause of the fourteenth, next to be considered."

Miller's opinion is sometimes cited as embracing an unenumerated rights theory of the Privileges or Immunities Clause.[112] For example, the above quote makes it appear that Miller read the Privileges or Immunities Clause as protecting, among other things, the unenumerated right to travel. But Miller nowhere mentions such a nontextual right. Instead, Miller speaks of the "right to use the navigable waters of the United States."[113] This, of course, is not a substantive unenumerated right, but a matter wholly under the regulatory control of the US Congress.[114] In fact, Miller opens this part of his opinion by referring the reader to Miller's 1867 opinion in *Crandall v. State of Nevada*.[115] *Crandall* held that states could not prevent individuals from traveling out of

> this mode to impede or embarrass the constitutional operations of that government, or the rights which its citizens hold under it, has been uniformly denied.

Crandall, 73 U.S. at 44. This passage from *Crandall* refers to Supremacy Clause constraints that prevent states from "imped[ing] or embarrass[ing]" the operations of the federal government. *See id.* at 45 (citing *McCulloch v. Maryland*).

[111] Notice that Miller reads the citizenship clause as securing to the individual "the same rights as other citizens of that State." This is a different kind of rights than those secured by the Equal Protection Clause, which recent scholarship suggests are limited to rights of *protection* rather than securing a right to "equal laws." See Christopher R. Green, *The Original Sense of the (Equal) Protection Clause: Pre-enactment History*, 19 Geo. Mason U. Civ. Rts. L. J. 1 (2008); Christopher R. Green, *The Original Sense of the (Equal) Protection Clause: Subsequent Interpretation and Application*, 19 Geo. Mason U. Civ. Rts. L. J. 219 (2009).

[112] *See, e.g.*, Jack Balkin, Living Originalism 208, 208 n.116 (2011) (citing as examples Miller's protection of "the right to travel to the nation's capitol, the right of access to seaports, the right to access federal facilities, the right to protection on the high seas or in foreign lands, and the right to use the navigable waters of the United States").

[113] *The Slaughter-House Cases*, 83 U.S. 36, 79 (1873).

[114] *See, e.g.*, Gibbons v. Ogden, 22 U.S. 1 (1824) (federal power to regulate interstate commerce includes the power to regulate commerce moving in the navigable waters of the United States); United States v. Darby Lumber Co., 312 U.S. 100 (1941) (power to regulate interstate commerce includes the power to determine what is allowed move in interstate commerce).

[115] 73 U.S. 35 (1867).

the state but only because this would impede the exercise *of enumerated federal authority*. Here are the relevant passages in *Crandall*:

> The people of these United States constitute one nation. They have a government in which all of them are deeply interested. This government has necessarily a capital established by law, where its principal operations are conducted. Here sits its legislature, composed of senators and representatives, from the States and from the people of the States. Here resides the President, directing through thousands of agents, the execution of the laws over all this vast country. Here is the seat of the supreme judicial power of the nation, to which all its citizens have a right to resort to claim justice at its hands. Here are the great executive departments, administering the offices of the mails, of the public lands, of the collection and distribution of the public revenues, and of our foreign relations. These are all established and conducted under the admitted powers of the Federal government. That government has a right to call to this point any or all of its citizens to aid in its service, as members of the Congress, of the courts, of the executive departments, and to fill all its other offices; and this right cannot be made to depend upon the pleasure of a State over whose territory they must pass to reach the point where these services must be rendered. The government, also, has its offices of secondary importance in all other parts of the country. On the sea-coasts and on the rivers it has its ports of entry. In the interior it has its land offices, its revenue offices, and its subtreasuries. In all these it demands the services of its citizens, and is entitled to bring them to those points from all quarters of the nation, and no power can exist in a State to obstruct this right that would not enable it to defeat the purposes for which the government was established.
>
> The Federal power has a right to declare and prosecute wars, and, as a necessary incident, to raise and transport troops through and over the territory of any State of the Union.
>
> If this right is dependent in any sense, however limited, upon the pleasure of a State, the government itself may be overthrown by an obstruction to its exercise. Much the largest part of the transportation of troops during the late rebellion was by railroads, and largely through States whose people were hostile to the Union. If the tax levied by Nevada on railroad passengers had been the law of Tennessee, enlarged to meet the wishes of her people, the treasury of the United States could not have paid the tax necessary to enable its armies to pass through her territory.
>
> But if the government has these rights on her own account, the citizen also has correlative rights. He has the right to come to the seat of government to assert any claim he may have upon that government, or to transact any business he may have with it. To seek its protection, to share its offices, to

engage in administering its functions. He has a right to free access to its sea-ports, through which all the operations of foreign trade and commerce are conducted, to the sub-treasuries, the land offices, the revenue offices, and the courts of justice in the several States, and this right is in its nature independent of the will of any State over whose soil he must pass in the exercise of it.

The views here advanced are neither novel nor unsupported by authority. The question of the taxing power of the States, as its exercise has affected the functions of the Federal government, has been repeatedly considered by this court, and the right of the States in this mode to impede or embarrass the constitutional operations of that government, or the rights which its citizens hold under it, has been uniformly denied.

The leading case of this class is that of *McCulloch* v. *Maryland*.[116]

This entire passage is about how the proper exercise of enumerated federal power, under the Supremacy Clause,[117] constrains the power of the states. Because the proper exercise of federal power includes the power to call citizens to the seat of the federal government if "necessary and proper," as well as the power to create institutions whose doors may be open to American citizens, states may not impede the exercise of these federal powers by forbidding out-of-state travel unless a citizen pays the state a special "tax."[118] It is the enumeration and exercise of enumerated federal power that creates the "correlative rights" of citizens. So, for example, Congress may *forbid* travel on navigable waterways, just as Congress may forbid access to "sub-treasuries, the land offices, the revenue offices, and the courts of justice in the several States." The rights are "correlative" in the sense that they are fully dependent on the enumeration and exercise of federal authority. If there is any doubt that Miller was referring to the constraining effect of enumerated federal power, notice how Miller punctuates his entire analysis with a closing citation to *McCulloch* v. *Maryland*, the preeminent case about limiting state power to interfere with the enumerated powers of the federal government.

In *Slaughter-House*, Justice Miller uses his own "correlative rights" analysis from *Crandall* as part of his definition of what constitutes the "privileges or immunities of citizens of the United States." In doing so, Miller does not abandon a text-based definition of "privileges or immunities" – he simply

---

[116] *Id.* at 43–45.

[117] U.S. Const. art. VI, cl. 2 ("This Constitution, and the Laws of the United States which shall be made in pursuance thereof; and all treaties made, or which shall be made, under the authority of the United States, shall be the supreme law of the land; and the judges in every state shall be bound thereby, anything in the constitution or laws of any state to the contrary notwithstanding.").

[118] The specific state law at issue in *Crandall*.

expands the list of enumerated rights by including those rights secured under the exercise of enumerated federal power.[119] Some might view this portion of Miller's opinion as "padding," rather than a good faith enumeration of the privileges or immunities of citizens of the United States. However, there is nothing clearly incorrect about including statutorily established rights as a portion of the constitutionally secured "privileges or immunities" of citizens of the United States. I do not believe this portion of Miller's opinion captures the *best* reading of the Clause only because the discussions of national privileges and immunities in 1866 focused on constitutionally secured personal rights. Regardless, there is nothing in his opinion that suggests Miller read the Privileges or Immunities Clause as securing against the states a non-unenumerated individual right to travel.[120]

Miller's textualism, constitutionally enumerated powers and constitutionally enumerated rights, mirrors that of John Bingham, who insisted that the "amendment takes from no State any rights that ever pertained to it" and protected rights "provided for and guarantied in your Constitution."[121] Bingham's effort was not to grant new rights, but to hold states accountable for protecting those rights that the people had already identified as deserving special protection. In dissent, Justice Stephen Field accused Miller of having reduced the Privileges or Immunities Clause to a "vain and idle" enactment by limiting its reach to only those rights already announced in the Constitution. But Field's criticism carries a sting only if those rights had already been *properly secured*. The woeful experience of life under the slave power, and the ongoing efforts to

---

[119] All of the rights mentioned in this part of Miller's opinion can be traced back to his list in *Crandall*, from the right to travel to the seat of government, to the rights of access to national seaports, to the rights of federal protection (*Crandall*, 73 U.S. at 43–44), every one of which Miller declared were "established and conducted under the admitted powers of the Federal government." *Id.* at 43.

[120] The Supreme Court grounds its protection of the right to travel on both an erroneous reading of the historical record and an erroneous reading of Miller's opinion. In *Saenz v. Roe*, 526 U.S. 489 (1999), Justice Stevens wrote that John Bingham "modeled the [Privileges or Immunities] Clause upon the 'Privileges and Immunities' Clause found in Article IV." *Id.* at 502 n.15 (Stevens, J.). In support of this claim, Stevens cites Bingham's introduction of the *first* draft of the Fourteenth Amendment. *See id.* (citing to CONG. GLOBE, 39th Cong., 1st Sess. 1033–1034 [1866]). This, of course, is the draft Bingham withdrew and replaced with one that he expressly *distinguished* from the Comity Clause of Article IV. Stevens also tried to use Miller's reference to the enumerated right to establish state citizenship through residency as precedent for an unenumerated right to travel, although he admitted that "Justice Bradley, in *dissent*, used even stronger language to make the same point." *Id.* at 503. As Stevens noted, aspects of the constitutional right to travel can be located in Congress's power to regulate interstate travel and the equal access principles of the Comity Clause of Article IV. There is no evidence, however, that either John Bingham or Samuel Miller embraced a free-floating substantive individual right to travel.

[121] CONG. GLOBE, 39th Cong., 1st Sess. 2542 (1866).

suppress constitutionally enumerated rights in the former confederate states, suggested otherwise. Field had an incentive to downplay this obvious point to make it appear that the Clause would be useless unless it protected unenumerated rights such as the right to pursue a trade. As Field put it, "[g]rants of exclusive privileges . . . are opposed to the whole theory of free government, and it requires no aid from the bill of rights to render them void."[122] Justice Bradley's dissent echoed the same supratextualist point, arguing that "[i]t was not necessary to say in words that the citizens of the United States should have and exercise all the privileges of citizens; the privilege of buying, selling, and enjoying property; the privilege of engaging in any lawful employment for a livelihood."[123] But to Bingham and Miller, textual definition was a critical prerequisite to properly cabin the powers of the central government.[124]

Miller's opinion is not clear about which textual rights are protected or how they are protected. Although Miller includes rights enumerated in the First Amendment as protected Privileges or Immunities (the right to assemble and petition government for redress of grievances), he does not repeat John Bingham's and Jacob Howard's listing of all of the rights of the first eight amendments. Still, Miller notes his list is not exhaustive (he is listing only "some" protected privileges and immunities), and the logic of this part of Miller's opinion suggests that all constitutionally enumerated rights should be considered national privileges and immunities. Miller does not say whether enumerated privileges like the rights of assembly ran only against the federal government. The Supreme Court would adopt this restricted interpretation in *Cruikshank*, and most scholars have read this anti-incorporation reading back into Miller's opinion. There is nothing in Miller's opinion, however, that requires such a reading.[125] Miller expressly maintains that the Privileges

---

[122] *The Slaughter-House Cases*, 83 U.S. 36, 111 (1873) (Field, J. dissenting).

[123] *Id.* at 119 (Bradley, J., dissenting).

[124] Justice Bradley, and a number of scholars, take Miller to task for rewriting the Comity Clause as involving "citizens of the several states" rather than, as in Article IV, "citizens in the several states." See Slaughter-House, 83 U.S. at 117 ("It is pertinent to observe that both the clause of the Constitution referred to, and Justice Washington in his comment on it, speak of the privileges and immunities of citizens *in* a State; not of citizens *of* a State"). *See also* Louis Lusky, By What Right?: A Commentary on the Supreme Court's Power to Revise the Constitution 194–95 (1975); Richard L. Aynes, *Unintended Consequences of the Fourteenth Amendment and What They Tell Us About Its Incorporation*, 39 Akron L. Rev. 289, 299 (2006). Miller's presentation of the Comity Clause, however, simply distilled the standard antebellum understanding of the "privileges and immunities of citizens in the several states." *See* Chapter 2; *see also* Philip Hamburger, *Privileges or Immunities*, 105 Nw. U. L. Rev. 61, 69 n.26 (2011) (Miller's "rewriting" was simply an attempt to "clarify the meaning of the Clause").

[125] Although mid-twentieth century scholarship tended to view Miller's opinion as denying incorporation of the Bill of Rights, more recent scholarship recognizes that Miller's opinion can be read as including rights in the first eight amendments as Privileges or Immunities of citizens

or Immunities Clause, properly read, declares that "no state shall make or enforce any law abridging" "[t]he right to peaceably assemble and petition for redress of grievances." If the next decision by the Supreme Court struck down a state law forbidding "peaceful assemblies" as a violation of the Privileges or Immunities Clause, the Court could cite this passage in *Slaughter-House* in support of its ruling.

The next case, however, was *United States v. Cruikshank*.[126] Instead of developing the textual possibilities of *Slaughter-House*, the Supreme Court expressly rejected the idea that the rights of the first eight amendments equally bound both state and federal governments. It is because of *Cruikshank* that scholars tend to view *Slaughter-House* as the first anti-incorporation case. But it was not Justice Samuel Miller's opinion that destroyed Bingham's dream of a truly national Bill of Rights; it was the opinion of Chief Justice Morrison Waite.

C. United States v. Cruikshank

Handed down a decade after the framing of the Fourteenth Amendment, Justice Stephen Bradley's opinion in *Cruikshank* ended any Reconstruction-era hope of holding states accountable for protecting the enumerated privileges and immunities of citizens of the United States. It is hard to imagine a more striking rejection of the goals that originally fueled the ratification of the Fourteenth Amendment. In the summer of 1866, a Louisiana mob attacked and killed a group of freedmen exercising their constitutional right of assembly. The New Orleans massacre highlighted the need for an amendment protecting constitutionally enumerated rights and helped fuel the 1866 Republican victory and the eventual ratification of the Fourteenth Amendment. In the spring of 1873, another Louisiana mob attacked and killed a group of freedmen exercising their constitutional rights of peaceful assembly. According to the Supreme Court, however, the Fourteenth Amendment had nothing to do with the matter.

The case involved a mob-driven attack on a group of freedmen who had taken refuge in a local courthouse as part of an ongoing dispute regarding who represented the legally elected officials of the State of Louisiana.[127] Despite

---

of the United States. *See* Bryan H. Wildenthal, *The Lost Compromise: Reassessing the Early Understanding in Court and Congress on Incorporation of the Bill of Rights in the Fourteenth Amendment*, 61 OHIO ST. L. J. 1051 (2000); Kevin Newsom, *Setting Incorporation Straight: A Reinterpretation of the Slaughter-House Cases*, 109 YALE L. J. 643, 666 (2000).

[126] 92 U.S. 542 (1876).

[127] *See* FONER, *supra* note 36, at 261–63; In her recent book, *Rethinking the Judicial Settlement of Reconstruction*, *supra* note 96, Pamela Brandwein argues that the Court's opinion in *Cruikshank* left the door open to federal enforcement of civil rights in the states by way of the

their surrender, up to 165 black Louisianans were killed before the attack had ended.[128] The attackers were indicted for conspiring to "injure, oppress, threaten, or intimidate any citizen, with intent to prevent or hinder his free exercise and enjoyment of any right or privilege granted or secured to him by the constitution or laws of the United States" in violation of the federal Enforcement Act of 1870.[129] Among other things, the defendants were alleged to have conspired to violate the victims' right to assemble for redress of grievances and their right to bear arms as applied against the states by Section One of the Fourteenth Amendment.[130]

Writing for the Court, Chief Justice Waite began by echoing Justice Miller's *Slaughter-House* distinction between the rights of state citizenship and the rights of national citizenship.

> We have in our political system a government of the United States and a government of each of the several States. Each one of these governments is distinct from the others, and each has citizens of its own who owe it allegiance, and whose rights, within its jurisdiction, it must protect. The same person may be at the same time a citizen of the United States and a citizen of a State, but his rights of citizenship under one of these governments will be different from those he has under the other. *Slaughter-House Cases*, 16 Wall. 74.[131]

Moving from the nature of rights to the nature of power, Waite pointed out that the federal government was one of "delegated powers alone. Its authority is defined and limited by the Constitution. All powers not granted to it by that instrument are reserved to the States or the people."[132] Congressional authority

---

now-forgotten doctrine of "state neglect." *Id.* at 119–21. Brandwein's work provides an important revisionist account of equal protection jurisprudence in the Reconstruction-era Supreme Court, and she illuminates an important historical distinction between "secured" pre-existing rights such as those announced in the Bill of Rights and "conferred" rights created by the Constitution itself and subject to greater federal enforcement. *See, e.g., id.* at 97. Brandwein does not, however, address the original meaning of the Privileges or Immunities Clause, nor does her account conflict with the conclusions presented here.

[128] *See* LeeAnna Keith, The Colfax Massacre: The Untold Story of Black Power, White Terror, and the Death of Reconstruction 109 (2009). According to Eric Foner, the Colfax massacre was "the bloodiest single act of carnage in all of Reconstruction." Foner, *supra* note 36, at 530; *see also* Charles Lane, The Day Freedom Died, The Colfax Massacre, The Supreme Court, and the Betrayal of Reconstruction (2008).

[129] United States v. Cruikshank, 92 U.S. 542, 548 (1875).

[130] *Id.*

[131] *Id.* at 549. It appears that the attribution to *Slaughter-House* was not in Waite's initial draft, but was added at Miller's prompting. Charles Fairman, Reconstruction and Reunion, 1864–88, Part Two, 273 fn.153 (Macmillan, 1987) (The Oliver Wendell Holmes Devise History of the Supreme Court of the United States, vol. 7) [hereinafter Fairman, Part Two].

[132] *Cruikshank*, 92 U.S. at 551.

to pass the Enforcement Act thus depended on the scope of power granted to that body under the original Constitution and under the newly enacted Fourteenth Amendment. Citing *Barron v. Baltimore*,[133] Waite explained that, although the "right of the people to assemble and to petition the government for a redress of grievances" was among the "privileges or immunities of citizens of the United States," this right was limited to protecting assemblies whose purpose was to petition the federal government for redress of grievances.[134] Because the indictment alleged a "conspiracy . . . to prevent a meeting for *any lawful purpose whatever*," it was overbroad and exceeded the scope of constitutionally granted federal power.[135] In a few short paragraphs, Waite thus removed from the scope of the Privileges and Immunities Clause the very violation of life and liberty that fueled the ratification of the Fourteenth Amendment.

The dog that does not bark in Waite's opinion is *Slaughter-House*. In support of his assertion that the Bill of Rights binds only the federal government, Waite cites antebellum cases like *Barron*. In support of his assertion that the Privileges or Immunities Clause is similarly restricted, he cites nothing at all.[136] If Waite's colleague Justice Miller had already written an opinion suggesting the first eight amendments were not to be applied against the states by way of the Privileges or Immunities Clause, it is surprising that Waite did not say so. Miller's opinion in *Slaughter-House* even specifically mentions the right at issue in *Cruikshank* – the right to assemble for the purpose of petitioning government for redress of grievances. In this critical part of his opinion, Waite treats the issue as if it is one of first impression.[137]

---

[133] *Id.* at 552. Waite emphasizes that the rights of peaceful assembly preexisted the federal Constitution and were merely secured in the Bill of Rights against federal abridgment. *Id.* His point is that the First Amendment confers no general power of federal enforcement.

[134] *Id.* ("The particular amendment now under consideration assumes the existence of the right of the people to assemble for lawful purposes, and protects it against encroachment by Congress. The right was not created by the amendment; neither was its continuance guaranteed, except as against congressional interference. For their protection in its enjoyment, therefore, the people must look to the States."). In the next part of his opinion, Waite also reads the Second Amendment as binding only the States, a holding that remained in place until 2010. *See* McDonald v. Chicago, 561 U.S. 3025 (2010) (interpreting the Due Process Clause of the Fourteenth Amendment as protecting against state abridgement an individual right to bear arms).

[135] *Id.*

[136] *See id.* at 552–53.

[137] Waite cites *Slaughter-House* earlier in his opinion for the proposition that one must distinguish the rights of federal and state citizenship. He does not cite *Slaughter-House* when discussing whether the First Amendment right of assembly is one of the protected rights of federal citizenship. We also know that Miller was not timid about prompting Waite to cite *Slaughter-House* when Miller thought it appropriate to do so. *See* FAIRMAN, PART TWO, *supra* note 131, at 273 n.153.

The Privileges or Immunities Clause never recovered from *Cruikshank*. Although the Supreme Court later developed its interpretation of the Due Process Clause in a manner that protected various enumerated and unenumerated rights against state abridgement, the Privilege or Immunities Clause remained, and remains, an obscure and generally forgotten aspect of the Fourteenth Amendment.

IV. THE BLAINE AMENDMENT

In 1875, President Grant recommended amending the Constitution to forbid "the teaching in [public] schools of religious, atheistic, or pagan tenets; and prohibiting the granting of any school funds, or school taxes . . . for the benefit or in aid, directly or indirectly, of any religious sect or denomination."[138] A few days later, Republican Congressman James G. Blaine introduced to the House of Representatives the following proposed amendment to the Constitution:

> No state shall make any law respecting an establishment of religion or prohibiting the free exercise thereof; and no money raised by taxation in any State for the support of public schools, or derived from any public fund therefor, nor any public lands devoted thereto, shall ever be under the control of any religious sect, nor shall any money so raised or lands so devoted be divided between religious sects or denominations.[139]

Passed by the House, the proposal was amended during debate in the Senate to read:

> No State shall make any law respecting an establishment of religion, or prohibiting the free exercise thereof; and no religious test shall ever be required as a qualification to any office or public trust under any State. No public property and no public revenue of, nor any loan of credit by or under the authority of, the United States, or any State, Territory, District, or municipal corporation, shall be appropriated to or made or used for the support of any school, educational or other institution under the control of any religious or anti-religious sect, organization, or denomination, or wherein the particular creed or tenets of any religious or anti-religious sect, organization, or denomination shall be taught. And no such particular creed or tenets shall be read or taught in any school or institution supported in whole or in part by such revenue or loan of credit; and no such appropriation or loan of credit shall be made to any religious or anti-religious sect, organization, or denomination,

---

[138] Ulysses S. Grant, Seventh Annual Message, December 7, 1875, *reprinted in* ULYSSES S. GRANT, 1822–1885: CHRONOLOGY-DOCUMENTS-BIBLIOGRAPHICAL AIDS 92 (Philip R. Moran ed., 1968).
[139] 4 CONG. REC. 205 (1875).

or to promote its interests or tenets. This article shall not be construed to prohibit the reading of the Bible in any school or institution; and it shall not have the effect to impair rights of property already vested.[140]

Anti-incorporationist scholars argue that, if the Privileges or Immunities Clause already applied the first eight amendments against the states, then the first clause of the Blaine Amendment is redundant.[141] Pro-incorporationists respond that, by the time of the Blaine Amendment, Supreme Court decisions like the *Slaughter-House Cases* had eviscerated the scope of the Fourteenth Amendment. Thus, a Blaine-type amendment *in* 1875 would not be redundant.[142]

Both sides of this debate have evidence to support their views,[143] but in some ways the dispute is based on a false premise. The entire debate assumes that Senator Blaine's proposal was intended to make the norms of the federal religion clauses applicable against states. In reality, the Blaine Amendment would have amended the First Amendment to deny Roman Catholic schools equal education funding and entrench the use of the Protestant Bible in public schools. This was not a hidden purpose, but the main one: The *Congressional Record* reports the debates on Blaine's proposal involved the proposed "School Amendment."[144] Blaine's proposal was but one of a number of eighteenth-century attempts to amend state or federal law to prohibit equal education funding for Roman Catholic or "sectarian" schools.

In 1870, Missouri Representative Samuel Burdett introduced in the House of Representatives the following proposed constitutional amendment:

Section 1. No State or municipal corporation within any State of the United States shall levy, or collect any tax for the support or aid of any Sectarian,

---

[140] 44th Cong., 1st Sess., 4 Cong. Rec. 5453 (1876).

[141] *See, e.g.*, Berger, *supra* note 17, at 464–65; Raoul Berger, *The Fourteenth Amendment: Light from the Fifteenth*, 74 Nw. U.L. Rev. 311, 346–47 (1979); *see also* Hamburger, *supra* note 124, at 136–43.

[142] *See* Curtis, *supra* note 92, at 169–70.

[143] Both sides have evidence in support of their view. Anti-incorporationists can cite Senator Frelinghuysen's remarks in support of the Blaine Amendment, in which he notes that the Amendment "prohibits the States, for the first time, from the establishment of religion, from prohibiting its free exercise, and from making any religious test a qualification to office." 4 Cong. Rec. 5561 (1876). Pro-incorporationists can cite Senator Morton's lament that "the fourteenth and fifteenth amendments which we supposed broad, ample, and specific, have, I fear, been very much impaired by construction, and one of them in some respects almost destroyed by construction." *Id.* at 5585. Morton therefore suggested that the Blaine Amendment be made as specific as possible to avoid a similar fate at the hands of the Supreme Court. *Id.* Although I believe the pro-incorporationists have the better of the argument, it is more for the reasons stated in the text than on the basis of Morton's lament.

[144] *Id.*

Denominational or Religious School or educational establishment; nor shall the legislature of any State or the corporate authorities of any municipality within any State appropriate any money, or make any donation from the public funds or property of such State or Municipality for the support of or aid of any Sectarian, Religious, or Denominational school or educational establishment.[145]

Burdett's Amendment (which, like Blaine's, failed to win congressional approval) does not mention the religion clauses at all. Instead, the Burdett Amendment tracks the language of similar state constitutional amendments that were adopted during the same period.[146] They reflected a widespread effort to deny Roman Catholic parochial schools an equal share of educational funding.[147]

Protestant religious exercises were ubiquitous in the common schools of the mid-nineteenth century.[148] Catholics, when given the choice between a free Protestant education and no education at all, often chose the latter.[149] Although some states flirted with the idea of equal funding for public and private schools, Nativist opposition barred any efforts in that direction.[150] To prevent any future attempts at equal funding, Nativists sponsored constitutional amendments that prohibited educational aid to sectarian institutions.[151]

Sometimes cited by scholars (and the Supreme Court) as reflecting the inexorable evolution of Jeffersonian Separatism,[152] these provisions were actually attempts to give the Protestant majority an educational monopoly. The most flagrant example of this is found in the Senate's version of the Blaine Amendment itself. Although educational funds were denied to "sectarian" (meaning

---

[145] H.J. Res. 254, CONG. GLOBE, 41st Cong., 2d Sess. 2754 (Apr. 18, 1870).

[146] According to Anson P. Stokes, "[f]rom 1844 on, all states amending their constitutions, and new states when admitted to the Union (except West Virginia, which later corrected the omission), decreed in their fundamental laws against any diversion of public funds to denominational purposes." 4 ANSON PHELPS STOKES, CHURCH AND STATE IN THE UNITED STATES 271 (1950).

[147] *See generally* PHILIP HAMBURGER, SEPARATION OF CHURCH AND STATE 219–29 (2002).

[148] *See* Kurt T. Lash, *The Second Adoption of the Establishment Clause*, 27 ARIZ. ST. L. J. 1085, 1120–22 (1995).

[149] *See* G. Alan Tarr, *Church and State in the States*, 64 WASH. L. REV. 73, 91 (1989). Tarr points out that although the Roman Catholic hierarchy encouraged the establishment of parochial schools, the poverty of the immigrant Catholic Church in America prevented the immediate institution of a widespread parochial school system. *Id.*

[150] For example, in 1842, the New York Legislature prohibited public funding of any school in New York City in which "any religious sectarian doctrine or tenet shall be taught, inculcated, or practiced." *Id.* at 92. This blocked attempts by the New York City Assembly to permit funding for Catholic parochial schools in districts where Catholics were a majority.

[151] 4 Stokes, *supra* note 146, at 271.

[152] *See id.*

Roman Catholic) schools, the amendment was not to be "construed to prohibit the reading of the Bible (meaning the Protestant King James version)
in any school or institution." This echoes the 1856 Know Nothing election
platform, which also called for "schools without sectarian influence" while
at the same time opposing Catholic attempts to remove the Bible from the
public schools.[153]

By constitutionalizing the use of the Protestant Bible and prohibiting public
funds to "sectarian" institutions, the Blaine Amendment would have significantly amended contemporary First Amendment norms. For the first time, the
Constitution would have recognized and protected state power to coercively
indoctrinate students in the tenets of a particular religion. Not only were such
provisions adopted alongside of compulsory education laws, but the day was
not far off when anti-Catholic animus would result in the passage of laws
that attempted to shut down private schools and force attendance at public
school.[154]

Those who participated in the debates over the Blaine Amendment were
well-aware of the real issue underlying the proposal. Senator Morton declared
that America was a "Protestant country" and warned of a "large and growing class of people in this country who are utterly opposed to our present
system of common schools, and who are opposed to any school that does
not teach their religion." Democrats ridiculed the Republicans' attempts to
bootstrap an anti-Catholic amendment into the Constitution by attaching it
to the uncontroversial proposition that states may not establish a religion.[155]
According to Democratic Senator Eaton, it was already the case that "no State

---

[153] The full text of the 1856 Know Nothing platform reads:

> The education of the youth of our country in schools provided by the State, which
> schools shall be common to all, without distinction of creed or party, and free from any
> influence or direction of a denominational or partisan character.

> And inasmuch as Christianity, by the Constitutions of nearly all the States; by the
> decisions of most eminent judicial authorities, and by the consent of the people of
> America, is considered an element of our political system, and the Holy Bible is at
> once the source of Christianity and the depository and fountain of all civil and religious
> freedom, we oppose every attempt to exclude it from the schools thus established in the
> states.

   Reprinted in 2 Stokes, *supra* note 146, at 67–68. For a discussion of the link between Nativists,
   the Know Nothing Party, and anti-Catholic politics, *see* Hamburger, *supra* note 124, at 135.
[154] *See* Pierce v. Society of Sisters, 268 U.S. 510 (1925) (invalidating one such law on the basis of
   the Liberty Clause of the Fourteenth Amendment).
[155] 4 Cong. Rec. 5589, 5589 (1876) (remarks of Senator Bogy) ("The Pope, the old Pope of Rome,
   is to be the great bull we are all to attack"); *id.* at 5583 (remarks of Senator Whyte) ("[The
   amendment is] nearly an accusation against a large body of fellow-citizens.").

can pass any law respecting religion or prohibiting the free exercise thereof."[156] In remarks made just before the proposal's defeat, Senator Saulsbury deplored the Republicans' cynical support of the amendment:

> When I listened to-day to the debates upon this question, when I heard the appeals that were made by the Senators to the religious prejudices and passions of mankind, I trembled for the future of my country.... Have not religious persecutions and appeals to religious prejudices stained the earth with blood and wrung from the hearts of millions the deepest agonies? Yet I see springing up in my own country for the base purposes of a party, to promote a presidential election, a disposition to drag down the sacred cross itself and make it subservient to party ends. I appeal to Heaven to thwart the purpose of all such partisans![157]

The rank bigotry and political opportunism that inspired the so-called Blaine Amendment makes it a poor contender for representing the original understanding of the Privileges or Immunities Clause. With little pre-adoption evidence available at the time to serve as a counter-balance, however, the Blaine Amendment once played a disproportionately large role in scholarly discussion of the historical Fourteenth Amendment. Given the large body of historical evidence now available to scholars studying the original understanding of the Privileges or Immunities Clause, it is hard to see the Blaine Amendment playing much, if any, role at all in determining the original meaning of the Fourteenth Amendment. Its proponents (Republicans) had every reason to discount or ignore the Privileges or Immunities Clause as applying the religion clauses against the states because doing so would rob them of the main argument in favor of adopting an "extended version" of the Amendment. Opponents of the Amendment had every reason to discount or ignore the Privileges or Immunities Clause as a source of broad constitutional constraints on the actions of the states because their party continued to be devoted to a narrow construction of the Fourteenth Amendment.

V. LEGAL TREATISES

Scholarly commentary on the Fourteenth Amendment was mixed, at least in terms of whether Section One applied substantive enumerated constitutional rights against the states. Even here, however, recent scholarship has revealed substantial support for the Bingham-Howard reading of the rights of national

---

[156] 4 Cong. Rec. 5592 (1876).
[157] 4 Cong. Rec. 5594 (1876).

citizenship.[158] For example, of the four constitutional treatises published clos-
est to the adoption of the Fourteenth Amendment (and therefore the least
affected by Supreme Court decisions like *Cruikshank*), only one seems to
have not believed that the Privileges or Immunities Clause protected substantive enumerated constitutional rights. The 1868 edition of Thomas Cooley's
Constitutional Limitations did not discuss the Fourteenth Amendment.[159] The
second edition, published in 1871, does not specifically discuss whether the
Privileges or Immunities Clause binds the states to follow the Bill of Rights,
but it does include a footnote indicating Colley's belief that states did not have
to provide a trial by jury in either criminal or civil cases.[160]

Other treatises expressly agreed with John Bingham that the Fourteenth
Amendment reversed *Barron v. Baltimore's* holding that states were not bound
by the Bill of Rights. John Norton Pomeroy's *Introduction to the Constitutional Law of the United States* described Section One of the Fourteenth
Amendment, an amendment "now pending before the people," as the proper
"remedy" for the "unfortunate" decision in *Barron v. Baltimore*.[161] According
to Pomeroy, the Amendment "would give the nation complete power to protect its citizens against local injustice and oppression; a power which it does
not now adequately possess, but which beyond all doubt, should be conferred
upon it. Nor would this amendment interfere with any of the rights, privileges
and functions which properly belong to the individual states."[162] In the 1869
edition of Timothy Farrar's *Manual of the Constitution of the United States*,
Farrar praised the fact that the Fourteenth Amendment had "entirely swept

[158] For an outstanding and exhaustive discussion of post-adoption Fourteenth Amendment commentary, *see* Bryan H. Wildenthal, *Nationalizing the Bill of Rights: Scholarship and Commentary on the Fourteenth Amendment in 1867–1873*, 18 J. CONTEMP. LEG. ISSUES 153 (2009).

[159] *See* THOMAS M. COOLEY, A TREATISE ON THE CONSTITUTIONAL LIMITATIONS WHICH REST
UPON THE LEGISLATIVE POWER OF THE STATES OF THE AMERICAN UNION (Little, Brown
[Boston], 1868) (preface dated Sept. 1868). Cooley served as Chief Justice of the Michigan
Supreme Court before becoming the Dean of the University of Michigan Law School. According to Bryan Wildenthal, Cooley's "Constitutional Limitations" is "widely hailed as one of the
most influential books on American constitutional law of the 19th century." Wildenthal, *supra*
note 158, at 171.

[160] THOMAS M. COOLEY, CONSTITUTIONAL LIMITATIONS 20 [*19] n.1 (Little, Brown [Boston], 2d
ed. 1871).

[161] JOHN NORTON POMEROY, AN INTRODUCTION TO THE CONSTITUTIONAL LAW OF THE UNITED
STATES § 235, at 149; § 237, at 151 (Houghton, Osgood & Co. [Boston], 1868). A law pro-
fessor at New York University before accepting the inaugural chair at Hastings College of
Law, Pomeroy's "major treatises dominated their fields until well into the twentieth century."
Stephen A. Siegel, *Historicism in Late Nineteenth-Century Constitutional Thought*, 1990 WIS.
L. REV. 1431, 1454. *See also* Wildenthal, *supra* note 158, at 192.

[162] POMEROY, *supra* note 161, at § 237, at 151.

away" the doctrine of *Barron v. Baltimore.*"[163] In his third edition, Farrar added that "[a]ll the rights, privileges, and immunities, guarantied and held under and by virtue of the Constitution of the United States, are necessarily placed beyond the reach of State or any other inferior authority; but, by the fourteenth Amendment, the States are expressly prohibited from abridging any of them."[164]

Finally, George W. Paschal's 1868 *Annotated Constitution of the United States* also agreed that the adoption of the Fourteenth Amendment would overturn the doctrine of *Barron v. Baltimore.*[165] According to Paschal,

> Section One . . . defines national citizenship, and thus makes organic what had already been declared law by the first section of the Civil Rights Bill. All else in this section has already been guarantied in the second and fourth sections of the fourth article [the Comity and Republican Guarantee Clauses]; and in the thirteenth amendment. The new feature declared is that the general principles, which had been construed to apply only to the national government, are thus imposed upon the States. Most of the States, in general terms, had adopted the same bill of rights in their own constitutions.[166]

Paschal's 1868 letter in the *New York Herald-Tribune* (mentioned in Chapter 4) echoes this same idea: Where once cases like *Barron v. Baltimore* left it to the states to adopt some form of the Bill of Rights on a state level, where it may or may not be enforced, we now have a constitutional provision that directly applies the Bill of Rights against the states:

> The lines defining American citizenship will no longer be a matter of doubt. Nor is the remaining guarantee in this clause less important. "No state shall make or enforce any law abridging the privileges or immunities of citizens of the United States; nor shall any State deprive any person of life, liberty or property without due process of law, nor deny to any person within its jurisdiction the equal protection of the laws."

> Law readers are so accustomed to see similar provisions in the State Constitutions, that they underrate this national guaranty. They should have lived

---

[163] TIMOTHY FARRAR, MANUAL OF THE CONSTITUTION OF THE UNITED STATES OF AMERICA 546 (Little, Brown [Boston], 2d ed. 1869). Judge, statesman, and law partner of Daniel Webster, Farrar's *Manual of the Constitution* was praised by Charles Sumner "for signaling 'the great change in our history.'" FRANCIS N. STITES & TIMOTHY FARRAR, 7 AMERICAN NATIONAL BIOGRAPHY [ANB] 742 (John A. Garraty & Mark C. Carnes eds., Oxford Univ. Press, 24 vols., 1999).

[164] Farrar, *supra* note, at 504.

[165] GEORGE W. PASCHAL, THE CONSTITUTION OF THE UNITED STATES DEFINED AND CAREFULLY ANNOTATED § 279, at 290 (W. H. & O. H. Morrison [Washington, D.C.], 1868).

[166] *Id.* (citations omitted).

in the South, where there was always a class of "persons" for whom there was a summary and barbarous code; they should know that the national bill of rights has, by a common error, been construed not to apply to or control the States; they should have seen and felt that for 30 years there was even half the area of the Union where no man could speak, write, or think against the institution of Slavery; they should know that even now to be called a "Radical" is to endanger life.[167]

VI. SUMMARY

It is not the purpose of this chapter to develop evidence of the original meaning of the Privileges or Immunities Clause. That evidence is presented in Chapters 2–4. Instead, my purpose has been to explore post-adoption cases and commentary that have played a significant role in prior histories of the Fourteenth Amendment and determine if we can understand this history better in light of what we now know of the Amendment's pre-adoption history and post-adoption politics. For example, given what we now know about John Bingham's theory of the Privileges or Immunities Clause, scholars have been wrong to criticize Justice Miller's opinion in the *Slaughter-House Cases* as departing from the drafters' understanding of the text. Bingham's second draft of the Privileges or Immunities Clause was a self-conscious attempt to distinguish the protections of the Clause from those provided by the Comity Clause of Article IV. Justice Miller correctly picked up on this textual distinction and correctly rejected efforts to read the Privileges or Immunities Clause as nationalizing the unenumerated common law rights afforded equal protection under the Comity Clause. Whether or not one accepts the Bingham reading as the proper interpretation of the text, scholars must now realize that much of the criticism leveled at Miller is actually criticism of the man who drafted the clause.

We also know that the Bingham-Howard reading of the text found its way into high-profile legal treatises and judicial case law. As is to be expected, there was neither scholarly nor political unanimity regarding the meaning of the Privileges or Immunities Clause. Still, if the Bingham-Howard reading represents the best reading of the text in light of the original meaning of the term "privileges or immunities of citizens of the United States," it would be odd if no one advocated such a reading in the period immediately following its adoption. We now know that many did. The fact that advocates put forward a variety of claims about the newly adopted amendment simply sends us back

---

[167] *The Fourteenth Article*, N.Y. Herald-Trib., *published as* N.Y. Daily Trib., Aug. 6, 1868, at 2 (printing letter by George W. Paschal, Austin, Tex., July 24, 1868).

to the evidence supplied in the earlier chapters of this book to determine which of these many readings most likely represents the original meaning of the Privileges or Immunities Clause. In the end, and rather unsurprisingly, it appears that the men most responsible for drafting and presenting the clause to the public were the men who articulated the most likely original meaning of the text.

6

Text and Theory

I. A SHORT REVIEW

The goal of this book is to identify the likely original meaning of the Privileges or Immunities Clause. I have defined original meaning as the likely original understanding of the text at the time of its adoption by competent speakers of the English language who are aware of the context in which the text was communicated for ratification.[1] Rather than seeking framers' intentions or linguistically possible interpretations, my effort has been to identify patterns of usage that signal commonly accepted meaning. The methodology has been empirical: I have identified historical public usage of the terms "privileges and immunities" in the periods just prior to, during, and immediately following the ratification of the Fourteenth Amendment.

In Chapter 2, I identified two separate strains of privileges and immunities that emerged in antebellum law and political rhetoric: those belonging to "citizens in the several states" (covered by the Comity Clause of Article IV) and those belonging to citizens of the United States (such as those identified in the Louisiana Cession Act of 1803). Chapter 3 showed how this distinction carried over into the framing debates and informed John Bingham's decision to abandon his initial draft, which relied on the language of the Comity Clause, and replace it with a draft that used the familiar language of US treaties – language that had entered the public debate that spring by way of President Andrew Johnson's widely published veto of the Civil Rights Act. According to Jacob

---

[1] *See* Lawrence B. Solum, *Originalism and Constitutional Construction*, Fordham L. Rev. (2013), *available at* http://papers.ssrn.com/sol3/papers.cfm?abstract_id=2307178 ("'Public Meaning Originalism' names the version of originalist theory holding that the communicative content of the constitutional text is fixed at the time of origin by the conventional semantic meaning of the words and phrases in the context that was shared by the drafters, ratifiers, and citizens.").

Howard's presentation of the Amendment to the Senate and to the public, the "privileges and immunities of citizens of the United States" involved textually enumerated personal rights such as those covered by the Comity Clause and those enumerated in the first eight amendments to the Constitution. Chapter 4 recounted the political debates of 1866 and what became a national referendum on the meaning and desirability of the Fourteenth Amendment, with both proponents and opponents viewing the Privileges or Immunities Clause as nationalizing enumerated rights such as the First Amendment rights of free speech and assembly. The accepted understanding of the Clause that informed these debates further supports an original meaning that ties the Privileges or Immunities Clause to enumerated constitutional rights. Finally, Chapter 5 discussed post-ratification case law and commentary. Although different political factions pressed for different readings of the Clause, John Bingham continued to distinguish the set of state-secured privileges and immunities covered by the Comity Clause from the national privileges and immunities protected under the Privileges or Immunities Clause. In the first Supreme Court case to interpret the Fourteenth Amendment, a majority of the Court followed the Bingham-Howard distinction between the Comity Clause and the Privileges or Immunities Clause and expressly left the door open to future judicial protection of enumerated constitutional "privileges or immunities."

A reasonable conclusion from this history is that common usage distinguished "privileges and immunities *of citizens in the several states*" (the full term used in the Comity Clause of Article IV) from "privileges or immunities *of citizens of the United States*" (the full term used in the Fourteenth Amendment). From its earliest use in legal and political rhetoric, the content of rights covered by the term "privileges and immunities" differed depending on the identity and nature of the protected individual or group. "Privileges and immunities of citizens in the several states" protected under the Comity Clause were widely viewed as involving a limited set of state-secured rights that must be equally extended to visiting citizens from other states. According to decisions like *Corfield v. Coryell*, it was not the underlying right that was guaranteed, but the right of equal access *if* a state granted such a right to its own citizens. This "equal protection of state secured-rights" reading of the Comity Clause remained the consensus interpretation throughout the nineteenth century, both before and after the Civil War.

The "privileges and immunities *of citizens of the United States,*" however, was a term used in reference to a set of substantive national rights secured by the Constitution and common to all US citizens. This included both the equal protection rights of the Comity Clause and those rights announced in the first eight amendments to the federal Constitution. Although the underlying rights granted equal protection by the Comity Clause differed from place to place depending on state law, the "privileges and immunities" of citizens of the United States were, or ought to be, the same for all US citizens wherever they traveled.

The earliest antebellum discussions of the rights of national citizenship distinguished this set of rights from those protected under the Comity Clause. Major federal reports prior to the Civil War maintained the distinction, as did President Johnson in his message vetoing the Civil Rights Act. The man who presented the Clause to the Senate and country, Jacob Howard, expressly described national privileges and immunities as including rights secured by the Comity Clause and by the enumerated rights in the first eight amendments. In the 1866 public debate on the need for the Fourteenth Amendment, both opponents and proponents of the Amendment accepted Howard's description, disagreeing only on whether such a clause was necessary. In 1871, the drafter of the Privileges or Immunities Clause, John Bingham, expressly distinguished the state-secured privileges and immunities granting equal protection under the Comity Clause from the substantive privileges and immunities of citizens of the United States protected under the Fourteenth Amendment. Finally, a majority of the Supreme Court embraced this same distinction in the very first Supreme Court case to consider the Clause.

This is the *Enumerated Rights* reading of the Privileges or Immunities Clause. It is not the only possible reading of the Clause, but it is the reading that best fits the full text of the Clause and the historical context in which it was enacted. Even if correct, this meaning does not tell us everything about the Clause; for example, it does not provide a complete and specific list of constitutional provisions that constitute protected privileges or immunities. However, the enumerated rights reading does establish both a minimum and a maximum scope of rights falling within the protection of the text.

II. THE ARCHITECTURE OF THE PRIVILEGES OR IMMUNITIES CLAUSE

A. *Ceilings and Floors*

The Enumerated Rights reading of the Privileges or Immunities Clause is quite different from the two interpretations that have dominated scholarly discussion of the Clause over the past half-century. Ever since the mid-twentieth-century debate over the Supreme Court's incorporation of the Bill of Rights into the Fourteenth Amendment, the two most influential theories of the Privileges or Immunities Clause have both relied on the Comity Clause and Justice

Washington's opinion in *Corfield v. Coryell* as guides to understanding the rights of national citizenship. These competing interpretations, which I call the *Equal Rights* reading and the *Fundamental Rights* reading, both attempt to merge the Comity Clause and the Privileges or Immunities Clause, although to very different ends. Although both theories represent possible readings of the Privileges or Immunities Clause, neither represents the best or most likely original meaning. The Equal Rights interpretation is unduly narrow, and the Fundamental Rights reading is unduly broad. Put another way, these alternative readings violate the textually established "floor" and "ceiling" of the Privileges or Immunities Clause. The floor requires, at a minimum, the inclusion of textually enumerated rights such as those listed in the first eight amendments. The ceiling limits protected rights to those expressly secured by the text of the federal Constitution.

1. Beneath the Floor: The Equal Rights Reading

The Equal Rights reading of the Privileges or Immunities Clause views both the Comity Clause and the Privileges or Immunities Clause as equal rights provisions that protect the same set of "privileges and immunities."[2] This approach rejects the idea that the Fourteenth Amendment incorporates the substantive protections of the first eight amendments. As Equal Rights theorist Philip Hamburger argues, "the Privileges or Immunities Clause concerned Comity Clause rights rather than incorporation."[3] The Equal Rights interpretation reduces the Privileges or Immunities Clause to a restatement of the Comity Clause but with the addition of federal enforcement power. Again, according to Hamburger, "the Fourteenth Amendment's Privileges or Immunities Clause had to reassert what the Comity Clause had already guaranteed."[4]

There is, in fact, a great deal of evidence to suggest that the rights of the Comity Clause were included within the protection of the Privileges or Immunities Clause.[5] Equal Rights theorists insist, however, that the Privileges or Immunities Clause involves *nothing more* than an equal rights provision.[6] This exclusivist reading of the Privileges or Immunities Clause is problematic

---

[2] For examples of equal rights theories of the Privileges or Immunities Clause, *see* John Harrison, *Reconstructing the Privileges or Immunities Clause*, 101 YALE L.J. 1385 (1992); Philip Hamburger, *Privileges or Immunities*, 105 Nw. U. L. REV. 61 (2011).

[3] Hamburger, *supra* note 2, at 71.

[4] *Id.* at 71.

[5] One of the most important pieces of evidence would be Jacob Howard's influential speech introducing the Fourteenth Amendment in which he included the rights of the Comity Clause along with the first eight amendments as examples of the privileges or immunities of citizens of the United States. See CONG. GLOBE, 39th Cong., 1st Sess. 2765 (1866).

[6] *Id.*

on a number of levels. To begin with, equating the Comity Clause and the Privileges or Immunities Clause seems contradicted by the texts themselves. Although both clauses speak of "privileges" and "immunities," they use very different language when referring to the groups whose rights are being protected: "citizens in the several states" versus "citizens of the United States." One could make the clauses refer to the same group by adding an unstated "ellipsis" to both provisions so that the Comity Clause refers to the "privileges and immunities of citizens (of the United States) in the several States," and the Privileges or Immunities Clause refers to the "privileges or immunities of citizens of the United States (in the several states)." But there is no textual justification for doing so, and the historical record strongly counsels against it.

John Bingham based his first draft of the Fourteenth Amendment on his early belief that the Comity Clause obligated the states to protect those rights listed in the first eight amendments. He abandoned the language of the Comity Clause when it became clear that most of his colleagues had a very different understanding of the Comity Clause; radicals read it as opening the door to federal enforcement of *Corfield*ian civil rights, and conservatives insisted that the language would do nothing more than enforce the traditional equal rights understanding of *Corfield* and the Comity Clause.[7] Bingham found both views equally objectionable, with the radical view going too far and the conservative view not going far enough. Accordingly, Bingham jettisoned the language of the Comity Clause and replaced it with the language of national citizenship. According to Jacob Howard, this language protected far more than just the equal protection principles of the Comity Clause; it also included the enumerated protections of the first eight amendments to the Constitution.[8] Throughout the debates of 1866, John Bingham insisted that his goal was to enforce the Bill of Rights against the states, and the record strongly suggests that he altered the language of the amendment to ensure that would be the case. If John Bingham and Jacob Howard correctly understood the second and final draft, then the Equal Rights reading is unduly narrow – it violates the textual floor established by the language of the Privileges or Immunities Clause.

Perhaps, however, Bingham and Howard were wrong about the meaning of the second draft. If our goal is to identify the original meaning of the text, then the particular private intentions of the framers are relevant only to the degree that they inform our understanding of the public meaning of the text. If the final language of the Privileges or Immunities Clause was commonly understood as only referring to the equally protected state-secured rights of

---

[7] *See* discussion in Chapter 3.
[8] *See* CONG. GLOBE, 39th Cong., 1st Sess. 2765 (1866).

the Comity Clause, then this would be the original meaning regardless of
Bingham's hopes or Howard's declarations. Professor Philip Hamburger makes
precisely this argument and claims that Bingham's second draft was simply
another form of the Comity Clause.[9] Thus, the final draft, as a matter of textual
meaning, protected nothing other than Comity Clause rights.

The problems with Hamburger's theory are threefold. First, the texts are not
the same, which would seem to require significant historical evidence that the
differently worded Privileges or Immunities Clause protects Comity Clause
rights and *nothing but* Comity Clause rights. Second, there is the abundant
evidence presented in Chapters 2, 3, and 4 that indicate the terms of these two
clauses carried different meanings. Third, and most fatally for Hamburger's
theory, his primary piece of evidence fatally undercuts his own argument.
Hamburger relies heavily on a bill introduced in the Thirty-Ninth Congress
by Samuel Shellabarger. Titled *A Bill to Declare and Protect All the Privi-*
leges and Immunities of Citizens of the United States in the Several States, the
bill protected only those rights covered by the Comity Clause.[10] Hamburger
claims that this bill and its content is evidence that the language of Privileges
or Immunities Clause ("of citizens of the United States") was understood as
referring to nothing more than rights covered by the Comity Clause. More,
Hamburger claims that John Bingham himself may have been inspired to use
the language of the Bill in his second draft of the Privileges or Immunities
Clause.[11] What Hamburger does not say is that Shellabarger's bill was never
debated or discussed at all, much less acted on.[12] This makes it a poor candidate

---

[9] *See* Hamburger, *supra* note 2, at 73 ("[A]lready before the Civil War, Americans not only
defended the Comity Clause rights of free blacks on the ground that they were citizens of the
United States but also began to describe Comity Clause rights as 'the privileges and immunities
of citizens of the United States.'"); *id.* at 124 ("The [Privileges or Immunities Clause] was thus
a succinct and familiar label for the Comity Clause rights that Bingham had already attempted
to protect in the Fourteenth Amendment.").

[10] *Id.*; see also A Bill to Declare and Protect All the Privileges and Immunities of Citizens of the
United States in the Several States, H.R. 437, 39th Cong. §1 (as reported by H. Comm. on the
Judiciary, Apr. 2, 1866, Printers No. 116).

[11] Hamburger, *supra* note 2, at 119, 123–24.

[12] Following Shellabarger's initial submission on April 2, 1866, the bill was sent to committee
without comment. *See* CONG. GLOBE, 39th Cong., 1st Sess. at 1719. Days later, James F. Wilson
proposed amending the Bill to clarify "[t]hat the enumeration of the privileges and immunities
of citizenship in this act contained shall not be deemed a denial or abridgment of *any other*
rights, privileges, or immunities which appertain to citizenship under the Constitution." *See*
39th Cong., 1st Sess. H.R. 437 (May 7, 1866) (Wilson's amended version of Shellabarger's
Bill) (emphasis added). Wilson's amended version was reported back to the House on July
25, long after the debates on the Fourteenth Amendment. *See* CONG. GLOBE, 39th Cong.,
1st Sess. at 4148. However, the House had more pressing matters to attend to and Wilson
successfully suggested that the Bill be tabled until the next session. Shellabarger had no
objection to Wilson's amendment and he agreed with the postponement. *Id.* Because this

for "inspiring" John Bingham or anyone else. But most devastating for Hamburger's argument is the fact that, only days after its submission, James F. Wilson added an amendment to the bill that clarified "[t]hat the enumeration of the privileges and immunities of citizenship in this act contained shall not be deemed a denial or abridgment of *any other* rights, privileges, or immunities which appertain to citizenship under the Constitution."[13] Instead of supporting an exclusivist Equal Rights reading of "privileges and immunities of citizens of the United States," the amended version of Shellabarger's Bill suggests that members of the Thirty-Ninth Congress did not believe the rights of the Comity Clause were the only privileges or immunities of national citizenship.

Neither the text nor the pre-ratification history of the Privileges or Immunities Clause suggest it was understood as the mirror image of the Comity Clause, protecting nothing other than the equal protection principles traditionally associated with that Clause. There is just too much historical evidence to the contrary. Given the antebellum use of this language to refer to enumerated rights, congressional debates declaring that this language referred to enumerated rights, and public debates assuming this language referred to enumerated rights, the historical evidence strongly suggests the existence of a textual "floor": At the very minimum, the original meaning of the Privileges or Immunities Clause includes substantive rights, in particular the rights listed in the first eight amendments to the Constitution.

2. Above the Ceiling: The Fundamental Rights Reading

Like the Equal Rights reading, the Fundamental Rights reading presumes that the Comity Clause and the Privileges or Immunities Clause refer to the same set of "privileges and immunities." Unlike the Equal Rights reading, however, the Fundamental Rights reading interprets the Privileges or Immunities Clause as protecting both constitutionally enumerated rights and unenumerated "fundamental" common law rights, such as those listed by Justice Bushrod Washington in *Corfield v. Coryell.* For example, according to Akhil Amar, "the language of section 1 opens up broader possibilities" than just

---

    denied Shellabarger the chance to make a speech explaining the bill, he asked that his remarks be added to the official record in the appendix of the *Congressional Globe. See* Cong. Globe, 39th Cong., 1st Sess. at 4148 (July 25). Wilson brought the bill forward the next session with the same amendment but, again, no action was taken and the bill apparently died. *See* 39th Cong., 2d Sess., H.R. 1037 (Jan. 23, 1867) (Wilson of the Judiciary Committee reporting Shellabarger's Bill).

[13] *See* 39th Cong., 1st Sess. H.R. 437 (May 7, 1866) (Wilson's amended version of Shellabarger's Bill) (emphasis added).

the "protection of enumerated rights"[14] and should be viewed as embracing "*Corfield*'s nonexhaustive list of fundamental rights."[15] Similarly, Randy Barnett links the Privileges or Immunities Clause to Justice Washington's list in *Corfield* and also to the "other rights" referred to in the Ninth Amendment.[16] According to Barnett, "[t]he quotations from Justice Washington and others suggest that 'privileges or immunities' is a broader term including both natural or inherent rights as well as those particular 'positive' procedural rights created by the Bill of Rights."[17]

Fundamental Rights advocates generally cite the early statements by radical Republicans in support of the original version of the Civil Rights Act, particularly those of Lyman Trumbull and James Wilson.[18] As we have seen, however, the efforts by radical Republicans to characterize *Corfield*'s list as a reference to substantive national rights were immediately challenged with irrefutable citations to antebellum case law and treatises, to the point that radical Republicans stopped relying on *Corfield* altogether.[19] Moderates were so concerned about federal intrusion into the general subject of civil rights in the states that they forced James Wilson to remove the term "civil rights" from the Civil Rights Act.[20] Radicals failed to secure an override of Johnson's veto of the Freedman's Bureau Bill and, in the spring of 1866, they had no chance at all of securing the rights of suffrage for newly freed blacks.[21] In short, it was not the views of radicals like James Wilson or Lyman Trumbull that

---

[14] Akhil Reed Amar, The Bill of Rights: Creation and Reconstruction 177 (1998).

[15] *Id.*

[16] Randy Barnett, Restoring the Lost Constitution: The Presumption of Liberty 61–68 (2004).

[17] *Id.* at 66. A related view is one that maintains that the Privileges or Immunities Clause protects a set of judicially identified common law rights. *See, e.g.*, Michael W. McConnell, *The Importance of Humility in Judicial Review: A Comment on Ronald Dworkin's "Moral Reading" of the Constitution*, 65 FORDHAM L. REV. 1269, 1286 (1997) ("In other words, the privileges and immunities of citizens of the United States were conceived against a common law backdrop, gradually evolving over time as circumstances and public mores change"); Steven G. Calabresi, *Two Cheers for Professor Balkin's Originalism*, 103 NW. U. L. REV. 663, 670 (2009) ("Privileges or immunities includes not only all the common law rights but also other related fundamental rights as discussed in Justice Bushrod Washington's opinion in Corfield v. Coryell"). This common law approach shares the same problems as those described earlier in regard to the Fundamental Rights reading of the Clause. Both approaches, for example, rely on a *Corfield*-based reading of the Privileges or Immunities Clause. *See id.*

[18] AMAR, *supra* at 14, and 178 n. 57 (citing Lyman Trumbull's speech of January 29 and James Wilson's speech of March 1); BARNETT, *supra* note 16, at 63, 64 (same).

[19] *See* discussion in Chapter 3.

[20] *Id.*

[21] According to Eric Foner, "[w]hen Congress reassembled in December [1865], the issue of black suffrage was, for the moment, politically dead." ERIC FONER, RECONSTRUCTION: AMERICA'S UNFINISHED REVOLUTION 1863–1877, at 224 (1988).

controlled the outcome of debates in the Thirty-Ninth Congress but those held by Republican moderates. Proposals that federalized, or that could be construed as federalizing, natural or "fundamental" common law rights in the states would have been (and were) opposed and defeated.[22]

Republican moderates were well aware of the dangers posed by future interpretation, and they were especially anxious not to pass an amendment that would place the control of civil rights in the states in the hands of a future Congress that might be under Democrat control. Most of all, moderates opposed on federalist grounds any effort to nationalize the substance of civil rights in the states. Bingham, of course, never once mentioned *Corfield* during the amendment debates of 1866, much less adopted a radical Republican reading of the case. Jacob Howard referred to *Corfield* as a case explaining the Comity Clause, but Howard also rejected the radical Republican effort to transform the rights of *Corfield* into a set of unenumerated national rights.[23] In sum, of all the assertions about the Privileges or Immunities Clause, one of the least plausible is the claim that the radical Republican reading of *Corfield* informed Congress's and the public's understanding of the original meaning of the Privileges or Immunities Clause. A proposal understood as even possibly authorizing future nationalization of unenumerated "fundamental" civil rights in the states would never have made it out of committee, much less have been passed by a two-thirds majority of the Thirty-Ninth Congress.

Some scholars might try to escape the textual ceiling of the Privileges or Immunities Clause by distinguishing original *meaning* (which is binding) from original *expected application* (which, arguably, is not binding).[24] One might argue, for example, that even if the framers of the Privileges or Immunities

---

[22] It was to avoid just this kind of possible construction that the term "civil rights" was removed from the Civil Rights Act.

[23] Scholars sometime quote Jacob Howard's assertion that "privileges and immunities" "are not and cannot be fully defined in their entire extent and precise nature" as evidence that the Privileges or Immunities Clause was understood as protecting unenumerated rights. *See* JACK BALKIN, LIVING ORIGINALISM 208 (2011; BARNETT, *supra* note 16, at 65. As a quick glance at the full quote makes clear, however, Howard was referring to state secured "privileges and immunities" "spoken of in the second section of the fourth article of the Constitution," not the substantive rights guaranteed by the Privileges or Immunities Clause. *See* CONG. GLOBE, 39th Cong., 1st Sess. at 2765. There was nothing particularly controversial about noting that state-secured rights granted equal protection by the (single) Comity Clause "are not and cannot be fully defined in their entire extent and precise nature," and Howard treated his description as an aside. He was not, however, making what would have been received as the explosive claim that the substantive rights nationalized by the Privileges or Immunities Clause and placed under federal political control "cannot be fully defined in their entire extent and precise nature." As explained in Chapter 3, Howard himself would have opposed such a radical measure. *See* Chapter 3 at notes 370–73 and accompanying text.

[24] *See* BALKIN, *supra* note 23, at 14.

Clause did not expect it would be applied to unenumerated fundamental rights, their limited expectations should not control the current application of the Clause. As long as a current application is consistent with the original meaning of the text, then it should not matter whether its application was expected at the time of the text's adoption.[25]

In some ways, this is a perfectly valid point. Original meaning originalism does not seek "original intentions" or "original expected applications." It is the actual language, not a particular expected application, that determines the meaning of the text, and it is quite possible that the meaning of the text embraces more or different possible applications than those anticipated by a particular framer. Originalist applications of the text, however, cannot contradict original meaning. In the case of the Privileges or Immunities Clause, applying the text in a manner that identifies and protects a right nowhere enumerated in the Constitution is inconsistent with the original meaning of the text because it exceeds definitional boundaries established by the original meaning of the term "privileges or immunities of citizens of the United States." There may be nonoriginalist theories that justify applying the Clause in a manner that enforces a nonenumerated right, from theories of judicial authority to entrench evolving ideas of morality[26] to theories that embrace the principles of *stare decisis*.[27] No such application, however, is consistent with original meaning if it violates the range of permissible application established by the text itself.

It is theoretically possible, of course, that the framers might purposefully choose vague and indeterminate terms due an inability of members to come to agreement on more specific language. These same framers might be willing to allow future courts (or future congresses) to identify and enforce their preferred ideas of government power and individual freedom. The historical evidence strongly suggests that this was not the case in the Thirty-Ninth Congress. Members forced a change in the language of the Civil Rights Act precisely because they were concerned about unduly broad future construction.[28] In the case of the Privileges or Immunities Clause, members initially considered a draft that carried the linguistic possibility of either unduly narrow or unduly broad future application. The first draft's use of Comity Clause language could be read as embracing Justice Bushrod Washington's analysis in *Corfield v. Coryell*, and *Corfield* could be understood as protecting either nothing more than the principles of equal protection (the conservative reading) or as federalizing the

---

[25] *Id.*
[26] *See* DAVIS A. STRAUSS, THE LIVING CONSTITUTION 92 (2010).
[27] *See* Planned Parenthood v. Casey, 505 U.S. 833, 854 (1992).
[28] See discussion in Chapter 3.

entire range of fundamental common law right in the states (the radical reading). This range of meaning was unacceptable to Republican moderates in general and John Bingham in particular, so Bingham withdrew his initial draft and replaced it with language that contained an entirely different meaning with a more constrained range of possible application.

It is Bingham's abandonment of the Comity Clause and his embrace of the language of national treaties that poses a problem for proponents of the Fundamental Rights/Expected Application theory. To make room for unenumerated rights as permissible (if unexpected) applications, these theorists rely on interpretations that (1) link the Privileges or Immunities Clause to the Comity Clause and to Bushrod Washington's opinion in *Corfield v. Coryell*[29] and (2) embrace the radical Republican "unenumerated national rights" reading of the Comity Clause and *Corfield*.[30] This *Corfield*ian reading of the Privileges or Immunities Clause creates space for the application of "unexpected" unenumerated rights. The historical record, however, contradicts both of these essential pillars.

Antebellum usage divided privileges and immunities "of citizens in the several states" from privileges and immunities of "citizens of the United States." The texts themselves use distinctly different language. The man who drafted the Privileges or Immunities Clause explained why the two clauses use distinctly different language. The first Supreme Court opinion to discuss the clause embraced this same distinction. Even if, despite all this evidence to the contrary, we still concluded that the Privileges or Immunities Clause somehow mirrors the Comity Clause, the historical evidence overwhelmingly suggests that the result would be a clause that represents the traditional reading of the Comity Clause as providing nothing other than a degree of equal protection for state-secured rights. In the end, the Fundamental Rights reading and its attendant unexpected applications are overwhelmed by the historical record. Without the ability to fold the Privileges or Immunities Clause into the Comity Clause and rely on the seemingly open-ended language of *Corfield v. Coryell*, the Fundamental Rights/Expected Applications theory finds no purchase. This is not what the text of the Privileges or Immunities Clause means.

B. *Furnishing the Room: The Privileges or Immunities of Citizens of the United States*

So what are the "privileges or immunities of citizens of the United States"? The historical record supports some conclusions about the general nature of

---

[29] *See, e.g.,* BALKIN, *supra* note 23, at 208–09.
[30] *Id.*

these rights, and it provides paradigmatic examples of both protected rights and excluded rights. The historical record does not, however, present us with a fully worked-out theory of the clause or an exhaustive list of protected rights. No one at the time attempted to create an exhaustive list, and there remain too many unanswered questions to allow the creation of such a list post hoc with a sufficient degree of confidence. That said, a *non*exhaustive list is not the same thing as an *in*exhaustive list. We know that the text establishes both a floor and a ceiling for the protected rights of the Privileges or Immunities Clause. Between these textual barriers there is room for debate and judicial construction.[31]

The "room" beyond which the Clause cannot expand is established by the four corners of the Constitution. The enumerated privileges or immunities of citizens of the United States may include "natural rights," common law rights, or positive political rights. What they have in common is not their particular nature but the document that secures them. As John Bingham's hero Daniel Webster explained,

> The rights, advantages and immunities here spoken of [in The Louisiana Cession Act] must, from the very force of the terms of the clause, be such as are recognized or communicated by the Constitution of the United States; such as are common to all citizens, and are uniform throughout the United States. The clause cannot be referred to rights, advantages and immunities derived exclusively from the State Government, for these do not depend upon the federal Constitution.[32]

John Bingham's goal in drafting the clause was to require the states to protect the enumerated rights of citizenship, such as those listed in the first eight amendments to the Constitution, along with the natural rights of due process and equal protection. There may be unenumerated rights one holds against the national government (consider, for example, the Ninth Amendment[33]). Rights held against the *state* government, however, must be expressly declared, otherwise decisional authority over the matter is retained by people in the states. This is the lesson of *Barron v. Baltimore*, a case Bingham believed was correctly decided and which guided his second draft of the Privileges or Immunities

---

[31] For the difference between original meaning and judicial construction, *see* Solum, *supra* note 1.

[32] *Daniel Webster et al., A Memorial to the Congress of the United States, On the Subject of Restraining the Increase of Slavery in New States to be Admitted Into the Union* (1819), reprinted *in* THE NEBRASKA QUESTION 9, 15 (N.Y., Redfield 1854.).

[33] *See* KURT T. LASH, THE LOST HISTORY OF THE NINTH AMENDMENT 343–51 (2009).

Clause. By using a legal term historically used in reference to textually enumerated rights, Bingham presented a clause that would be attractive to moderates like himself who wished to protect nationally recognized individual rights in the states without erasing the federalist division of powers between local and national governments. Again, it is not Bingham's desires or the preferences of moderates that set the meaning of the Clause; these considerations merely explain why Bingham chose the particular language of the text. It is the text itself that establishes its original meaning and that meaning points to the document that establishes and declares the rights of American citizenship: the Constitution.

The paradigmatic example of protected privileges or immunities would be those rights listed in the first eight amendments to the Constitution. For decades prior to the Civil War, legal and political commentators had described enumerated rights like speech and assembly as privileges and immunities of citizens of the United States. For example, consider again the 1849 description of the privileges and immunities of citizens of the United States by abolitionist Joel Tiffany:

> What are the privileges, and immunities of citizenship, of the United States?
>
> We have already seen that to be a citizen of the United States, is to be entitled to the benefit of all the guarantys of the Federal Constitution for personal security, personal liberty, and private property. . . .
>
> But what further guarantys, for personal security and liberty, could a government provide, than the constitution of the United States has already provided? It has secured the right of petition, – the right to keep and bear arms, the right to be secure from all unwarrantable seizures and searches, – the right to demand, and have a presentment or indictment found by a grand jury before he shall be held to answer to any criminal charge, – the right to be informed beforehand of the nature and cause of accusation against him, the right to a public and speedy trial by an impartial jury of his peers, – the right to confront those who testify against him, – the right to have compulsory process to bring in his witnesses, – the right to demand and have counsel for his defence, – the right to be exempt from excessive bail, or fines, &c., from cruel and unusual punishments, or from being twice jeopardized for the same offence; and the right to the privileges of the great writ of Liberty, the Habeas Corpus.[34]

Tiffany's definition of national privileges and immunities as the "guarantys of the Federal Constitution for personal security, personal liberty, and private

---

[34] *See* JOEL TIFFANY, TREATISE ON THE UNCONSTITUTIONALITY OF AMERICAN SLAVERY 97–99 (Cleveland, Ohio: J. Calyer, 1849).

property" is echoed in John Bingham's declaration that "no state may deny to any person the equal protection of the laws, including all *the limitations for personal protection of every article and section of the Constitution.*"[35] Likewise, Jacob Howard described the privileges and immunities of citizens of the United States as including "the personal rights guarantied and secured by the first eight amendments of the Constitution."[36]

These definitions reflect the antebellum understanding of the rights of national citizenship, as well as the controlling ideas of moderate Republicans in the Thirty-Ninth Congress. Thus, in addition to requiring textual enumeration, it seems reasonable to further define the Fourteenth Amendment rights of national citizenship as involving *personal* rights.[37] This would explain why key proponents of the Amendment included the first eight amendments as paradigmatic examples of protected privileges or immunities, but omitted the Ninth and Tenth Amendments – provisions not obviously involving personal rights.

1. The Ten Amendments

The term "privileges or immunities of citizens of the United States" refers to *all* constitutionally enumerated personal rights. To date, the Supreme Court has used a "selective incorporation" approach whereby provisions in the Bill of Rights are selected for incorporation only if they pass a judicially constructed test for sufficient "fundamentality." For example, in *Duncan v. Louisiana*, the Court declared that, to be worthy of incorporation, a right must be "fundamental to the American scheme of justice."[38] In other words, even if a provision in the Bill of Rights can properly be characterized as a "personal right," it may not be applied against the states unless it meets an additional test that establishes its particular importance in American law.

Nothing about this test has anything to do with the original meaning of the Privileges or Immunities Clause. The *Duncan* test is a remnant of the substantive due process approach first constructed by the Lochner Court, whereby

---

[35] CONG. GLOBE, 39th Cong., 1st Sess. 811 (1866) (emphasis added). The historical roots of this "tripartite" protection of "personal liberty," "personal security," and property go back to Blackstone's *Commentaries* and his chapter on the "Absolute Rights of Individuals." *See* 1 WILLIAM BLACKSTONE, COMMENTARIES ON THE LAWS OF ENGLAND *127–45 (1765). *See also* AMAR, *supra* note 14, at 261.

[36] CONG. GLOBE, 39th Cong., 1st Sess. 2765 (1866).

[37] According to Akhil Amar, enumerated rights should be included within the protection of the Privileges or Immunities Clause if "the provision really guarantees a privilege or immunity of individual citizens rather than a right of states or the public at large." *See* Akhil Reed Amar, *The Bill of Rights and the Fourteenth Amendment*, 101 YALE L. J. 1193, 1197 (1992).

[38] Duncan v. Louisiana, 391 U.S. 145, 149 (1968).

Fourteenth Amendment rights had to be "fundamental" and "implicit in the concept of ordered liberty."[39] The opening provisions of Section One, however, say nothing about fundamentality. The reference is to "privileges or immunities of citizens of the United States," and *this* term includes all constitutionally enumerated rights. If the Constitution enumerates the personal right "to skip down the sidewalk," this would constitute a privilege and immunity of citizens of the United States, whether or not such a right is "fundamental to the American scheme of justice."

As a matter of original textual meaning, then, every personal right listed in the Bill of Rights constitutes a "privilege or immunity" of citizens of the United States. This would include everything from the Third Amendment's immunity from nonconsensual quartering of troops in times of peace[40] to the Seventh Amendment's right to jury trial in "suits at common law, where the value in controversy shall exceed twenty dollars."[41] The resulting jurisprudence would essentially mirror the "total incorporation" theory first advanced by Justice Hugo Black in *Adamson v. California*.[42] Rejecting the substantive due process analysis of his colleagues, Justice Black based his theory on a historical investigation of the Privileges or Immunities Clause.[43] Black's opinion triggered decades of debate, but it remains remarkably prescient given his limited access to the full historical record.

It may well be the case that few people in 1868 thought deeply about the implications of imposing on the states an obligation to respect all constitutionally enumerated personal rights.[44] But here, the point about "expected applications" carries the day. The meaning of the Privileges or Immunities Clause fixes its protection of enumerated personal rights. The particular expectations of the time focused on the Amendment's impact on the protection of speech, press, and assembly in the southern states. These rights were merely examples of the

---

[39] *See* Palko v. Connecticut, 302 U.S. 319, 325–28 (1937). *See also* Twining v. New Jersey, 211 U.S. 78 (1908) (limiting protected rights to those involving "fundamental principles of liberty and justice").

[40] U.S. CONST. amend. III.

[41] U.S. CONST. amend. VII.

[42] Adamson v. California, 332 U.S. 46, 68–71 (1947) (Black, J., dissenting).

[43] *Id.*

[44] Charles Fairman, for example, argued that the country never would have accepted an amendment they believed would incorporate the "federal provisions on grand jury, criminal jury, and civil jury." Charles Fairman, *Does the Fourteenth Amendment Incorporate the Bill of Rights?*" 2 STAN. L. REV. 5, 197 (1949). For a response to the "grand jury" argument against incorporation, see Bryan Wildenthal, *Nationalizing the Bill of Rights: Revisiting the Original Understanding of the Fourteenth Amendment in 1866–67*, 68 OHIO ST. L. J. 1509, 1601–08 (2007); Bryan Wildenthal, *Nationalizing the Bill of Rights: Scholarship and Commentary on the Fourteenth Amendment in 1867–73*, 18 J. CONTEMP. LEG. ISSUES 153, 177–86 (2009).

rights of national citizenship and were especially salient in light of tragic riot in New Orleans. But this fact does not alter the text's inclusion of all enumerated personal rights or their application outside of the southern states.[45]

It is possible, of course, that not all of the provisions in the Bill of Rights constitute "personal rights" covered by the Clause. Akhil Amar, for example, advocates a theory of "refined incorporation" whereby some, but not all, of the provisions in the Bill of Rights count as protected "privileges or immunities of citizens of the United States."[46] Amar points in particular at the Establishment Clause as a provision that might not represent an "incorporatable" personal right.[47] Other scholars oppose the incorporation of the Second Amendment, insisting that the provision represented a federalist guarantee to the states and not a promised personal right to individual citizens.[48]

Determining whether a provision counts as a personal right of American citizenship falling within the original meaning of the Privileges or Immunities Clause depends on the common understanding of that provision when the people ratified the Fourteenth Amendment. This is true whether the provision is inside or outside the Bill of Rights. So, for example, whether the individual right to bear arms constitutes a personal right of American citizens protected under the Privileges or Immunities Clause depends on whether the constitutionally enumerated Second Amendment was understood as declaring a personal right at the time of the ratification of the Fourteenth Amendment.[49] The same would be true for the Establishment Clause.[50]

The method by which provisions are determined to be properly included in the protections of the Privileges or Immunities Clause has implications for determining content and scope of the protected right. Take, for example, the Establishment Clause. There is considerable historical evidence that this clause, originally, represented nothing other than the value of leaving the

---

[45] Including the Third Amendment. *See Engblom v. Carey*, 677 F.2d 957 (2d Cir. 1982).

[46] AMAR, *supra* note 14, at 213–14, 218–30.

[47] *See* AMAR, *supra* note 14, at 41–42, 246–57.

[48] *See, e.g.,* Brief of Historians and Legal Scholars as Amicus Curiae in Support of Respondent City of Chicago, McDonald v. Chicago, No. 08–1521, 2010 WL 59034; *see also* Lawrence Rosenthal, *Second Amendment Plumbing After Heller: Of Standards of Scrutiny, Incorporation, Well-Regulated Militias, and Criminal Street Gangs*, 41 URB. LAW 1 (2009).

[49] There is good reason to think the Second Amendment was understood as declaring a personal right in 1868. *See id.* at 257–68. The Supreme Court "incorporated" the Second Amendment into its substantive due process jurisprudence in *McDonald v. Chicago*, 561 U.S. 3025 (2010).

[50] For an argument that the Establishment Clause was understood as declaring an individual right in 1868 see Kurt T. Lash, *The Second Adoption of the Establishment Clause*, 27 ARIZ. ST. L. J. 1085 (1995).

issue of religious establishments to the people in the several states and out of the hands of the federal government.[51] If this original federalist understanding of the Establishment Clause remained the common understanding in 1868, then it would be inappropriate to consider state nonestablishment to be a constitutionally enumerated privilege or immunity of citizens of the United States. Conversely, if the Establishment Clause in 1868 was understood as declaring not a principle of federalism but a personal right of citizens to be free from government-imposed religious establishments, then this would be properly viewed as a protected "privilege or immunity of citizens of the United States." Notice, however, that the courts would not be enforcing the original understanding of the Establishment Clause, but the original understanding of the Privileges or Immunities Clause.

The reason for this would be because the meaning of the Privileges or Immunities Clause does not "incorporate" the original understanding of the Establishment Clause (whatever that might have been) but instead represents the common understanding of the rights of American citizenship in 1868. If the people of 1868 did not view nonestablishment as a personal right of citizenship, then no such right would be enforced against the states. If the people did understand the Establishment Clause as declaring a personal right, then *this* understanding becomes part of the original meaning of the Privileges or Immunities Clause.

This renders moot much of the Supreme Court's struggle to determine whether the "incorporated" Establishment Clause should be read as reflecting the original views of James Madison, Thomas Jefferson, or George Washington.[52] In fact, there would be no original views to "incorporate" at all. Instead, the endeavor would be determining the understanding of nonestablishment at the time of Reconstruction. In this case, one place to begin might be the summation of antebellum nonestablishment principles in the 1872 Supreme Court case *Watson v. Jones*. There, Judge Miller summed up the nation's contemporary understanding of religious liberty with the declaration:

> In this country the full and free right to entertain any religious belief, to practice any religious principle, and to teach any religious doctrine which does not violate the laws of morality and property, and which does not infringe

---

[51] *See* STEVEN D. SMITH, FOREORDAINED FAILURE: THE QUEST FOR A CONSTITUTIONAL PRINCIPLE OF RELIGIOUS FREEDOM (1995).

[52] *See, e.g.*, Everson v. Bd. of Ed. of Ewing Township, 330 U.S. 1, 11–12 (1947) (Black, J.) (relying on the views of James Madison and Thomas Jefferson to determine the meaning of the incorporated Establishment Clause).

personal rights, is conceded to all. The law knows no heresy, and is committed to the support of no dogma, the establishment of no sect.[53]

Whether or not Miller's opinion accurately represents the original understanding of nonestablishment as a right of national citizenship, Miller's discussion of the evolved understanding of religious freedom since the time of the Founding would be directly relevant to determining this aspect of the Privileges or Immunities Clause. This is not to say that the views of Madison, Jefferson, and Washington are necessarily irrelevant to determining the meaning of Fourteenth Amendment nonestablishment. It is to say that their views would be relevant *only to the extent* that they informed the common understanding of the personal right of nonestablishment in 1868. Even here, one would have to proceed carefully to make sure one was recovering not the "true" view of Thomas Jefferson, but the 1868 understanding of "Jefferson's views" and the degree to which they were accepted as informing the meaning of constitutionally protected nonestablishment. Other constitutionally enumerated aspects of Fourteenth Amendment privileges and immunities would have to be viewed in the same Reconstruction-era light.

Theoretically, this could create an interpretive rift between the original meaning of an enumerated right as a limitation on federal power and the original meaning of the same right as an aspect of the Privileges or Immunities Clause's limitation on state power. For example, suppose that the original Second Amendment was not commonly understood as protecting an individual right, but represented a federalist guarantee not to disarm the state militia. Further suppose that, by the time Congress considered the Fourteenth Amendment, the Second Amendment was commonly understood as representing the individual right to armed self-defense, particularly for newly freed blacks who faced increasing instances of private and state-directed violent attacks. In such a scenario, it is possible to view American citizens as being able to assert a right to bear arms against the actions of the state governments but perhaps not against the actions of the federal government.

The Supreme Court has rejected this kind of two-track theory of enumerated privileges and immunities.[54] This seems correct. The Fourteenth Amendment

---

[53] Watson v. Jones, 80 U.S. (13 Wall.) 679, 728 (1972); *see also* Kurt T. Lash, *The Fourteenth Amendment and the Bill of Rights: Beyond Incorporation*, 18 J. CONTEMP. LEG. ISSUES 447, 457 (2009).

[54] *See* Dist. of Columbia v. Heller, 554 U.S. 570 (2008) (finding that the Second Amendment secured an individual right to bear arms against abridgment by federal authorities); McDonald v. Chicago, 561 U.S. 3025 (2010) (finding that the Fourteenth Amendment also protects an individual right to bear arms).

did not simply address the relationship between citizens and the states; it also established one's relationship to the federal government. The opening sentence of the Amendment declares that all persons born or naturalized are *citizens of the United States.* It then asserts that no state shall abridge the privileges or immunities of citizens of the United States. This is, and was understood as, a declaration that the current rights of citizens of the United States shall not be abridged by the States. If we follow the anti-incorporationist reading of this sentence, there is nothing to apply against the states because the current enumerated rights in the Bill of Rights are not rights that constrain state action. We have already concluded, however, that this does not reflect the original meaning of the Privileges or Immunities Clause. If, then, the amendment properly understood includes the enumerated rights of the first eight amendments as now binding the states, this amounts to a *new communication* of the Bill of Rights, this time as an announcement of the Privileges or Immunities of citizens of the United States. In this way, the passage of the Fourteenth Amendment amounts to a second adoption of the Bill of Rights. That being the case, the privileges and immunities that bind the federal government are the same privileges or immunities that bind the States.[55]

2. Beyond Incorporation

If this is the correct way to think about the Privileges or Immunities Clause, then not only are the provisions of the original Bill of Rights not *incorporated into* the Fourteenth Amendment, these provisions are actually *reenacted by* the Fourteenth Amendment. The New Deal doctrine of textual incorporation, although correctly applying the personal rights of the early amendments against the states, misleadingly suggests that we are "incorporating" the original understanding of the Bill of Rights. Instead, the very opposite has occurred: By enacting the Fourteenth Amendment, the people entrenched their understanding of the rights of national citizenship and, in so doing, reconfigured the meaning and scope of the original Bill of Rights.

[55] We have seen this kind of reasoning before in the Supreme Court's reading of the Equal Protection Clause and the so-called "reverse incorporation" doctrine in *Bolling v. Sharpe*, 347 U.S. 497 (1954). In *Bolling*, the Supreme Court ruled that the principles of equal protection that prohibited government-directed segregation in the states under the Fourteenth Amendment's Equal Protection Clause also prohibited government-directed segregation in the District of Columbia under the Fifth Amendment's Due Process Clause. But where *Bolling* remains a difficult case because it is based on a different text than that relied on in *Brown*, incorporated rights cases involve the same textually announced "privileges or immunities of citizens of the United States."

If we are seeking the original meaning of the Privileges or Immunities Clause, then instead of asking whether a textual right ought to be incorporated into the Fourteenth Amendment Due Process Clause, we should be asking whether the claimed right was understood to be a privilege or immunity of citizens of the United States in 1868. If so, then in what manner was that right, at that time, understood to bind the actions of state and federal governments? It may well be that the original vision of a textual right continued to inform the 1868 meaning of a national privilege or immunity. In such a case, the original views of Founders like James Madison could be quite relevant. Whether this is true, however, would be a matter of historical investigation rather than doctrinal assumption.

3. The Ninth and Tenth Amendments

If it is correct that the Privileges or Immunities Clause applies against the states all constitutionally enumerated personal rights, then this suggests scholars may have been wrong to assume that not all of the Bill of Rights can be applied against the states. In fact, there is no textual reason why we cannot enforce the Ninth and Tenth Amendments as privileges and immunities of citizens of the United States.

In terms of the Ninth Amendment, fundamental rights scholars commonly point to the Ninth Amendment as the textual precursor to the Privileges or Immunities Clause, with both treated as proper textual vehicles for judicial enforcement of unenumerated substantive rights.[56] This reflects an erroneous understanding of both the original meaning of the Ninth Amendment and the Privileges or Immunities Clause. We know, for example, that the Privileges or Immunities Clause was not understood as a fount of unenumerated fundamental rights. More surprisingly, perhaps, is that neither was the Ninth Amendment. As I have detailed elsewhere, the original meaning of the Ninth Amendment declared that the limitations on federal power listed in the first eight amendments "shall not be construed" as the *only* limitations on federal power.[57] The effort was to avoid the undesired implication that, by adding the Bill of Rights, federal power would be construed as extending to every matter except those expressly placed off-limits in the Bill of Rights.[58] The effect of the Amendment, in other words, was to force a limited construction on

---

[56] *See, e.g.,* Barnett, *supra* note 16, at 54–68.

[57] Lash, *supra* note 33, at 86–87.

[58] *Id. See also* Kurt T. Lash, A Textual-Historical Theory of the Ninth Amendment, 60 Stan. L. Rev. 895 (2008).

enumerated federal power in order to preserve the people's retained right to local self-government.[59] The fact that neither John Bingham nor Jacob Howard included the Ninth Amendment in their description of the personal rights to be applied against the states suggests that this federalism-based understanding of the Ninth Amendment had not changed by 1866.[60]

But the fact that the Ninth Amendment in 1866 continued to be understood as reflecting federalism-based concerns does not by itself render the Amendment "unprotectable" as a privilege or immunity of citizens of the United States. To begin with, the text of the Ninth Amendment, even without incorporation, binds both the federal government and the states. For example, suppose that a state judge is faced with a claimed federal constitutional right nowhere enumerated in the Constitution. The Ninth Amendment would prevent the state judge from concluding that because the right was not enumerated in the Federal Constitution, it was therefore not retained by the people. In fact, all officials, whether state or federal, are bound by their oaths to support the Constitution, and this includes respecting the rule of construction announced by the Ninth Amendment.[61]

Construing the Ninth Amendment as preserving constitutional federalism is not inconsistent with viewing the Amendment as one of the people's enumerated personal rights. Federalism, as originally conceived, guarded the individual liberties of the people. As Samuel Adams wrote to Richard Henry Lee:

> I mean my friend, to let you know how deeply I am impressed with a sense of the Importance of Amendments; that the good People may clearly see the distinction, for there is a distinction, between the federal Powers vested in Congress, and the sovereign Authority belonging to the several States, which is the Palladium of the private, and personal rights of the Citizens.[62]

The same moderate Republicans who produced the Fourteenth Amendment also continued to embrace the principles of federalism as a critical component of American constitutionalism. As John Bingham announced during the debates of the Thirty-Ninth Congress, "this dual system of national and State government under the American organization is the secret of our strength and power. I do not propose to abandon it."[63] Any state action that supports an

---

[59] *Id.*

[60] There is good reason to believe it had not. *See* Lash, *supra* note 33, at 235–51.

[61] *See* Lash, *supra* note 58, at 904.

[62] Letter from Samuel Adams to Richard Henry Lee (Aug. 24, 1789), *in* Creating the Bill of Rights: The Documentary Record From the First Federal Congress 286 (Helen E. Veit et al. eds., 1991).

[63] Cong. Globe, 39th Cong., 2d Sess. 450 (1867).

unconstitutional exercise of federal power in a manner that affects the liberty of an individual citizen can be seen as violating both the Ninth Amendment and the Fourteenth Amendment's protection of the privileges and immunities of citizens of the United States.

This last point suggests that not only may the 1866 understanding of the Ninth Amendment be appropriately applied against the states, but so too can the 1866 understanding of the Tenth Amendment. For decades, scholars (including myself in earlier writing) have considered the Tenth Amendment to be "unincorporatable."[64] The very idea seems at first glance to be a contradiction in terms. How can an amendment that reserves power to the states be applied against the states? The answer lies in the original understanding of the Amendment as one of the two federalist guardians of individual liberty in the Bill of Rights. When the Adams administration passed the Sedition Act criminalizing criticism of President Adams and his administration, James Madison declared that such an abuse of federal power violated individual rights of the American people, including their right to reserve matters involving speech and press to the control of their local state governments under the Tenth Amendment.[65] As the slave power attempted to force slavery on the entire country as a matter of national law, abolitionists took refuge in the liberty-enhancing principles of federalism. According to abolitionist Wendell Philips, "I love State Rights; that doctrine is the corner-stone of individual liberty."[66] As noted earlier and in Chapter 3, moderate Republicans continued to embrace federalism as a critical constraint on the abuse of government power.

The current Supreme Court also views the federalism principle of the Tenth Amendment as implicating the personal liberties of the people. According to Justice Anthony Kennedy in *Bond v. United States*:[67]

> The federal system rests on what might at first seem a counterintuitive insight, that "freedom is enhanced by the creation of two governments, not one." The Framers concluded that allocation of powers between the National Government and the States enhances freedom, first by protecting the integrity

---

[64] AMAR, *supra* note 14, at 34 ("To my knowledge no scholar or judge has argued for incorporating the Tenth Amendment."). In earlier writing, I took the same position. *See, e.g.*, Kurt T. Lash, *The Second Adoption of the Establishment Clause: The Rise of the Nonestablishment Principle*, 27 ARIZ. ST. L. J. 1085, 1099 (1995).

[65] See Kurt T. Lash, *James Madison's Celebrated Report of 1800: The Transformation of the Tenth Amendment*, 74 GEO. WASH. L. REV. 165, 180–86 (2006).

[66] J. M. W. Yerrington, *Thirty Second Anniversary of the American Anti-Slavery Society*, NAT'L ANTI-SLAVERY STANDARD (N.Y.), May 15, 1865, at 2.

[67] 131 S. Ct. 2355 (2011).

of the governments themselves, and second by protecting the people, from whom all governmental powers are derived.[68]

According to Kennedy, "[f]ederalism is more than an exercise in setting the boundary between different institutions of government for their own integrity. . . . '[F]ederalism secures to citizens the liberties that derive from the diffusion of sovereign power.'"[69] Finally, just to drive home the link between local self-government and national liberty, Kennedy declared, "[b]y denying any one government complete jurisdiction over all the concerns of public life, federalism protects the liberty of the individual from arbitrary power. When government acts in excess of its lawful powers, that liberty is at stake."[70]

Although the federalism jurisprudence of the current Supreme Court is probably best viewed as an application of both the Ninth and Tenth Amendments,[71] the original understanding of both amendments, as well as their accepted meaning in 1866, allows for the application of both amendments against the state and federal governments as protected privileges or immunities of citizens of the United States. For example, if the actions of a state official commandeered by the federal government to enforce a federal policy injures an individual, that individual could challenge such action as an abridgment of his or her rights under the Ninth and Tenth Amendments.[72]

C. Toward a Jurisprudence of Original Meaning

Even if one can identify important aspects of the original meaning of the text, this does not in itself control current judicial application of the text to a current legal controversy. To begin with, not all scholars believe the current operations of government ought to be constrained by the original meaning of the text.[73] And even among those originalist scholars who believe the original meaning ought to constrain current application of the text are those who believe the principle of *stare decisis* should play a role in determining whether a prior case ought to be overruled.[74] Finally, even if the Privileges or Immunities Clause does not protect a particular right, it is possible that another provision

---

[68] *Id.* at 2364.

[69] *Id.*

[70] *Id.*

[71] See generally, Kurt T. Lash, *Federalism, Individual Rights, and Judicial Engagement*, 19 Geo. Mason L. Rev. 873 (2012).

[72] *See, e.g.,* Printz v. United States, 521 U.S. 898 (1997).

[73] *See, e.g.,* David A. Strauss, The Living Constitution (2010).

[74] See Kurt T. Lash, *Originalism, Popular Sovereignty and Reverse Stare Decisis*, 93 Va. L. Rev. 1437 (2007).

in the Fourteenth Amendment does. For example, even if the right of sexual autonomy is not covered by the Privileges or Immunities Clause, key aspects of that right may be covered by the Equal Protection Clause.[75] We cannot know the full impact of an originalist reading of the Privileges or Immunities Clause without knowing (1) the full original meaning of Section One of the Fourteenth Amendment, (2) whether originalism is a normatively attractive theory of constitutional adjudication, and (3) the proper role that *stare decisis* should play in those instances when a prior decision is contradicted by the original meaning of the text.

Still, some matters seem clear enough. A jurisprudence of the Privileges or Immunities Clause based on its original meaning would include the entire Bill of Rights, as well as other textually enumerated rights such as the great writ of habeas corpus and the equal protection coverage of the Comity Clause. An original meaning jurisprudence would not include unenumerated rights, whether progressive,[76] libertarian,[77] or conservative.[78] Unless covered under a separate clause in the Constitution, matters involving the rights of privacy, economic rights, and parental rights would remain subject to political debate in the several states. Some aspects of the right to privacy, sexual autonomy, and gay rights may be covered by the Equal Protection Clause[79] or preserved under the doctrine of *stare decisis*.[80] However, there is no plausible originalist understanding of the Privileges or Immunities Clause that would include such rights.[81]

---

[75] *Compare* Lawrence v. Texas, 539 U.S. 558 (2003) (Kennedy, J.) *with* Lawrence v. Texas, 539 U.S. 558, 579 (2003) (O'Connor, J., concurring).

[76] Roe v. Wade, 410 U.S. 113 (1973); Griswold v. Connecticut, 381 U.S. 479 (1965).

[77] Lochner v. New York, 198 U.S. 45 (1905).

[78] *See* Troxel v. Granville, 530 U.S. 57 (2000); Pierce v. Society of Sisters, 268 U.S. 510 (1925); Meyer v. Nebraska, 262 U.S. 390 (1923).

[79] *See* Planned Parenthood v. Casey, 505 U.S. 833, 856 (1992) (discussing equal protection aspects of the right to abortion); Lawrence v. Texas, 539 U.S. 558, 579 (2003) (O'Connor, J., concurring) (analyzing the right to homosexual sodomy under Equal Protection Clause).

[80] *See* Planned Parenthood v. Casey, 505 U.S. 833, 854 (1992) (discussing the role of *stare decisis* in deciding whether to uphold *Roe v. Wade*).

[81] Yale law professor Jack Balkin claims that the right to privacy, including a woman's right to obtain an abortion, can be viewed as consistent with an originalist understanding of the Fourteenth Amendment. *See* Jack M. Balkin, *Abortion and Original Meaning*, 24 CONST. COMM. 291 (2007). Whether or not one considers Balkin's unique theory to constitute a plausible form of originalism, he is not claiming that the right to privacy is part of the original *meaning* of the Privileges or Immunities Clause, only that such a reading is *consistent* with the original meaning. *Id.* at 328–30 (describing a "dynamic" reading of the "declaratory" Privileges or Immunities that allows courts to recognize and enforce nontextual rights that gain sufficient public acceptance over time). But even this lesser claim is incorrect given the interpretive ceiling imposed by the original meaning of the text.

III. CONCLUSION

The proposition pending before the House is simply a proposition to arm the Congress of the United States, by the consent of the people of the United States, with the power to enforce the bill of rights as it stands in the Constitution today. It "hath that extent – no more."[82]

John Bingham (1866)

The history of the Fourteenth Amendment in general and the Privileges or Immunities Clause in particular has been buried under decades of scholarship based on the assumption that the Clause was modeled on the "privileges *and* immunities" clause of Article IV (the Comity Clause). That single assumption has resulted in two equally erroneous theories about the Privileges or Immunities Clause, one pointing toward an equal rights–only reading of "fundamental" state-secured rights and the other pointing toward an ever-expanding list of judicially construed unenumerated substantive rights. One fails to credit the significant body of historical evidence linking the rights of national citizenship to the substantive rights listed in the Bill of Rights, and the other fails to credit the equally significant body of historical evidence suggesting that the people of 1866 remained committed to constitutional federalism.

The Fourteenth Amendment did signal a kind of revolution, but one reflecting the commitments of post-Civil War nineteenth-century Americans. Neither the same as us, nor wholly different from us, the people of 1866 occupied a place midway between the deep federalism of the Founding and the almost unlimited centralized power of the twentieth-century United States. Whether their accomplishments are adequate for our day is a matter for contemporary reflection and, perhaps, revolutionary activity of our own. What we cannot miss, however, is how the Privileges or Immunities Clause accomplished at least a partial revolution for their day.

For the first time, every person on American soil walked under the constitutional guarantee of Due Process and Equal Protection. And, also for the first time, American citizens carried with them every right announced in the federal Constitution, from the rights of free expression to the right to peacefully assemble to petition *any* government for redress of grievances, the right to keep and bear arms, the immunity from any taking of their private property without just compensation, freedom from illegal searches and seizures, and all the protections of constitutionally enumerated criminal procedure. All this and more – *every* right of citizens of the United States which were available for every person to see who could read the English language and who had

---

[82] CONG. GLOBE, 39th Cong., 1st Sess. 1088 (1866).

access to a current copy of the federal Constitution. Rights that could be held up to any government official, from the federal Commissioner of the Internal Revenue Service[83] to the mayor of New Orleans. This might not have been a total revolution, but it was a revolution nonetheless.

But revolutionaries cannot steer the course of a revolution nor guarantee its success. John Bingham's vision of the Privileges or Immunities Clause never came to pass. Had Justice Miller been an enthusiastic advocate of enumerated privileges and immunities, he might have written a lead opinion in *Slaughter-House* that clearly marked the protections of the Bill of Rights as privileges and immunities states no longer could deny, even if states remained in control of local commercial and labor laws. Instead, Miller's grudging and inscrutable list of the rights of national citizenship was easily ignored a few years later when the Supreme Court drove a stake through the heart of Bingham's Clause in *Cruikshank*. By that time, the wave of revolutionary reform that swept the country in the immediate aftermath of the Civil War had crested and receded. Only a few months after the ruling in *Cruikshank*, Republicans agreed to withdraw the federal troops overseeing Reconstruction in the South in exchange for securing the election of Rutherford B. Hayes.[84] Decades would pass before the Supreme Court would expand the protections of the Due Process Clause to include a handful of rights listed in the first eight amendments.[85] It was not until 2010 that the Supreme Court finally reversed *Cruikshank* and granted both black and white American citizens the right to bear arms for self-defense.[86] But even if the story of the rights of American citizenship is one of eventual (if still only partial) vindication,[87] the decades of denied protection cast a kind of shadow across the Constitution and our celebration of the Fourteenth Amendment.

It seems no more than an act of penance, then, to properly understand just what was achieved through the adoption of the Privileges or Immunities Clause. The rights of national citizenship are not hidden or discoverable only

---

[83] A position created by the Revenue Act of 1862, 12 Stat. 432.

[84] For a history of the tawdry Compromise of 1877, see FONER, *supra* note 21, at 564–87.

[85] *See, e.g.*, Everson v. Bd. of Education, 330 U.S. 1 (1947) (the Establishment Clause); Cantwell v. Connecticut, 310 U.S. 296 (1940) (free exercise of religion); Gitlow v. New York, 268 U.S. 652 (1925) (freedom of speech); Chicago, B. & Q. R. Co. v. Chicago, 166 U.S. 226 (1897) (the Takings Clause).

[86] McDonald v. Chicago, 130 S. Ct. 3020 (2010).

[87] The Supreme Court has not yet incorporated the Sixth Amendment right to a unanimous jury verdict, the Third Amendment's protection against quartering of soldiers, the Fifth Amendment's grand jury indictment requirement, the Seventh Amendment right to a jury trial in civil cases, or the Eighth Amendment's prohibition on excessive fines. *See* McDonald v. Chicago, 130 S. Ct. 3020, 3035 (2010).

by those versed in sophisticated theories of justice or in the artificial reason of the common law.[88] They are right where a US citizen would expect them to be: in the text of the citizen's charter, the American Constitution.

---

[88] *Prohibitions del Roy (Case of Prohibitions)* (1607), 77 Eng. Rep. 1342, 12 Co. Rep. 64, *reprinted in* 1 THE SELECTED WRITINGS AND SPEECHES OF SIR EDWARD COKE 478–81 (Steve Sheppard ed., 2003) (Edward Coke explaining to James I that "causes which concern the life, inheritance, or goods, or fortunes" of English subjects "are not to be decided by natural reason but by the artificial reason and judgment of law, which law is an act that requires long study and experience, before that a man can attain to the cognizance of it").

Index

Made in United States
Orlando, FL
17 February 2022

14915057R00178